the AMAZING SPIDER-MAN

Dead Language PART 2

Peter and his girlfriend Mary Jane Watson were transported to an alternate universe by the mad mathematician **BENJAMIN RABIN, A.K.A. THE EMISSARY!** As Rabin was about to transcend to godhood using Spider-Man's totem energy, MJ made the hard choice to save Peter instead of herself, sending him back to their own dimension on a one-way trip, leaving her and a mysterious man named **PAUL** stranded. Back in his home dimension, Peter's trip caused a nearly nuclear explosion, and Peter learned that while a week had passed in the dimension Rabin had trapped them in, not even a day had passed at home.

Knowing time was not on his side, Peter attempted to get the **FANTASTIC FOUR's** help, but when they attempted to hold him for details about his explosive situation, Peter went on the run. **CAPTAIN AMERICA** was the next hero to try and get Spider-Man to slow down and explain himself, which ended with Spidey assaulting and escaping from Cap. Realizing none of his usual allies would be able to help him fast enough, Peter turned to someone whose morals tend to be looser...**NORMAN OSBORN.**

Jennifer Grünwald COLLECTION EDITOR

Daniel Kirchhoffer ASSISTANT EDITOR

Lisa Montalbano ASSOCIATE MANAGER, TALENT RELATIONS

Jeff Youngquist VP PRODUCTION & SPECIAL PROJECTS

Adam Del Re MANAGER & SENIOR DESIGNER

Jay Bowen BOOK DESIGNER

David Gabriel SVP PRINT, SALES & MARKETING

C.B. Cebulski EDITOR IN CHIEF

AMAZING SPIDER-MAN BY ZEB WELLS VOL. 6: DEAD LANGUAGE PART 2. Contains material originally published in magazine form as AMAZING SPIDER-MAN (2022) #24-26, AMAZING SPIDER-MAN ANNUAL (2023) #1 and FALLEN FRIEND (2023) #1. First printing 2023. ISBN 978-1-302-94738-5. Published by MARVEL WORLDWIDE, INC., a subsidiary of MARVEL ENTERTAINMENT, LLC. OFFICE OF PUBLICATION: 1290 Avenue of the Americas, New York, NY 10104. © 2023 MARVEL No similarity between any of the names, characters, persons, and/or institutions in this book with those of any living or dead person or institution is intended, and any such similarity which may exist is purely coincidental. **Printed in the U.S.A.** KEVIN FEIGE, Chief Creative Officer; DAN BUCKLEY, President, Marvel Entertainment; DAVID BOGART, Associate Publisher & SVP of Talent Affairs; TOM BREVOORT, VP, Executive Editor; NICK LOWE, Executive Editor, VP of Content, Digital Publishing; DAVID GABRIEL, VP of Print & Digital Publishing; SVEN LARSEN, VP of Licensed Publishing; MARK ANNUNZIATO, VP of Planning & Forecasting; JEFF YOUNGQUIST, VP of Production & Special Projects; ALEX MORALES, Director of Publishing Operations; DAN EDINGTON, Director of Editorial Operations; RICKEY PURDIN, Director of Talent Relations; JENNIFER GRÜNWALD, Director of Production & Special Projects; SUSAN CRESPI, Production Manager; STAN LEE, Chairman Emeritus. For information regarding advertising in Marvel Comics or on Marvel.com, please contact Vit DeBellis, Custom Solutions & Integrated Advertising Manager, at vdebellis@marvel.com. For Marvel subscription inquiries, please call 888-511-5480. **Manufactured between 8/4/2023 and 9/5/2023 by SEAWAY PRINTING, GREEN BAY, WI, USA.**

10 9 8 7 6 5 4 3 2 1

the AMAZING SPIDER-MAN

Dead Language PART 2

AMAZING SPIDER-MAN 24-26

Zeb Wells WRITER

John Romita Jr. WITH
Kaare Andrews (25) PENCILERS

Scott Hanna WITH
Kaare Andrews (25) INKERS

Marcio Menyz WITH
Erick Arciniega (26) COLOR ARTISTS

FALLEN FRIEND

G. Willow Wilson, Mark Waid
& Saladin Ahmed WRITERS

Takeshi Miyazawa;
Humberto Ramos & Victor Olazaba;
AND **Andrea Di Vito** ARTISTS

Ian Herring &
Edgar Delgado COLOR ARTISTS

AMAZING SPIDER-MAN ANNUAL 1

"HAPPY BIRTHDAY, ANNA!"

Celeste Bronfman WRITER

David Lopez ARTIST

KJ Díaz COLOR ARTIST

"BREAK IN/BREAK OUT"

Erica Schultz WRITER

Julian Shaw ARTIST

Andrew Dalhouse COLOR ARTIST

"WELCOME TO OMAHA, SPIDER-MAN"

Rainbow Rowell WRITER

Álvaro López ARTIST

Andrew Crossley COLOR ARTIST

SPIDER-MAN CREATED BY
STAN LEE & STEVE DITKO

VC's **Joe Caramagna** (24-26, ANNUAL 1)
& Arian Maher (FALLEN FRIEND 1)
LETTERERS

Kaeden McGahey ASSISTANT EDITOR

Nick Lowe EDITOR

John Romita Jr., Scott Hanna &
Marcio Menyz (24-26);
Kaare Andrews (FALLEN FRIEND 1); AND
Corin Howell & Brian Reber
(ANNUAL 1) COVER ART

/////// WITH GREAT POWER THERE MUST ALSO COME GREAT RESPONSIBILITY /////

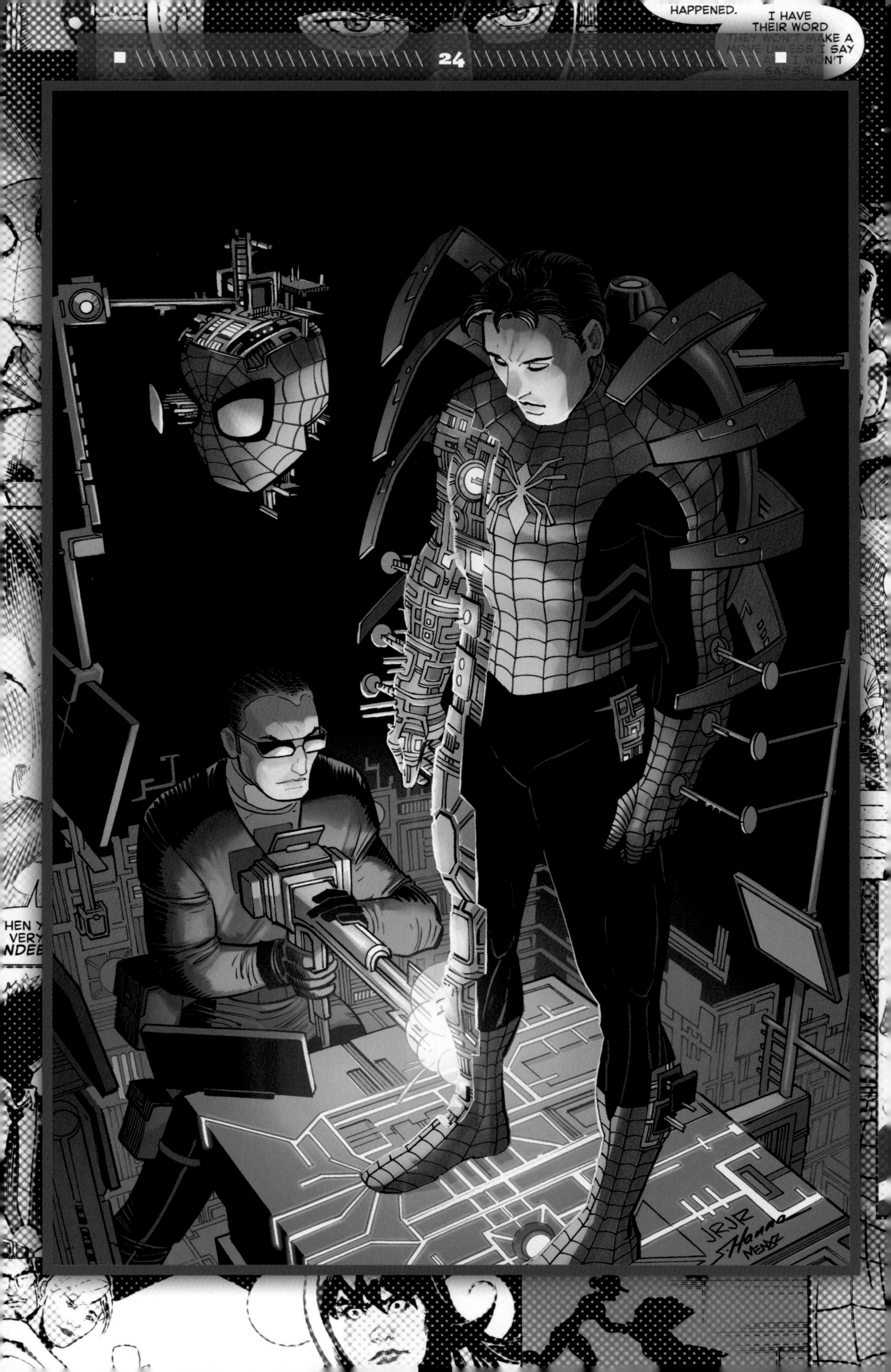
HAPPENED.
I HAVE THEIR WORD
JRJR

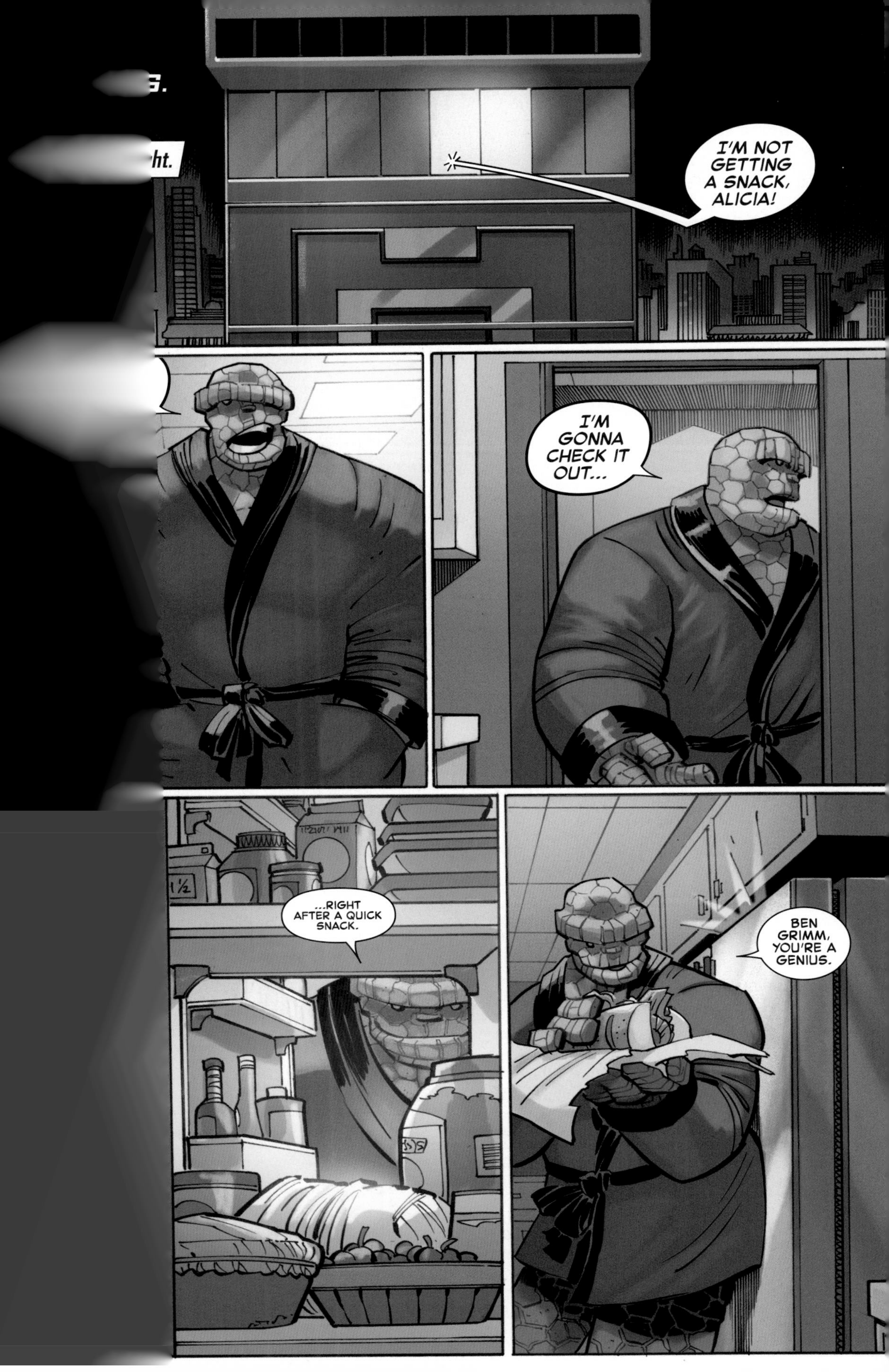

I'M NOT GETTING A SNACK, ALICIA!
I'M GONNA CHECK IT OUT...
...RIGHT AFTER A QUICK SNACK.
BEN GRIMM, YOU'RE A GENIUS.

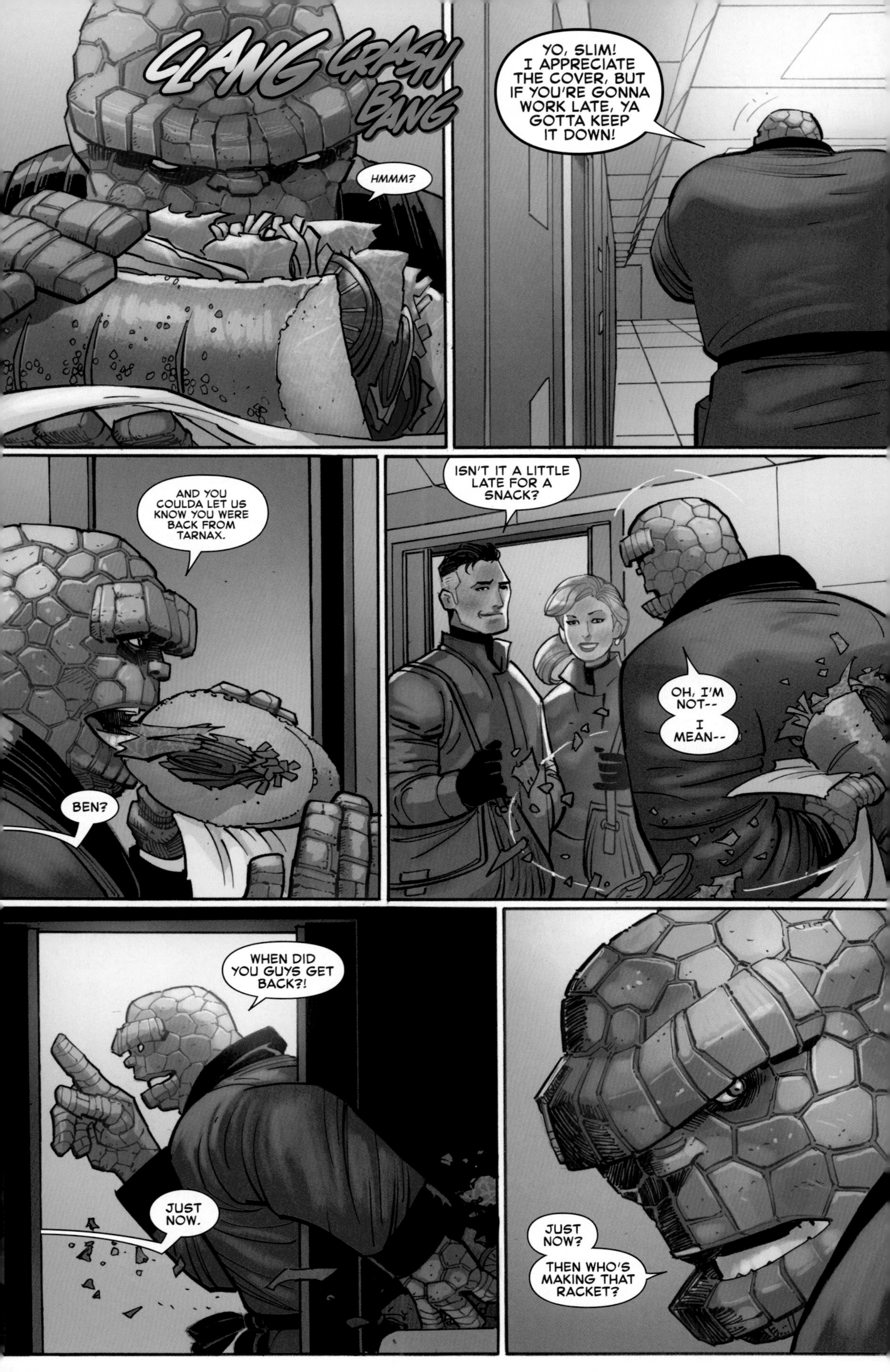
CLANG CRASH BANG
HMMM?
YO, SLIM! I APPRECIATE THE COVER, BUT IF YOU'RE GONNA WORK LATE, YA GOTTA KEEP IT DOWN!
AND YOU COULDA LET US KNOW YOU WERE BACK FROM TARNAX.
BEN?
ISN'T IT A LITTLE LATE FOR A SNACK?
OH, I'M NOT--
I MEAN--
WHEN DID YOU GUYS GET BACK?!
JUST NOW.
JUST NOW?
THEN WHO'S MAKING THAT RACKET?

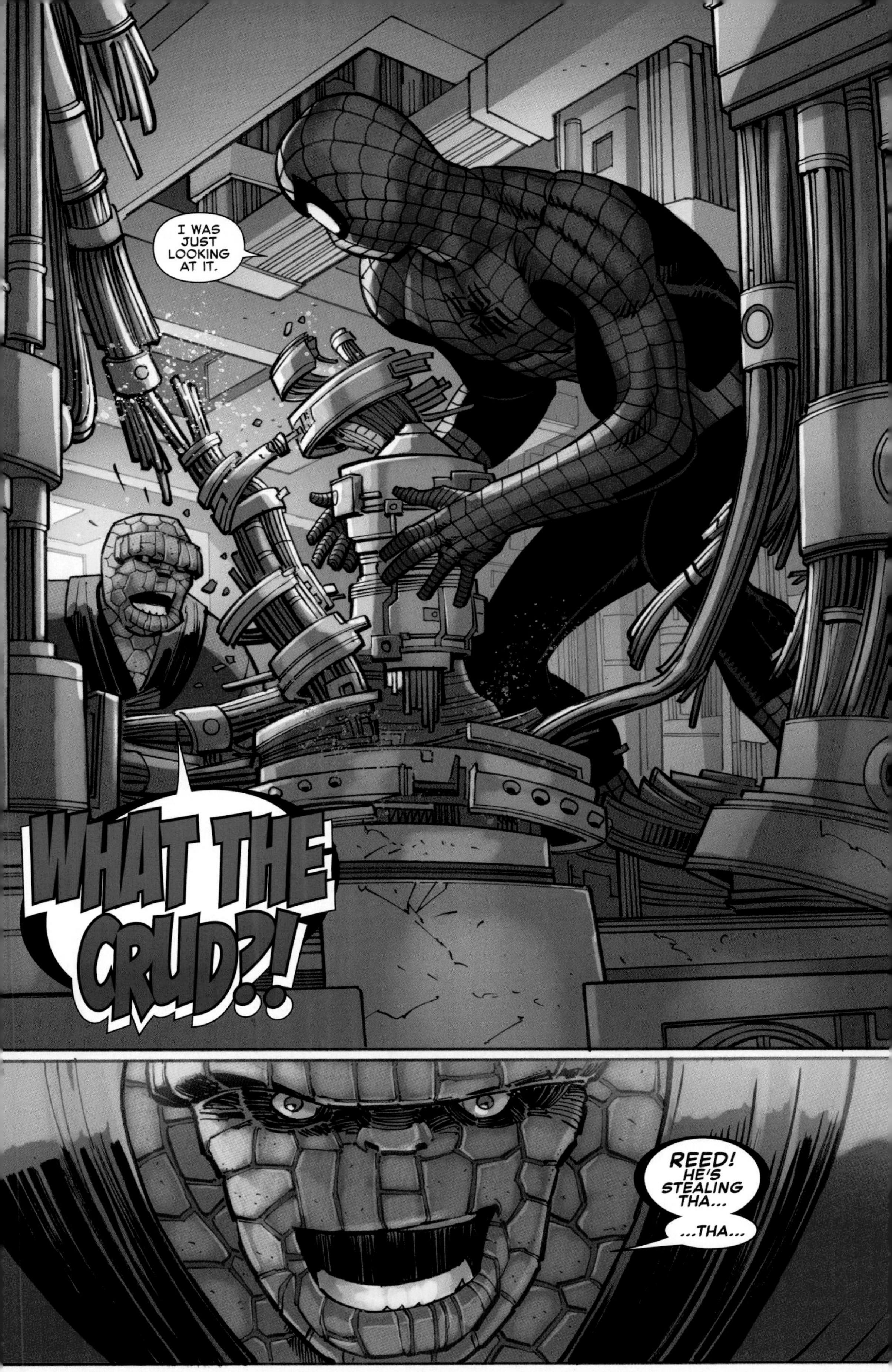
I WAS JUST LOOKING AT IT.
WHAT THE CRUD?!
REED! HE'S STEALING THA...
...THA...

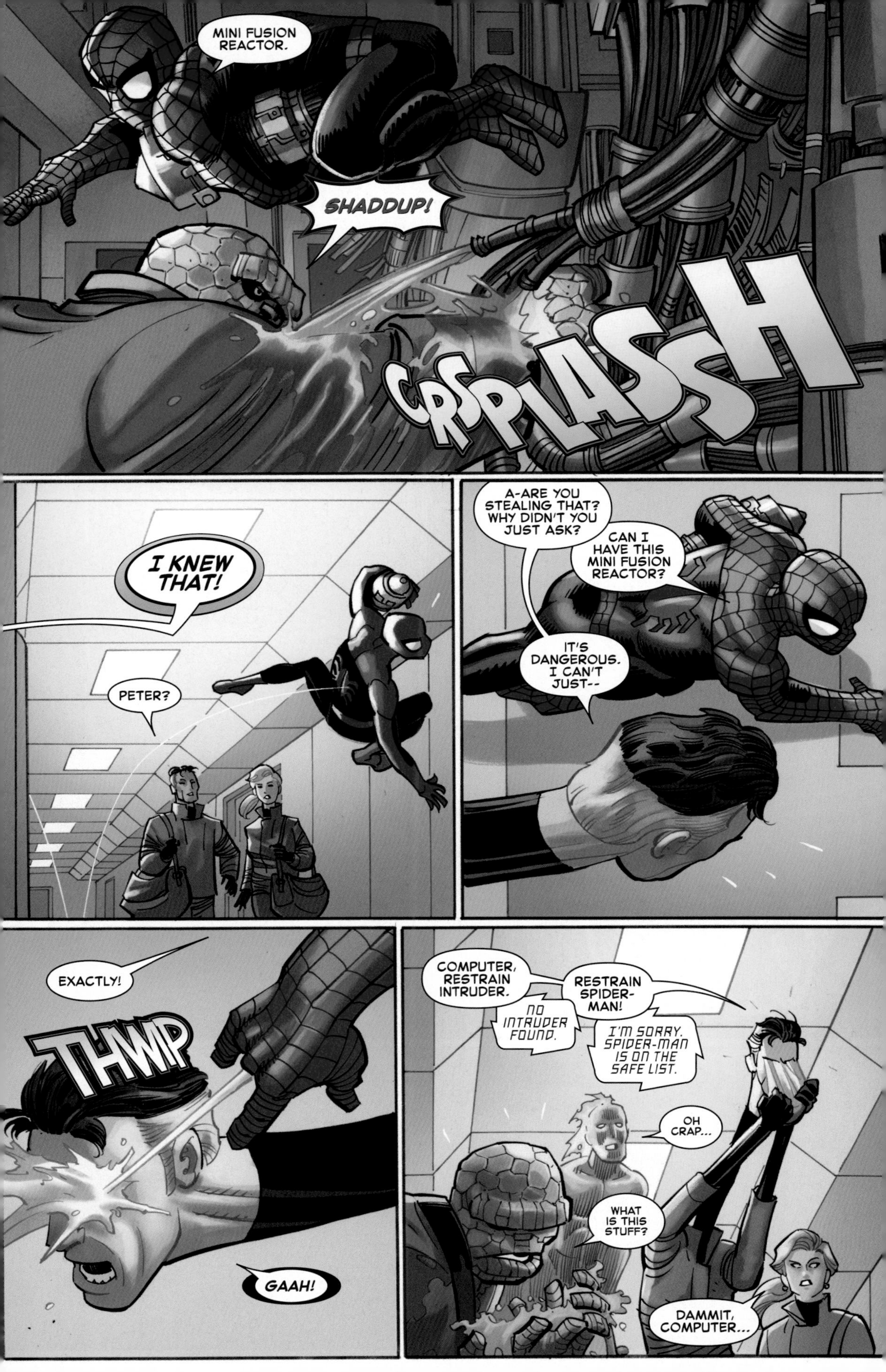
MINI FUSION REACTOR.
SHADDUP!
CRSPLASSH
I KNEW THAT!
PETER?
A-ARE YOU STEALING THAT? WHY DIDN'T YOU JUST ASK?
CAN I HAVE THIS MINI FUSION REACTOR?
IT'S DANGEROUS. I CAN'T JUST--
EXACTLY!
THWIP
GAAH!
COMPUTER, RESTRAIN INTRUDER.
NO INTRUDER FOUND.
RESTRAIN SPIDER-MAN!
I'M SORRY. SPIDER-MAN IS ON THE SAFE LIST.
OH CRAP...
WHAT IS THIS STUFF?
DAMMIT, COMPUTER...

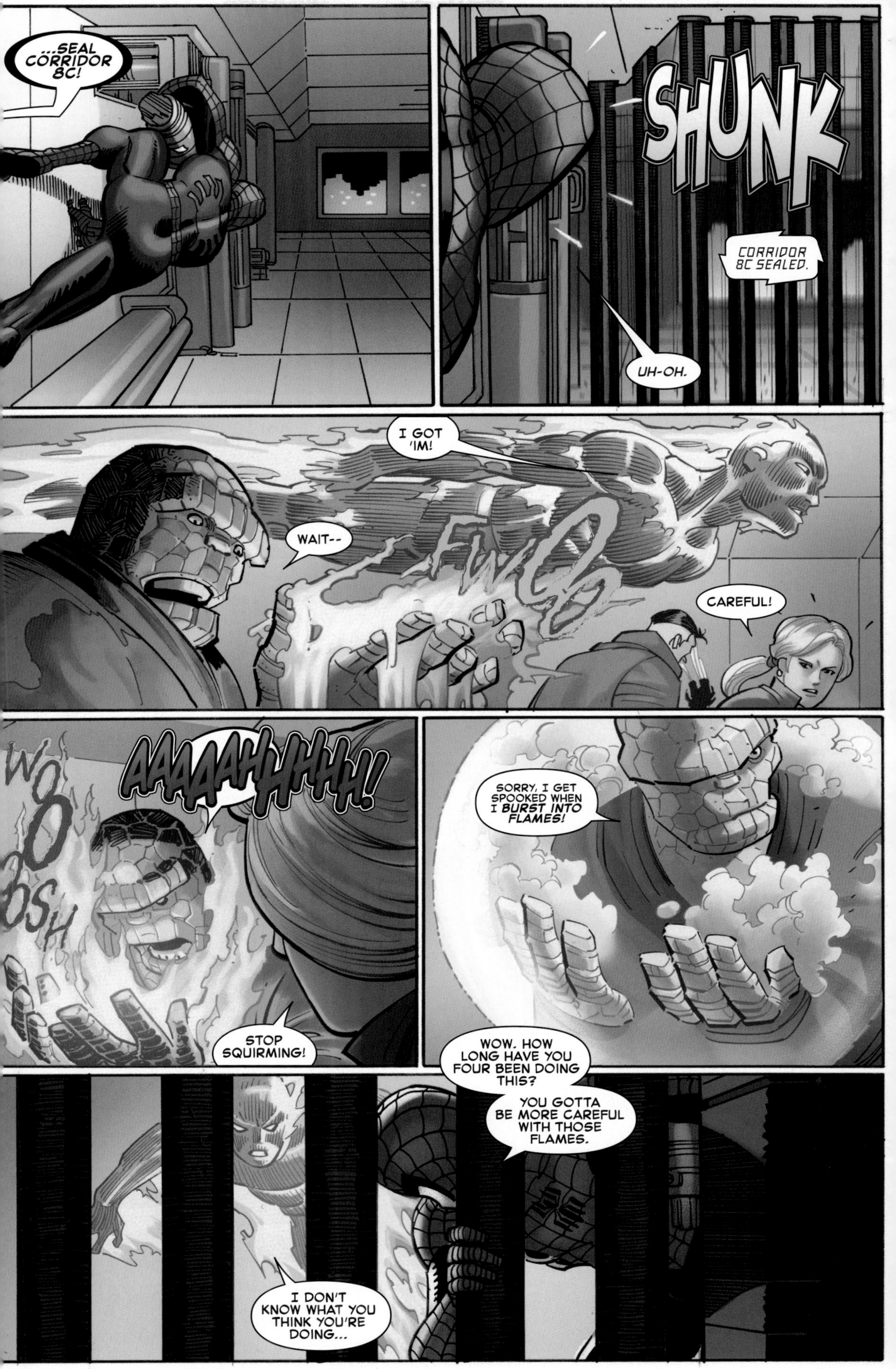
...SEAL CORRIDOR 8C!
SHUNK
CORRIDOR 8C SEALED.
UH-OH.
I GOT 'IM!
WAIT--
FWOOSH
CAREFUL!
AAAAAHHHHH!
WOOSH
STOP SQUIRMING!
SORRY, I GET SPOOKED WHEN I BURST INTO FLAMES!
WOW. HOW LONG HAVE YOU FOUR BEEN DOING THIS?
YOU GOTTA BE MORE CAREFUL WITH THOSE FLAMES.
I DON'T KNOW WHAT YOU THINK YOU'RE DOING...

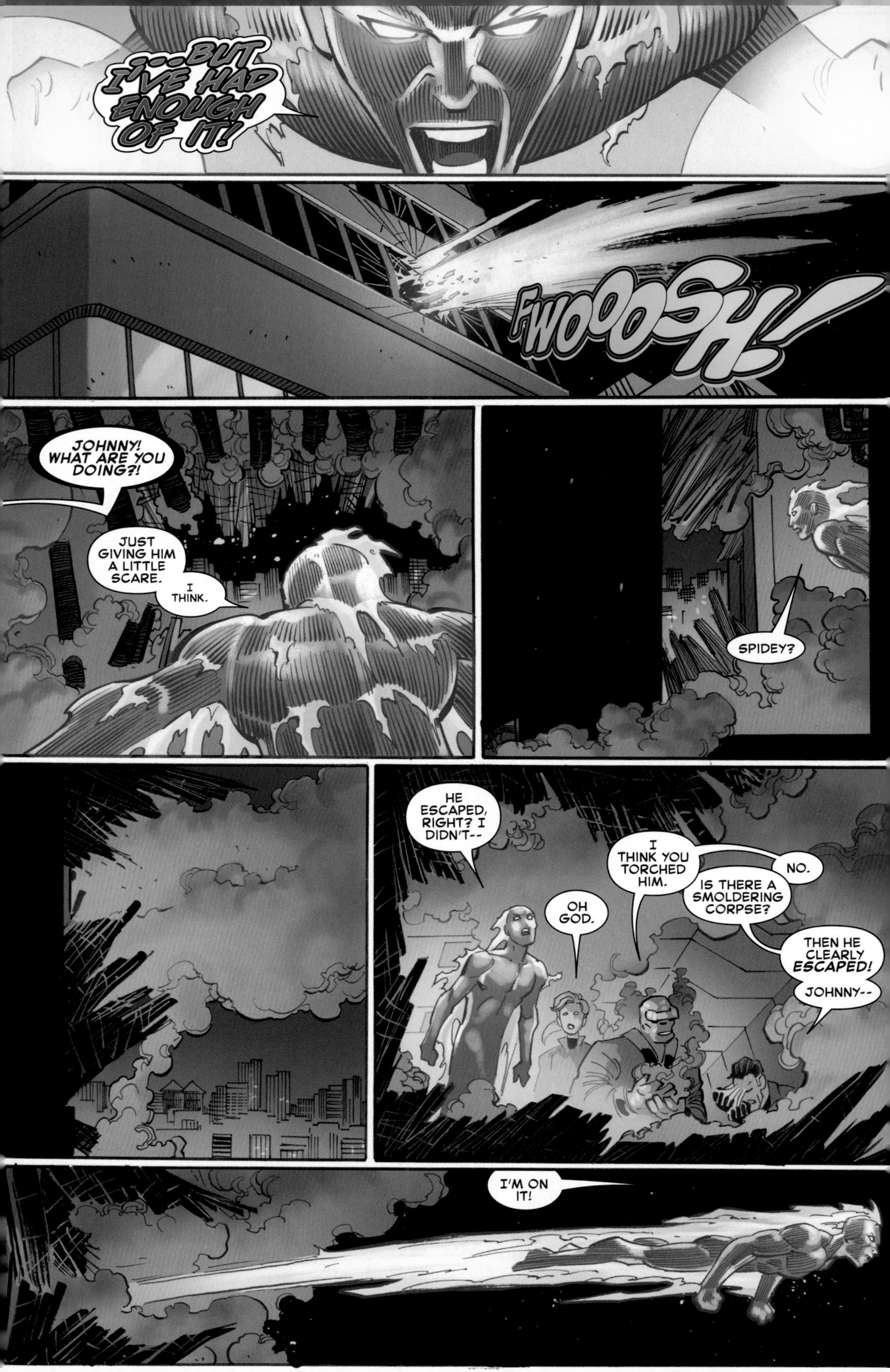
...BUT I'VE HAD ENOUGH OF IT!
FWOOOSH!
JOHNNY! WHAT ARE YOU DOING?!
JUST GIVING HIM A LITTLE SCARE.
I THINK.
SPIDEY?
HE ESCAPED, RIGHT? I DIDN'T--
OH GOD.
I THINK YOU TORCHED HIM.
NO.
IS THERE A SMOLDERING CORPSE?
THEN HE CLEARLY ESCAPED!
JOHNNY--
I'M ON IT!

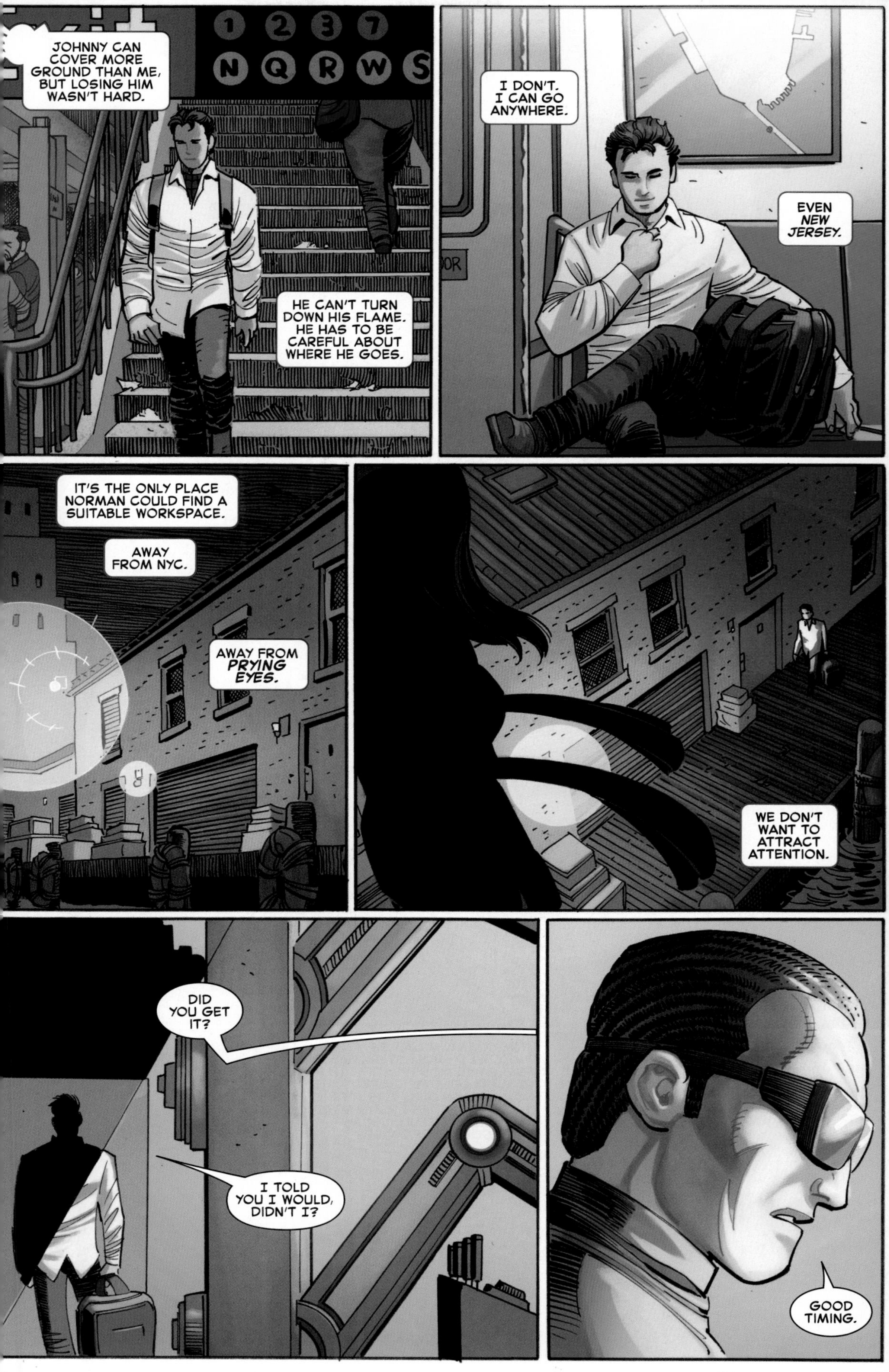
1 2 3 7
N Q R W S
JOHNNY CAN COVER MORE GROUND THAN ME, BUT LOSING HIM WASN'T HARD.
HE CAN'T TURN DOWN HIS FLAME. HE HAS TO BE CAREFUL ABOUT WHERE HE GOES.
I DON'T. I CAN GO ANYWHERE.
EVEN NEW JERSEY.
IT'S THE ONLY PLACE NORMAN COULD FIND A SUITABLE WORKSPACE.
AWAY FROM NYC.
AWAY FROM PRYING EYES.
WE DON'T WANT TO ATTRACT ATTENTION.
DID YOU GET IT?
I TOLD YOU I WOULD, DIDN'T I?
GOOD TIMING.

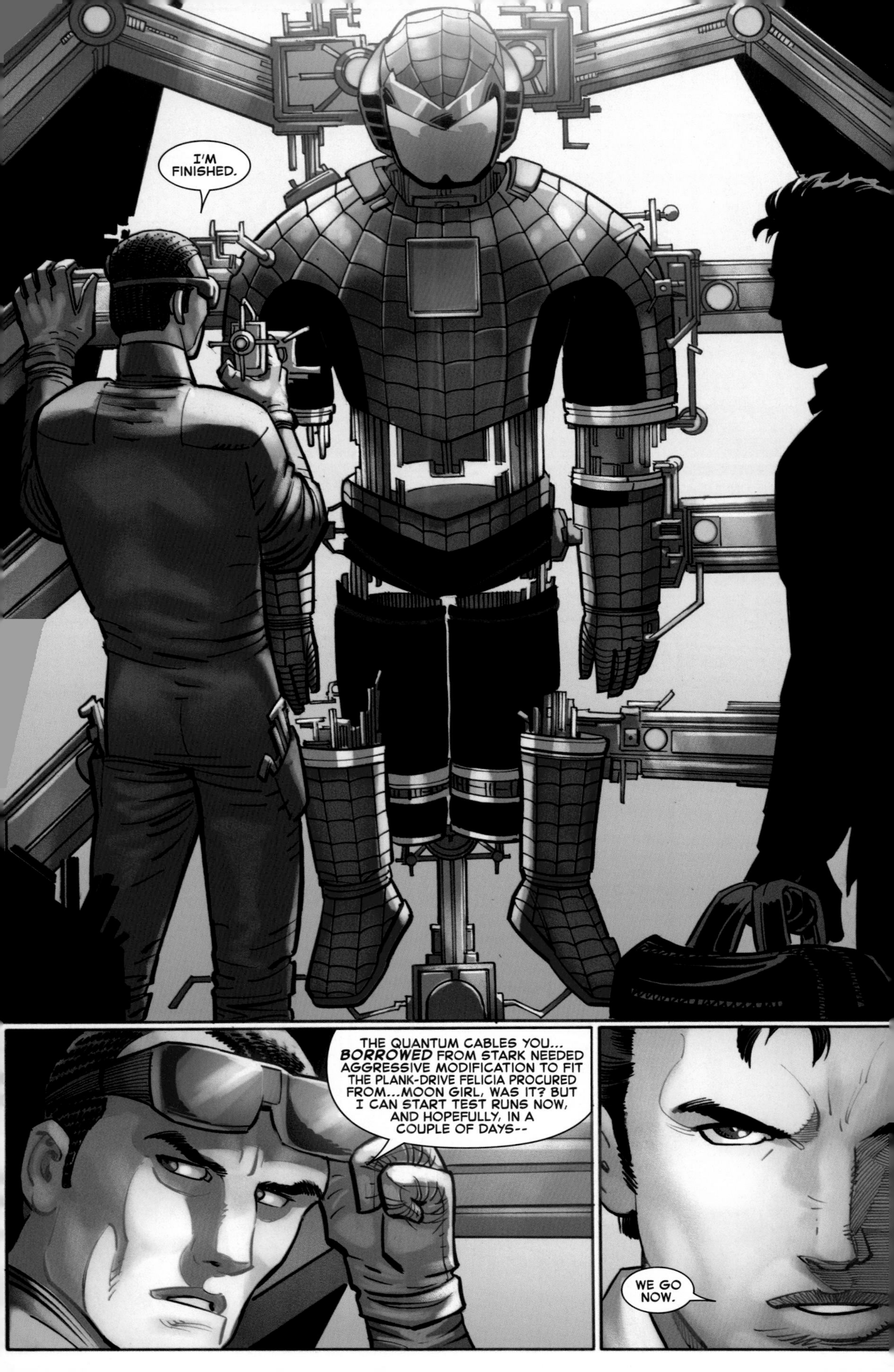

I'M FINISHED.
THE QUANTUM CABLES YOU... BORROWED FROM STARK NEEDED AGGRESSIVE MODIFICATION TO FIT THE PLANK-DRIVE FELICIA PROCURED FROM...MOON GIRL, WAS IT? BUT I CAN START TEST RUNS NOW, AND HOPEFULLY, IN A COUPLE OF DAYS--
WE GO NOW.

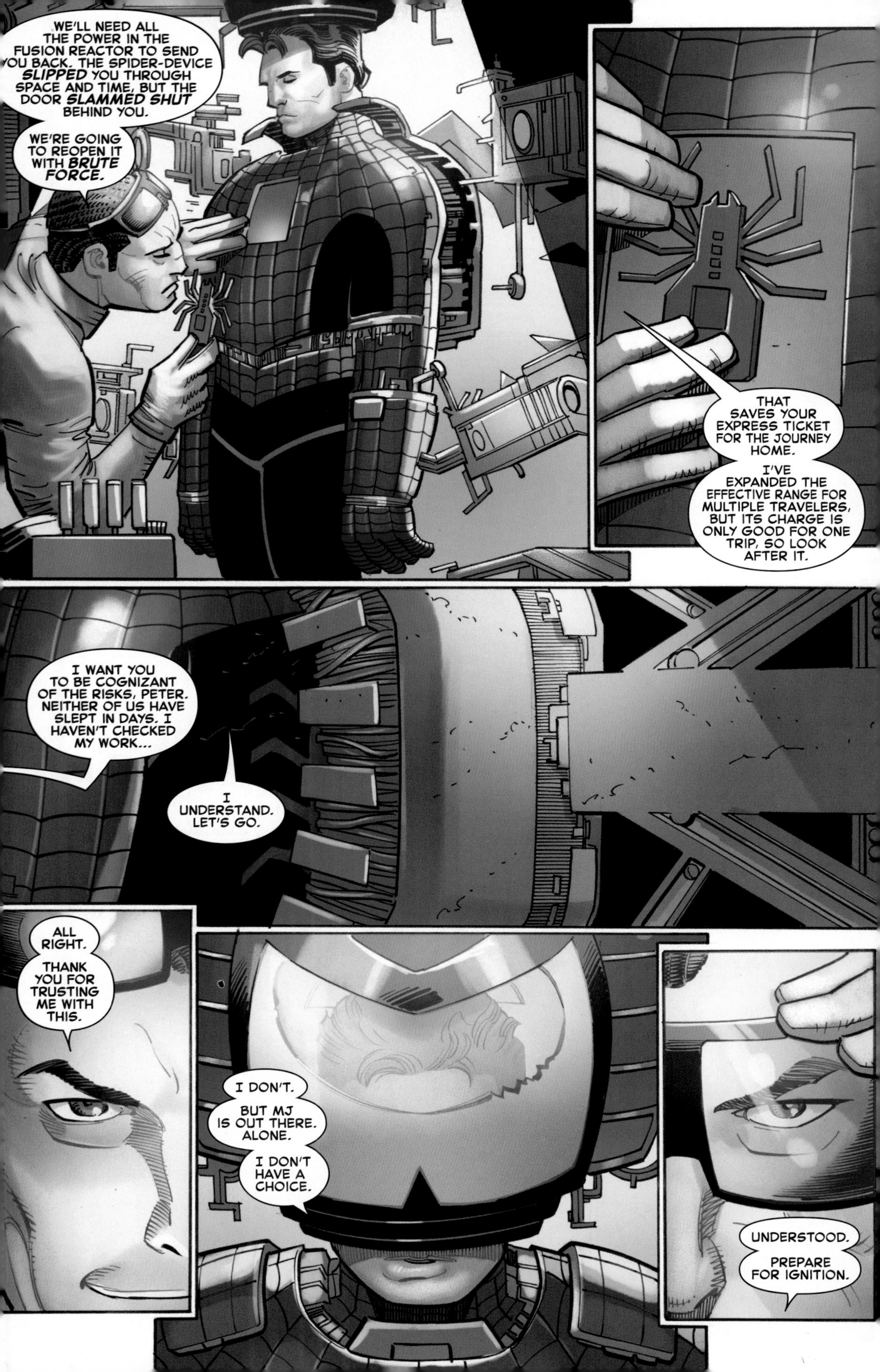
WE'LL NEED ALL THE POWER IN THE FUSION REACTOR TO SEND YOU BACK. THE SPIDER-DEVICE SLIPPED YOU THROUGH SPACE AND TIME, BUT THE DOOR SLAMMED SHUT BEHIND YOU.
WE'RE GOING TO REOPEN IT WITH BRUTE FORCE.
THAT SAVES YOUR EXPRESS TICKET FOR THE JOURNEY HOME.
I'VE EXPANDED THE EFFECTIVE RANGE FOR MULTIPLE TRAVELERS, BUT ITS CHARGE IS ONLY GOOD FOR ONE TRIP, SO LOOK AFTER IT.
I WANT YOU TO BE COGNIZANT OF THE RISKS, PETER. NEITHER OF US HAVE SLEPT IN DAYS. I HAVEN'T CHECKED MY WORK...
I UNDERSTAND. LET'S GO.
ALL RIGHT.
THANK YOU FOR TRUSTING ME WITH THIS.
I DON'T.
BUT MJ IS OUT THERE. ALONE.
I DON'T HAVE A CHOICE.
UNDERSTOOD.
PREPARE FOR IGNITION.

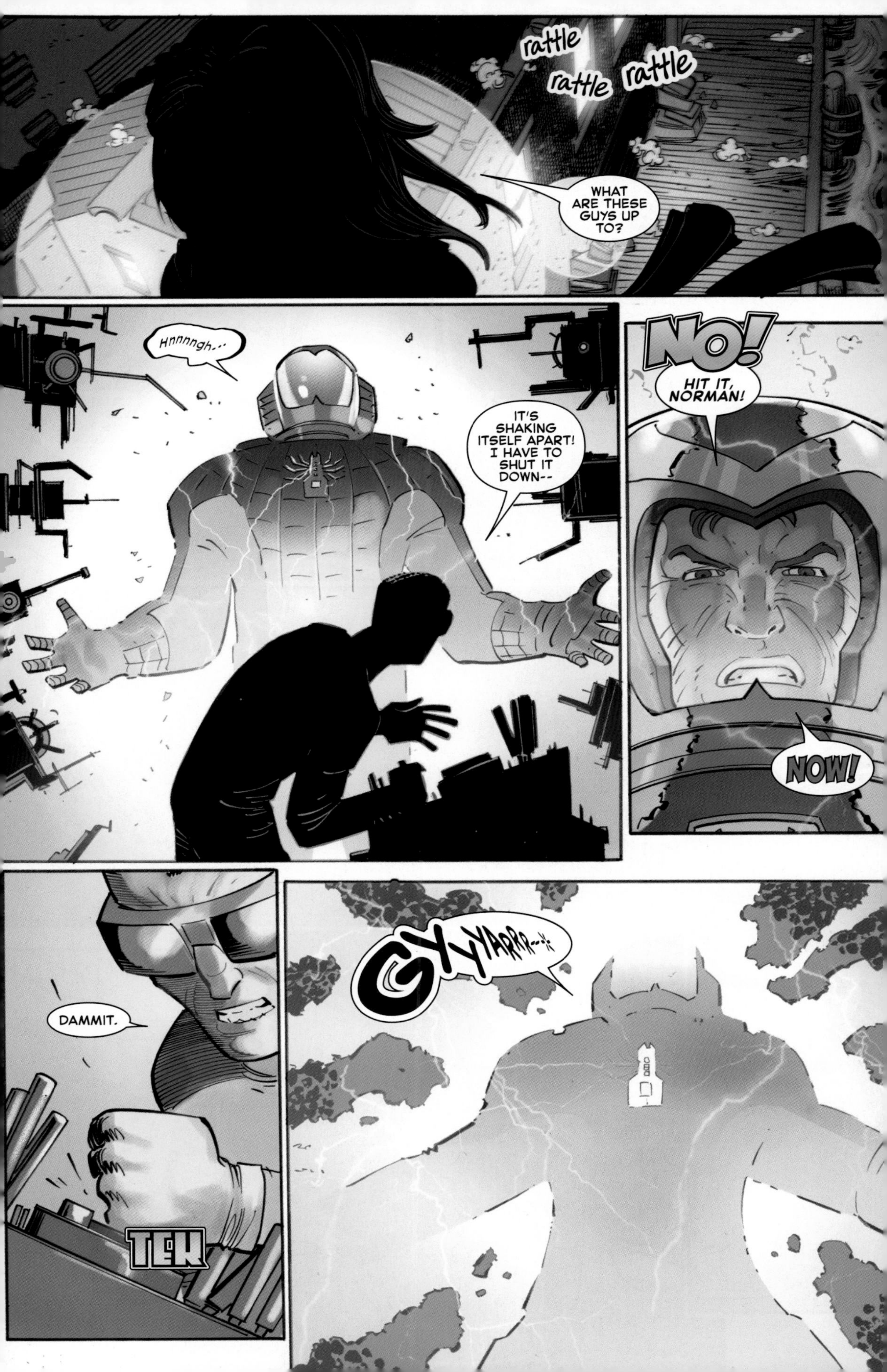
rattle
rattle rattle
WHAT ARE THESE GUYS UP TO?
Hnnnngh...
IT'S SHAKING ITSELF APART! I HAVE TO SHUT IT DOWN--
NO!
HIT IT, NORMAN!
NOW!
DAMMIT.
TEK
GYYYARRR--!!

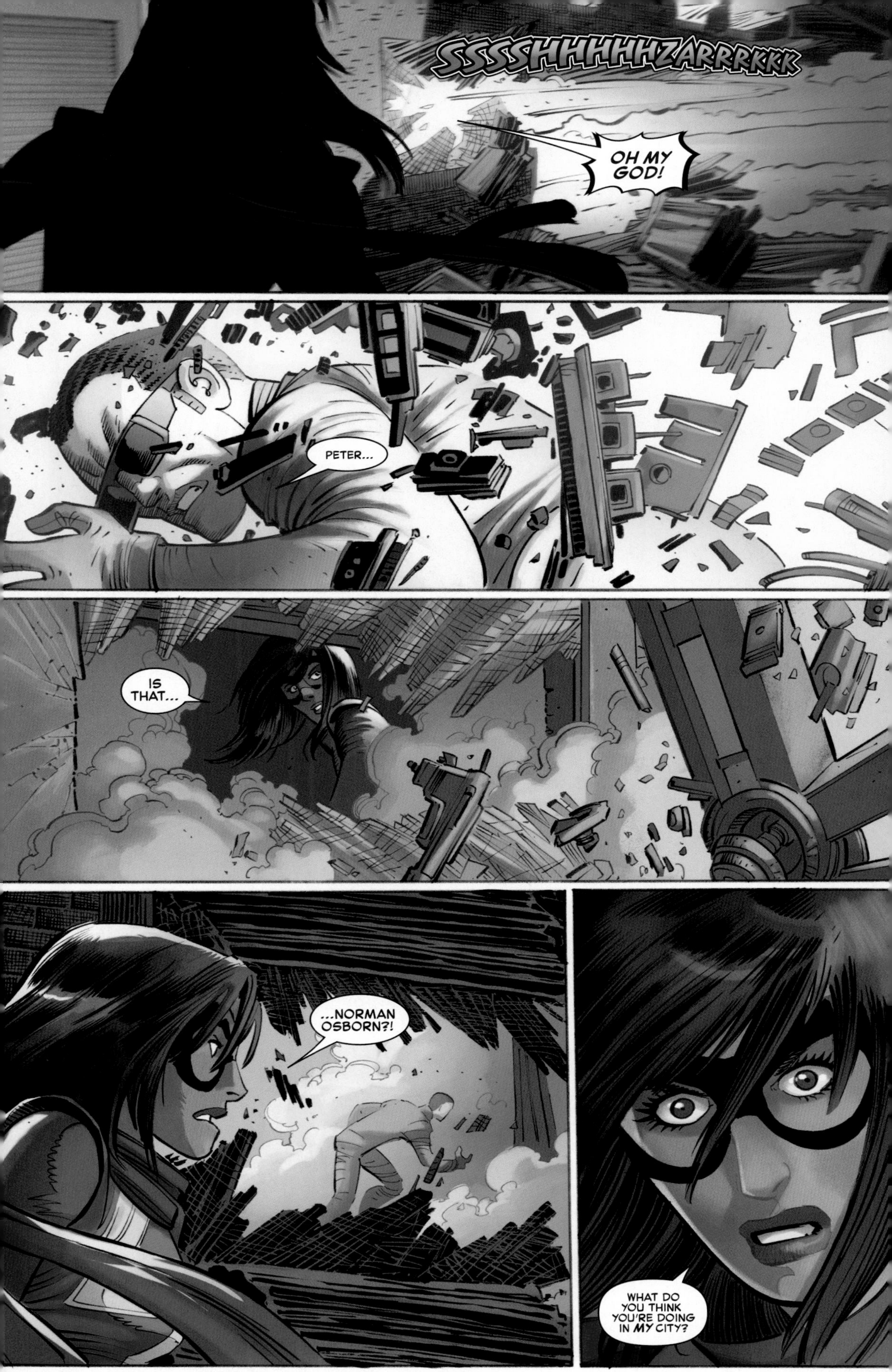
SSSSHHHHHZARRRKKK
OH MY GOD!
PETER...
IS THAT...
...NORMAN OSBORN?!
WHAT DO YOU THINK YOU'RE DOING IN *MY* CITY?

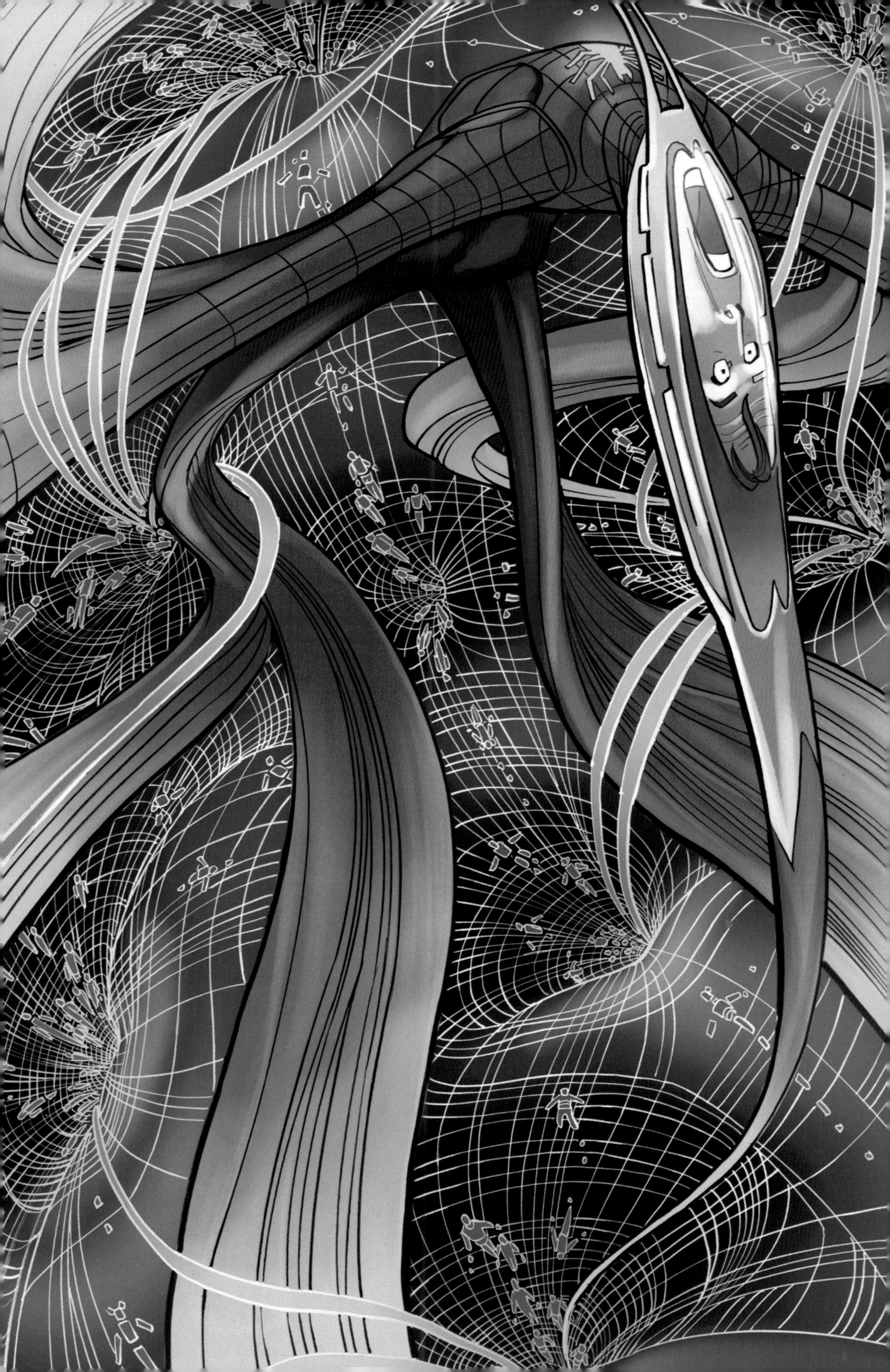

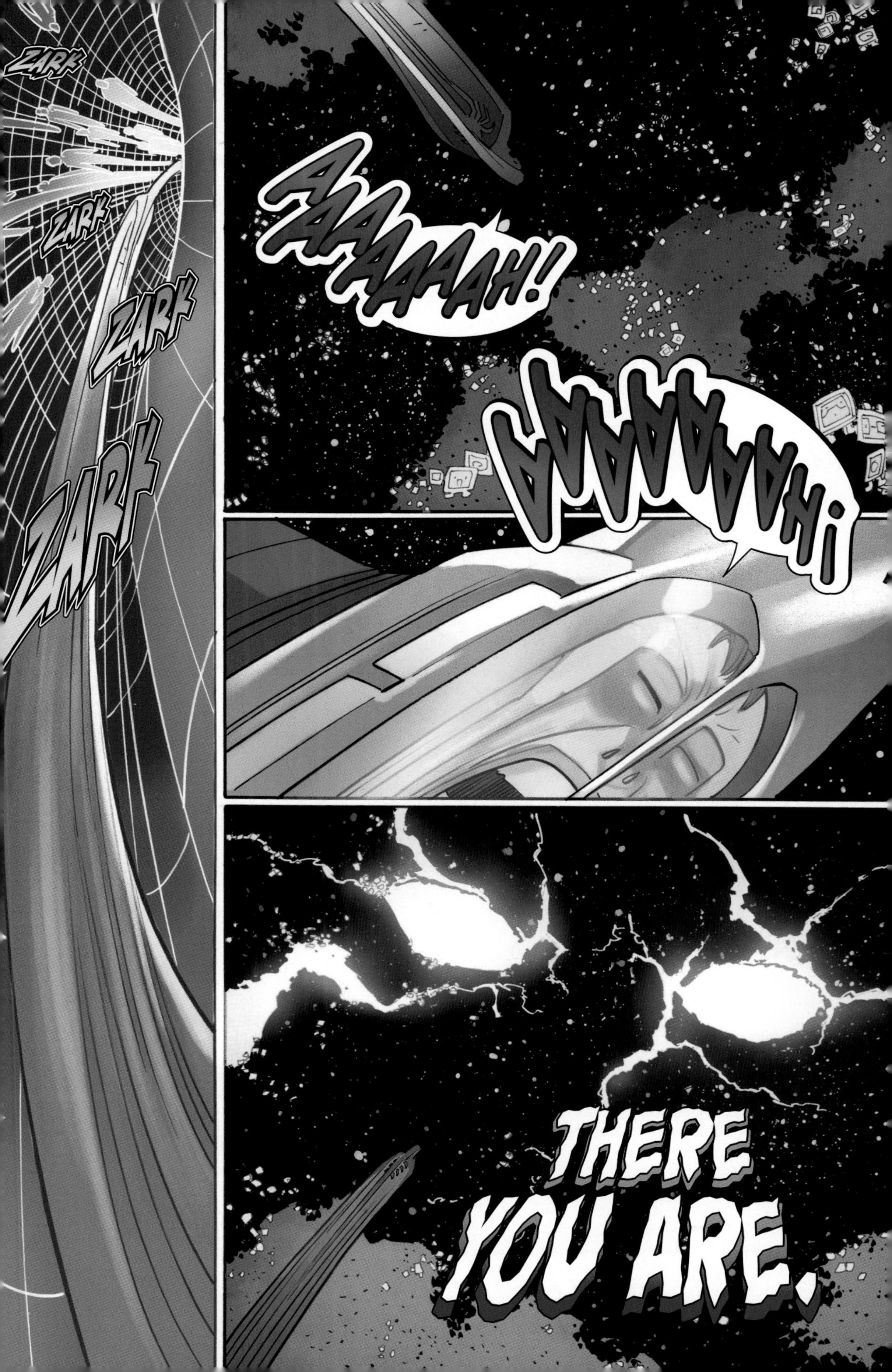

ZARK
ZARK
ZARK
ZARK
AAAAAAAH!
AAAAAAAH!
THERE YOU ARE.

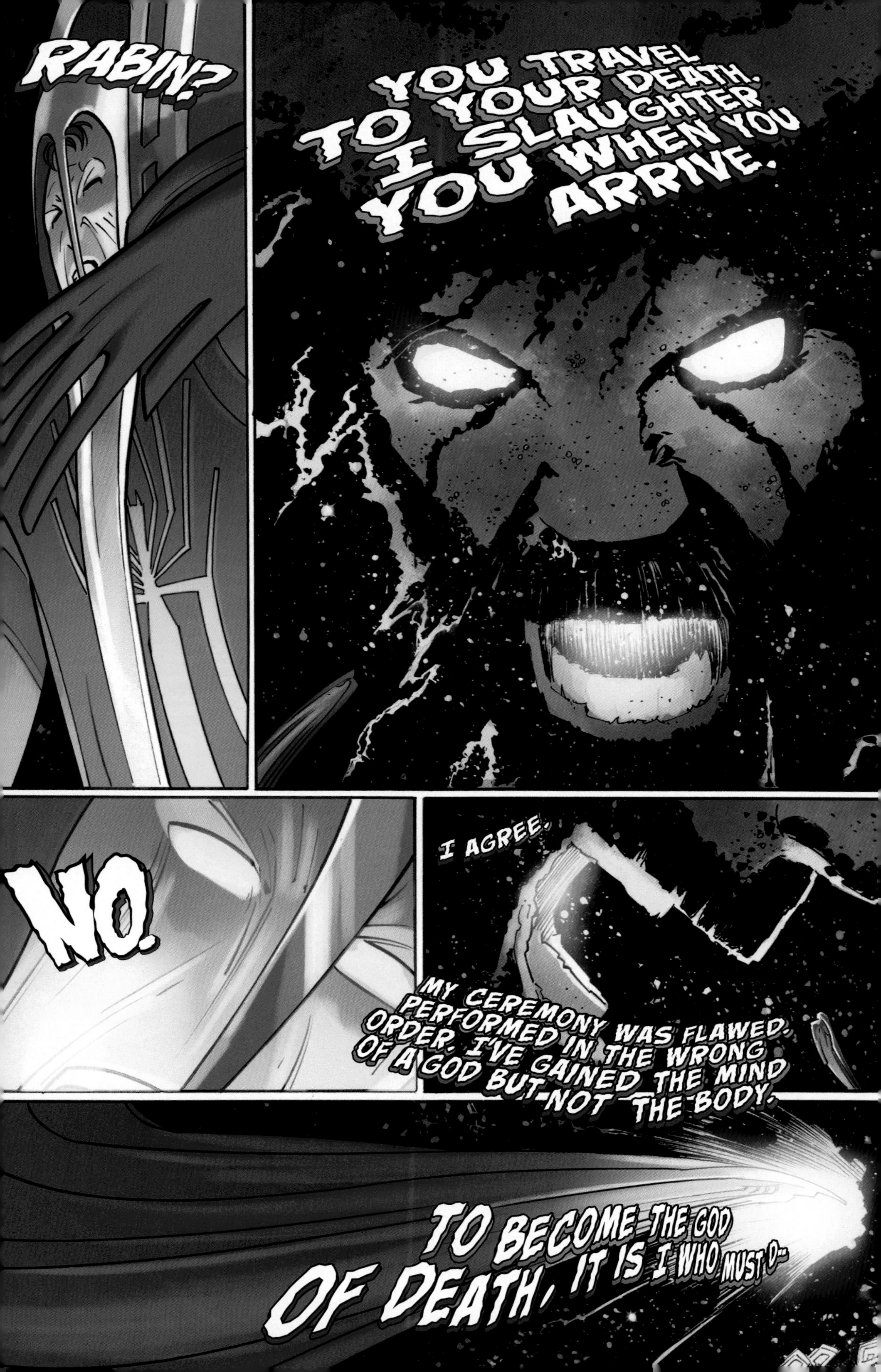
RABIN?
YOU TRAVEL TO YOUR DEATH. I SLAUGHTER YOU WHEN YOU ARRIVE.
NO.
I AGREE.
MY CEREMONY WAS FLAWED. PERFORMED IN THE WRONG ORDER. I'VE GAINED THE MIND OF A GOD BUT NOT THE BODY.
TO BECOME THE GOD OF DEATH, IT IS I WHO MUST D--

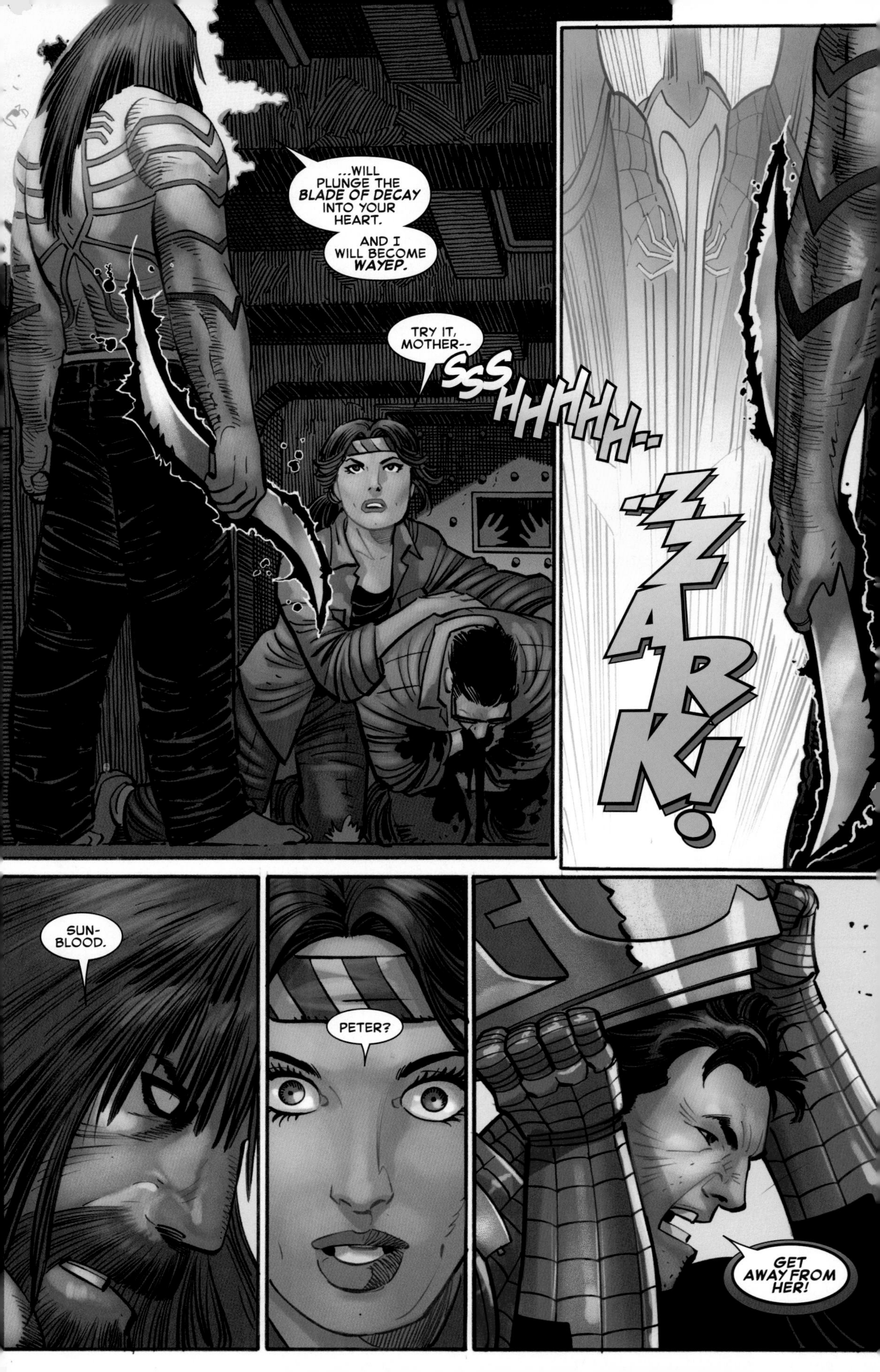
...WILL PLUNGE THE *BLADE OF DECAY* INTO YOUR HEART.
AND I WILL BECOME *WAYEP.*
TRY IT, MOTHER--
SSSHHHHHH--
--ZZARK!
SUN-BLOOD.
PETER?
GET AWAY FROM HER!

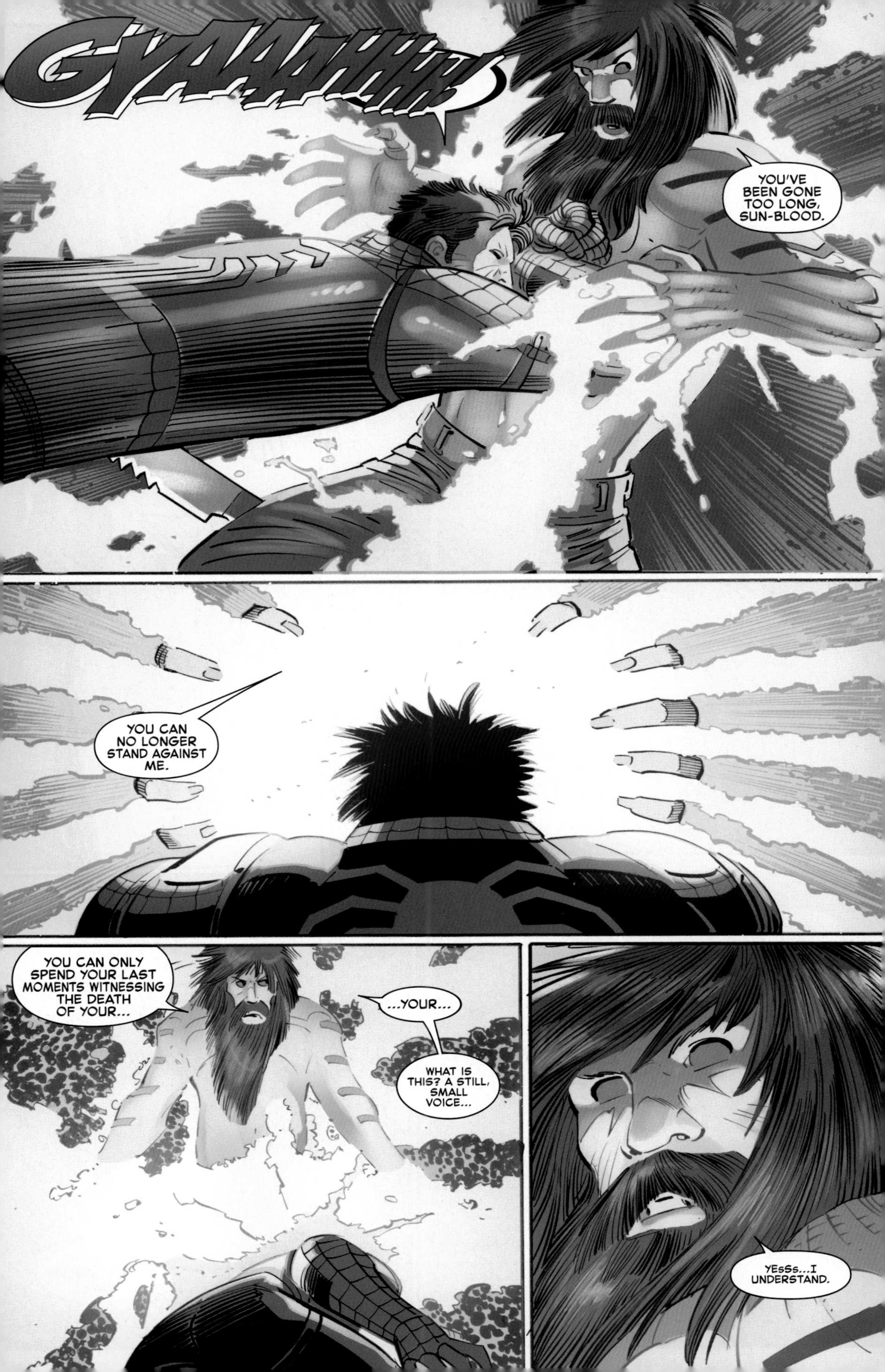
GYAAAHHHH!
YOU'VE BEEN GONE TOO LONG, SUN-BLOOD.
YOU CAN NO LONGER STAND AGAINST ME.
YOU CAN ONLY SPEND YOUR LAST MOMENTS WITNESSING THE DEATH OF YOUR...
...YOUR...
WHAT IS THIS? A STILL, SMALL VOICE...
YEsSs...I UNDERSTAND.

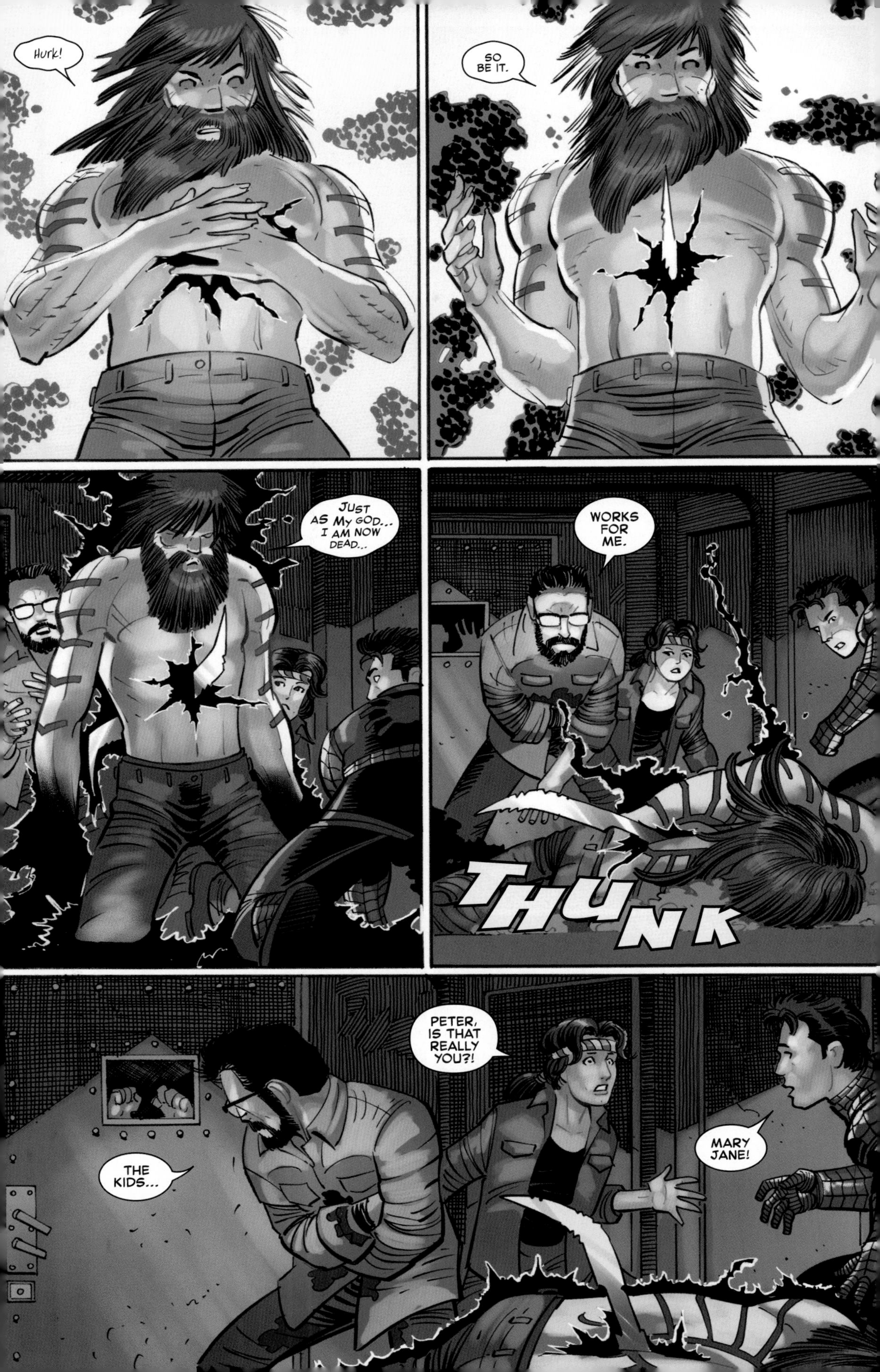
Hurk!
SO BE IT.
JUST AS MY GOD... I AM NOW DEAD...
WORKS FOR ME.
THUNK
PETER, IS THAT REALLY YOU?!
THE KIDS...
MARY JANE!

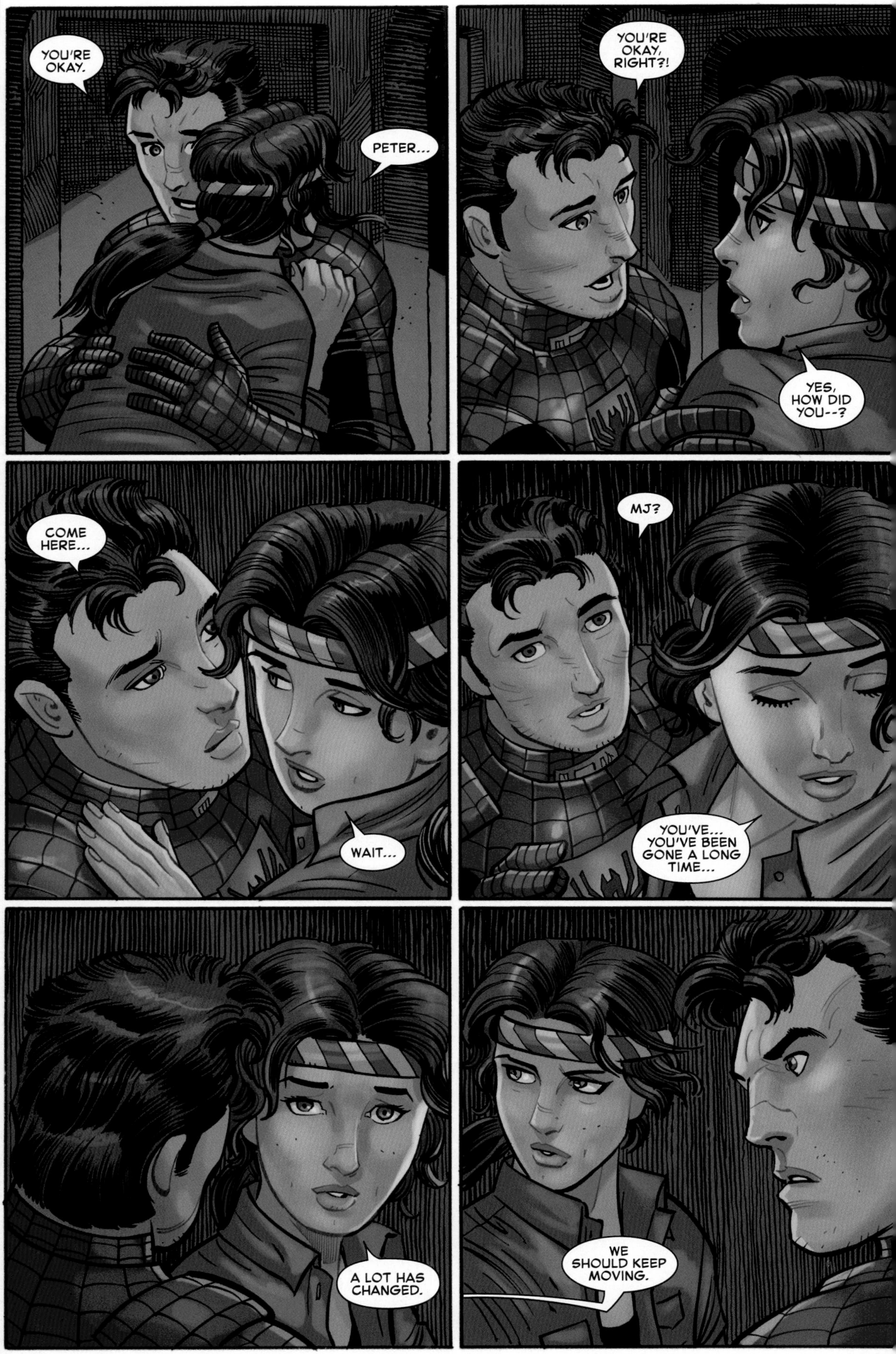
YOU'RE OKAY.
PETER...
YOU'RE OKAY, RIGHT?!
YES, HOW DID YOU--?
COME HERE...
WAIT...
MJ?
YOU'VE... YOU'VE BEEN GONE A LONG TIME...
A LOT HAS CHANGED.
WE SHOULD KEEP MOVING.

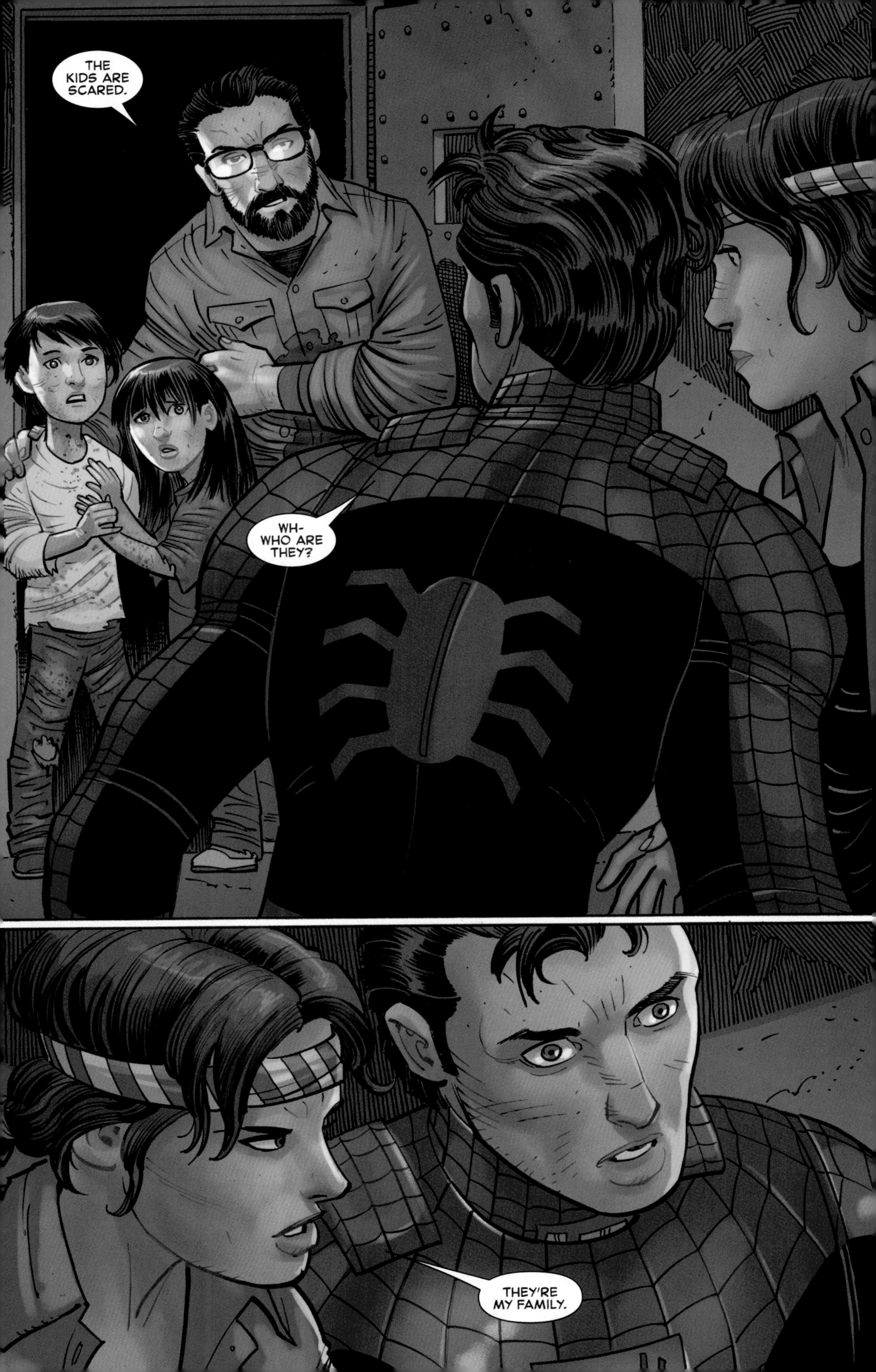
THE KIDS ARE SCARED.
WH- WHO ARE THEY?
THEY'RE MY FAMILY.

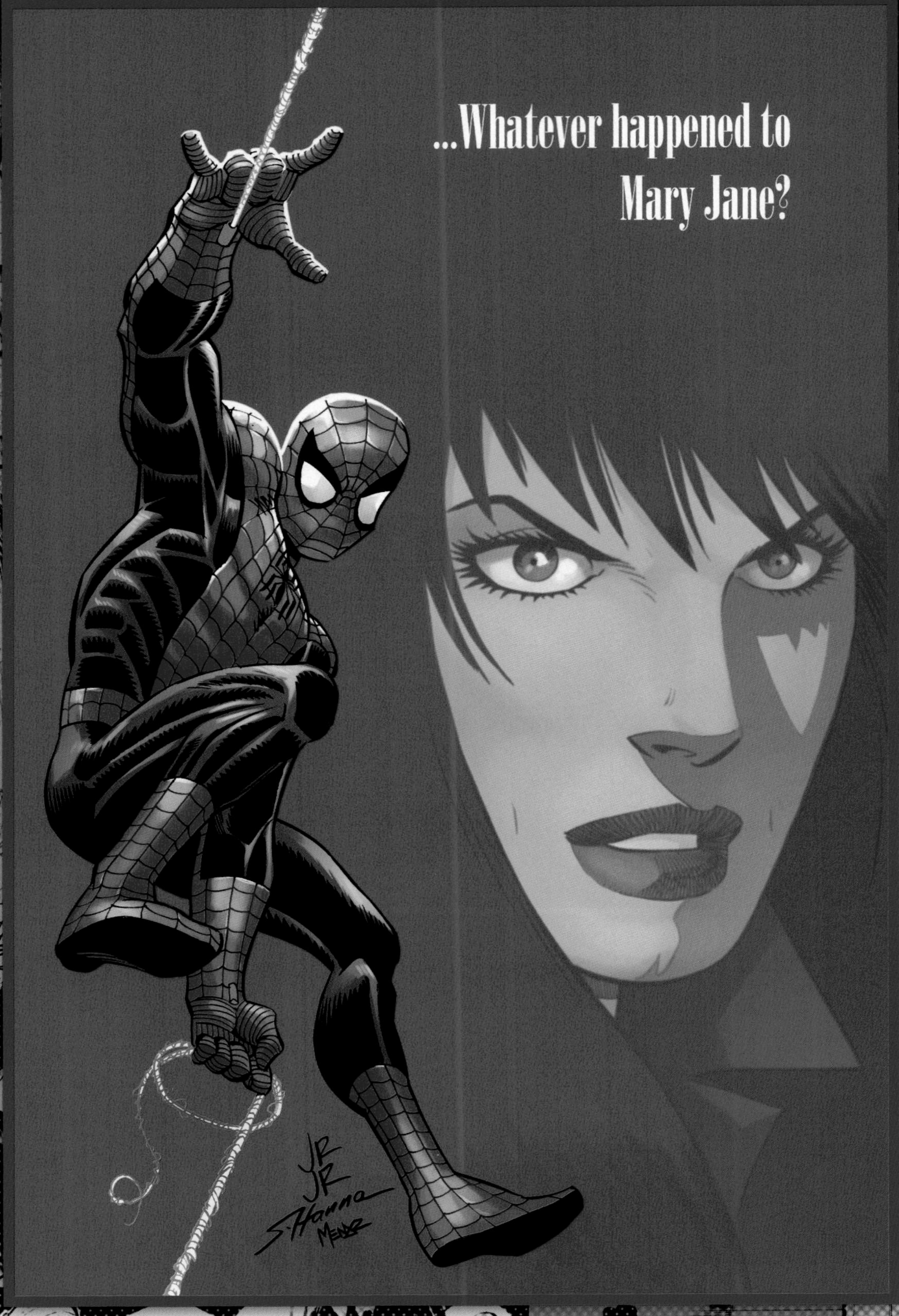
...Whatever happened to
Mary Jane?
JR JR
S. Hanna
Mendr

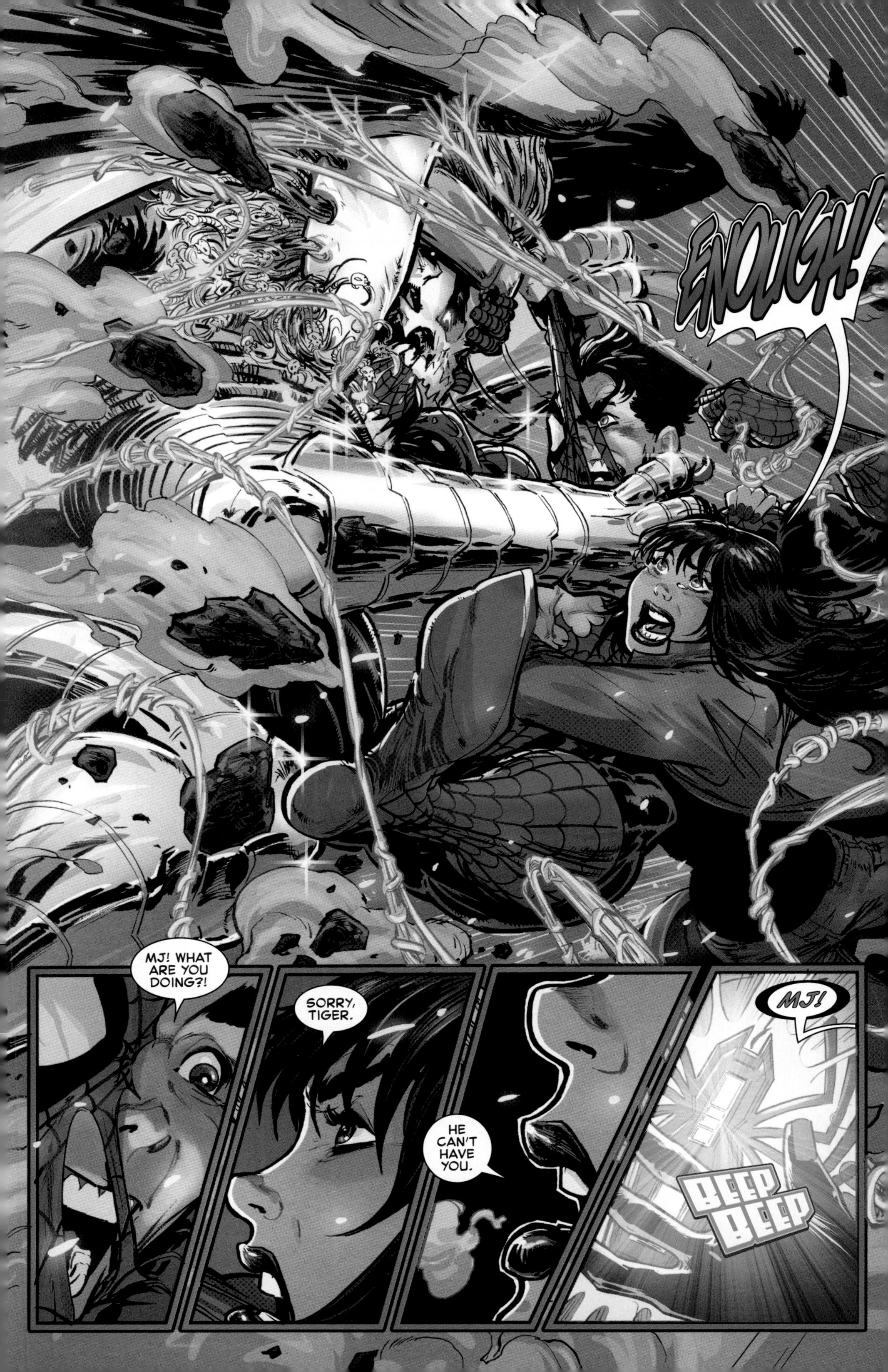
ENOUGH!
MJ! WHAT ARE YOU DOING?!
SORRY, TIGER.
HE CAN'T HAVE YOU.
MJ!
BEEP BEEP

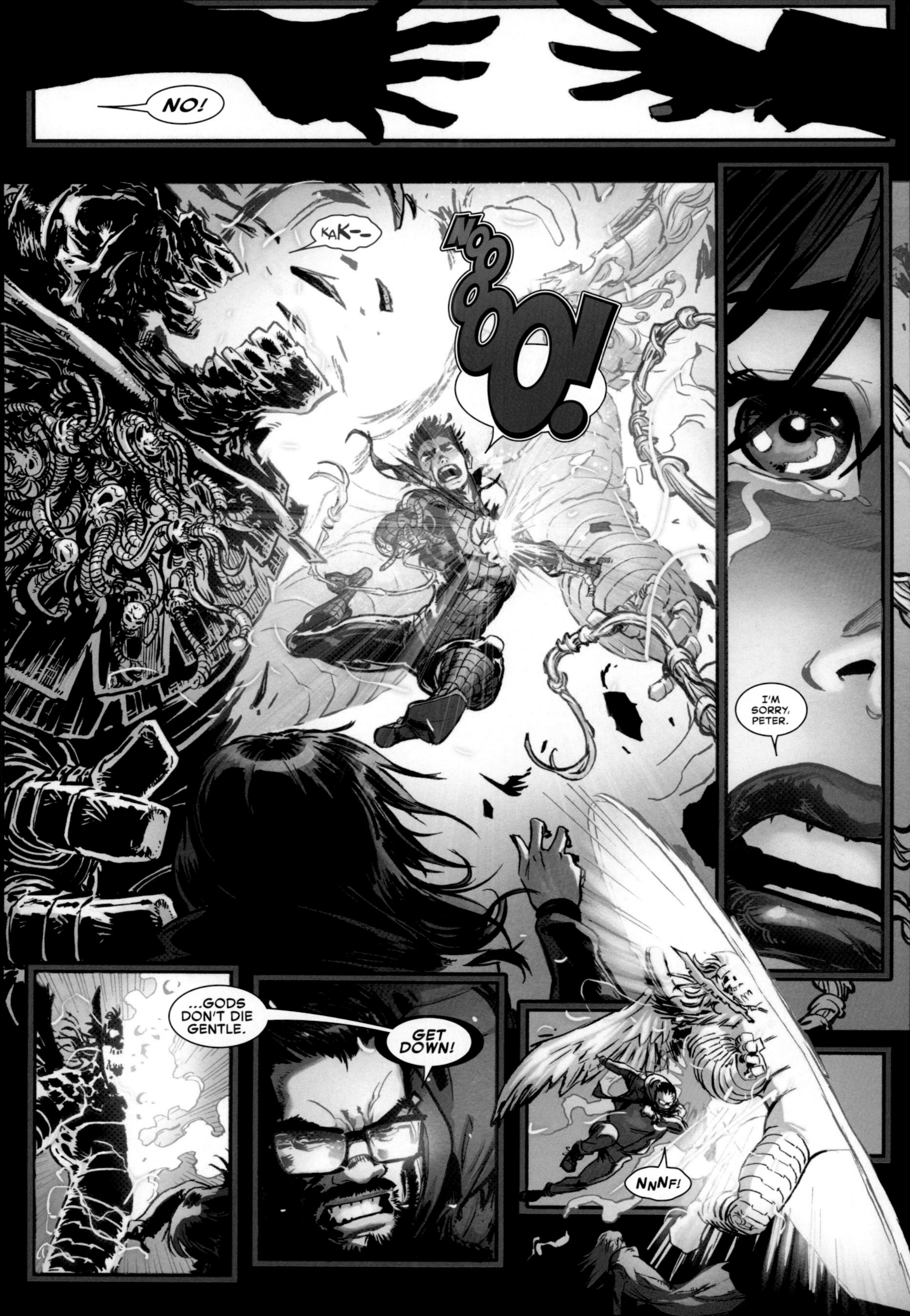
NO!
KAK--
NOOOOOO!
I'M SORRY, PETER.
...GODS DON'T DIE GENTLE.
GET DOWN!
NNNF!

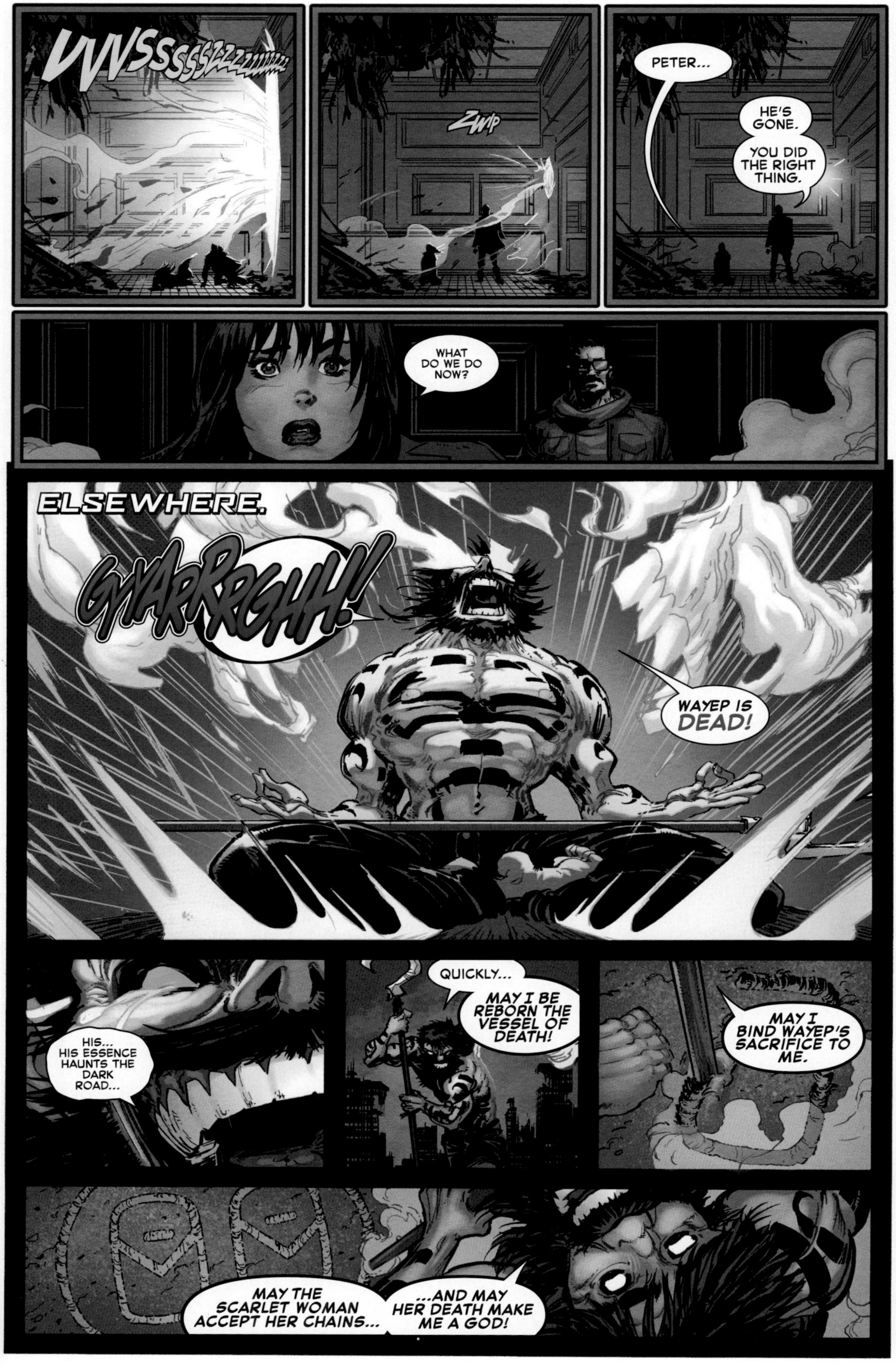
VVVSSSSSSZZZZZZZZZZZ
ZWIP
PETER...
HE'S GONE.
YOU DID THE RIGHT THING.
WHAT DO WE DO NOW?
ELSEWHERE.
GYARRRGHH!
WAYEP IS DEAD!
HIS... HIS ESSENCE HAUNTS THE DARK ROAD...
QUICKLY...
MAY I BE REBORN THE VESSEL OF DEATH!
MAY I BIND WAYEP'S SACRIFICE TO ME.
MAY THE SCARLET WOMAN ACCEPT HER CHAINS...
...AND MAY HER DEATH MAKE ME A GOD!

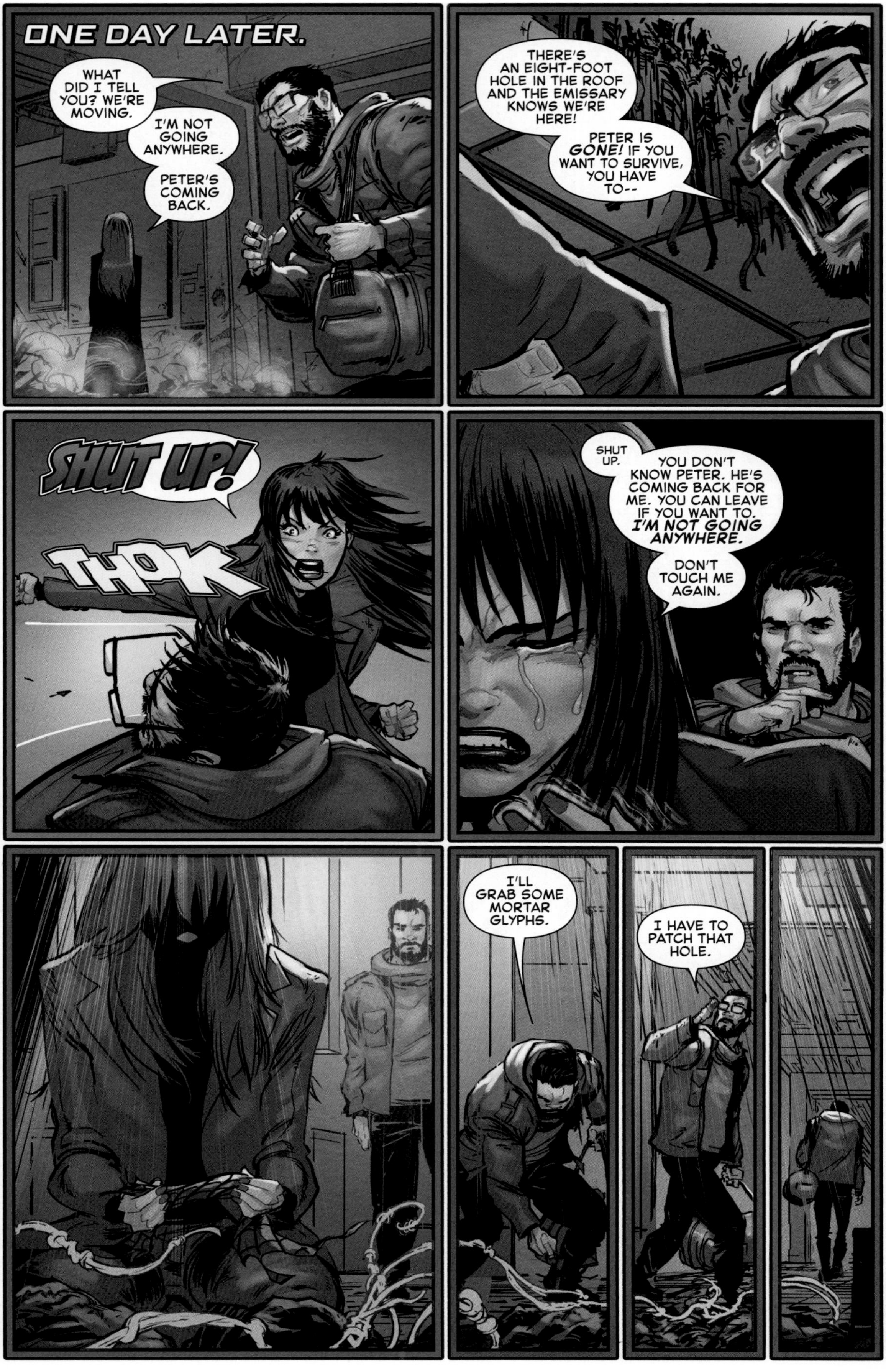
ONE DAY LATER.
WHAT DID I TELL YOU? WE'RE MOVING.
I'M NOT GOING ANYWHERE.
PETER'S COMING BACK.
THERE'S AN EIGHT-FOOT HOLE IN THE ROOF AND THE EMISSARY KNOWS WE'RE HERE!
PETER IS *GONE!* IF YOU WANT TO SURVIVE, YOU HAVE TO--
SHUT UP!
THOK
SHUT UP.
YOU DON'T KNOW PETER. HE'S COMING BACK FOR ME. YOU CAN LEAVE IF YOU WANT TO. ***I'M NOT GOING ANYWHERE.***
DON'T TOUCH ME AGAIN.
I'LL GRAB SOME MORTAR GLYPHS.
I HAVE TO PATCH THAT HOLE.

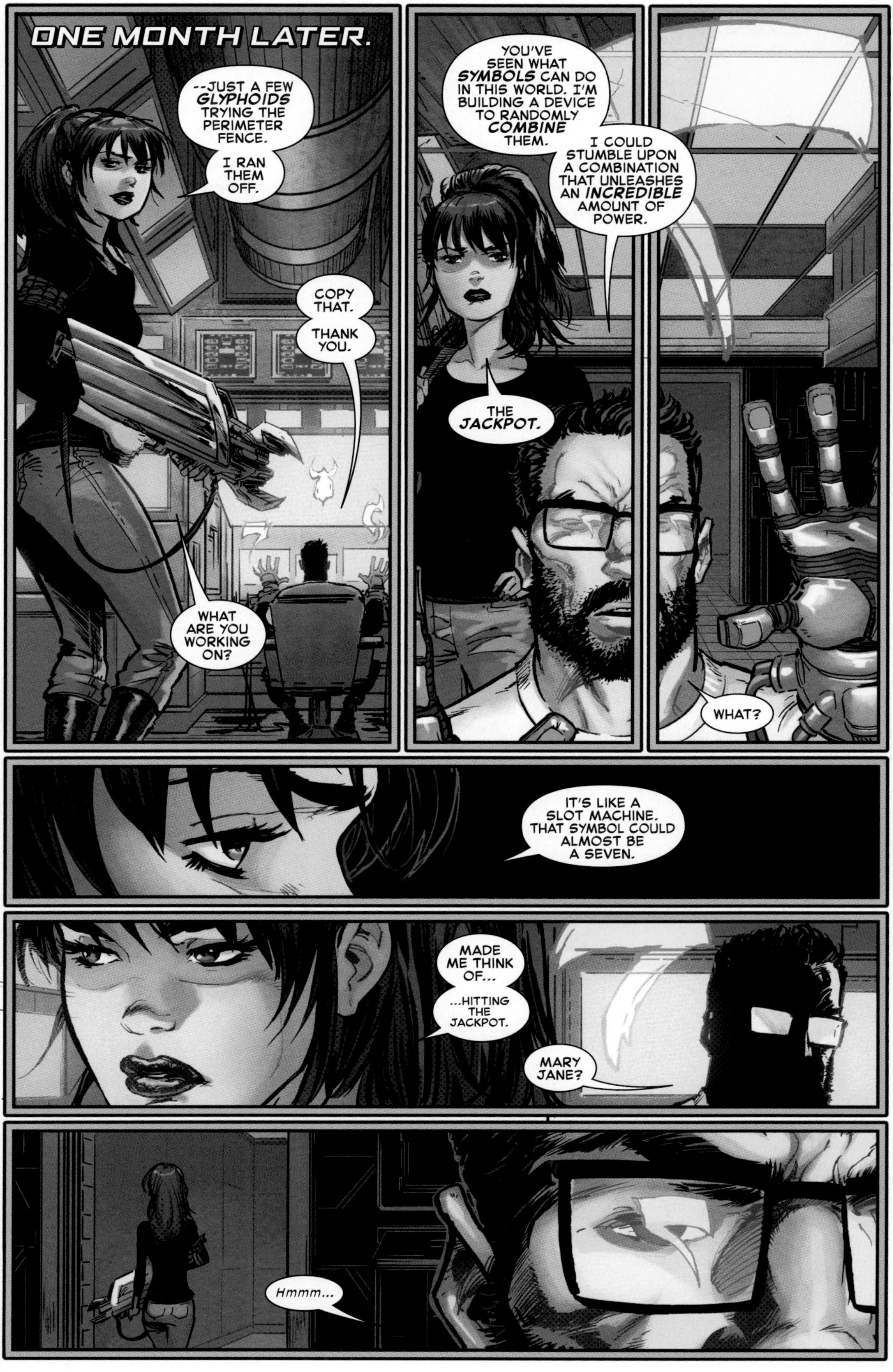
ONE MONTH LATER.
--JUST A FEW GLYPHOIDS TRYING THE PERIMETER FENCE.
I RAN THEM OFF.
COPY THAT.
THANK YOU.
WHAT ARE YOU WORKING ON?
YOU'VE SEEN WHAT SYMBOLS CAN DO IN THIS WORLD. I'M BUILDING A DEVICE TO RANDOMLY COMBINE THEM.
I COULD STUMBLE UPON A COMBINATION THAT UNLEASHES AN INCREDIBLE AMOUNT OF POWER.
THE JACKPOT.
WHAT?
IT'S LIKE A SLOT MACHINE. THAT SYMBOL COULD ALMOST BE A SEVEN.
MADE ME THINK OF...
...HITTING THE JACKPOT.
MARY JANE?
Hmmm...

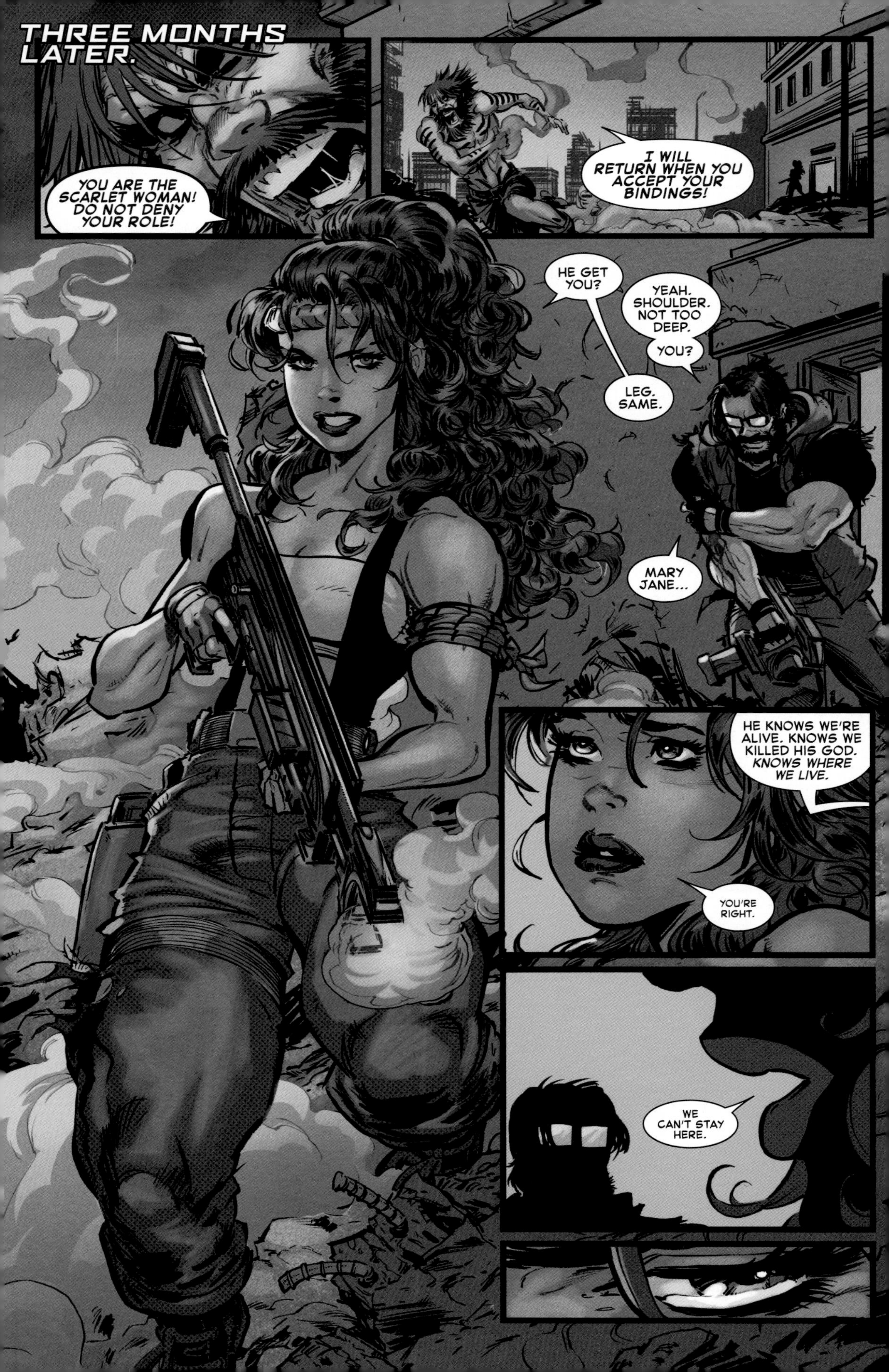
THREE MONTHS LATER.
YOU ARE THE SCARLET WOMAN! DO NOT DENY YOUR ROLE!
I WILL RETURN WHEN YOU ACCEPT YOUR BINDINGS!
HE GET YOU?
YEAH. SHOULDER. NOT TOO DEEP.
YOU?
LEG. SAME.
MARY JANE...
HE KNOWS WE'RE ALIVE. KNOWS WE KILLED HIS GOD. KNOWS WHERE WE LIVE.
YOU'RE RIGHT.
WE CAN'T STAY HERE.

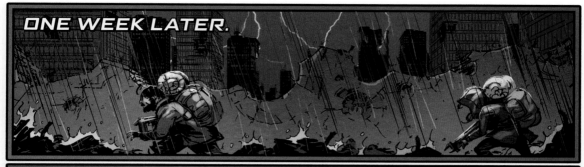

ONE WEEK LATER.

WHAT'S THE HOLD UP, TIGER?

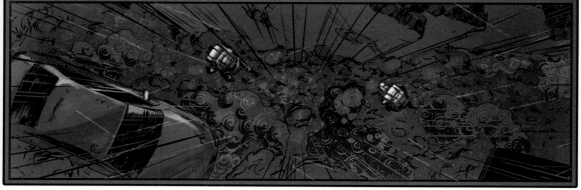

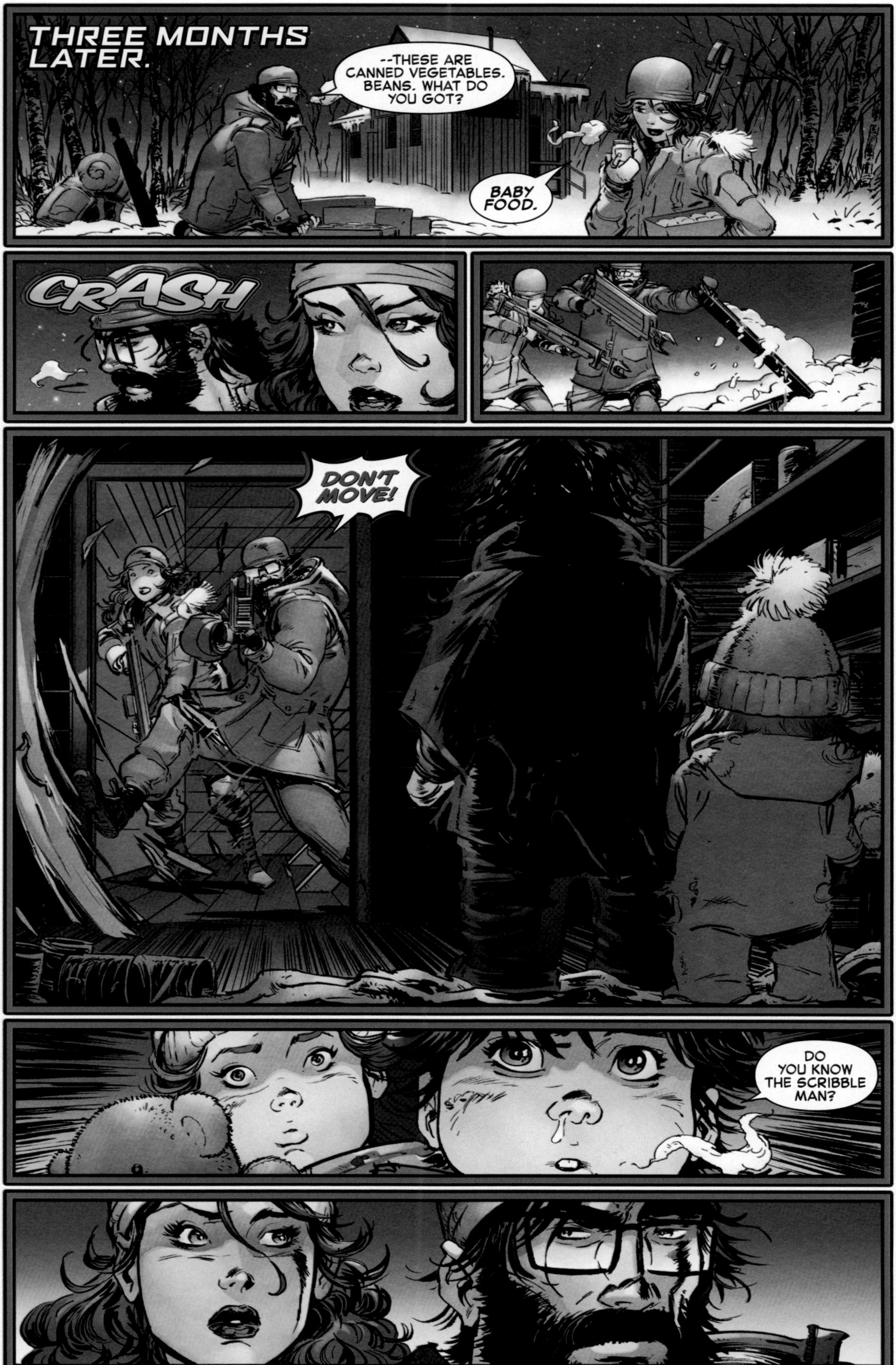
THREE MONTHS LATER.
--THESE ARE CANNED VEGETABLES. BEANS. WHAT DO YOU GOT?
BABY FOOD.
CRASH
DON'T MOVE!
DO YOU KNOW THE SCRIBBLE MAN?

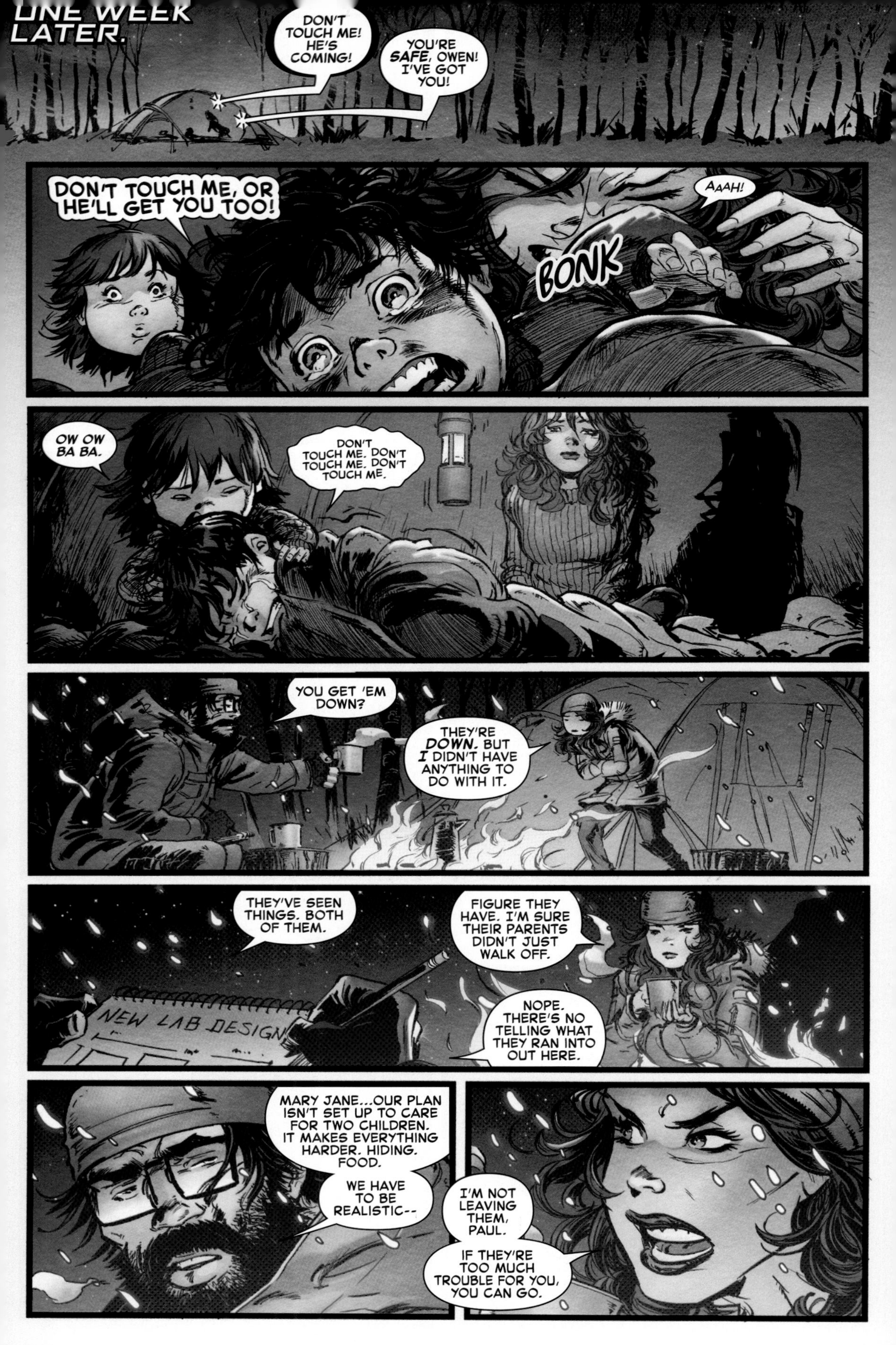
ONE WEEK LATER.
DON'T TOUCH ME! HE'S COMING!
YOU'RE SAFE, OWEN! I'VE GOT YOU!
DON'T TOUCH ME, OR HE'LL GET YOU TOO!
AAAH!
BONK
OW OW BA BA.
DON'T TOUCH ME. DON'T TOUCH ME. DON'T TOUCH ME.
YOU GET 'EM DOWN?
THEY'RE DOWN. BUT I DIDN'T HAVE ANYTHING TO DO WITH IT.
THEY'VE SEEN THINGS. BOTH OF THEM.
FIGURE THEY HAVE. I'M SURE THEIR PARENTS DIDN'T JUST WALK OFF.
NEW LAB DESIGN
NOPE. THERE'S NO TELLING WHAT THEY RAN INTO OUT HERE.
MARY JANE...OUR PLAN ISN'T SET UP TO CARE FOR TWO CHILDREN. IT MAKES EVERYTHING HARDER. HIDING. FOOD.
WE HAVE TO BE REALISTIC--
I'M NOT LEAVING THEM, PAUL.
IF THEY'RE TOO MUCH TROUBLE FOR YOU, YOU CAN GO.

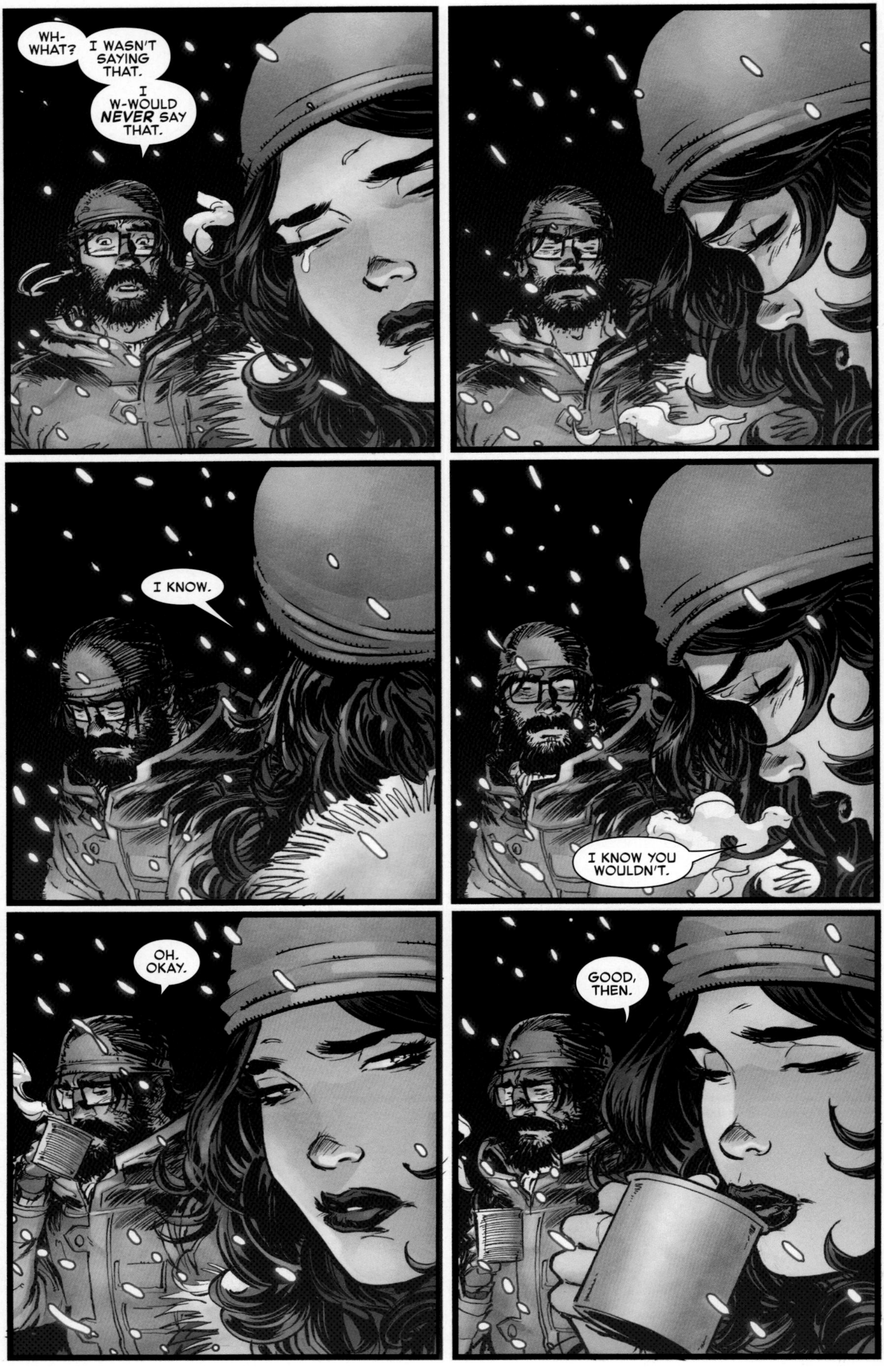
WH- WHAT?
I WASN'T SAYING THAT.
I W-WOULD NEVER SAY THAT.
I KNOW.
I KNOW YOU WOULDN'T.
OH. OKAY.
GOOD, THEN.

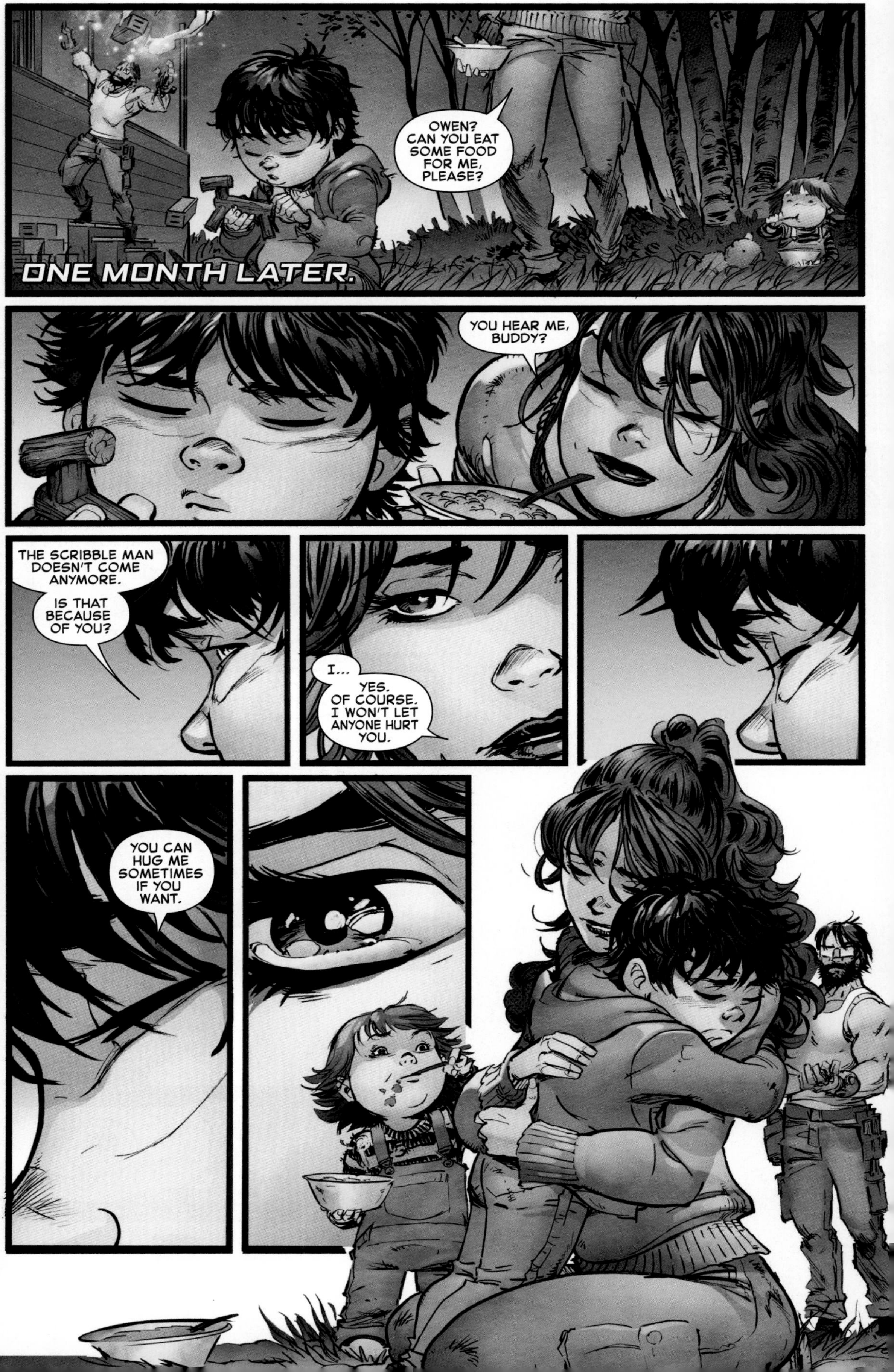
OWEN? CAN YOU EAT SOME FOOD FOR ME, PLEASE?
ONE MONTH LATER.
YOU HEAR ME, BUDDY?
THE SCRIBBLE MAN DOESN'T COME ANYMORE.
IS THAT BECAUSE OF YOU?
I...
YES. OF COURSE. I WON'T LET ANYONE HURT YOU.
YOU CAN HUG ME SOMETIMES IF YOU WANT.

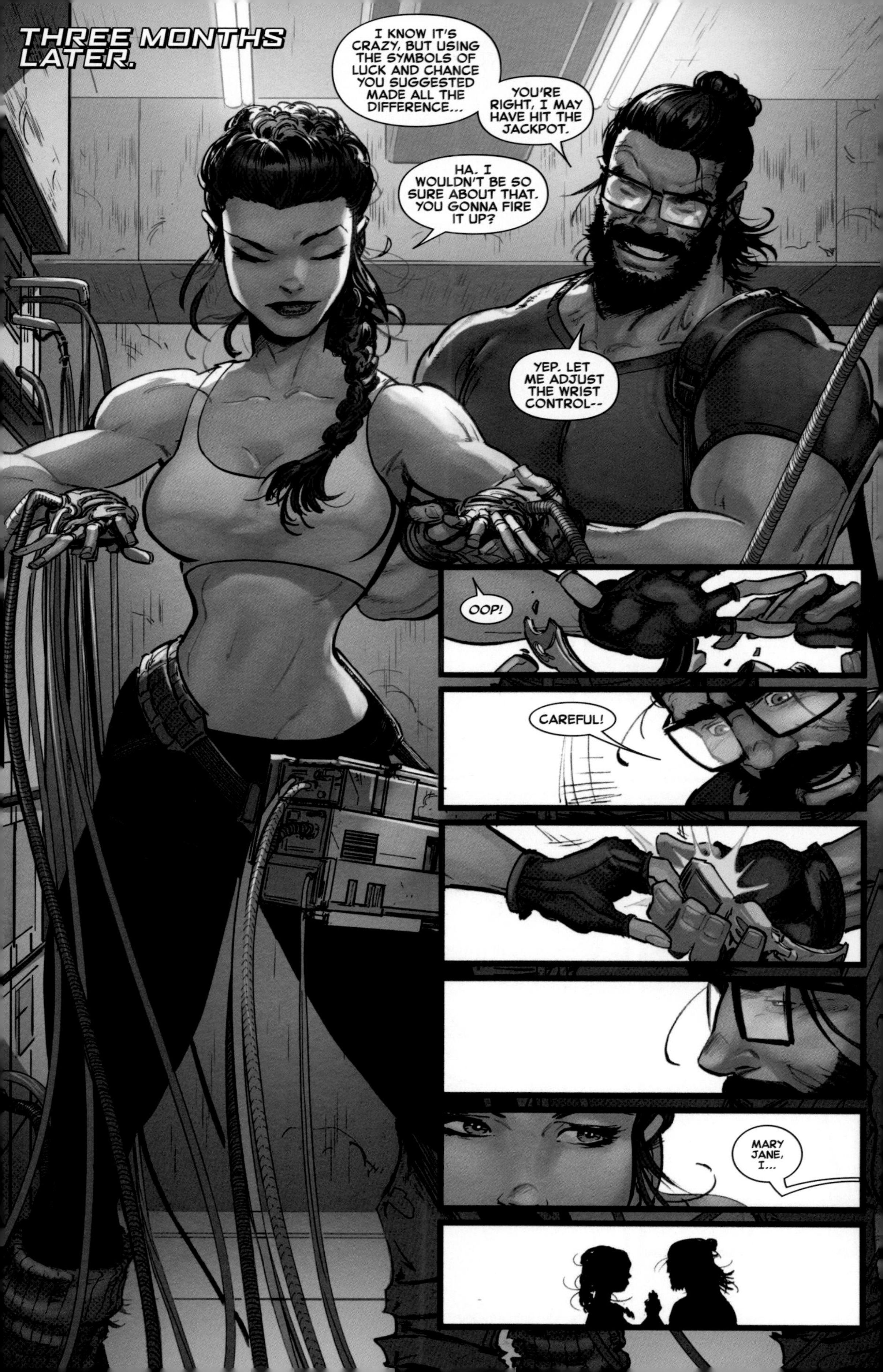
THREE MONTHS LATER.
I KNOW IT'S CRAZY, BUT USING THE SYMBOLS OF LUCK AND CHANCE YOU SUGGESTED MADE ALL THE DIFFERENCE...
YOU'RE RIGHT, I MAY HAVE HIT THE JACKPOT.
HA. I WOULDN'T BE SO SURE ABOUT THAT. YOU GONNA FIRE IT UP?
YEP. LET ME ADJUST THE WRIST CONTROL--
OOP!
CAREFUL!
MARY JANE, I...

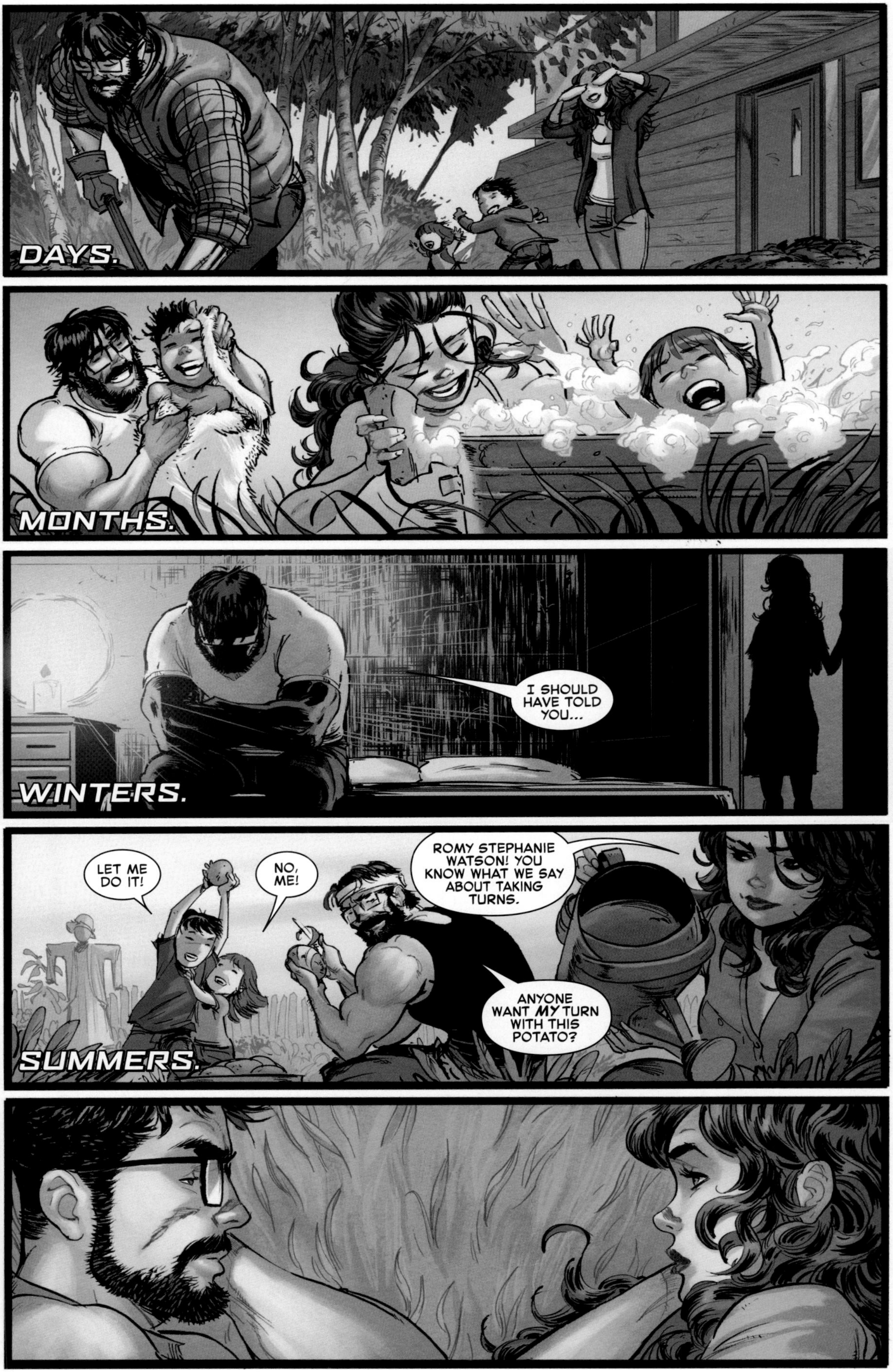
DAYS.
MONTHS.
I SHOULD HAVE TOLD YOU...
WINTERS.
LET ME DO IT!
NO, ME!
ROMY STEPHANIE WATSON! YOU KNOW WHAT WE SAY ABOUT TAKING TURNS.
ANYONE WANT MY TURN WITH THIS POTATO?
SUMMERS.

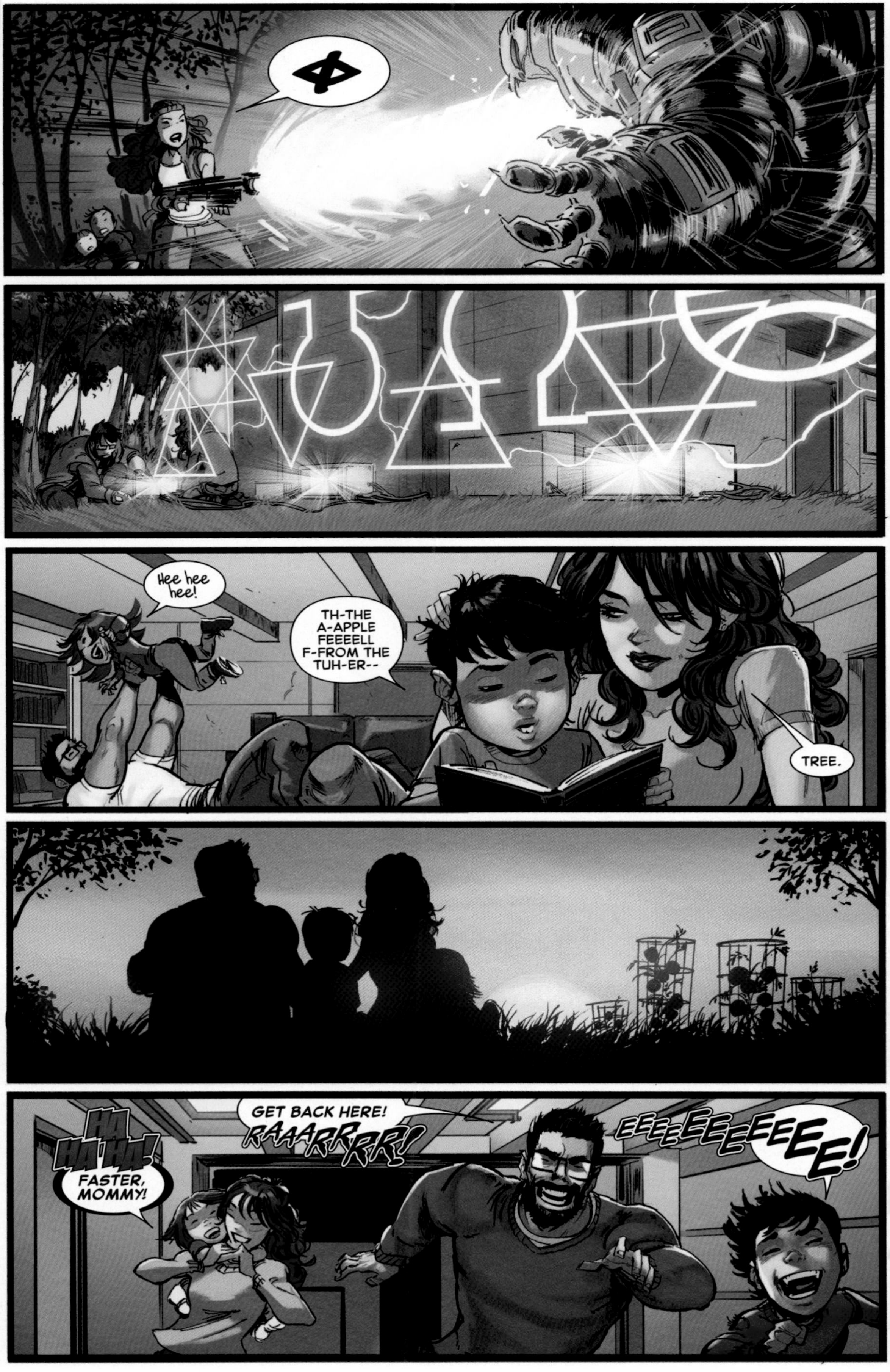

TH-THE A-APPLE FEEEELL F-FROM THE TUH-ER--
TREE.
Hee hee hee!
HA HA HA!
FASTER, MOMMY!
GET BACK HERE! RAAARRRRR!
EEEEEEEEEEEEE!

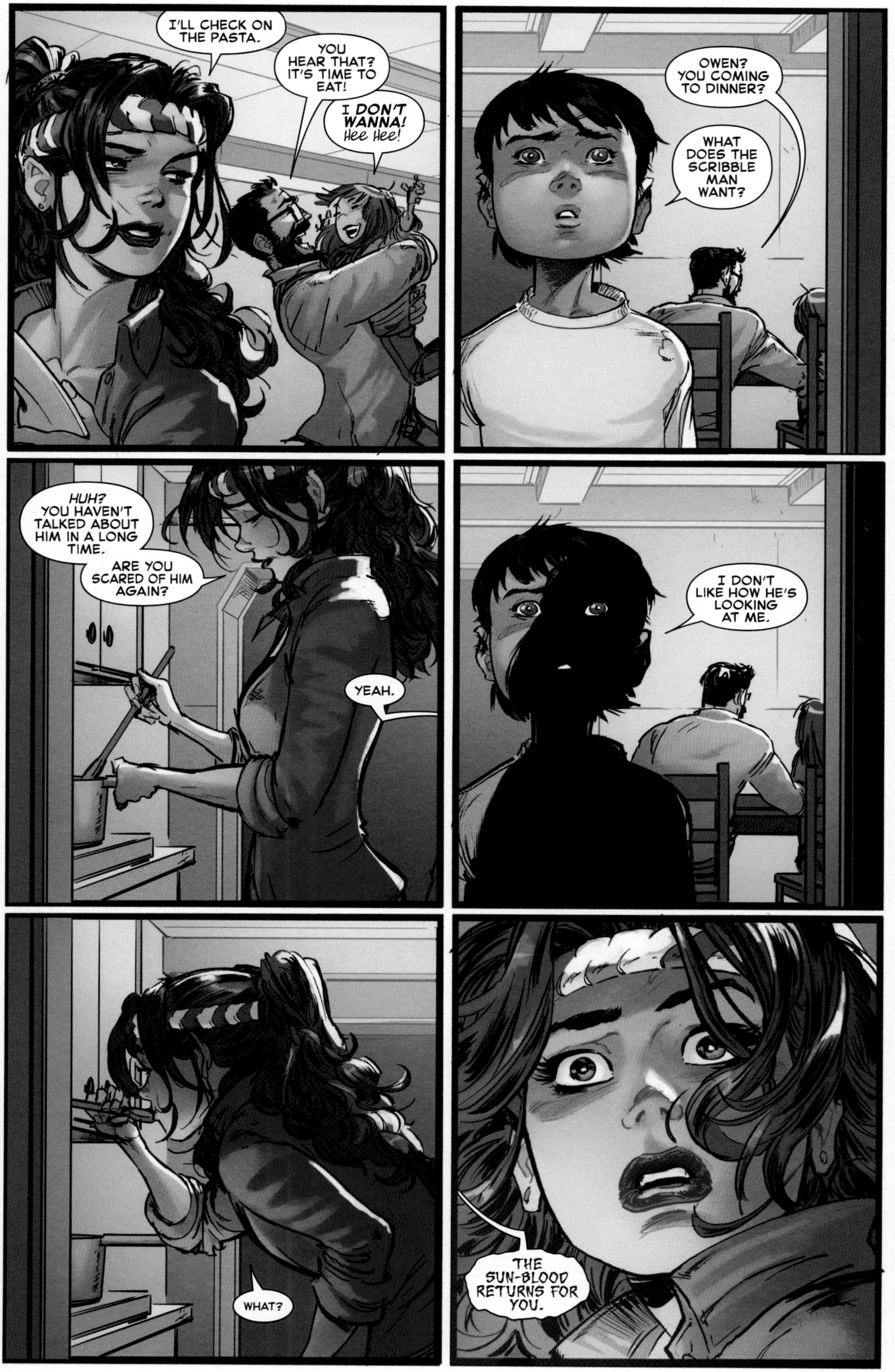
I'LL CHECK ON THE PASTA.
YOU HEAR THAT? IT'S TIME TO EAT!
I *DON'T WANNA!* Hee Hee!
OWEN? YOU COMING TO DINNER?
WHAT DOES THE SCRIBBLE MAN WANT?
HUH? YOU HAVEN'T TALKED ABOUT HIM IN A LONG TIME.
ARE YOU SCARED OF HIM AGAIN?
YEAH.
I DON'T LIKE HOW HE'S LOOKING AT ME.
WHAT?
THE SUN-BLOOD RETURNS FOR YOU.

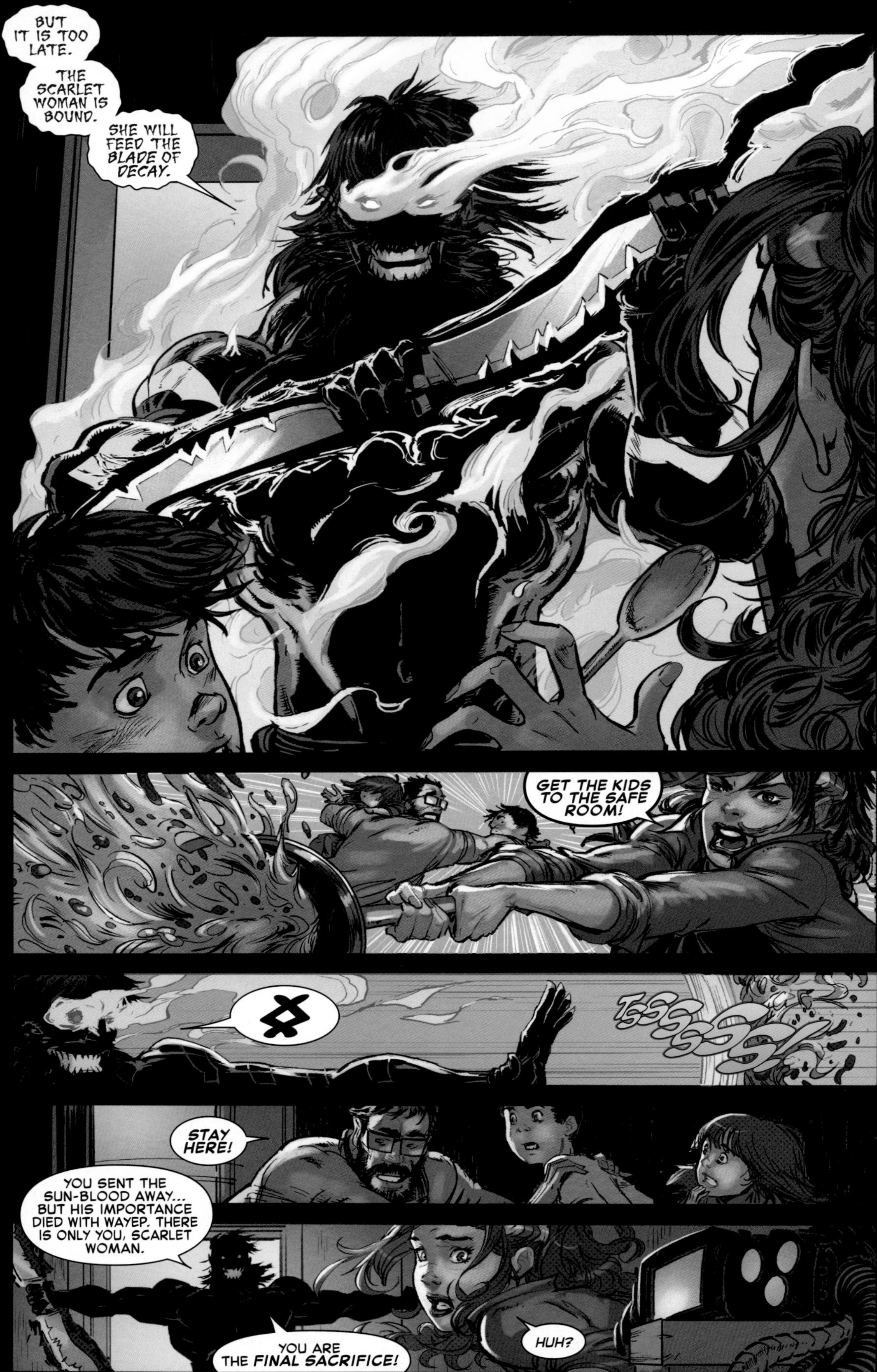
BUT IT IS TOO LATE.
THE SCARLET WOMAN IS BOUND.
SHE WILL FEED THE BLADE OF DECAY.
GET THE KIDS TO THE SAFE ROOM!
TSSSSSSS!
STAY HERE!
YOU SENT THE SUN-BLOOD AWAY... BUT HIS IMPORTANCE DIED WITH WAYEP. THERE IS ONLY YOU, SCARLET WOMAN.
YOU ARE THE FINAL SACRIFICE!
HUH?

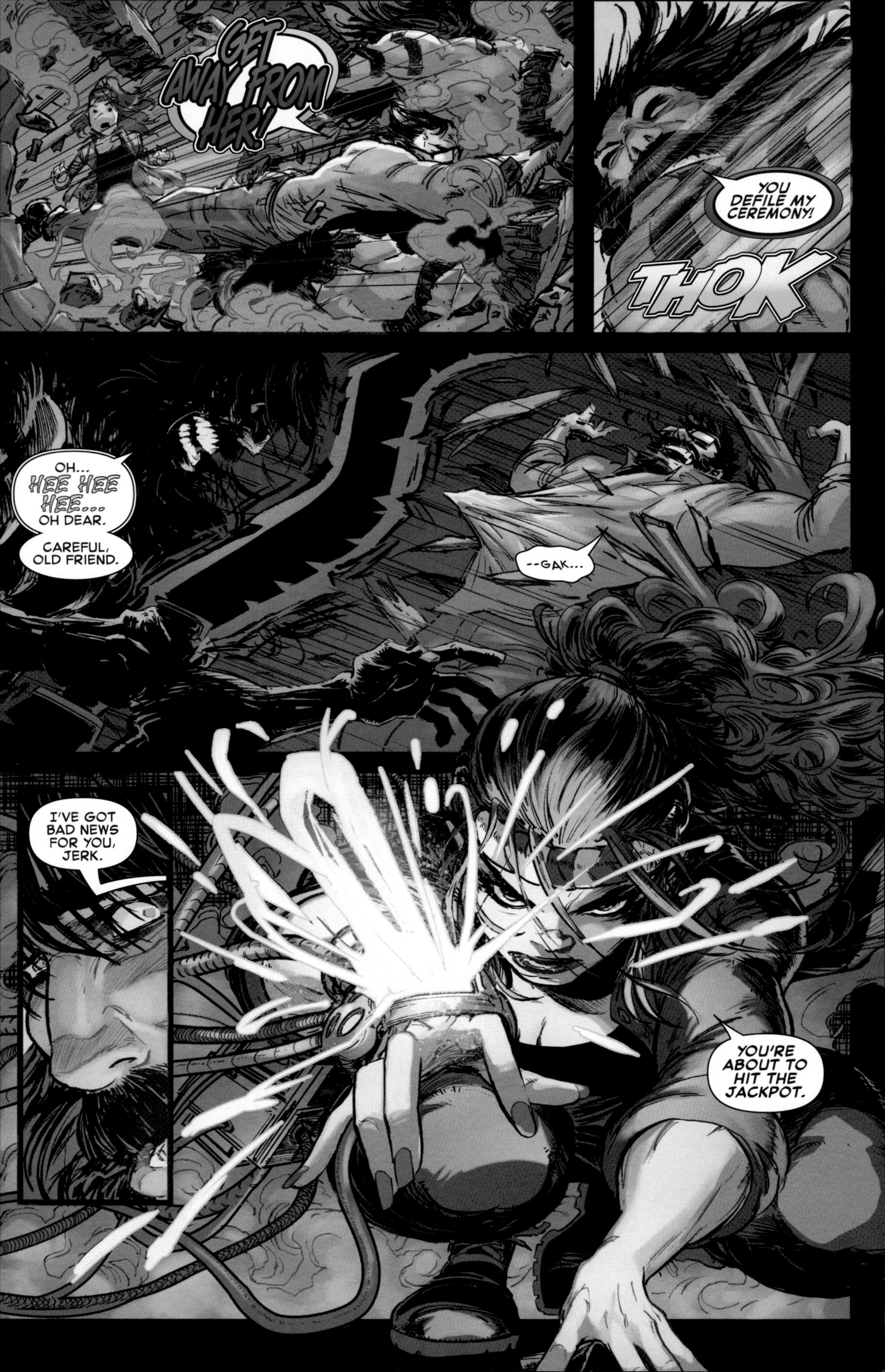
GET AWAY FROM HER!
YOU DEFILE MY CEREMONY!
THOK
OH... HEE HEE HEE... OH DEAR.
CAREFUL, OLD FRIEND.
--GAK...
I'VE GOT BAD NEWS FOR YOU, JERK.
YOU'RE ABOUT TO HIT THE JACKPOT.

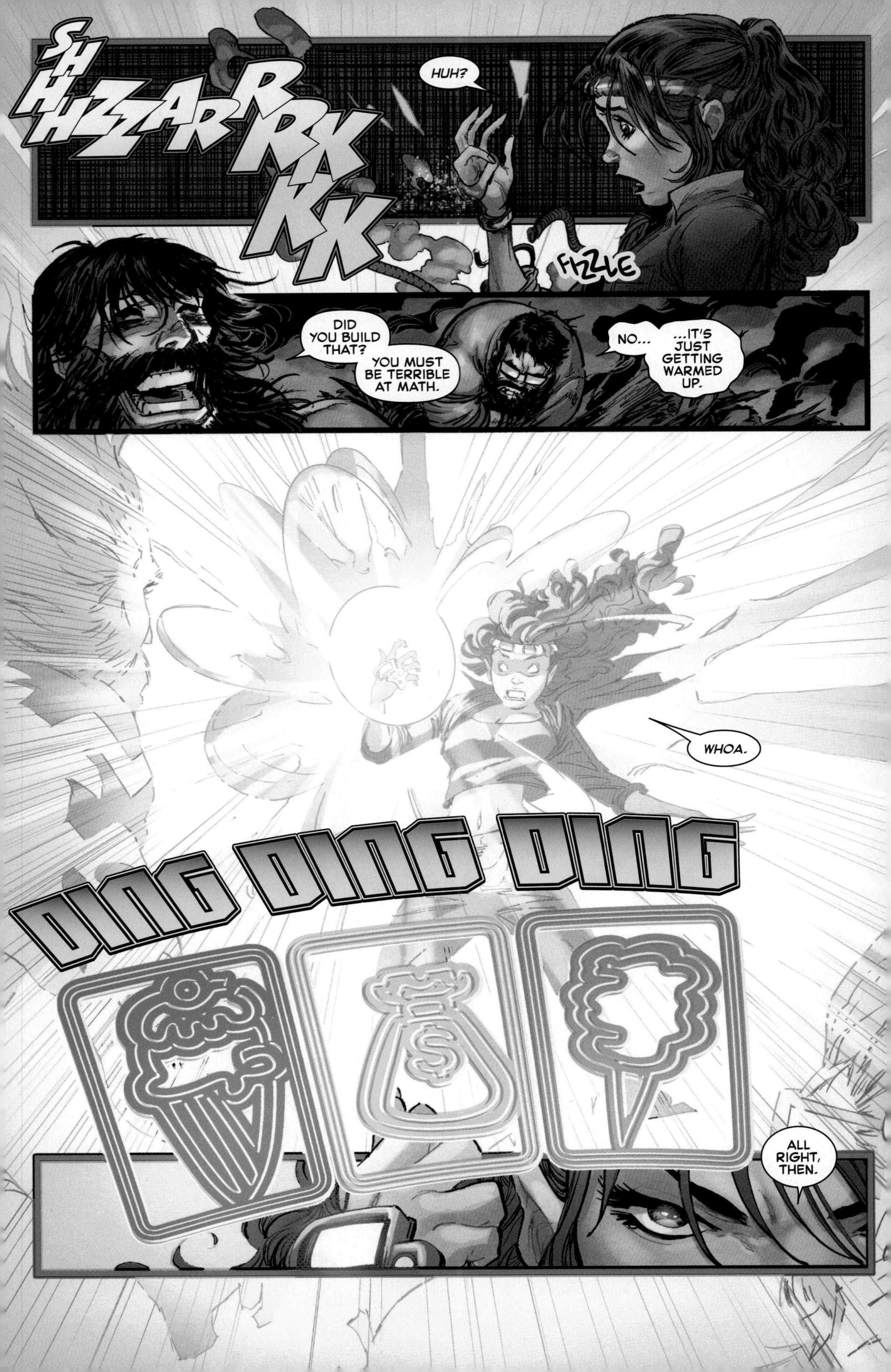
SHHZZARRRKKK
HUH?
FIZZLE
DID YOU BUILD THAT?
YOU MUST BE TERRIBLE AT MATH.
NO...
...IT'S JUST GETTING WARMED UP.
WHOA.
DING DING DING
ALL RIGHT, THEN.

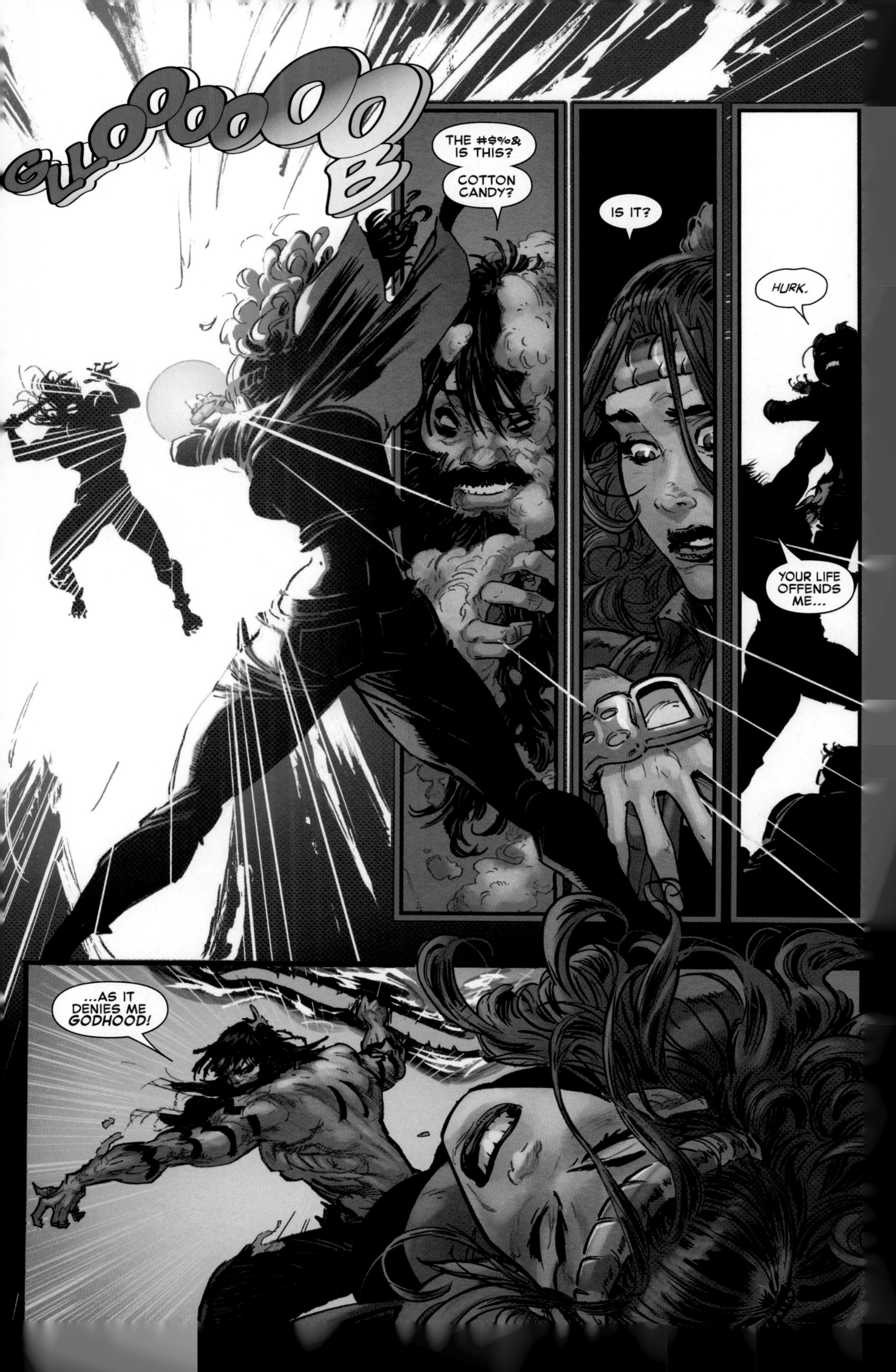
GLLOOOOOOOB
THE #$%& IS THIS?
COTTON CANDY?
IS IT?
HURK.
YOUR LIFE OFFENDS ME...
...AS IT DENIES ME GODHOOD!

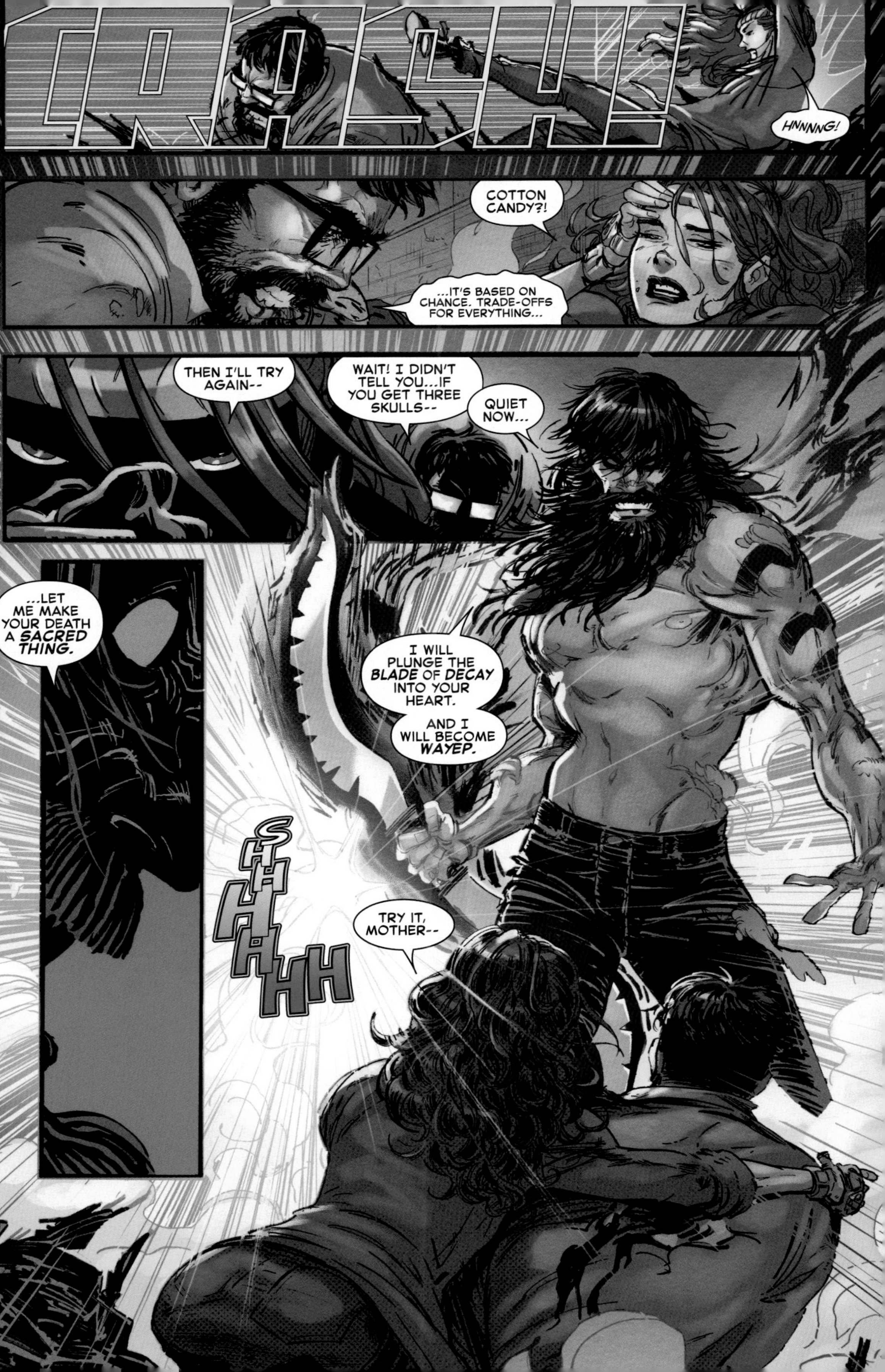
CRASH!
HNNNNG!
COTTON CANDY?!
...IT'S BASED ON CHANCE. TRADE-OFFS FOR EVERYTHING...
THEN I'LL TRY AGAIN--
WAIT! I DIDN'T TELL YOU...IF YOU GET THREE SKULLS--
QUIET NOW...
...LET ME MAKE YOUR DEATH A *SACRED THING.*
I WILL PLUNGE THE *BLADE* OF *DECAY* INTO YOUR HEART.
AND I WILL BECOME *WAYEP.*
SHHHHHHH
TRY IT, MOTHER--

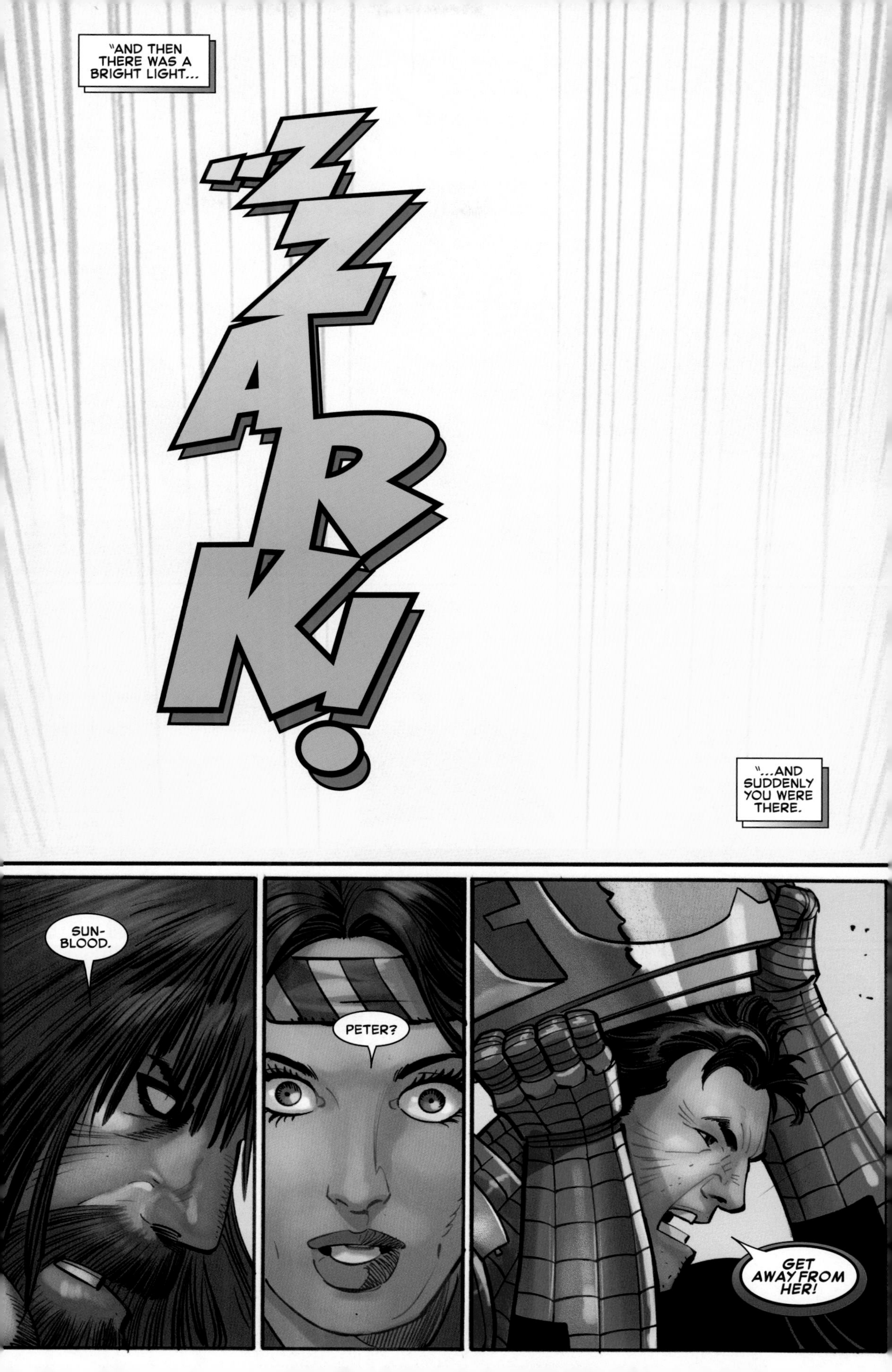
"AND THEN THERE WAS A BRIGHT LIGHT...
ZZZARK!
"...AND SUDDENLY YOU WERE THERE.
SUN-BLOOD.
PETER?
GET AWAY FROM HER!

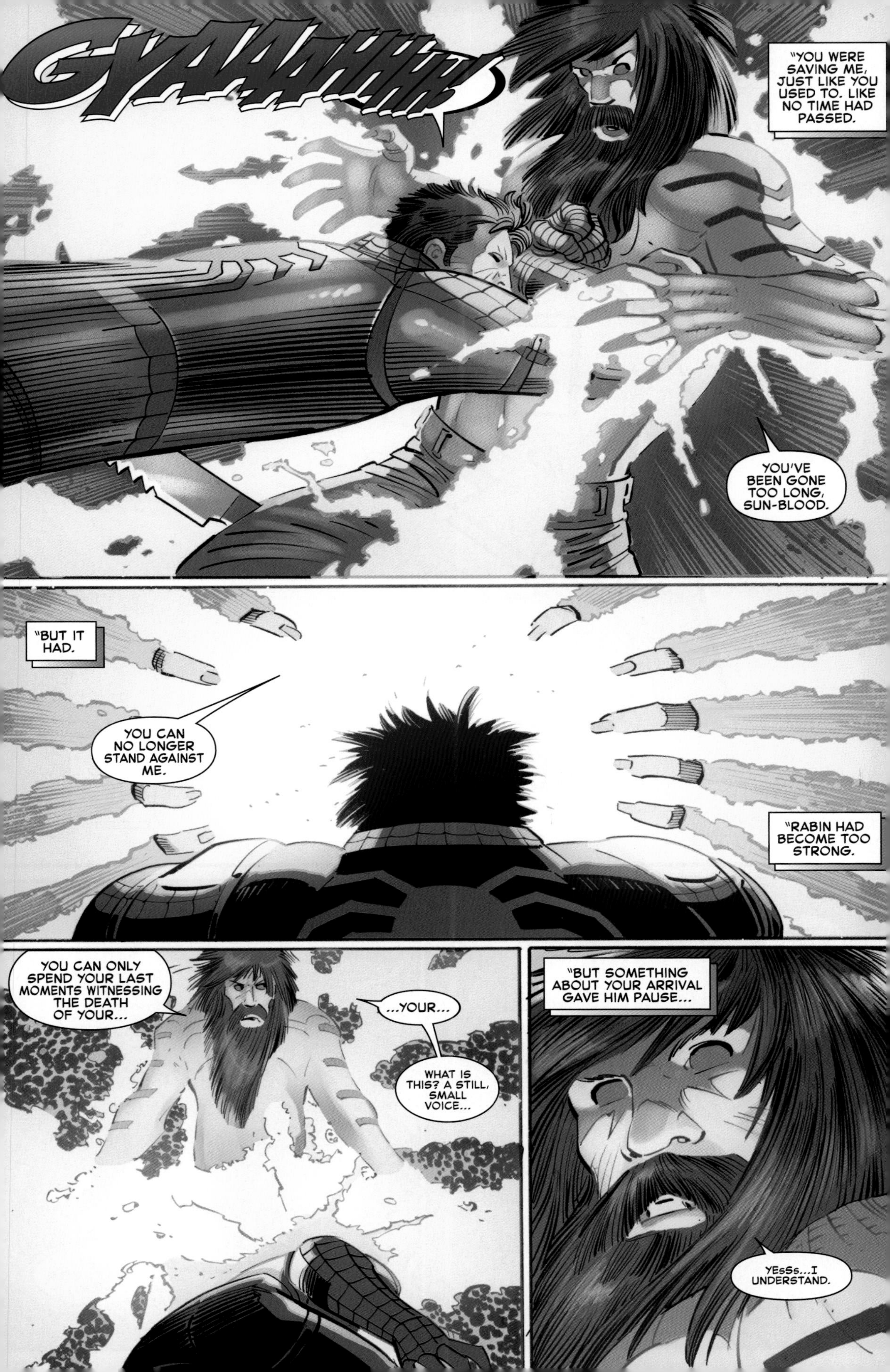
GYAAAHHH!
"YOU WERE SAVING ME, JUST LIKE YOU USED TO. LIKE NO TIME HAD PASSED.
YOU'VE BEEN GONE TOO LONG, SUN-BLOOD.
"BUT IT HAD.
YOU CAN NO LONGER STAND AGAINST ME.
"RABIN HAD BECOME TOO STRONG.
YOU CAN ONLY SPEND YOUR LAST MOMENTS WITNESSING THE DEATH OF YOUR...
...YOUR...
WHAT IS THIS? A STILL, SMALL VOICE...
"BUT SOMETHING ABOUT YOUR ARRIVAL GAVE HIM PAUSE...
YEsSs...I UNDERSTAND.

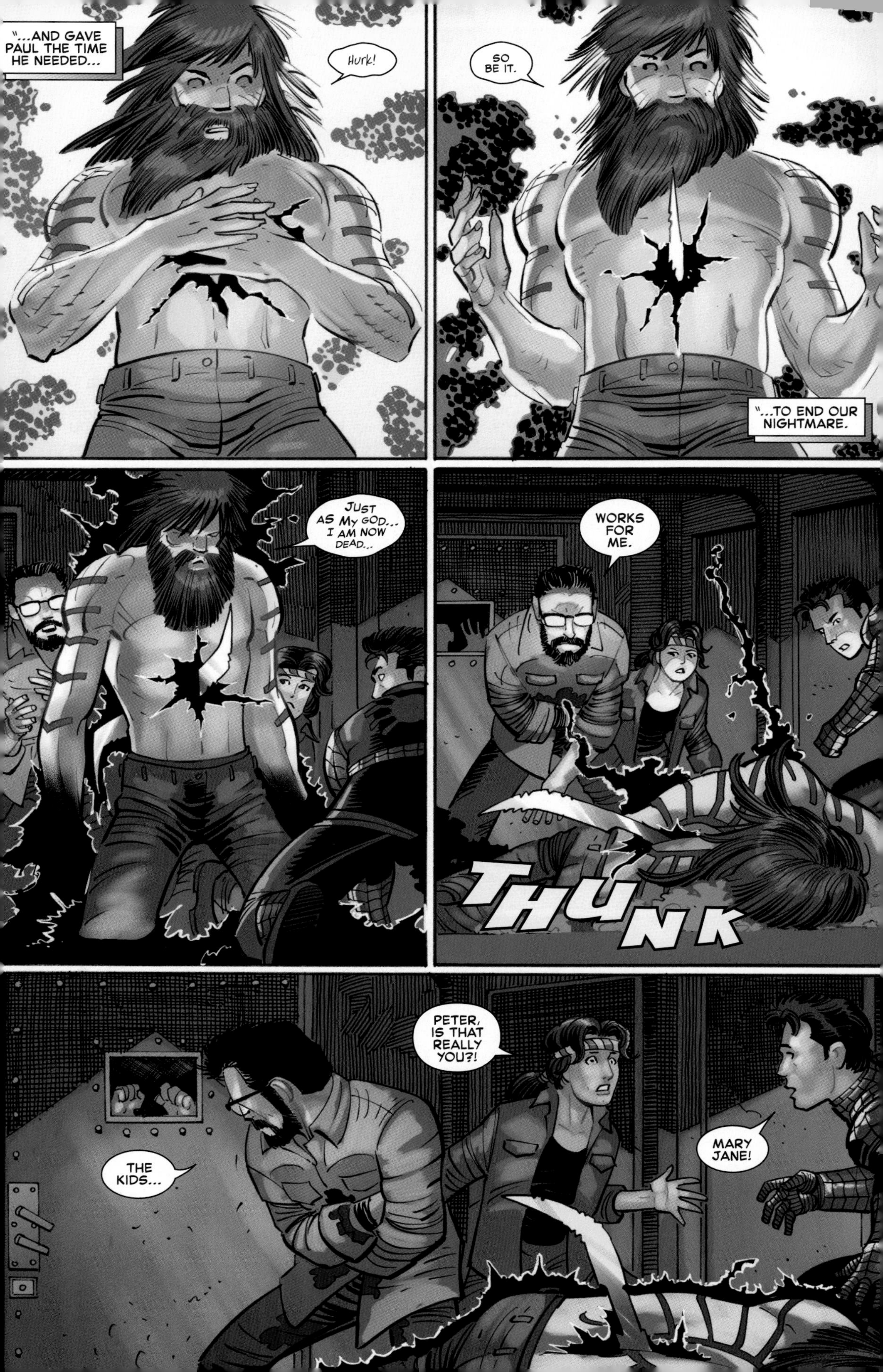
"...AND GAVE PAUL THE TIME HE NEEDED...
Hurk!
SO BE IT.
"...TO END OUR NIGHTMARE.
JUST AS MY GOD... I AM NOW DEAD...
WORKS FOR ME.
THUNK
PETER, IS THAT REALLY YOU?!
THE KIDS...
MARY JANE!

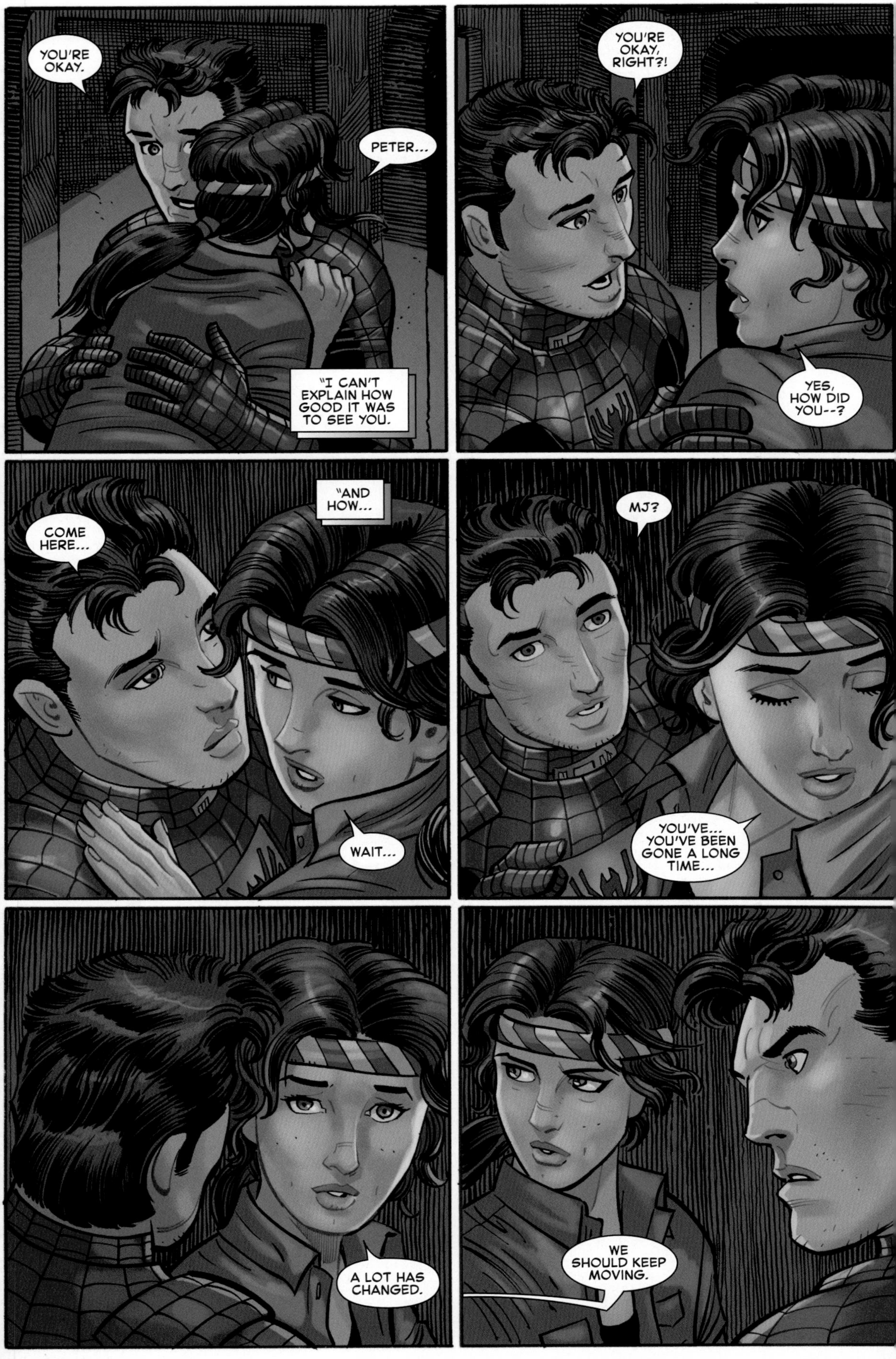
YOU'RE OKAY.
PETER...
"I CAN'T EXPLAIN HOW GOOD IT WAS TO SEE YOU.
YOU'RE OKAY, RIGHT?!
YES, HOW DID YOU--?
"AND HOW...
COME HERE...
WAIT...
MJ?
YOU'VE... YOU'VE BEEN GONE A LONG TIME...
A LOT HAS CHANGED.
WE SHOULD KEEP MOVING.

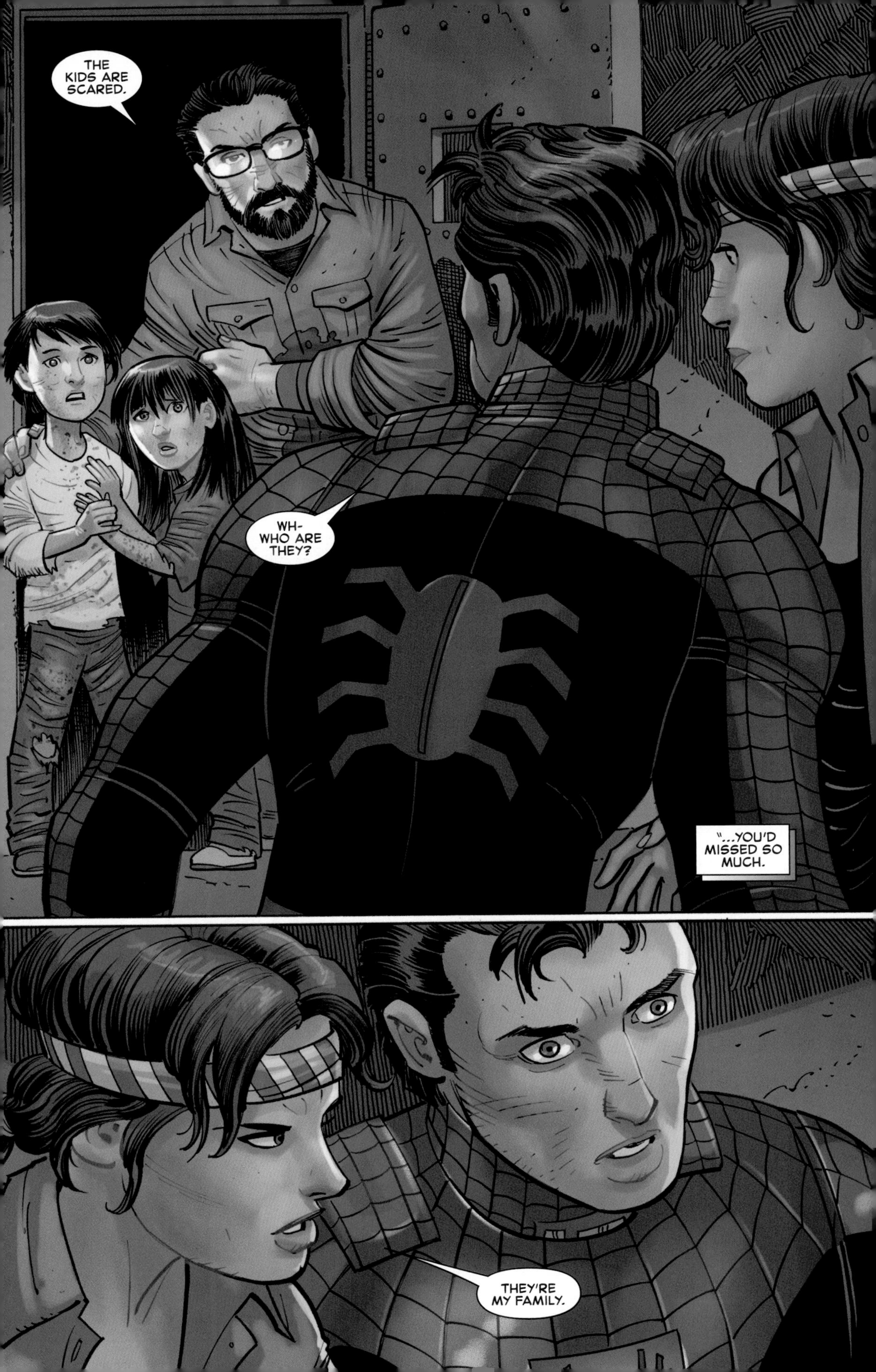
THE KIDS ARE SCARED.
WH- WHO ARE THEY?
"...YOU'D MISSED SO MUCH.
THEY'RE MY FAMILY.

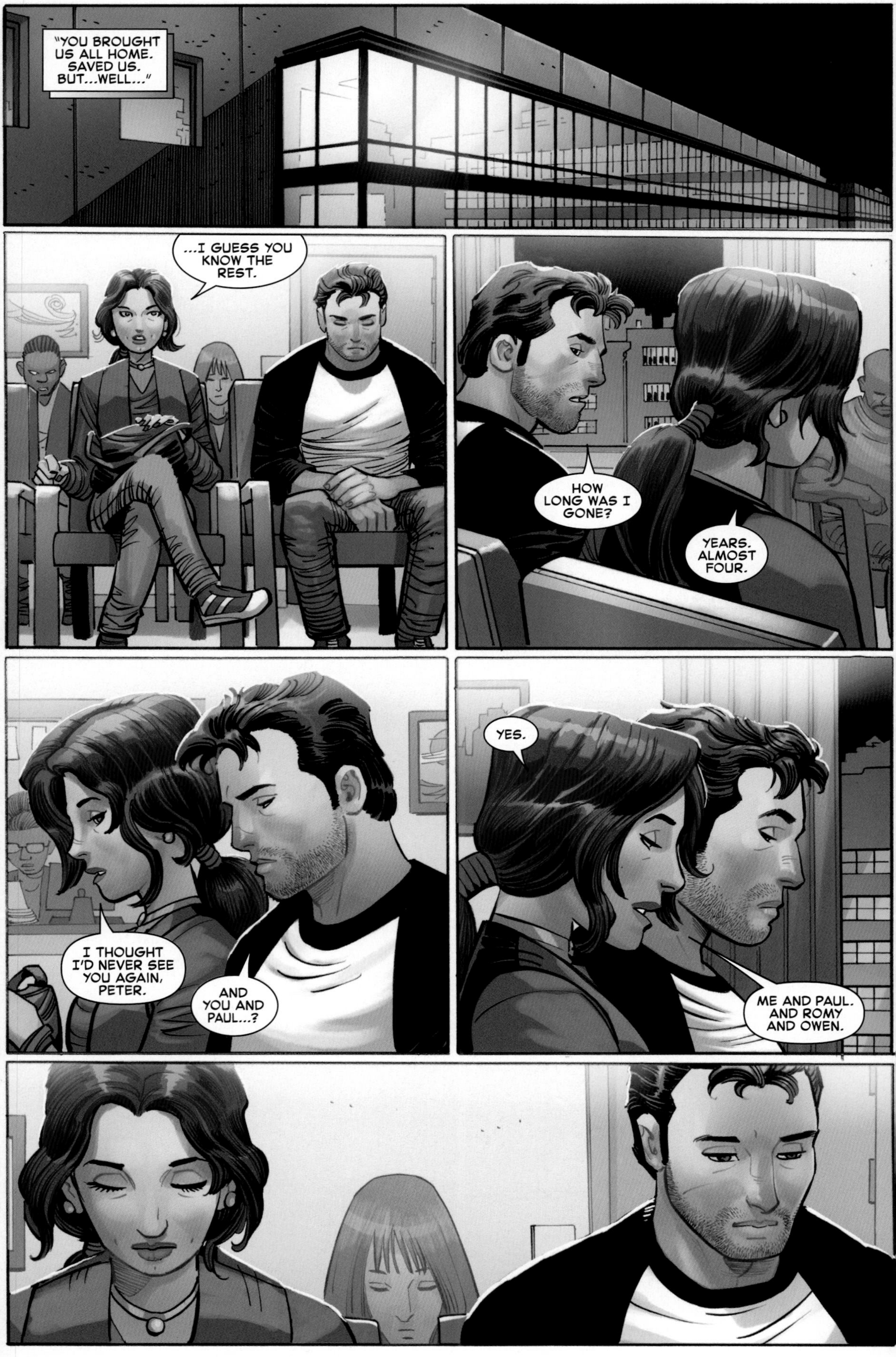
"YOU BROUGHT US ALL HOME. SAVED US. BUT...WELL..."
...I GUESS YOU KNOW THE REST.
HOW LONG WAS I GONE?
YEARS. ALMOST FOUR.
I THOUGHT I'D NEVER SEE YOU AGAIN, PETER.
AND YOU AND PAUL...?
YES.
ME AND PAUL. AND ROMY AND OWEN.

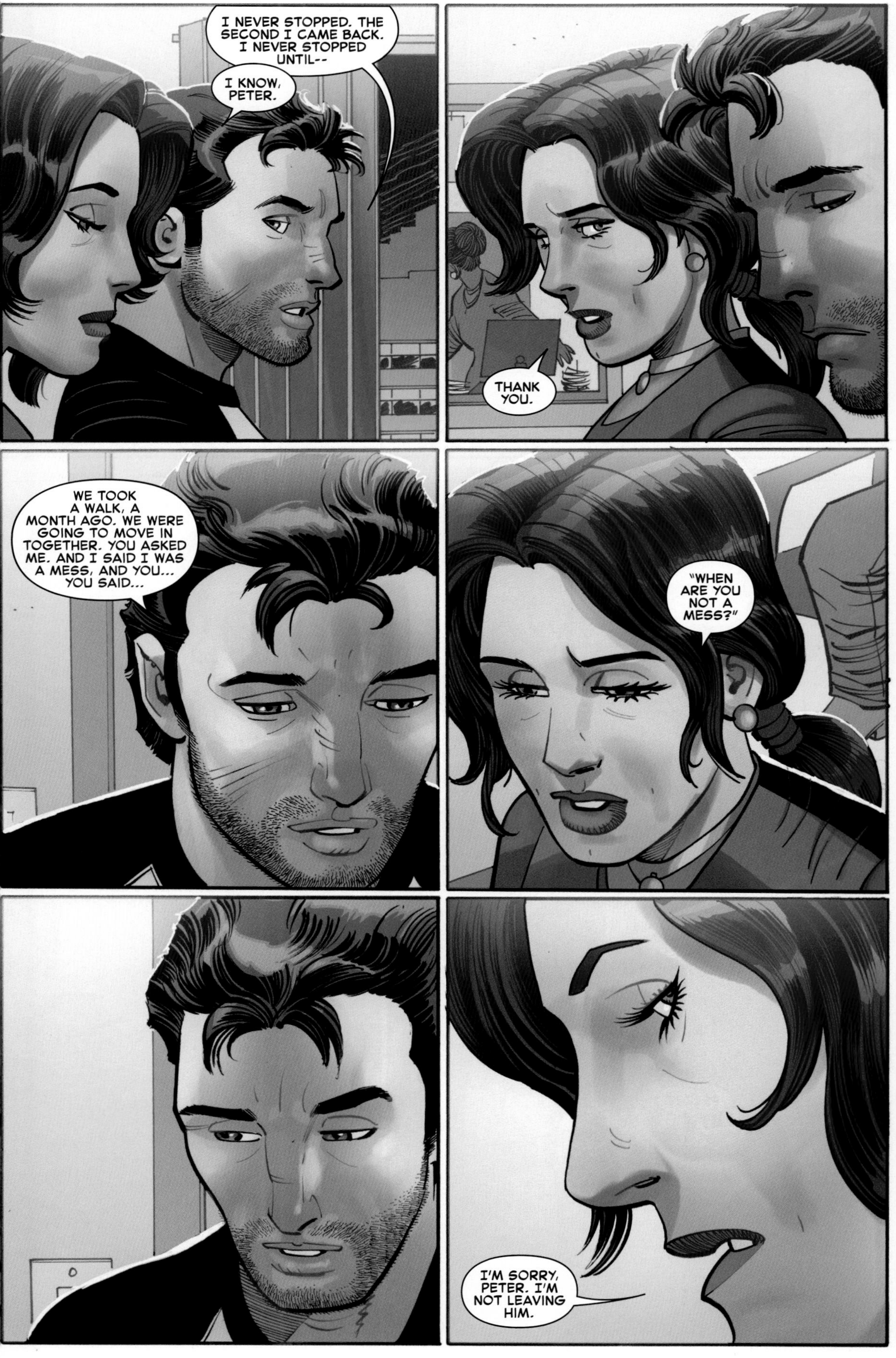
I NEVER STOPPED. THE SECOND I CAME BACK. I NEVER STOPPED UNTIL--
I KNOW, PETER.
THANK YOU.
WE TOOK A WALK, A MONTH AGO. WE WERE GOING TO MOVE IN TOGETHER. YOU ASKED ME. AND I SAID I WAS A MESS, AND YOU... YOU SAID...
"WHEN ARE YOU NOT A MESS?"
I'M SORRY, PETER. I'M NOT LEAVING HIM.

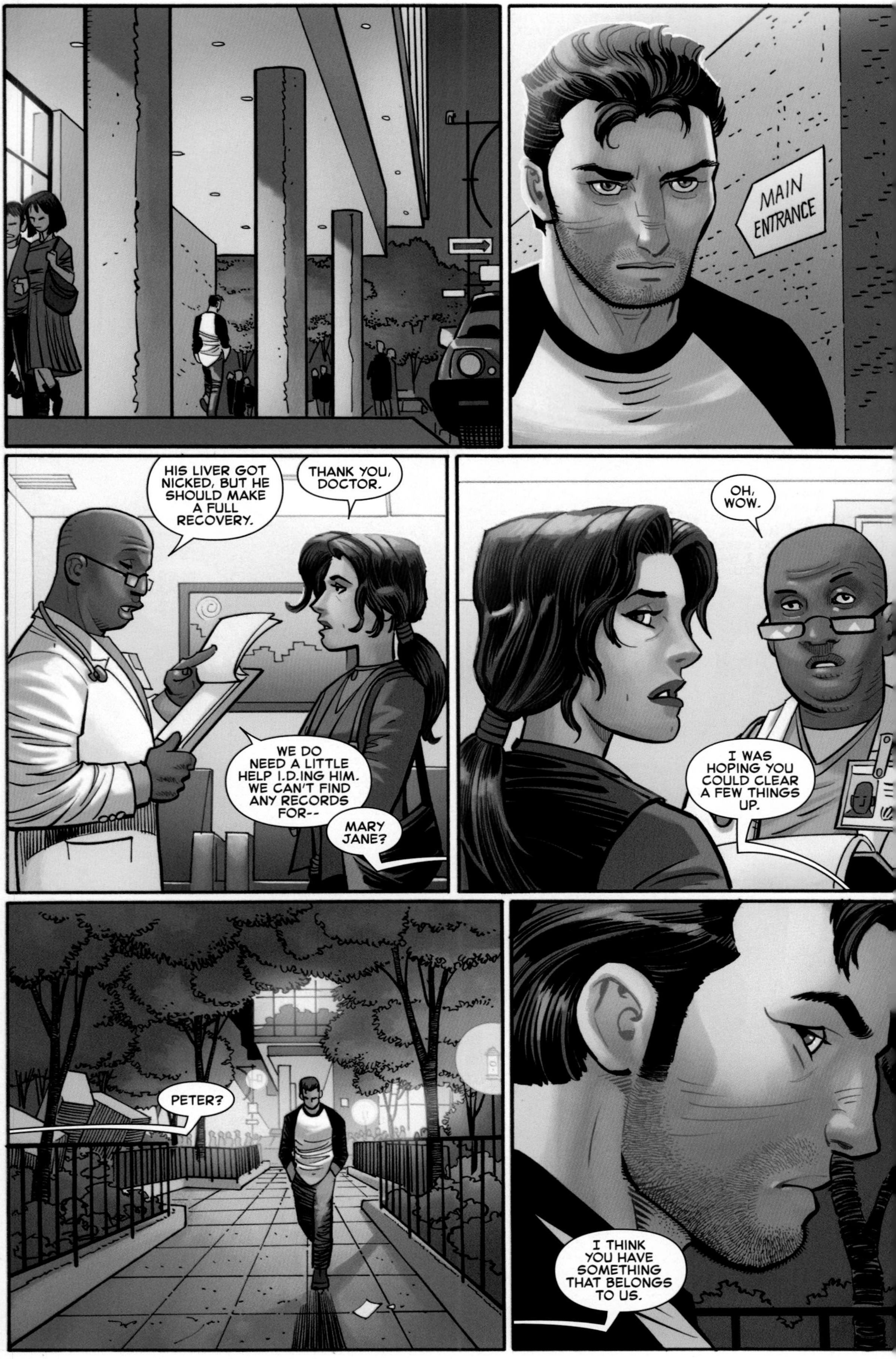
MAIN ENTRANCE
HIS LIVER GOT NICKED, BUT HE SHOULD MAKE A FULL RECOVERY.
THANK YOU, DOCTOR.
WE DO NEED A LITTLE HELP I.D.ING HIM. WE CAN'T FIND ANY RECORDS FOR--
MARY JANE?
OH, WOW.
I WAS HOPING YOU COULD CLEAR A FEW THINGS UP.
PETER?
I THINK YOU HAVE SOMETHING THAT BELONGS TO US.

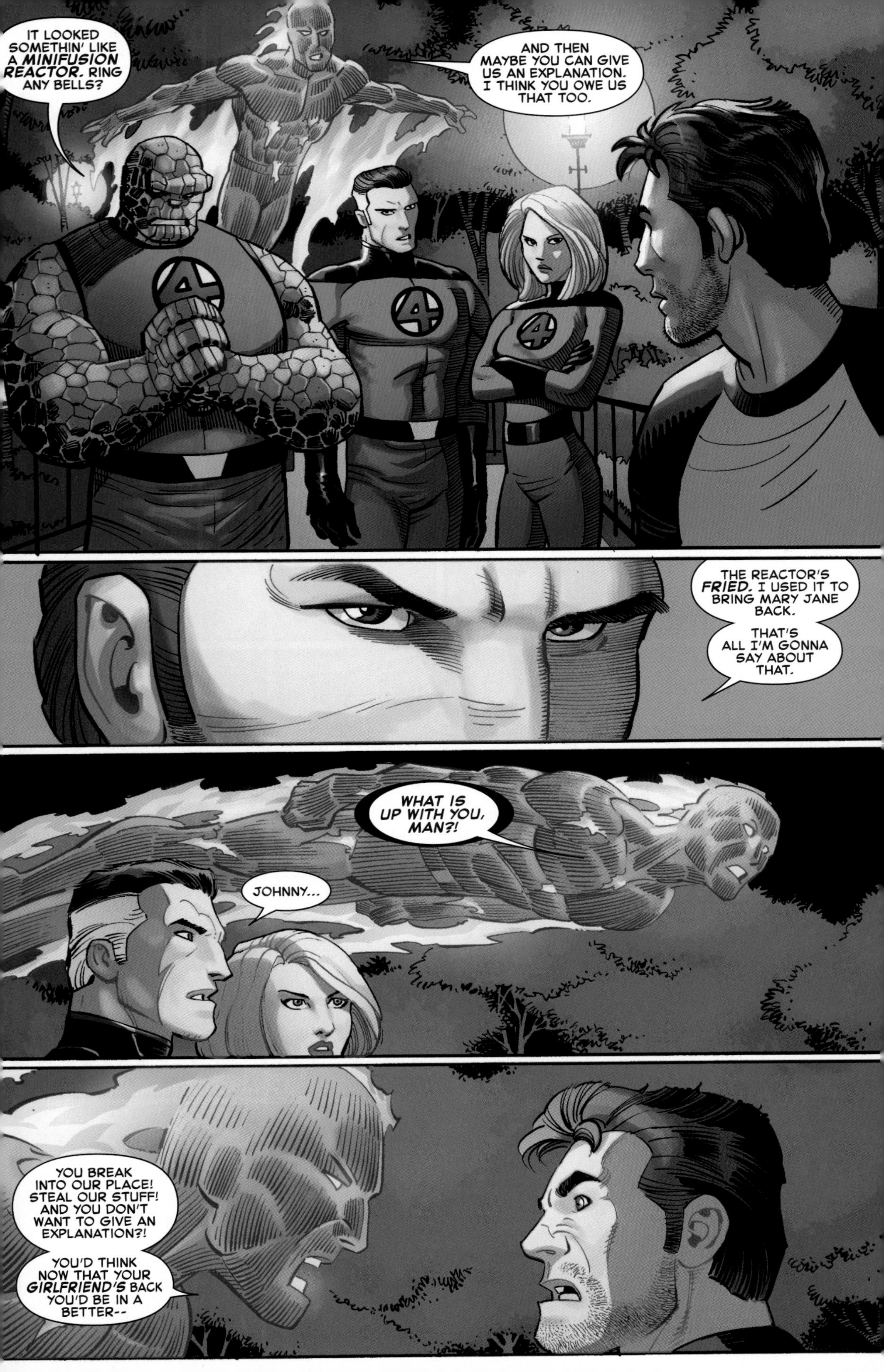
IT LOOKED SOMETHIN' LIKE A MINIFUSION REACTOR. RING ANY BELLS?
AND THEN MAYBE YOU CAN GIVE US AN EXPLANATION. I THINK YOU OWE US THAT TOO.
THE REACTOR'S FRIED. I USED IT TO BRING MARY JANE BACK.
THAT'S ALL I'M GONNA SAY ABOUT THAT.
WHAT IS UP WITH YOU, MAN?!
JOHNNY...
YOU BREAK INTO OUR PLACE! STEAL OUR STUFF! AND YOU DON'T WANT TO GIVE AN EXPLANATION?!
YOU'D THINK NOW THAT YOUR GIRLFRIEND'S BACK YOU'D BE IN A BETTER--

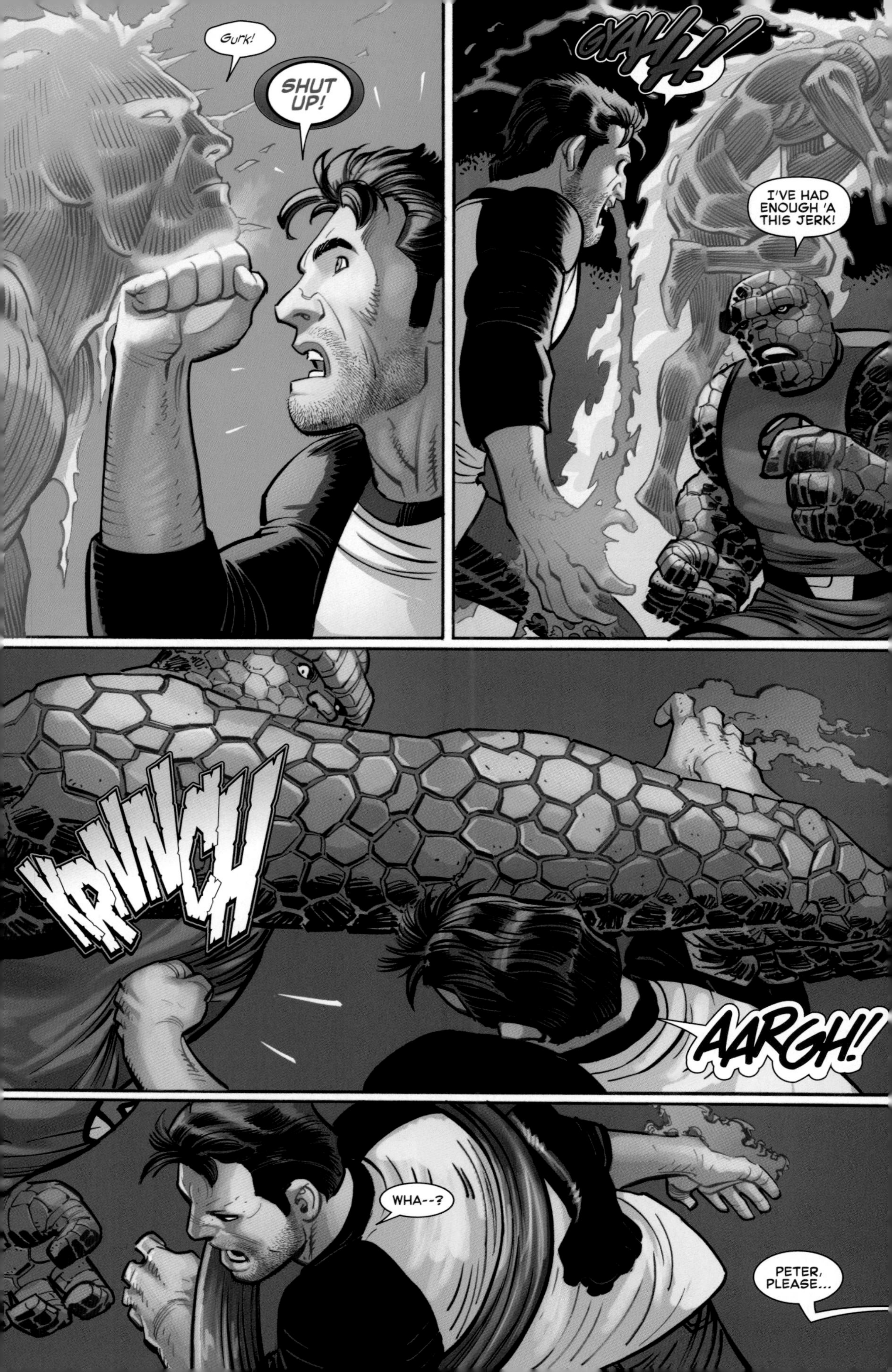
Gurk!
SHUT UP!
GYAHH!
I'VE HAD ENOUGH 'A THIS JERK!
KRUNCH
AARGH!
WHA--?
PETER, PLEASE...

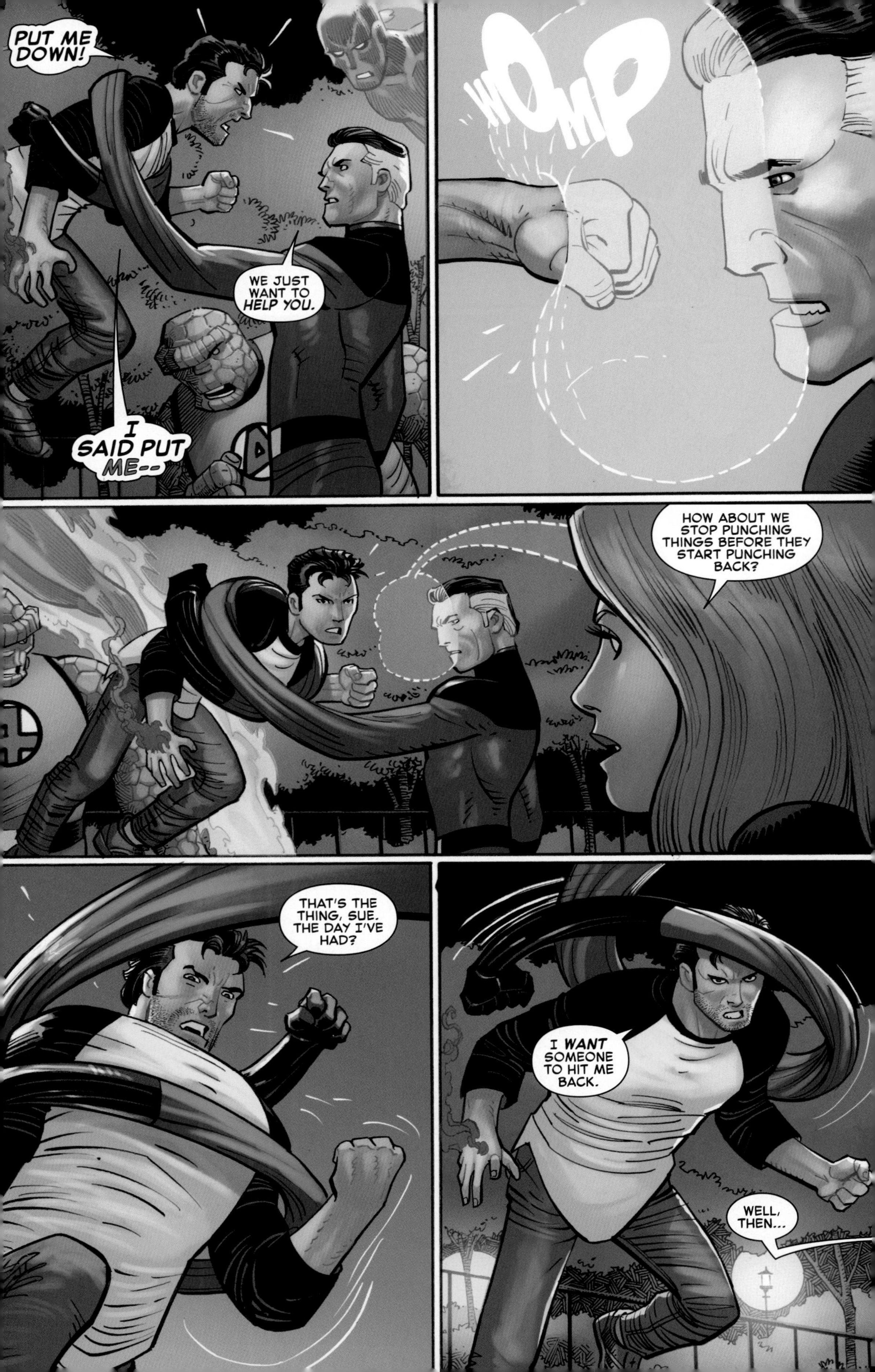
PUT ME DOWN!
WE JUST WANT TO HELP YOU.
I SAID PUT ME--
WOMP
HOW ABOUT WE STOP PUNCHING THINGS BEFORE THEY START PUNCHING BACK?
THAT'S THE THING, SUE. THE DAY I'VE HAD?
I WANT SOMEONE TO HIT ME BACK.
WELL, THEN...

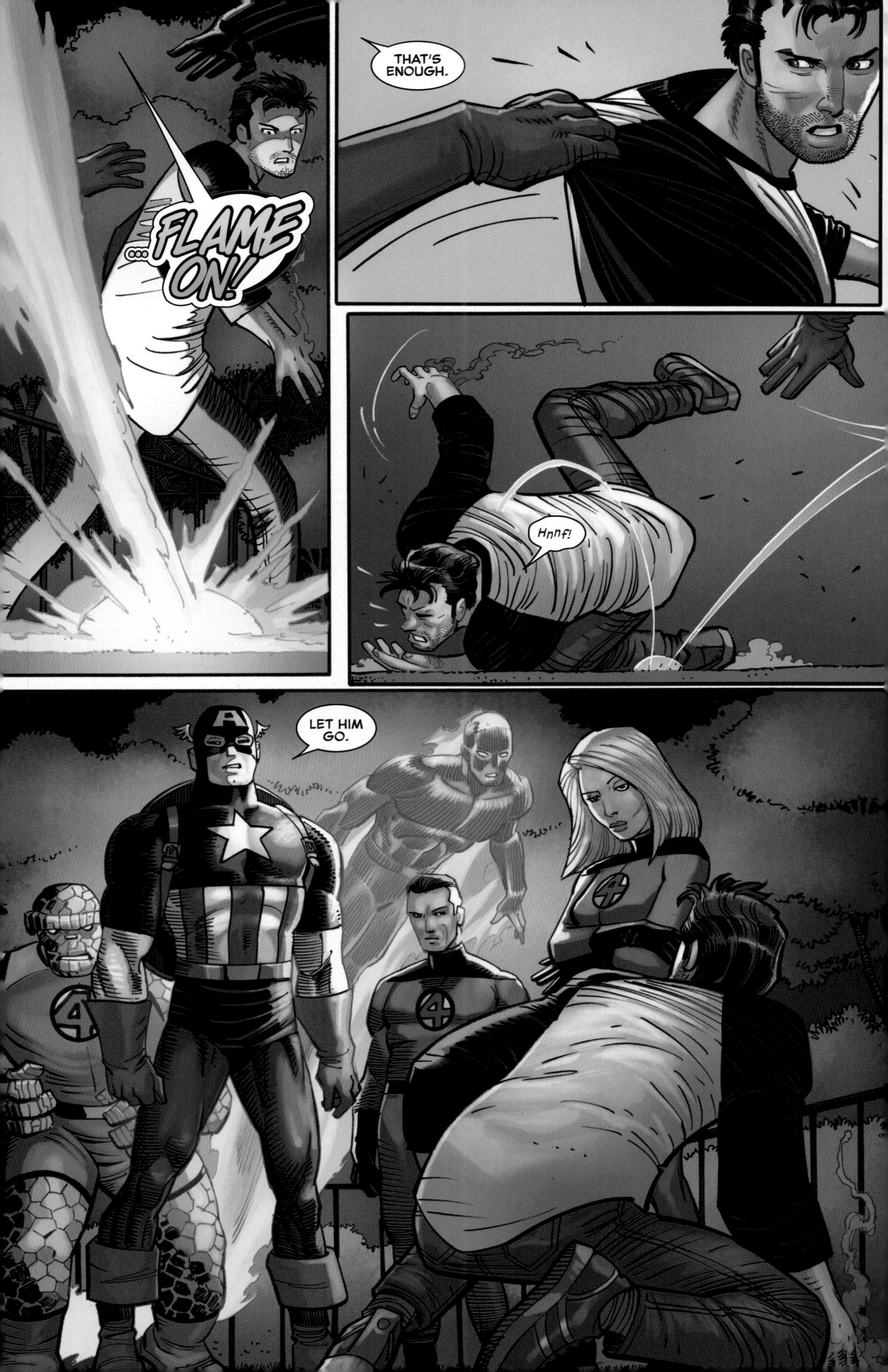
...FLAME ON!
THAT'S ENOUGH.
Hnnf!
LET HIM GO.

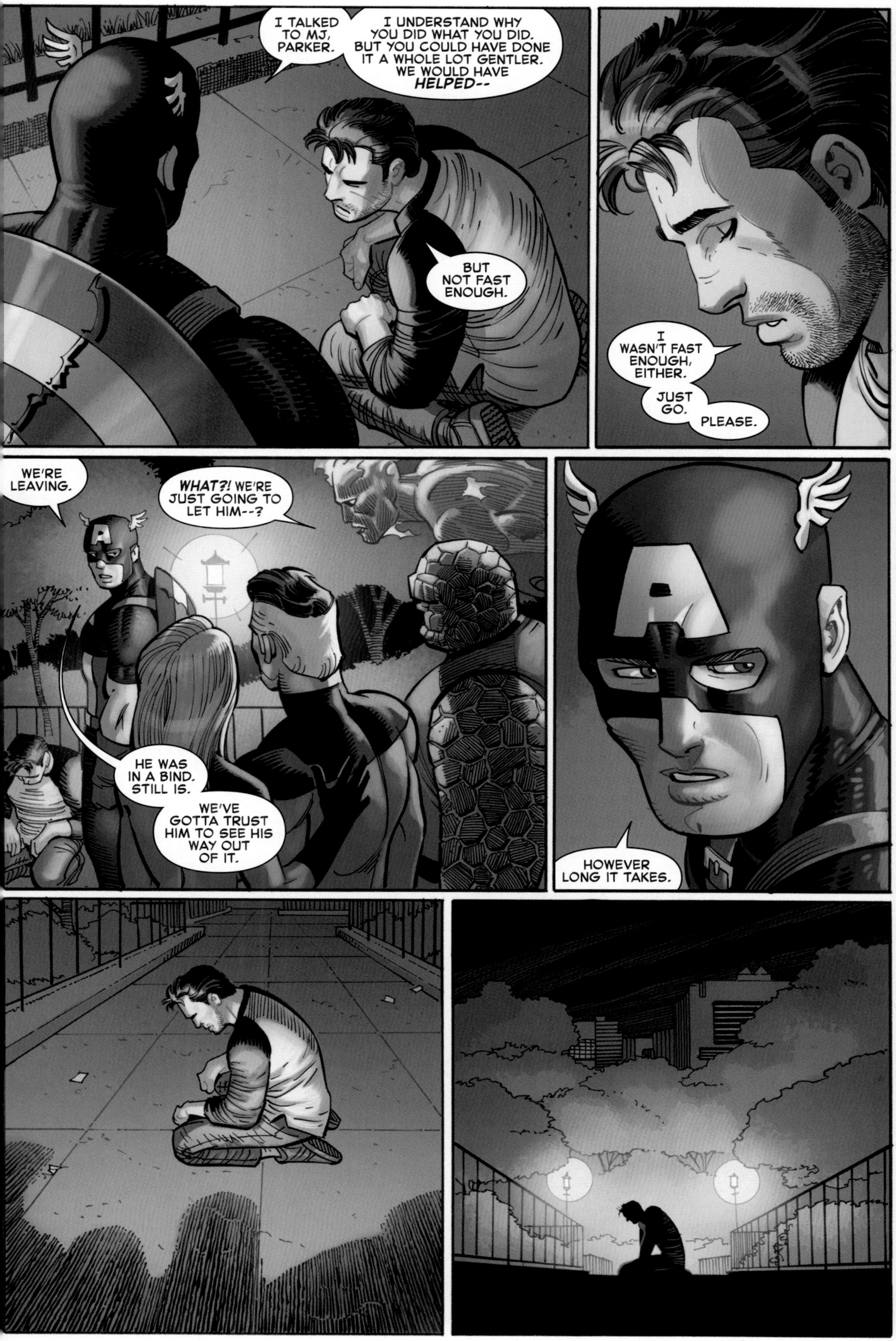
I TALKED TO MJ, PARKER.
I UNDERSTAND WHY YOU DID WHAT YOU DID. BUT YOU COULD HAVE DONE IT A WHOLE LOT GENTLER. WE WOULD HAVE *HELPED--*
BUT NOT FAST ENOUGH.
I WASN'T FAST ENOUGH, EITHER.
JUST GO.
PLEASE.
WE'RE LEAVING.
WHAT?! WE'RE JUST GOING TO LET HIM--?
HE WAS IN A BIND. STILL IS.
WE'VE GOTTA TRUST HIM TO SEE HIS WAY OUT OF IT.
HOWEVER LONG IT TAKES.

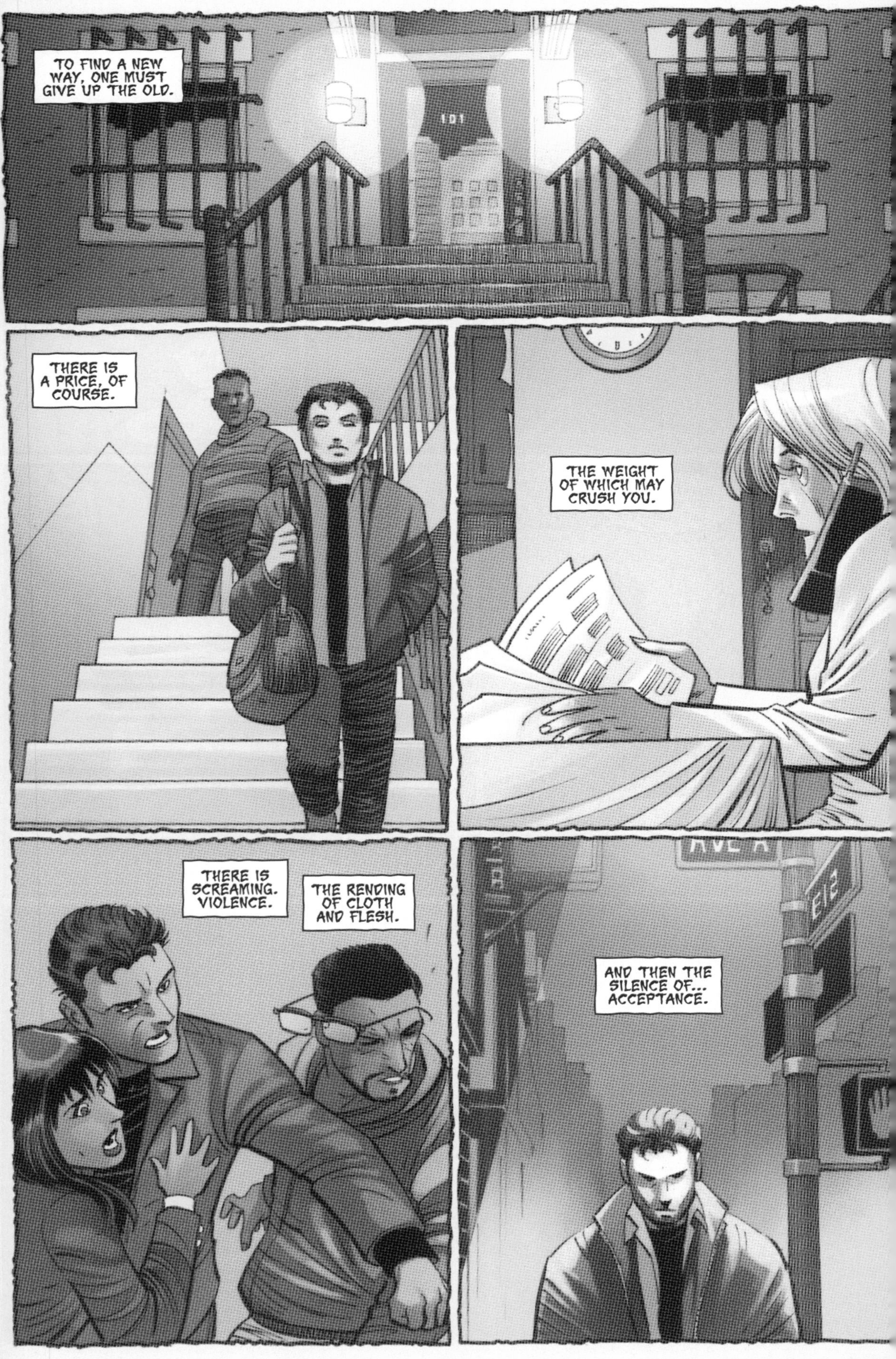
TO FIND A NEW WAY, ONE MUST GIVE UP THE OLD.
THERE IS A PRICE, OF COURSE.
THE WEIGHT OF WHICH MAY CRUSH YOU.
THERE IS SCREAMING. VIOLENCE.
THE RENDING OF CLOTH AND FLESH.
AND THEN THE SILENCE OF... ACCEPTANCE.

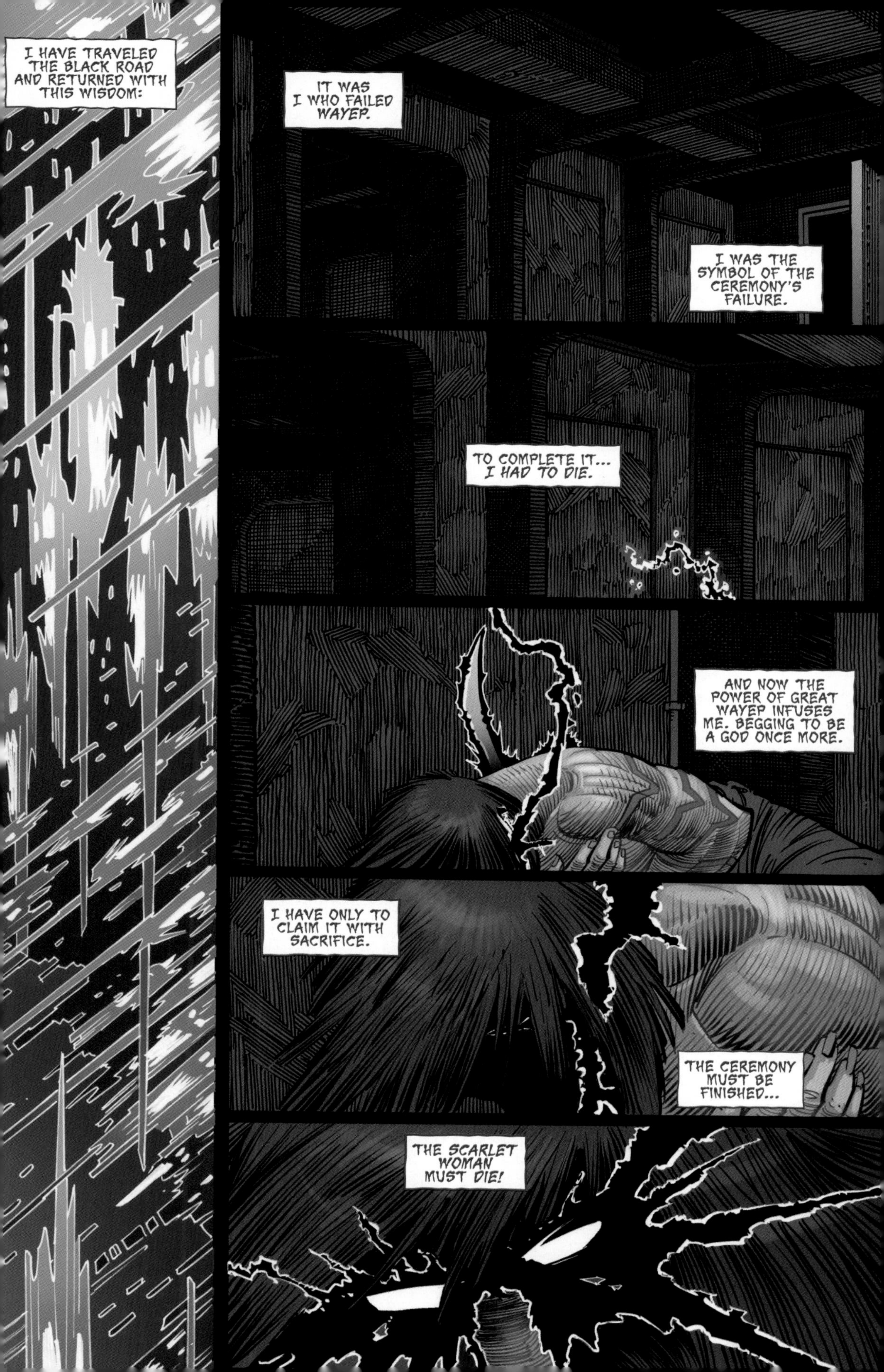
I HAVE TRAVELED THE BLACK ROAD AND RETURNED WITH THIS WISDOM:
IT WAS I WHO FAILED WAYEP.
I WAS THE SYMBOL OF THE CEREMONY'S FAILURE.
TO COMPLETE IT... I HAD TO DIE.
AND NOW THE POWER OF GREAT WAYEP INFUSES ME. BEGGING TO BE A GOD ONCE MORE.
I HAVE ONLY TO CLAIM IT WITH SACRIFICE.
THE CEREMONY MUST BE FINISHED...
THE SCARLET WOMAN MUST DIE!

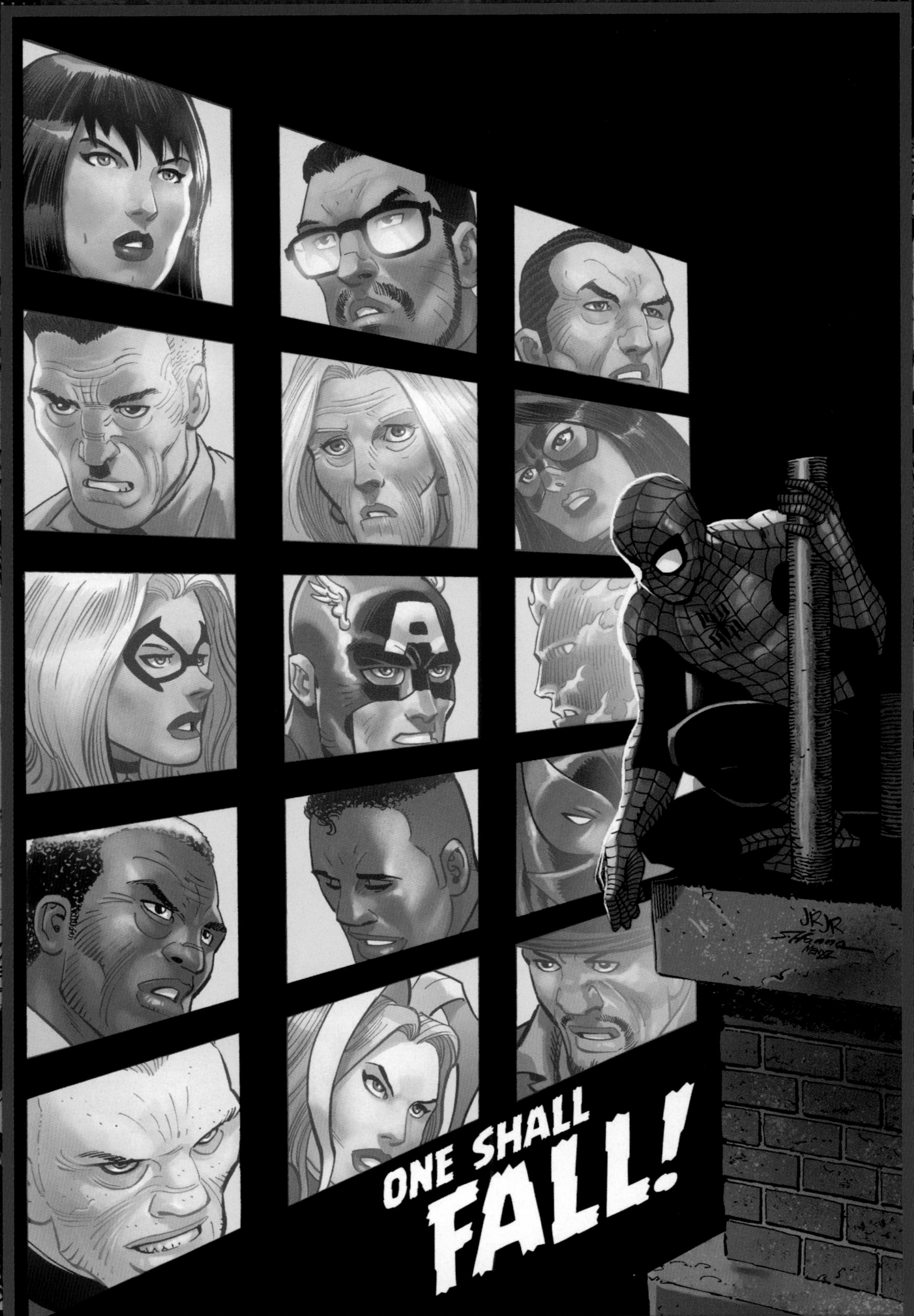
ONE SHALL
FALL!

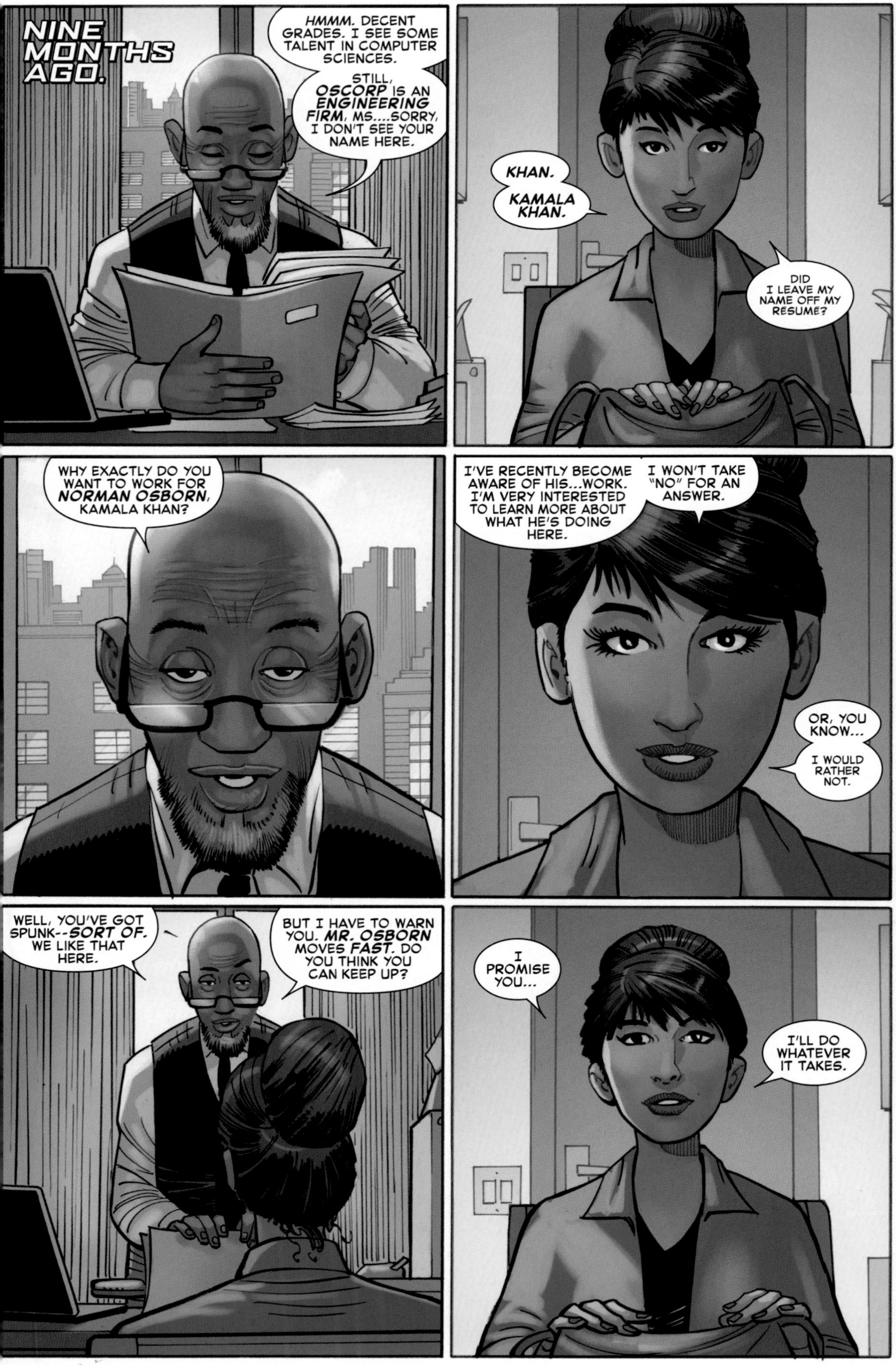
NINE MONTHS AGO.
HMMM. DECENT GRADES. I SEE SOME TALENT IN COMPUTER SCIENCES.
STILL, OSCORP IS AN ENGINEERING FIRM, MS....SORRY, I DON'T SEE YOUR NAME HERE.
KHAN.
KAMALA KHAN.
DID I LEAVE MY NAME OFF MY RESUME?
WHY EXACTLY DO YOU WANT TO WORK FOR NORMAN OSBORN, KAMALA KHAN?
I'VE RECENTLY BECOME AWARE OF HIS...WORK. I'M VERY INTERESTED TO LEARN MORE ABOUT WHAT HE'S DOING HERE.
I WON'T TAKE "NO" FOR AN ANSWER.
OR, YOU KNOW...
I WOULD RATHER NOT.
WELL, YOU'VE GOT SPUNK--SORT OF. WE LIKE THAT HERE.
BUT I HAVE TO WARN YOU. MR. OSBORN MOVES FAST. DO YOU THINK YOU CAN KEEP UP?
I PROMISE YOU...
I'LL DO WHATEVER IT TAKES.

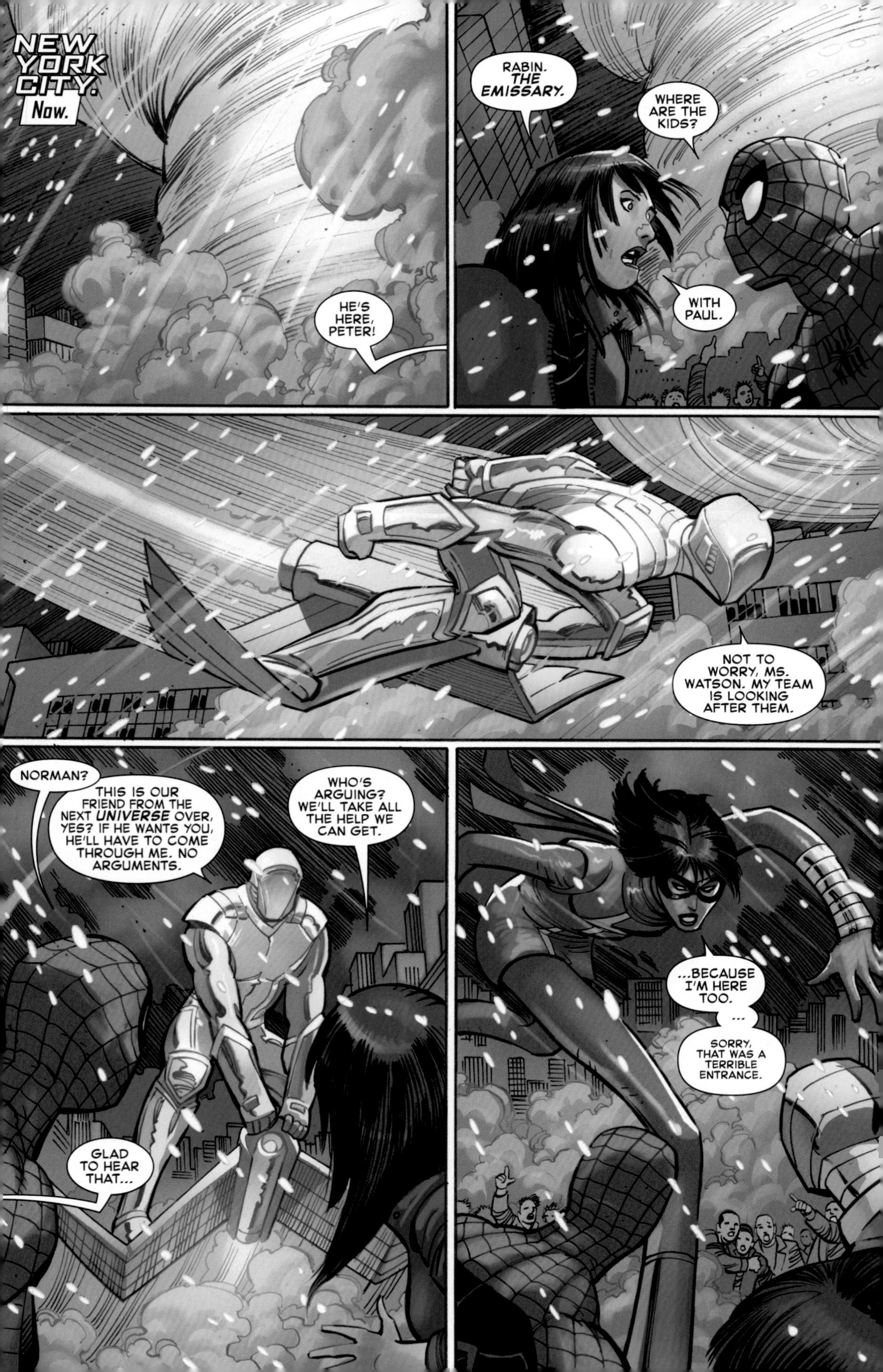
NEW YORK CITY.
Now.
HE'S HERE, PETER!
RABIN. THE EMISSARY.
WHERE ARE THE KIDS?
WITH PAUL.
NOT TO WORRY, MS. WATSON. MY TEAM IS LOOKING AFTER THEM.
NORMAN?
THIS IS OUR FRIEND FROM THE NEXT UNIVERSE OVER, YES? IF HE WANTS YOU, HE'LL HAVE TO COME THROUGH ME. NO ARGUMENTS.
WHO'S ARGUING? WE'LL TAKE ALL THE HELP WE CAN GET.
GLAD TO HEAR THAT...
...BECAUSE I'M HERE TOO.
...
SORRY, THAT WAS A TERRIBLE ENTRANCE.

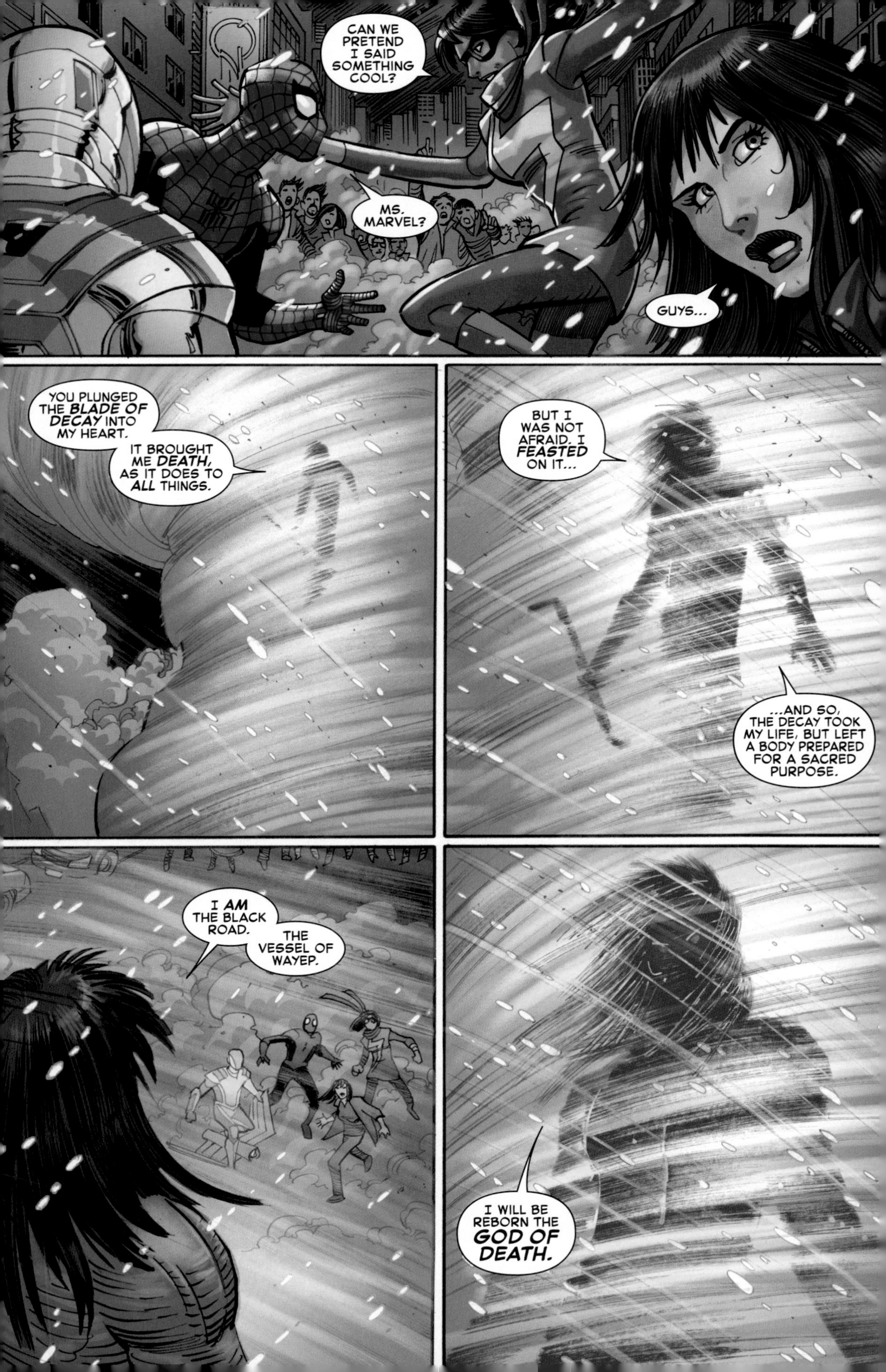
CAN WE PRETEND I SAID SOMETHING COOL?
MS. MARVEL?
GUYS...
YOU PLUNGED THE BLADE OF DECAY INTO MY HEART.
IT BROUGHT ME DEATH, AS IT DOES TO ALL THINGS.
BUT I WAS NOT AFRAID. I FEASTED ON IT...
...AND SO, THE DECAY TOOK MY LIFE, BUT LEFT A BODY PREPARED FOR A SACRED PURPOSE.
I AM THE BLACK ROAD.
THE VESSEL OF WAYEP.
I WILL BE REBORN THE GOD OF DEATH.

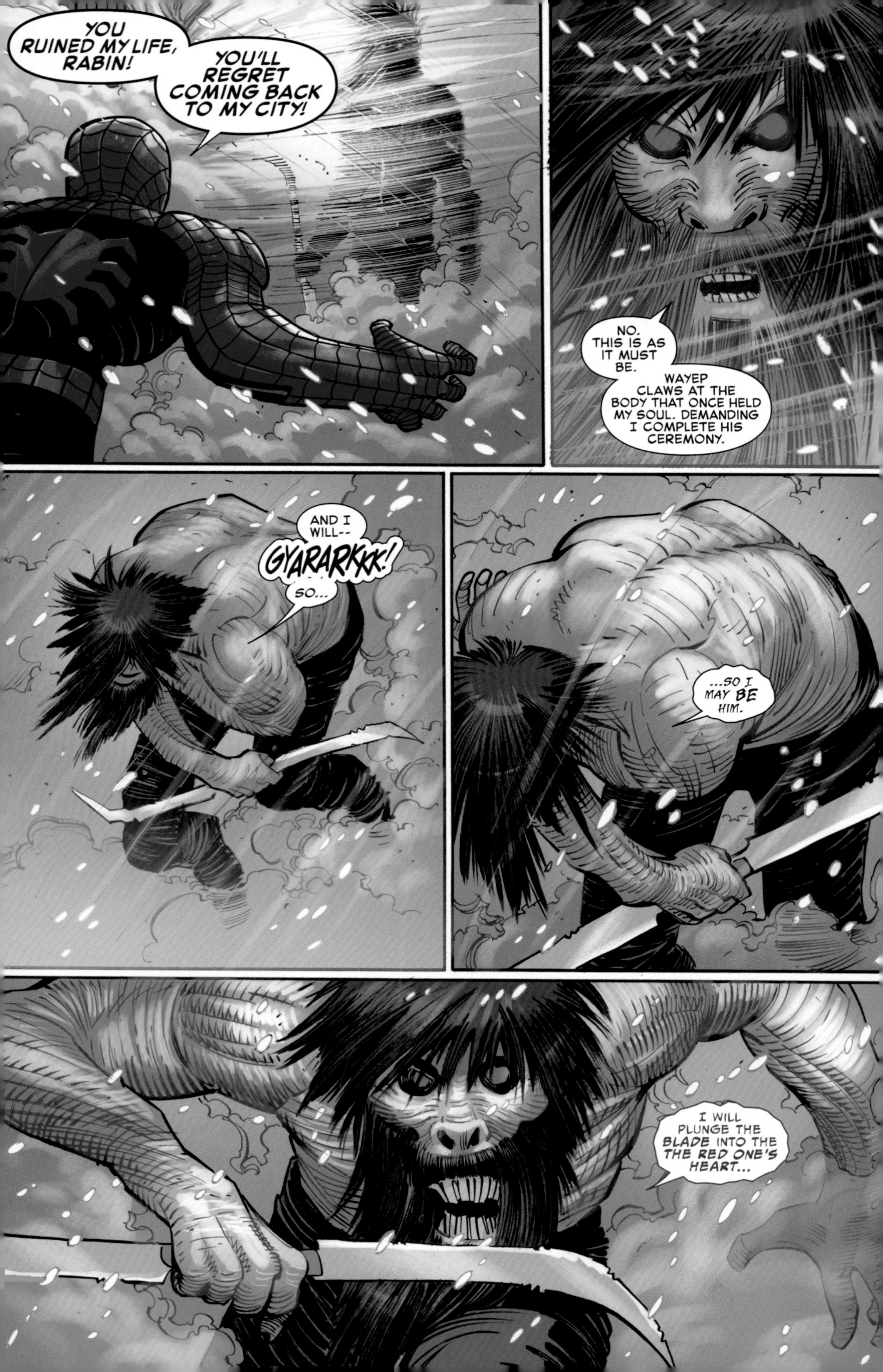
YOU RUINED MY LIFE, RABIN!
YOU'LL REGRET COMING BACK TO MY CITY!
NO. THIS IS AS IT MUST BE.
WAYEP CLAWS AT THE BODY THAT ONCE HELD MY SOUL. DEMANDING I COMPLETE HIS CEREMONY.
AND I WILL--
GYARARKKK!
SO...
...SO I MAY BE HIM.
I WILL PLUNGE THE BLADE INTO THE THE RED ONE'S HEART...

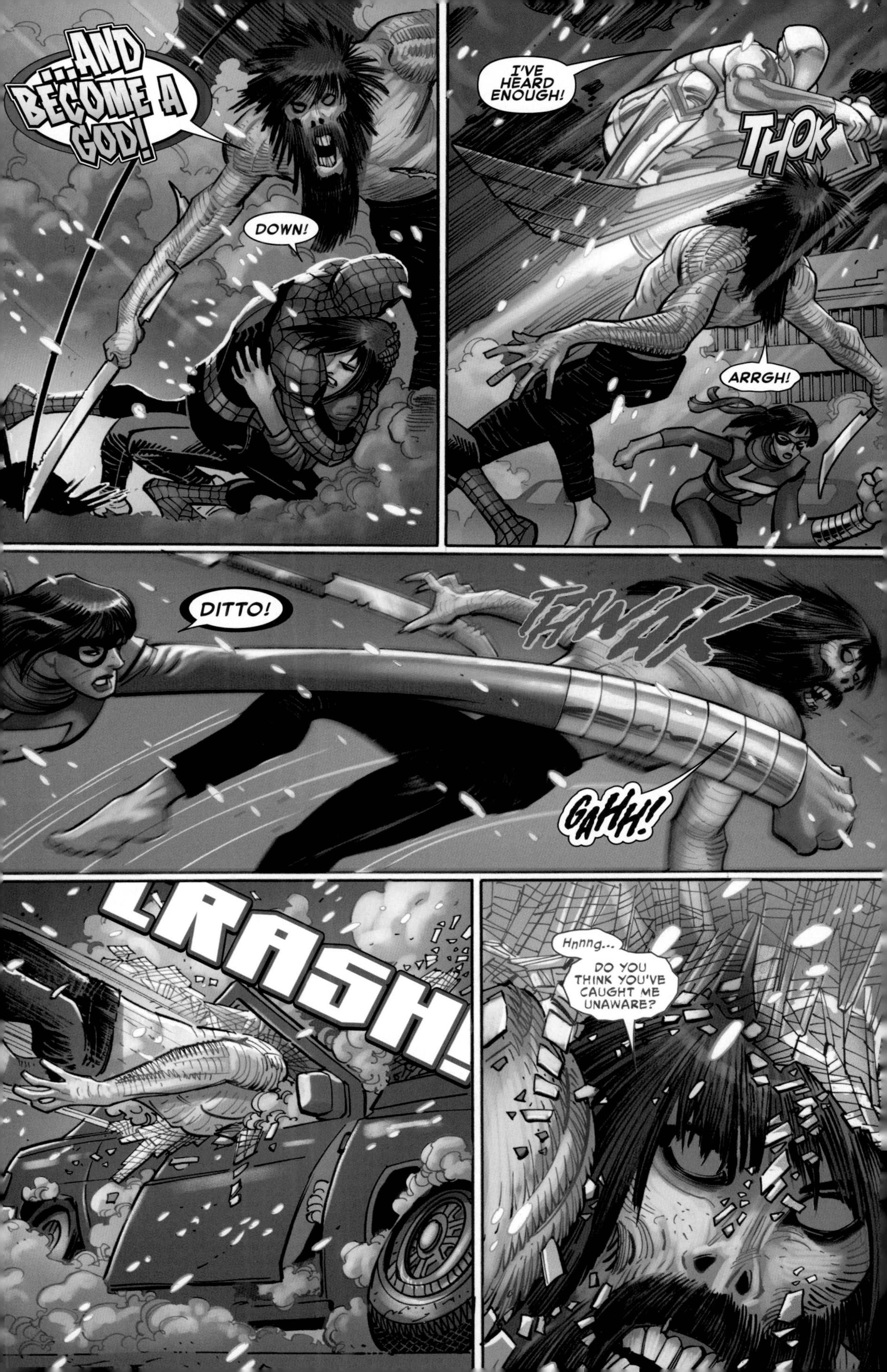
...AND BECOME A GOD!
DOWN!
I'VE HEARD ENOUGH!
THOK
ARRGH!
DITTO!
THWAK
GAHH!
CRASH!
Hnnng...
DO YOU THINK YOU'VE CAUGHT ME UNAWARE?

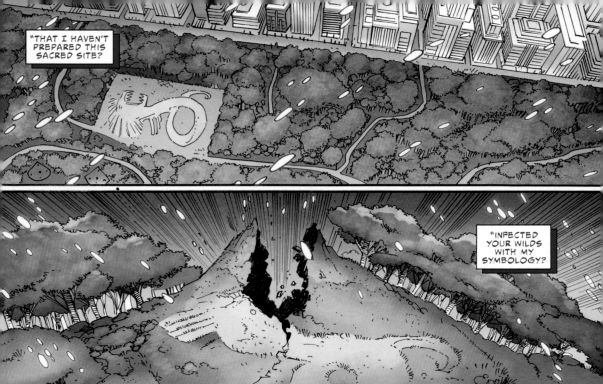

"THAT I HAVEN'T PREPARED THIS SACRED SITE?

"INFECTED YOUR WILDS WITH MY SYMBOLOGY?

"MY EQUATIONS... COUCHED IN GLYPHS... POWERFUL ENOUGH TO BRING FORTH *LIFE*.

"AND LIFE IS ONLY THE *SEED* OF *DEATH*.

"AND OH, HOW I HUNGER FOR *DEATH*."

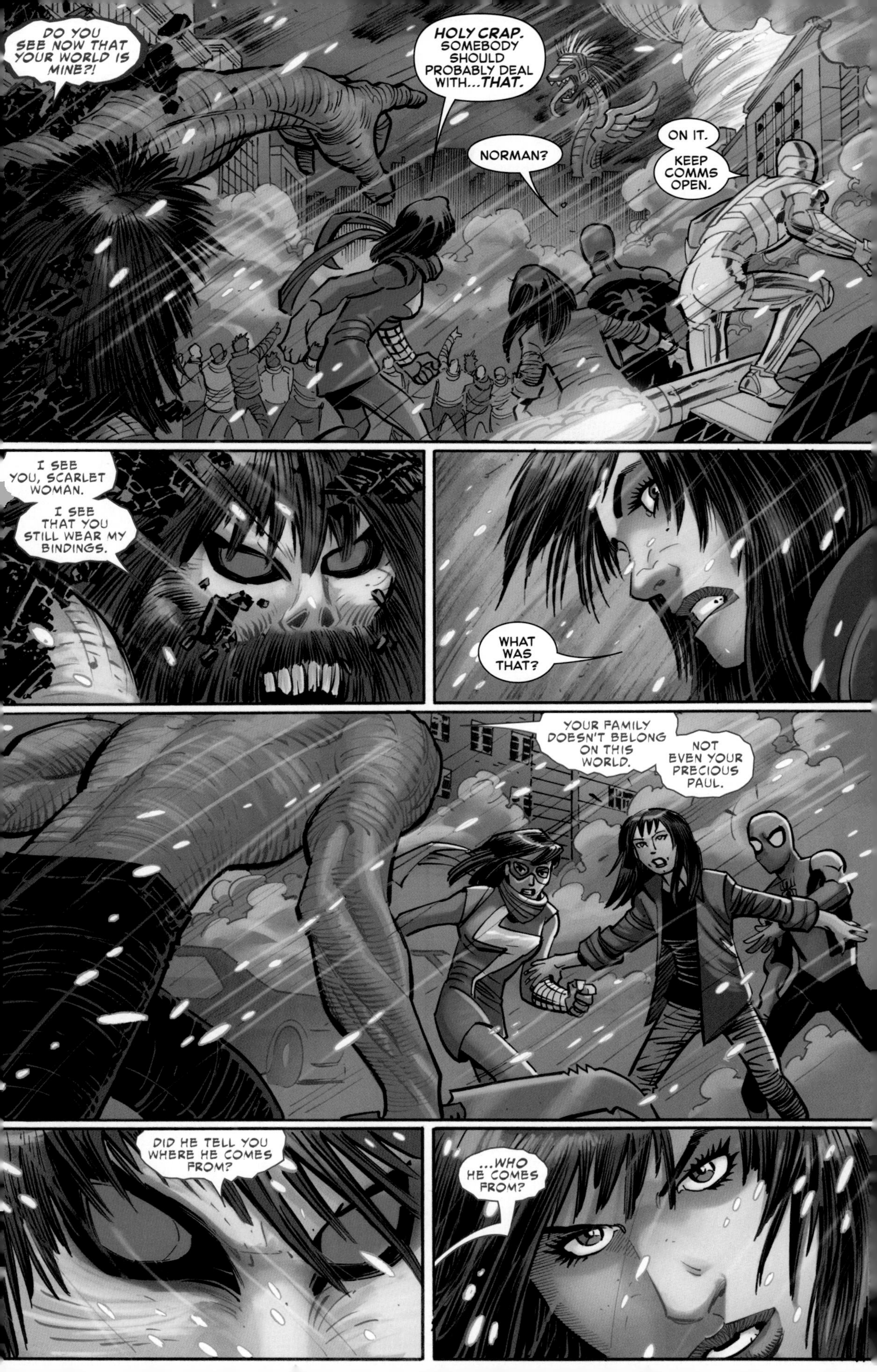
DO YOU SEE NOW THAT YOUR WORLD IS MINE?!
HOLY CRAP. SOMEBODY SHOULD PROBABLY DEAL WITH...THAT.
NORMAN?
ON IT.
KEEP COMMS OPEN.
I SEE YOU, SCARLET WOMAN.
I SEE THAT YOU STILL WEAR MY BINDINGS.
WHAT WAS THAT?
YOUR FAMILY DOESN'T BELONG ON THIS WORLD.
NOT EVEN YOUR PRECIOUS PAUL.
DID HE TELL YOU WHERE HE COMES FROM?
...WHO HE COMES FROM?

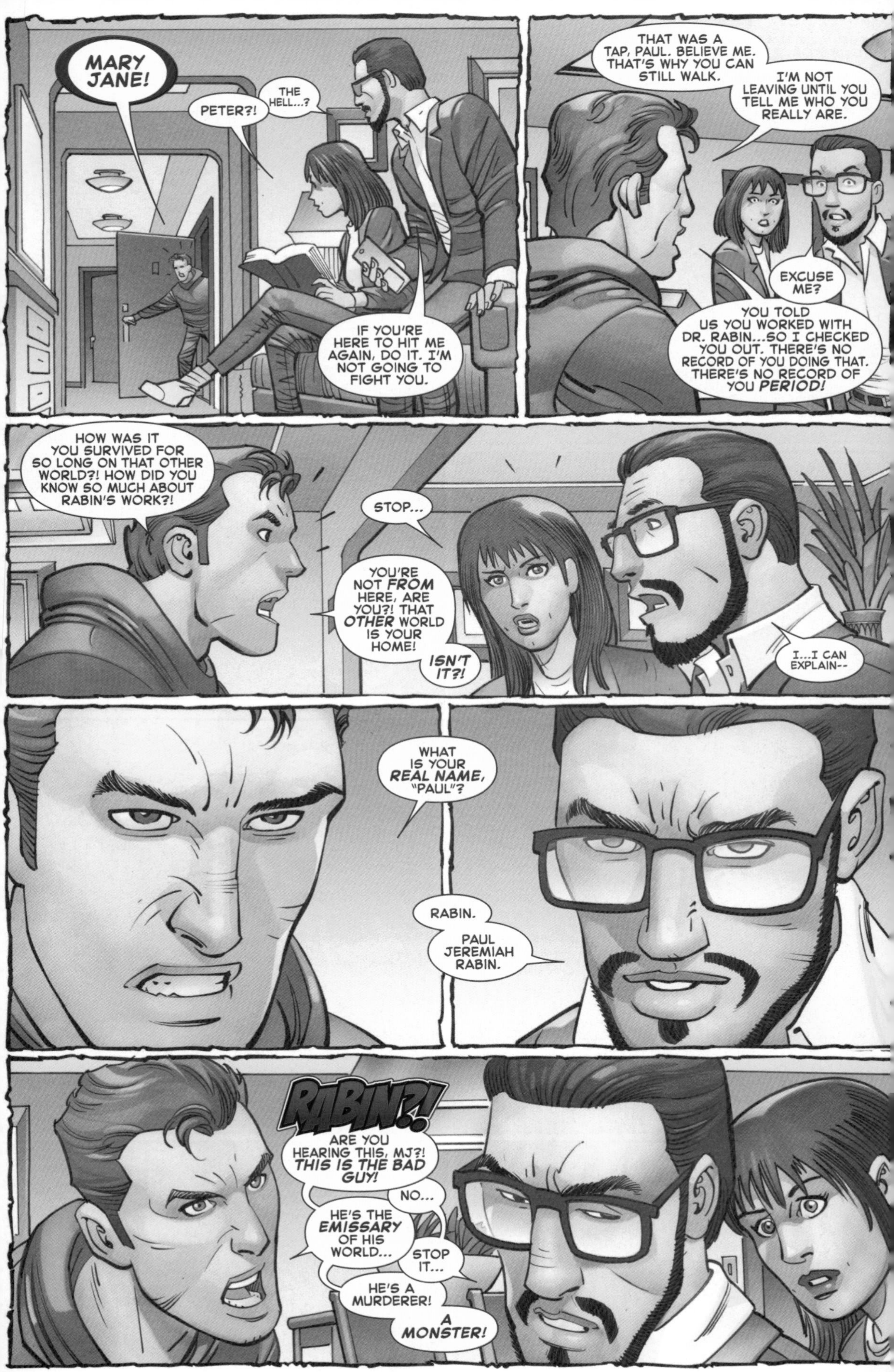
MARY JANE!
PETER?!
THE HELL...?
IF YOU'RE HERE TO HIT ME AGAIN, DO IT. I'M NOT GOING TO FIGHT YOU.
THAT WAS A TAP, PAUL. BELIEVE ME. THAT'S WHY YOU CAN STILL WALK.
I'M NOT LEAVING UNTIL YOU TELL ME WHO YOU REALLY ARE.
EXCUSE ME?
YOU TOLD US YOU WORKED WITH DR. RABIN...SO I CHECKED YOU OUT. THERE'S NO RECORD OF YOU DOING THAT. THERE'S NO RECORD OF YOU PERIOD!
HOW WAS IT YOU SURVIVED FOR SO LONG ON THAT OTHER WORLD?! HOW DID YOU KNOW SO MUCH ABOUT RABIN'S WORK?!
STOP...
YOU'RE NOT FROM HERE, ARE YOU?! THAT OTHER WORLD IS YOUR HOME!
ISN'T IT?!
I...I CAN EXPLAIN--
WHAT IS YOUR REAL NAME, "PAUL"?
RABIN.
PAUL JEREMIAH RABIN.
RABIN?!
ARE YOU HEARING THIS, MJ?! THIS IS THE BAD GUY!
NO...
HE'S THE EMISSARY OF HIS WORLD...
STOP IT...
HE'S A MURDERER!
A MONSTER!

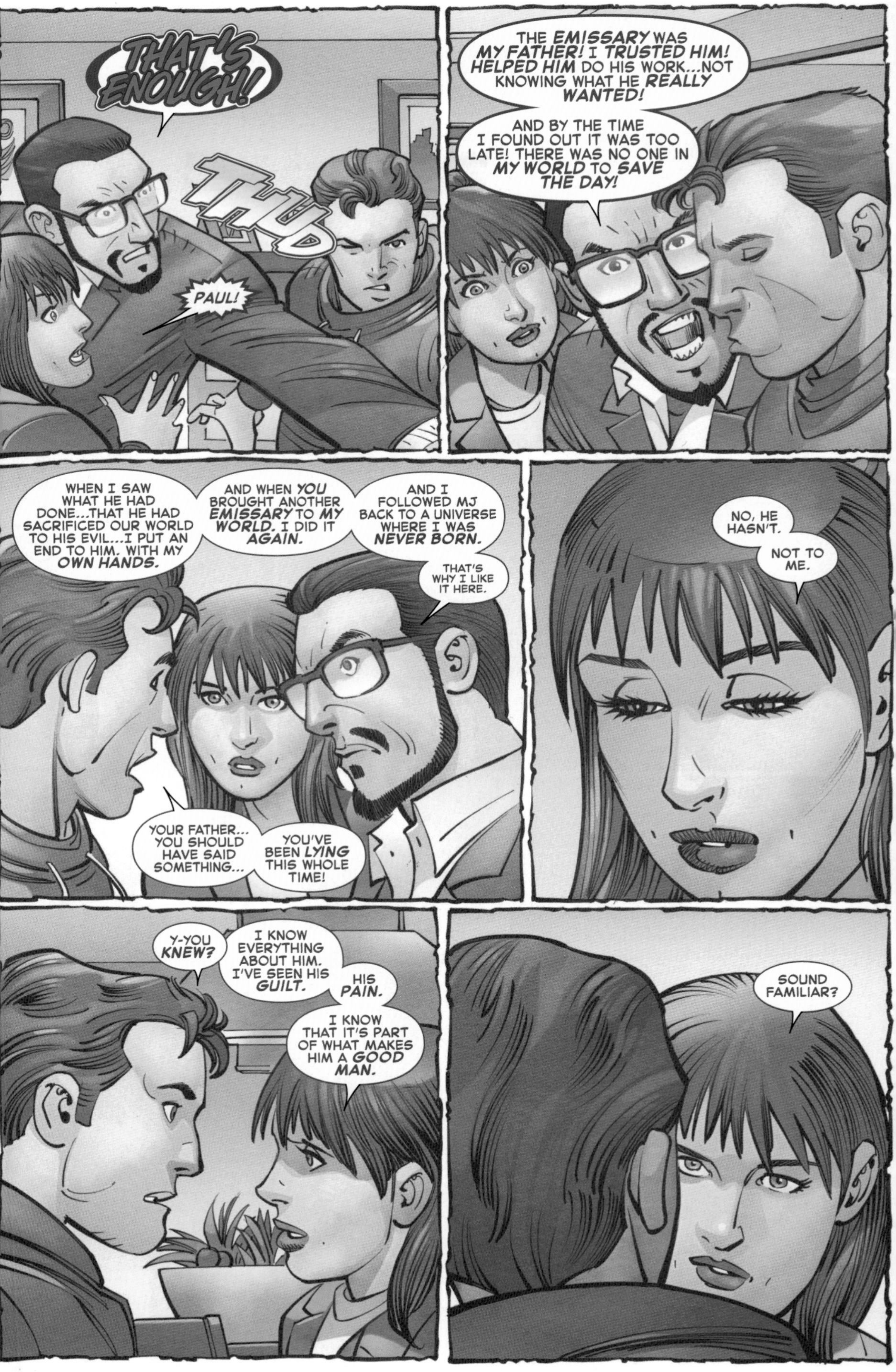
THAT'S ENOUGH!
THUD
PAUL!
THE EMISSARY WAS MY FATHER! I TRUSTED HIM! HELPED HIM DO HIS WORK...NOT KNOWING WHAT HE REALLY WANTED!
AND BY THE TIME I FOUND OUT IT WAS TOO LATE! THERE WAS NO ONE IN MY WORLD TO SAVE THE DAY!
WHEN I SAW WHAT HE HAD DONE...THAT HE HAD SACRIFICED OUR WORLD TO HIS EVIL...I PUT AN END TO HIM. WITH MY OWN HANDS.
AND WHEN YOU BROUGHT ANOTHER EMISSARY TO MY WORLD, I DID IT AGAIN.
AND I FOLLOWED MJ BACK TO A UNIVERSE WHERE I WAS NEVER BORN.
THAT'S WHY I LIKE IT HERE.
YOUR FATHER... YOU SHOULD HAVE SAID SOMETHING...
YOU'VE BEEN LYING THIS WHOLE TIME!
NO, HE HASN'T.
NOT TO ME.
Y-YOU KNEW?
I KNOW EVERYTHING ABOUT HIM. I'VE SEEN HIS GUILT.
HIS PAIN.
I KNOW THAT IT'S PART OF WHAT MAKES HIM A GOOD MAN.
SOUND FAMILIAR?

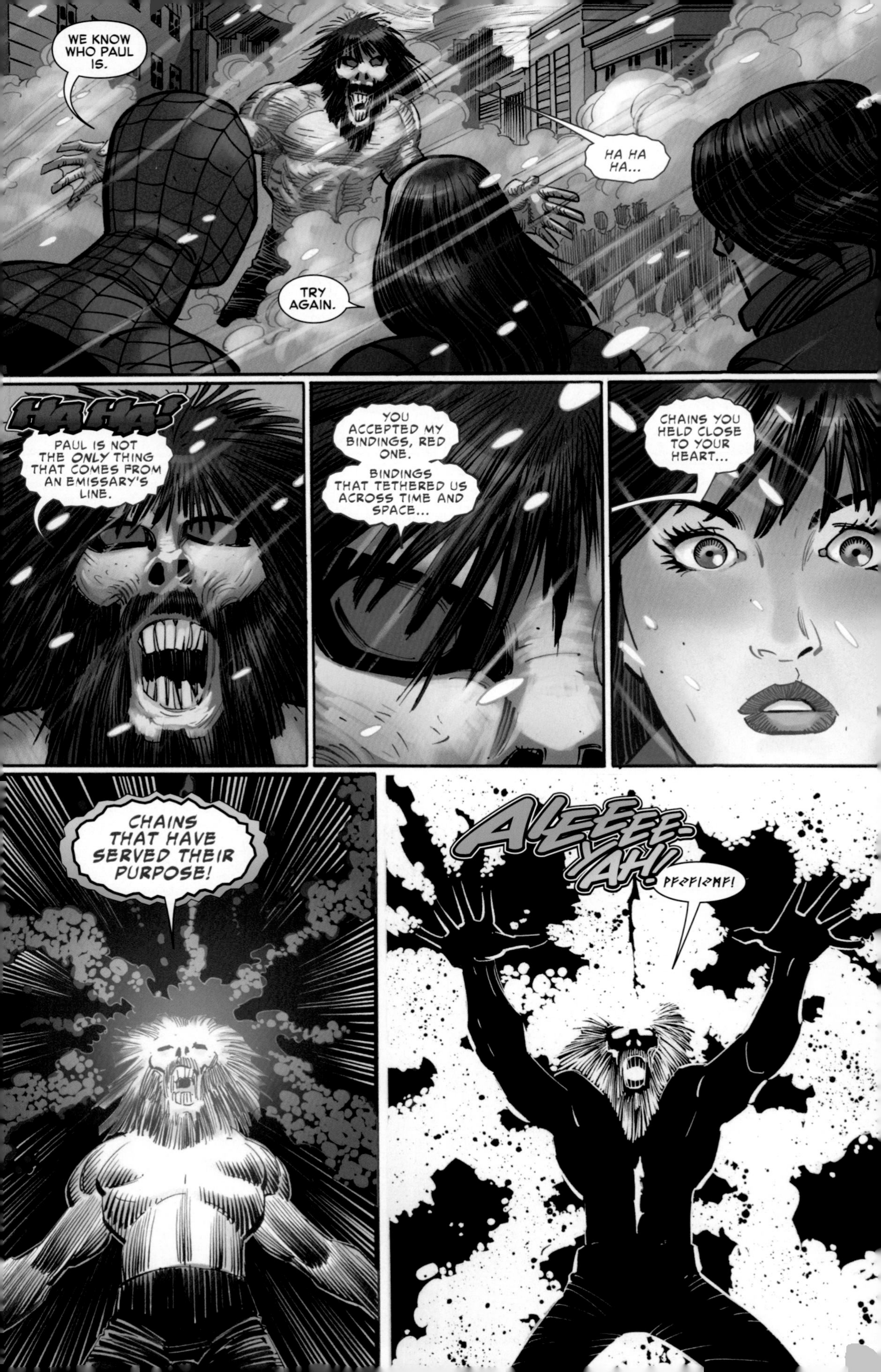
WE KNOW WHO PAUL IS.
HA HA HA...
TRY AGAIN.
HA HA!
PAUL IS NOT THE ONLY THING THAT COMES FROM AN EMISSARY'S LINE.
YOU ACCEPTED MY BINDINGS, RED ONE.
BINDINGS THAT TETHERED US ACROSS TIME AND SPACE...
CHAINS YOU HELD CLOSE TO YOUR HEART...
CHAINS THAT HAVE SERVED THEIR PURPOSE!
AIEEEE-YAH!

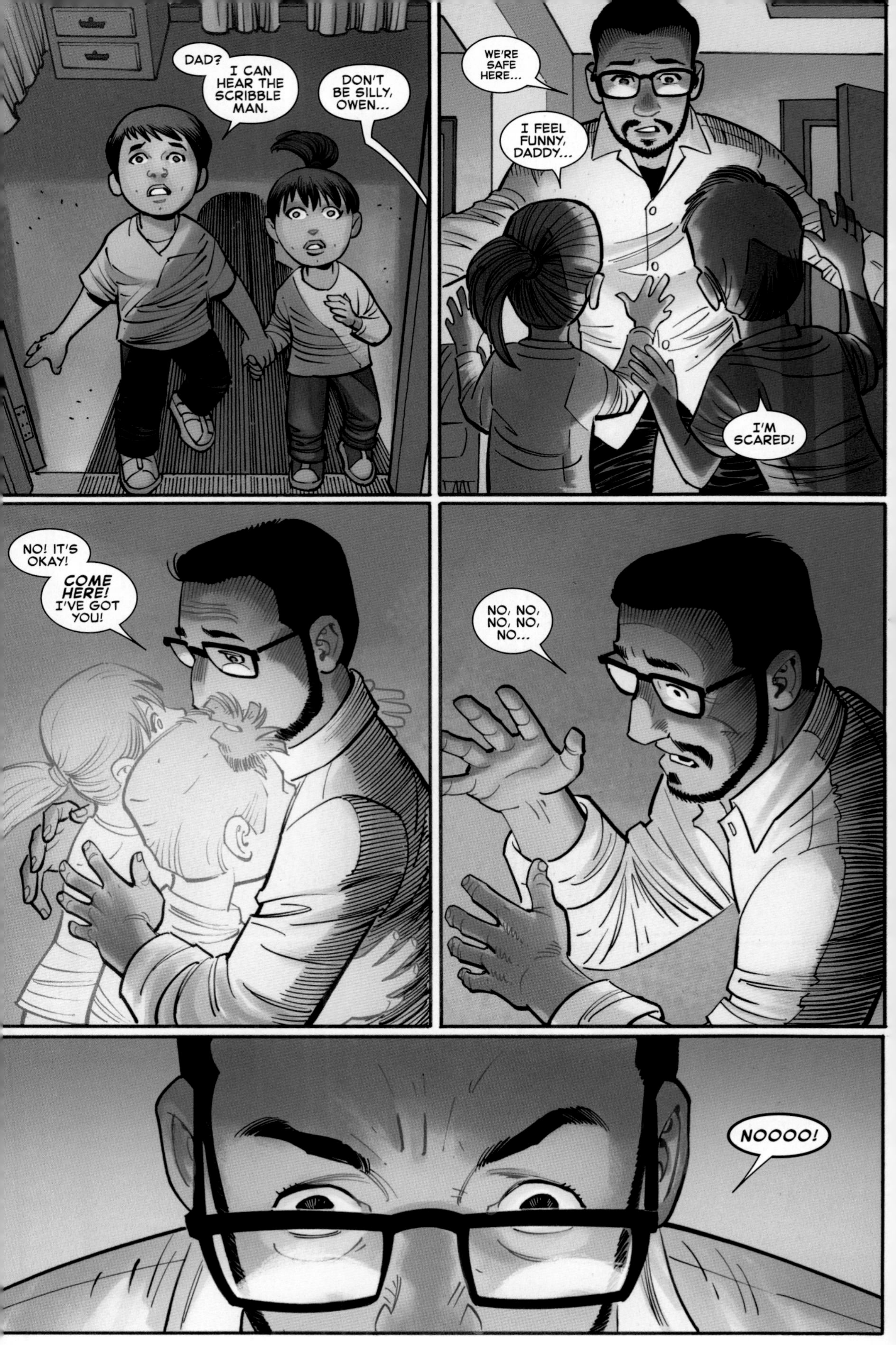
DAD? I CAN HEAR THE SCRIBBLE MAN.
DON'T BE SILLY, OWEN...
WE'RE SAFE HERE...
I FEEL FUNNY, DADDY...
I'M SCARED!
NO! IT'S OKAY!
COME HERE! I'VE GOT YOU!
NO, NO, NO, NO, NO...
NOOOO!

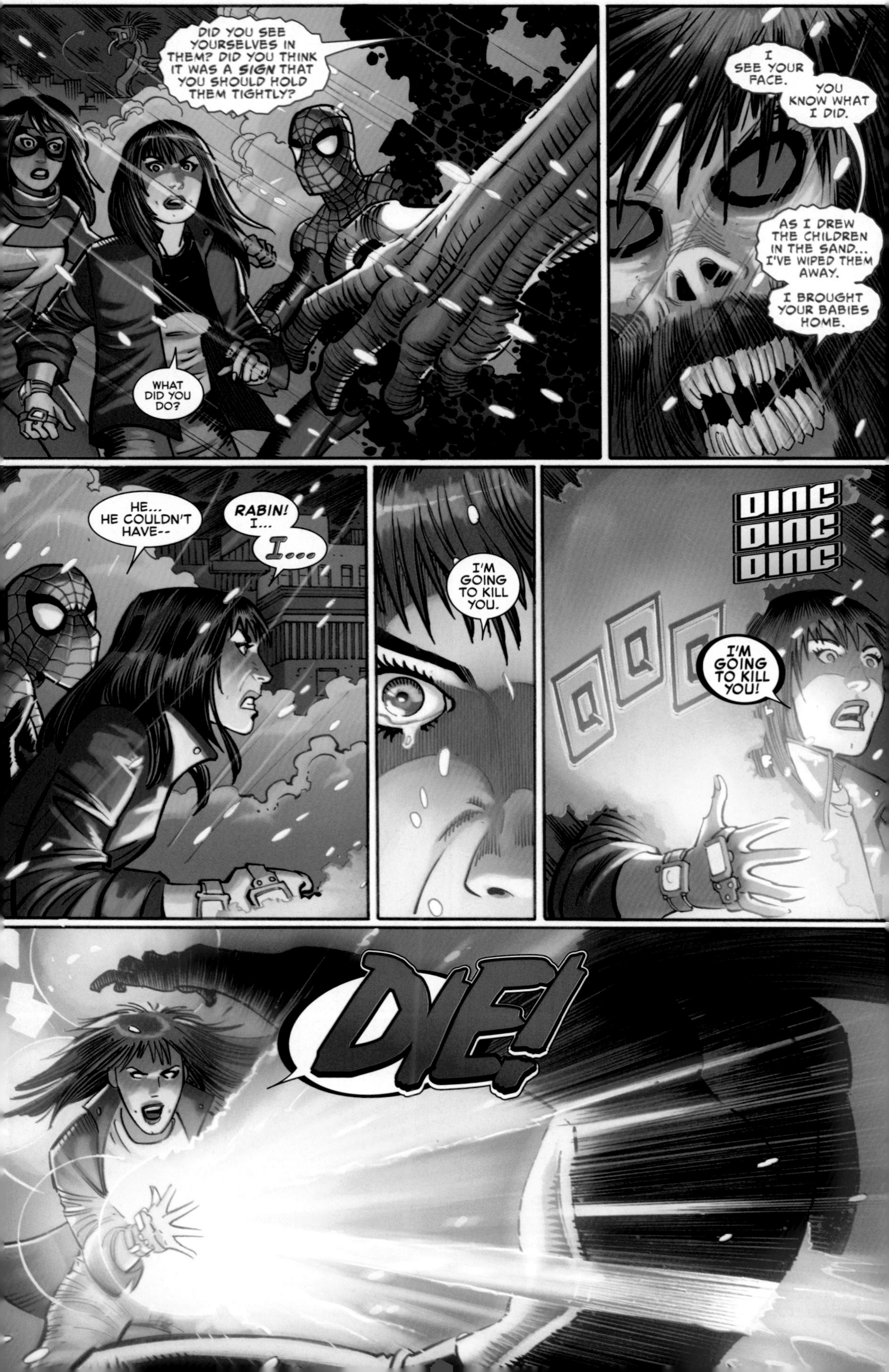
DID YOU SEE YOURSELVES IN THEM? DID YOU THINK IT WAS A SIGN THAT YOU SHOULD HOLD THEM TIGHTLY?
WHAT DID YOU DO?
I SEE YOUR FACE.
YOU KNOW WHAT I DID.
AS I DREW THE CHILDREN IN THE SAND... I'VE WIPED THEM AWAY.
I BROUGHT YOUR BABIES HOME.
HE... HE COULDN'T HAVE--
RABIN! I... I...
I'M GOING TO KILL YOU.
DING DING DING
I'M GOING TO KILL YOU!
DIE!

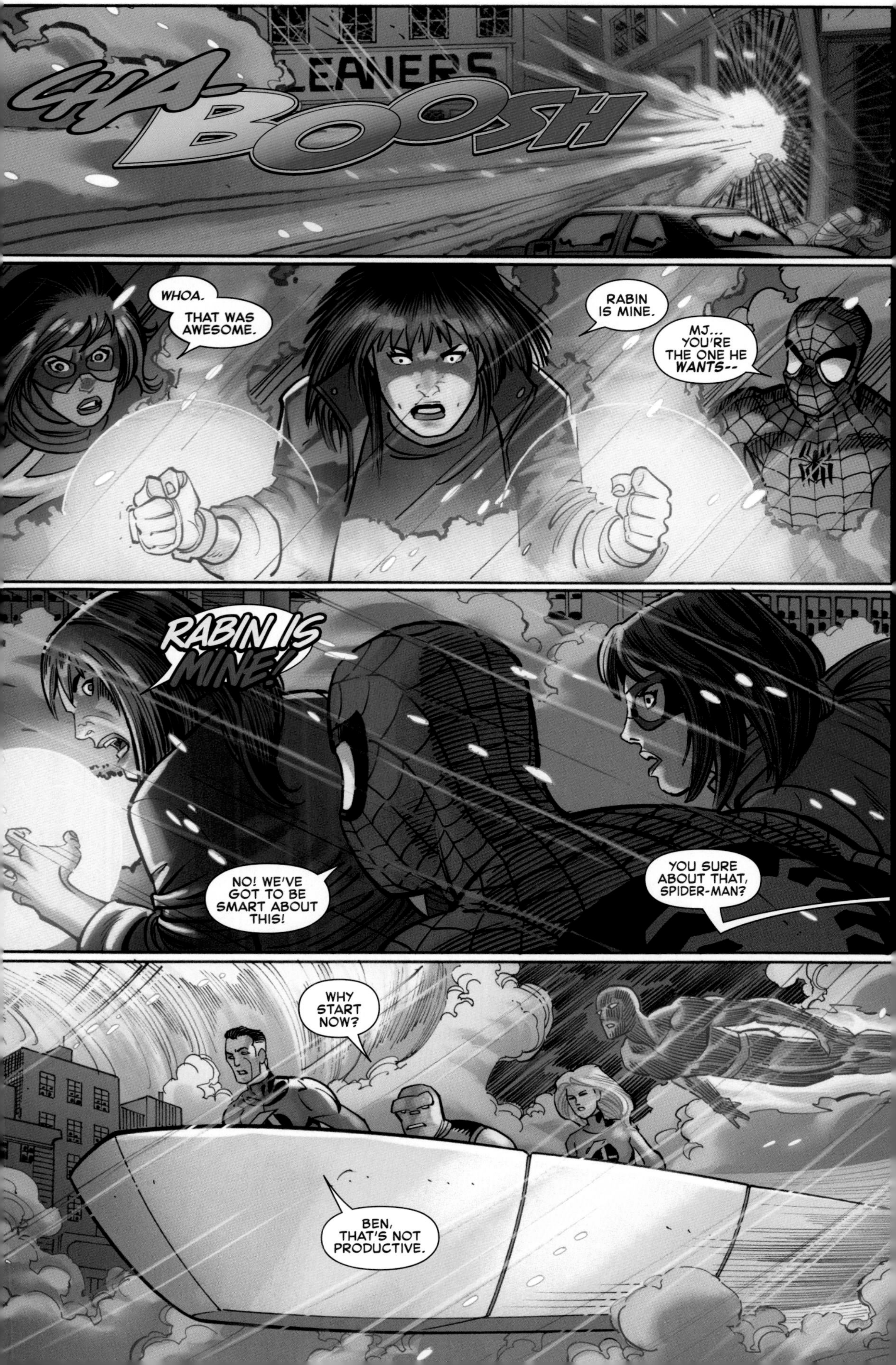
LEANERS
CHA BOOSH
WHOA.
THAT WAS AWESOME.
RABIN IS MINE.
MJ... YOU'RE THE ONE HE WANTS--
RABIN IS MINE!
NO! WE'VE GOT TO BE SMART ABOUT THIS!
YOU SURE ABOUT THAT, SPIDER-MAN?
WHY START NOW?
BEN, THAT'S NOT PRODUCTIVE.

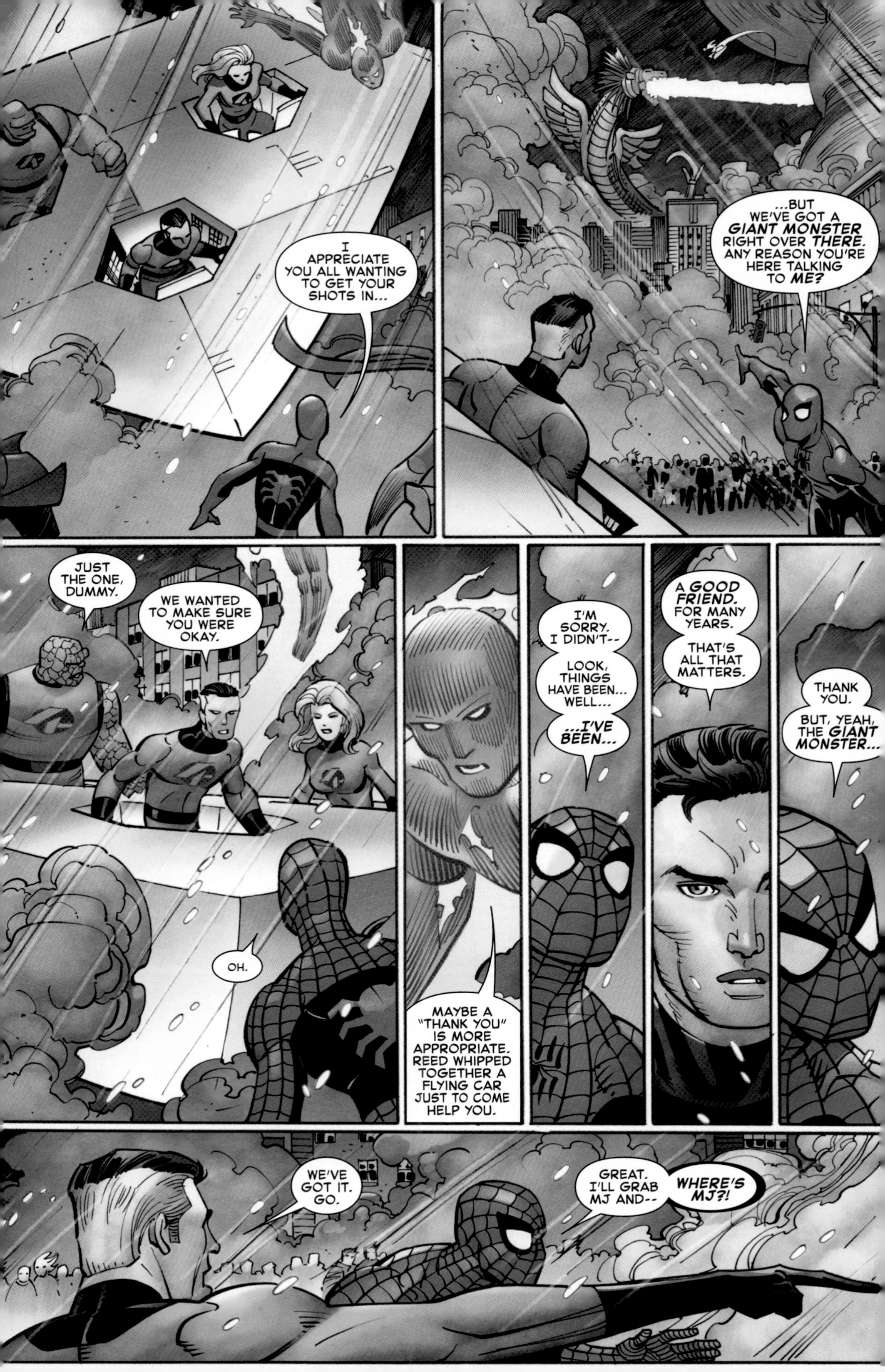
I APPRECIATE YOU ALL WANTING TO GET YOUR SHOTS IN...
...BUT WE'VE GOT A *GIANT MONSTER* RIGHT OVER *THERE.* ANY REASON YOU'RE HERE TALKING TO *ME?*
JUST THE ONE, DUMMY.
WE WANTED TO MAKE SURE YOU WERE OKAY.
OH.
MAYBE A "THANK YOU" IS MORE APPROPRIATE. REED WHIPPED TOGETHER A FLYING CAR JUST TO COME HELP YOU.
I'M SORRY. I DIDN'T--
LOOK, THINGS HAVE BEEN... WELL...
...I'VE BEEN...
A *GOOD FRIEND.* FOR MANY YEARS.
THAT'S ALL THAT MATTERS.
THANK YOU.
BUT, YEAH, THE *GIANT MONSTER...*
WE'VE GOT IT. GO.
GREAT. I'LL GRAB MJ AND--
WHERE'S MJ?!

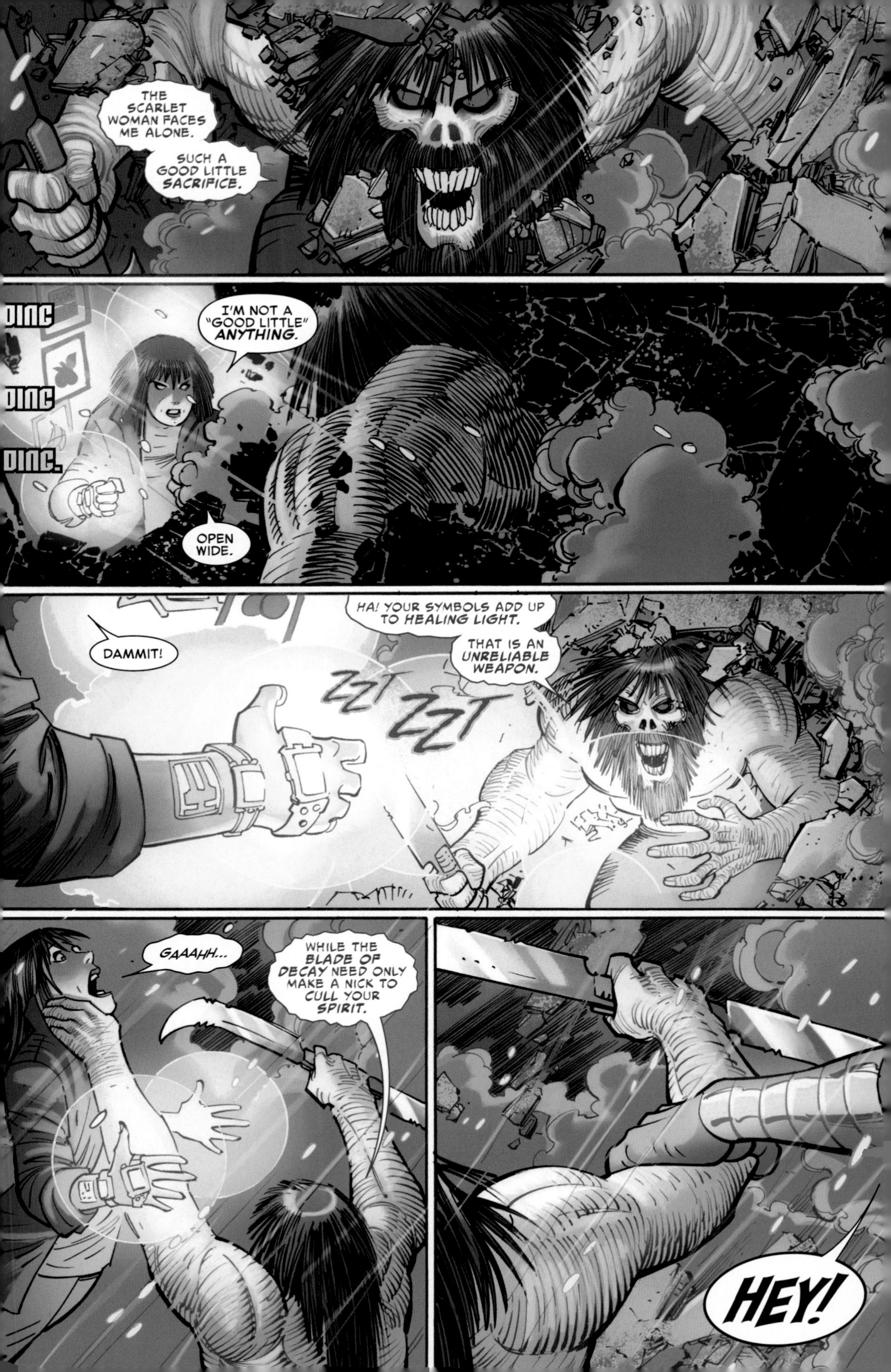
THE SCARLET WOMAN FACES ME ALONE.
SUCH A GOOD LITTLE SACRIFICE.
DINC
DINC
DINC.
I'M NOT A "GOOD LITTLE" ANYTHING.
OPEN WIDE.
DAMMIT!
HA! YOUR SYMBOLS ADD UP TO HEALING LIGHT.
THAT IS AN UNRELIABLE WEAPON.
ZZZT ZZZT
GAAAHH...
WHILE THE BLADE OF DECAY NEED ONLY MAKE A NICK TO CULL YOUR SPIRIT.
HEY!

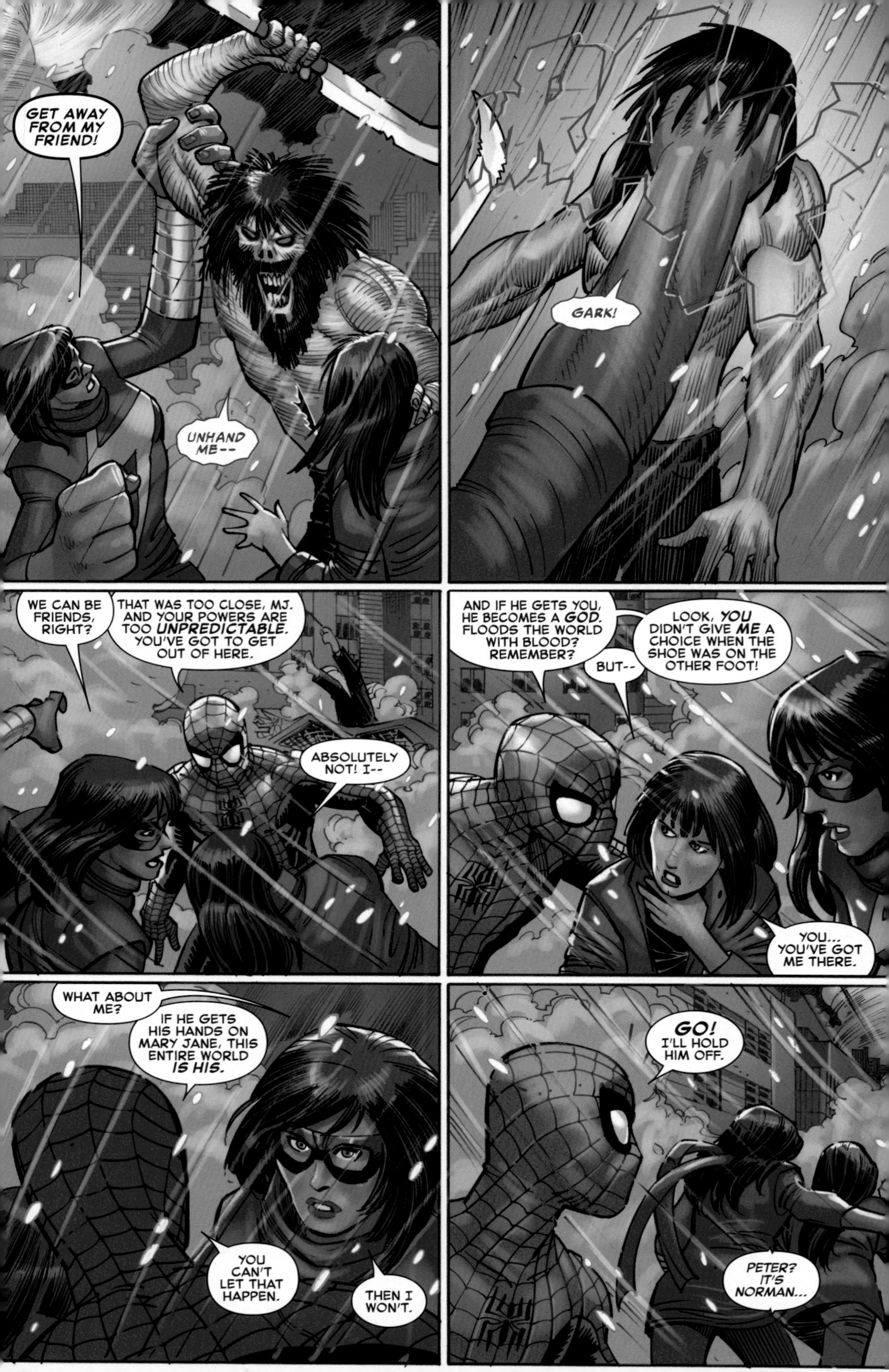
GET AWAY FROM MY FRIEND!
UNHAND ME--
GARK!
WE CAN BE FRIENDS, RIGHT?
THAT WAS TOO CLOSE, MJ. AND YOUR POWERS ARE TOO UNPREDICTABLE. YOU'VE GOT TO GET OUT OF HERE.
ABSOLUTELY NOT! I--
AND IF HE GETS YOU, HE BECOMES A GOD. FLOODS THE WORLD WITH BLOOD? REMEMBER?
BUT--
LOOK, YOU DIDN'T GIVE ME A CHOICE WHEN THE SHOE WAS ON THE OTHER FOOT!
YOU... YOU'VE GOT ME THERE.
WHAT ABOUT ME?
IF HE GETS HIS HANDS ON MARY JANE, THIS ENTIRE WORLD IS HIS.
YOU CAN'T LET THAT HAPPEN.
THEN I WON'T.
GO! I'LL HOLD HIM OFF.
PETER? IT'S NORMAN...

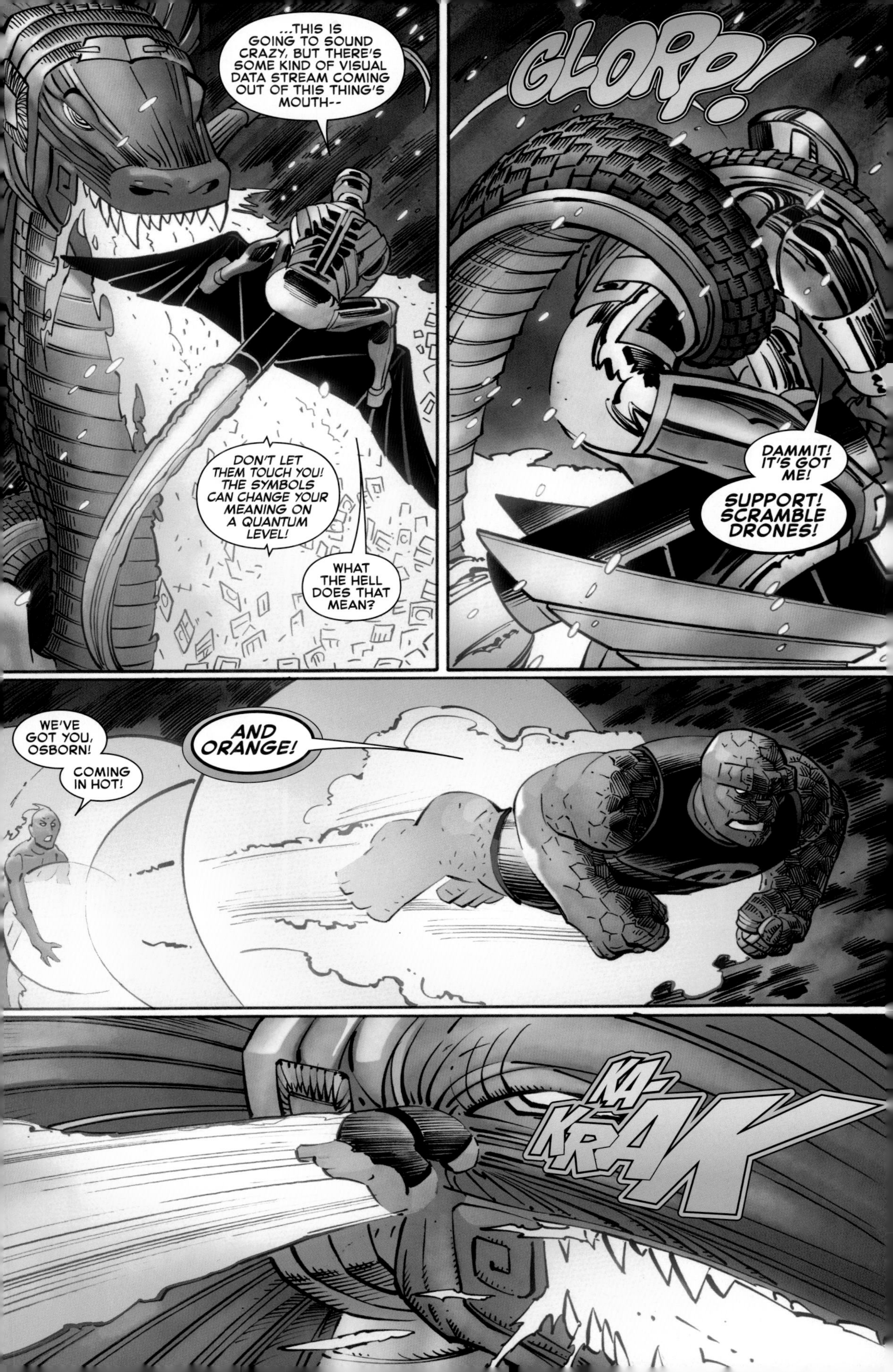
...THIS IS GOING TO SOUND CRAZY, BUT THERE'S SOME KIND OF VISUAL DATA STREAM COMING OUT OF THIS THING'S MOUTH--
DON'T LET THEM TOUCH YOU! THE SYMBOLS CAN CHANGE YOUR MEANING ON A QUANTUM LEVEL!
WHAT THE HELL DOES THAT MEAN?
GLORP!
DAMMIT! IT'S GOT ME!
SUPPORT! SCRAMBLE DRONES!
WE'VE GOT YOU, OSBORN!
COMING IN HOT!
AND ORANGE!
KA-KRAK

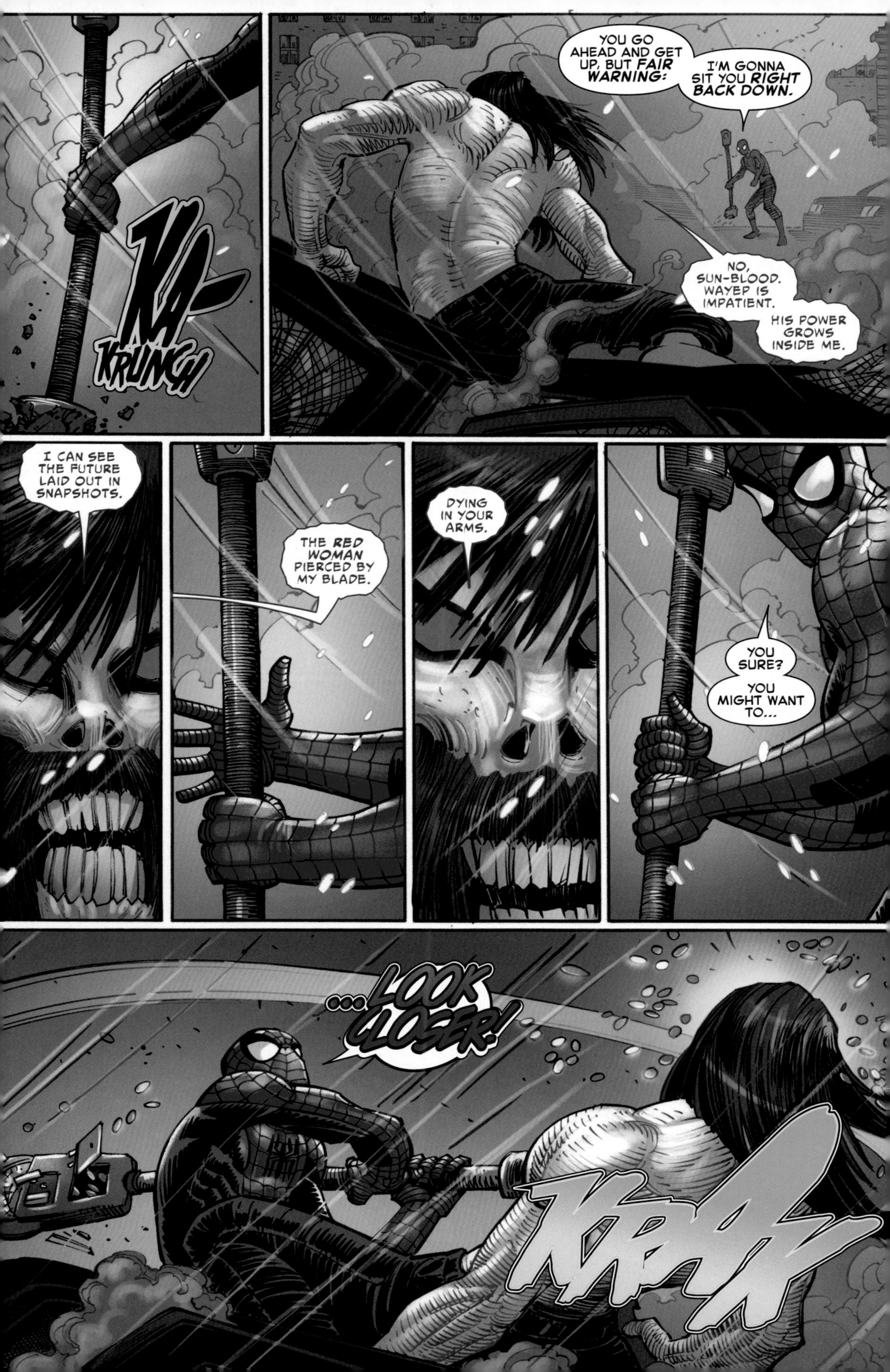
KA-KRUNCH
YOU GO AHEAD AND GET UP, BUT FAIR WARNING:
I'M GONNA SIT YOU RIGHT BACK DOWN.
NO, SUN-BLOOD. WAYEP IS IMPATIENT.
HIS POWER GROWS INSIDE ME.
I CAN SEE THE FUTURE LAID OUT IN SNAPSHOTS.
THE RED WOMAN PIERCED BY MY BLADE.
DYING IN YOUR ARMS.
YOU SURE?
YOU MIGHT WANT TO...
...LOOK CLOSER!
KRAK

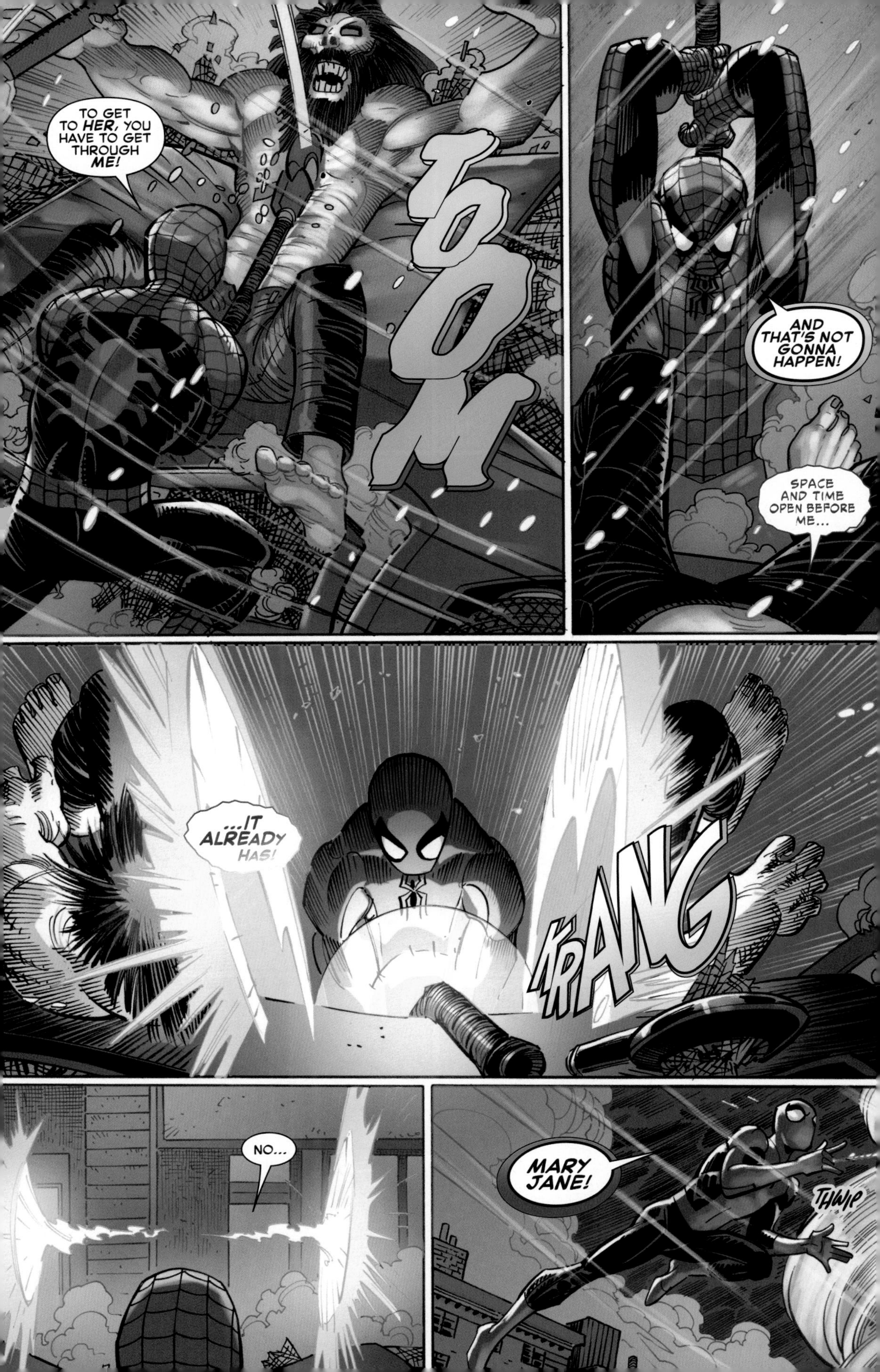
TO GET TO HER, YOU HAVE TO GET THROUGH ME!
TOOM
AND THAT'S NOT GONNA HAPPEN!
SPACE AND TIME OPEN BEFORE ME...
...IT ALREADY HAS!
KRANG
NO...
MARY JANE!
THWIP

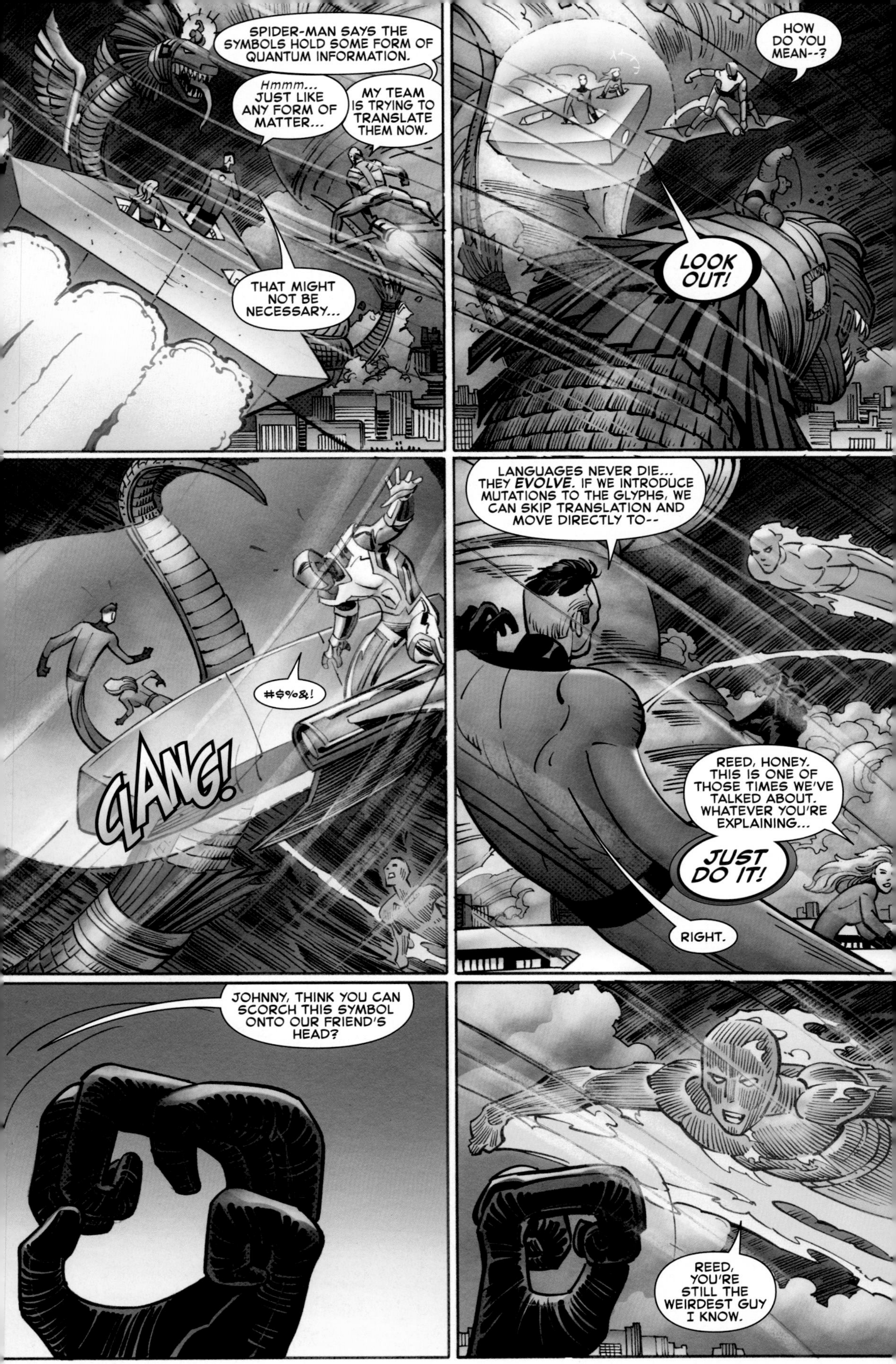
SPIDER-MAN SAYS THE SYMBOLS HOLD SOME FORM OF QUANTUM INFORMATION.
Hmmm... JUST LIKE ANY FORM OF MATTER...
MY TEAM IS TRYING TO TRANSLATE THEM NOW.
THAT MIGHT NOT BE NECESSARY...
HOW DO YOU MEAN--?
LOOK OUT!
#$%&!
CLANG!
LANGUAGES NEVER DIE... THEY EVOLVE. IF WE INTRODUCE MUTATIONS TO THE GLYPHS, WE CAN SKIP TRANSLATION AND MOVE DIRECTLY TO--
REED, HONEY. THIS IS ONE OF THOSE TIMES WE'VE TALKED ABOUT. WHATEVER YOU'RE EXPLAINING...
JUST DO IT!
RIGHT.
JOHNNY, THINK YOU CAN SCORCH THIS SYMBOL ONTO OUR FRIEND'S HEAD?
REED, YOU'RE STILL THE WEIRDEST GUY I KNOW.

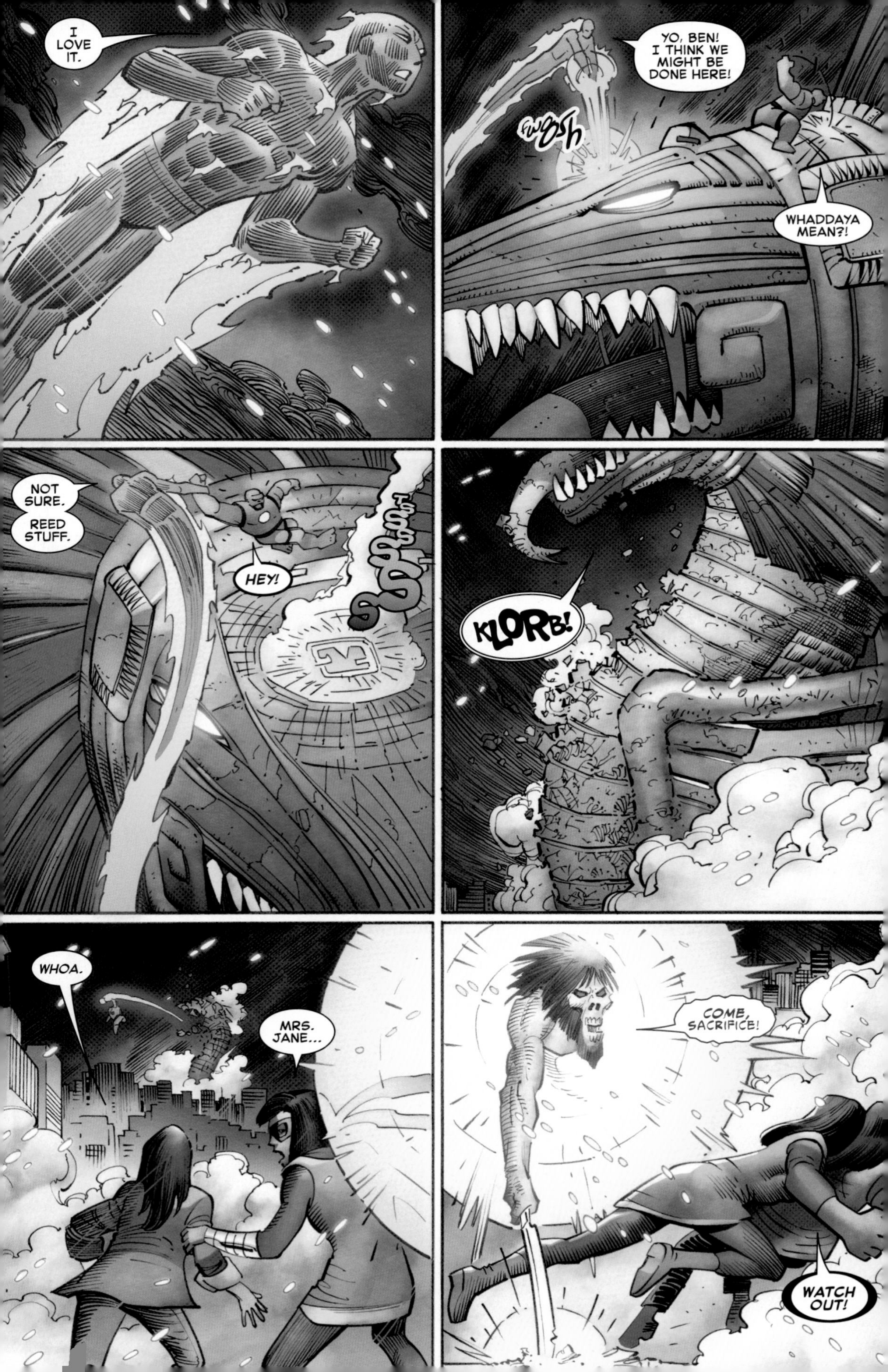

I LOVE IT.
YO, BEN! I THINK WE MIGHT BE DONE HERE!
WHADDAYA MEAN?!
NOT SURE.
REED STUFF.
HEY!
KLORB!
WHOA.
MRS. JANE...
COME, SACRIFICE!
WATCH OUT!

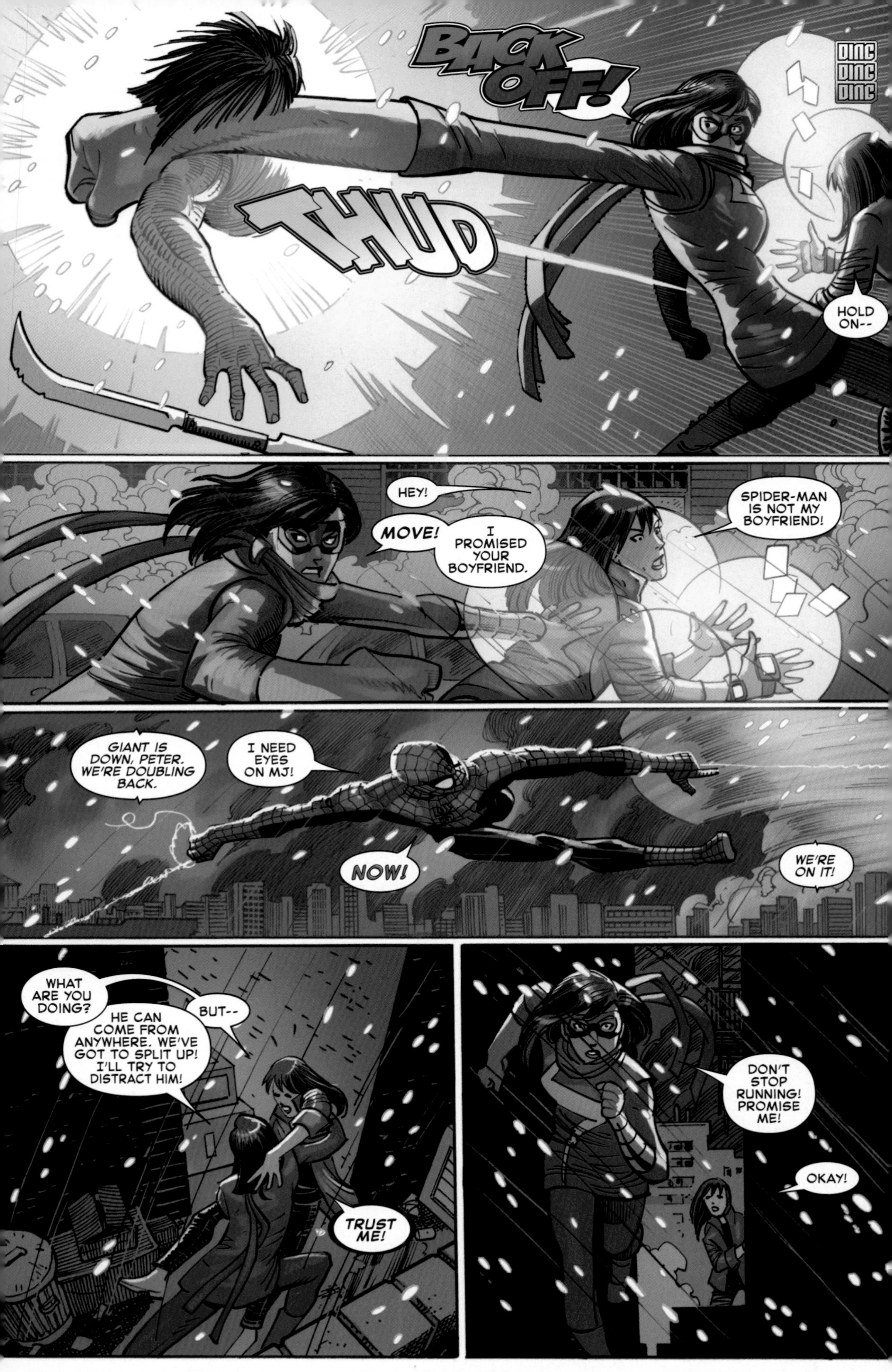

DINC DINC DINC
BACK OFF!
THUD
HOLD ON--
HEY!
MOVE!
I PROMISED YOUR BOYFRIEND.
SPIDER-MAN IS NOT MY BOYFRIEND!
GIANT IS DOWN, PETER. WE'RE DOUBLING BACK.
I NEED EYES ON MJ!
NOW!
WE'RE ON IT!
WHAT ARE YOU DOING?
BUT--
HE CAN COME FROM ANYWHERE. WE'VE GOT TO SPLIT UP! I'LL TRY TO DISTRACT HIM!
TRUST ME!
DON'T STOP RUNNING! PROMISE ME!
OKAY!

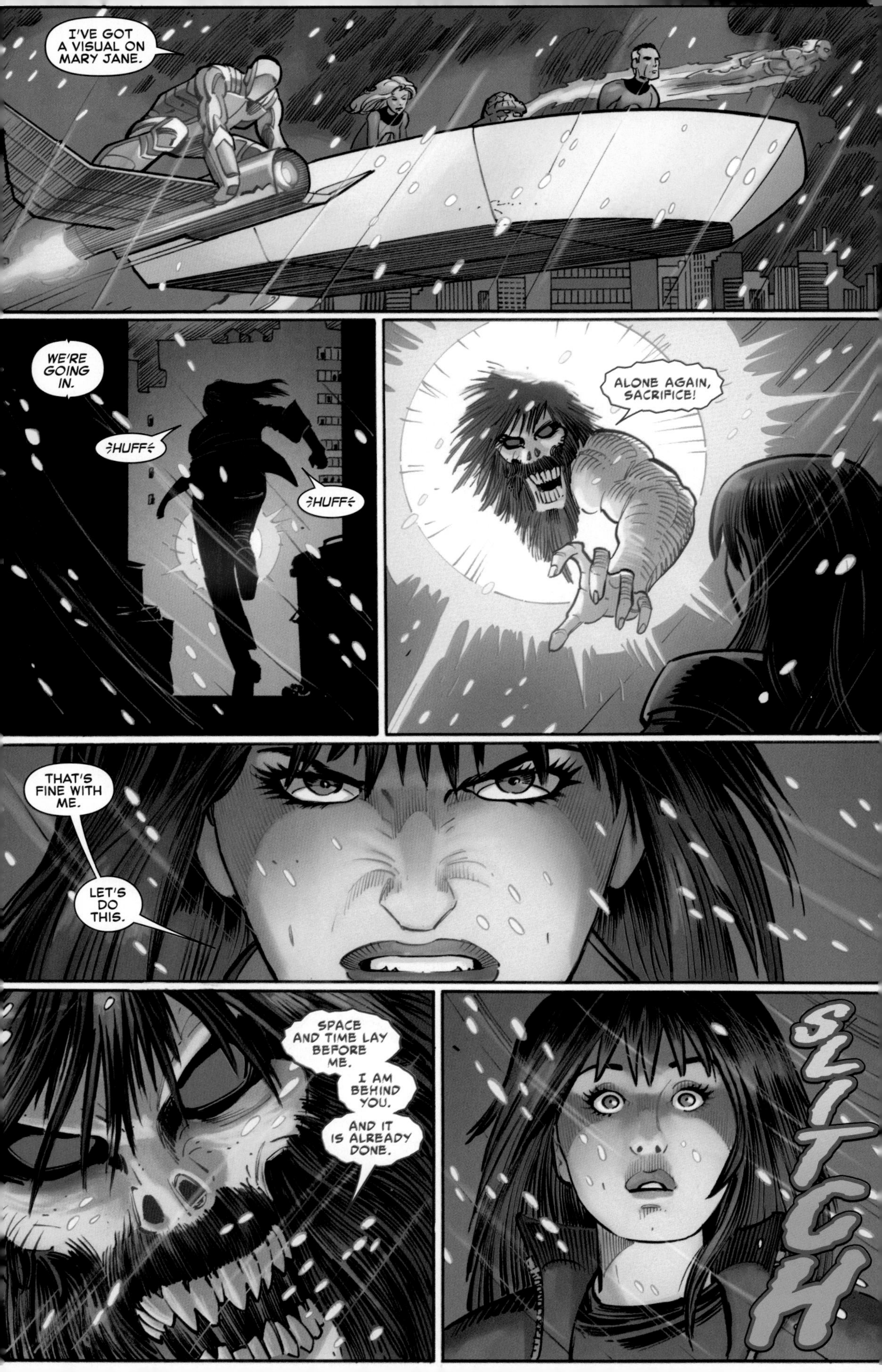
I'VE GOT A VISUAL ON MARY JANE.
WE'RE GOING IN.
HUFF
HUFF
ALONE AGAIN, SACRIFICE!
THAT'S FINE WITH ME.
LET'S DO THIS.
SPACE AND TIME LAY BEFORE ME.
I AM BEHIND YOU.
AND IT IS ALREADY DONE.
SLITCH

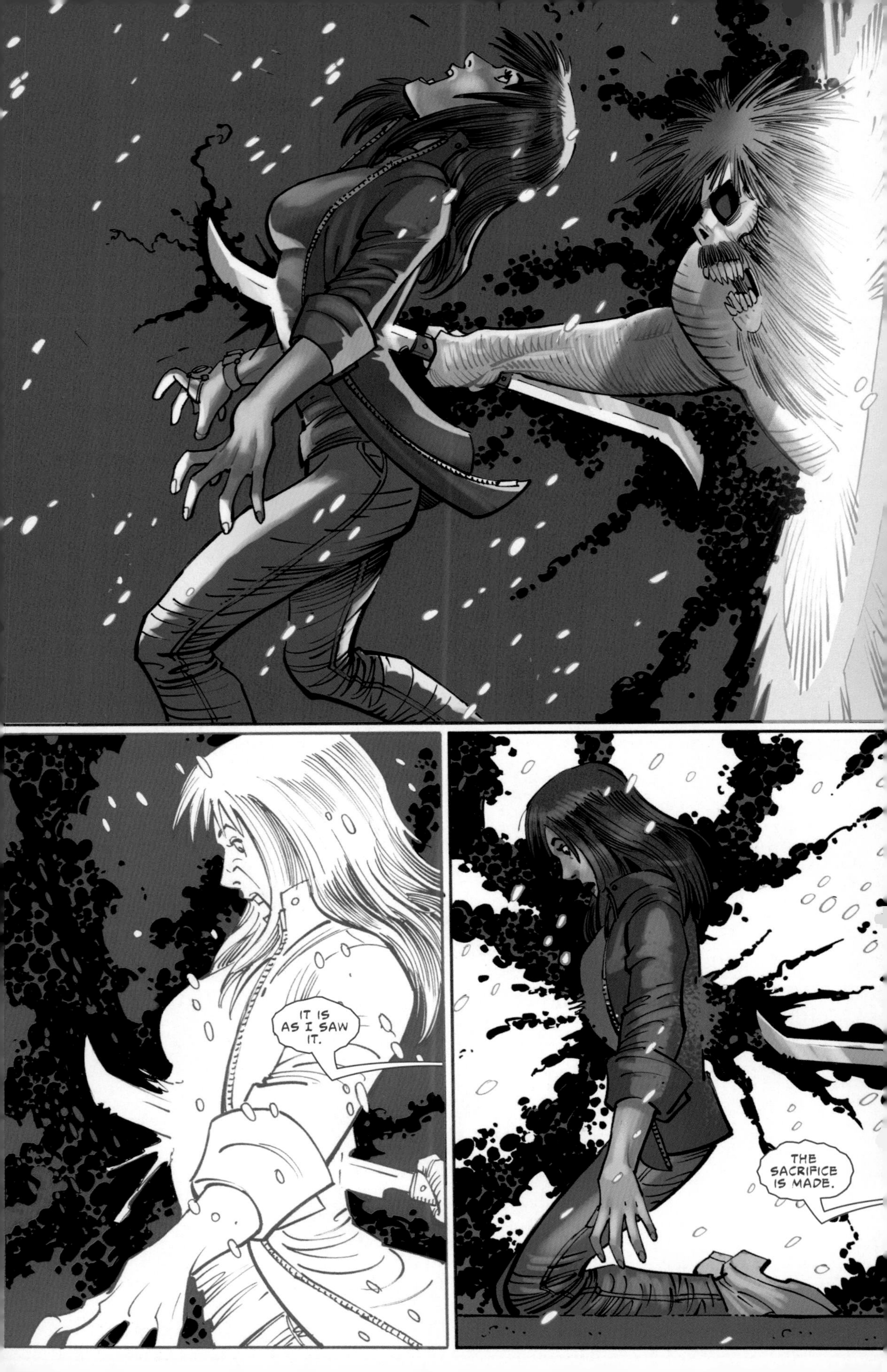
IT IS AS I SAW IT.
THE SACRIFICE IS MADE.

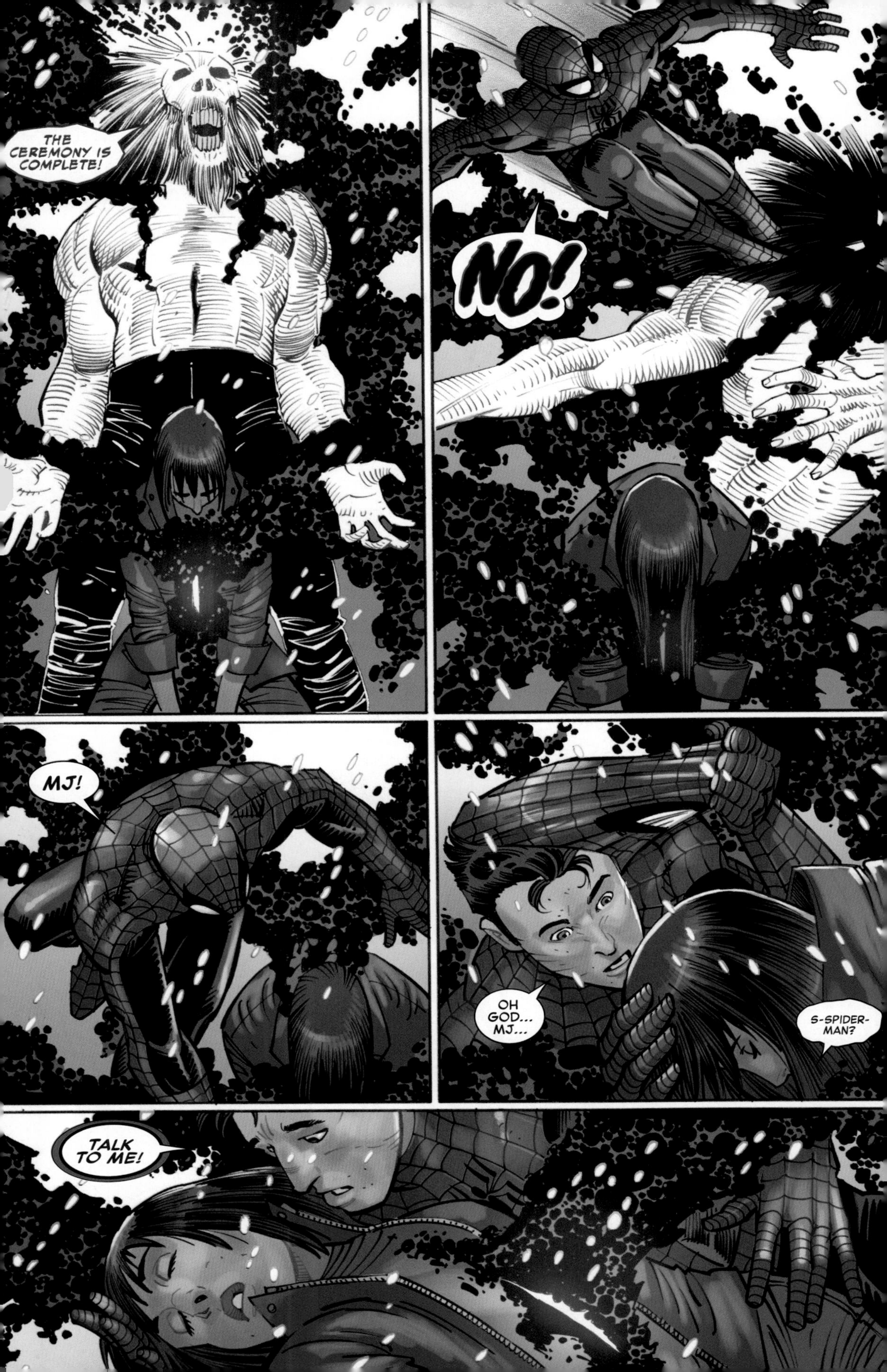
THE CEREMONY IS COMPLETE!
NO!
MJ!
OH GOD... MJ...
S-SPIDER-MAN?
TALK TO ME!

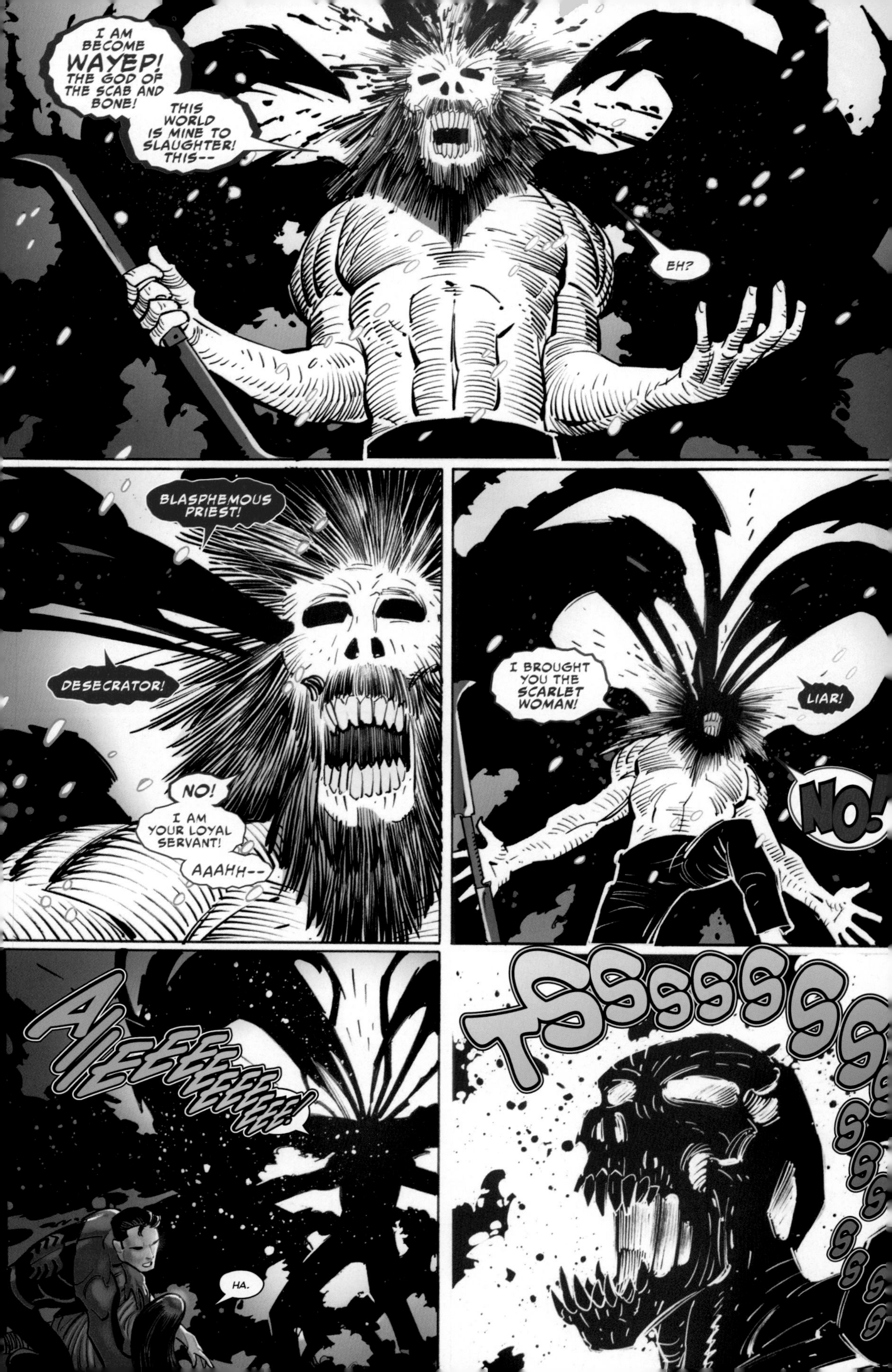
I AM BECOME WAYEP! THE GOD OF THE SCAB AND BONE!
THIS WORLD IS MINE TO SLAUGHTER! THIS--
EH?
BLASPHEMOUS PRIEST!
DESECRATOR!
NO!
I AM YOUR LOYAL SERVANT!
AAAHH--
I BROUGHT YOU THE SCARLET WOMAN!
LIAR!
NO!
AIIEEEEEEEEEEEE!
HA.
TSSSSSSSSSSSSSSSS

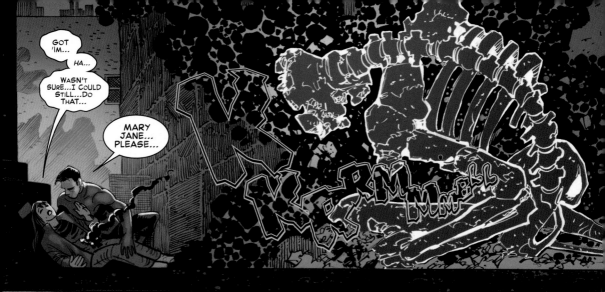

GOT 'IM...

HA...

WASN'T SURE...I COULD STILL...DO THAT...

MARY JANE... PLEASE...

PETER?

WHO... WHO IS THAT?

PETER?

MS. MARVEL...?

I--I'VE BEEN WORKING WITH... SPIDER-MAN HA...HA...

GUESS I DON'T NEED THIS ANYMORE.

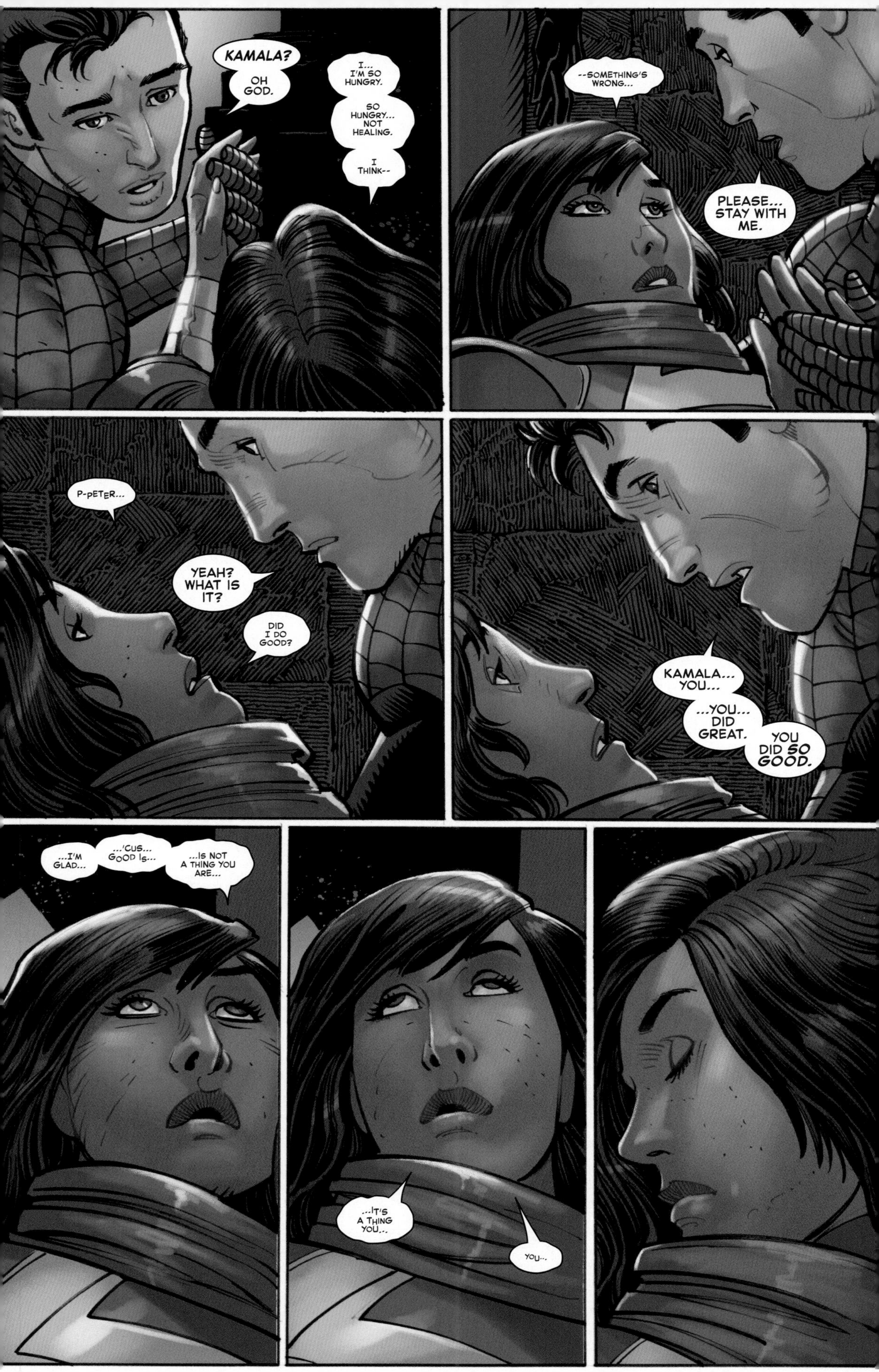
KAMALA?
OH GOD.
I... I'M SO HUNGRY.
SO HUNGRY... NOT HEALING.
I THINK--
--SOMETHING'S WRONG...
PLEASE... STAY WITH ME.
P-PETER...
YEAH? WHAT IS IT?
DID I DO GOOD?
KAMALA... YOU...
...YOU... DID GREAT.
YOU DID SO GOOD.
...I'M GLAD...
...'CUS... GOOD IS...
...IS NOT A THING YOU ARE...
...IT'S A THING YOU...
YOU...

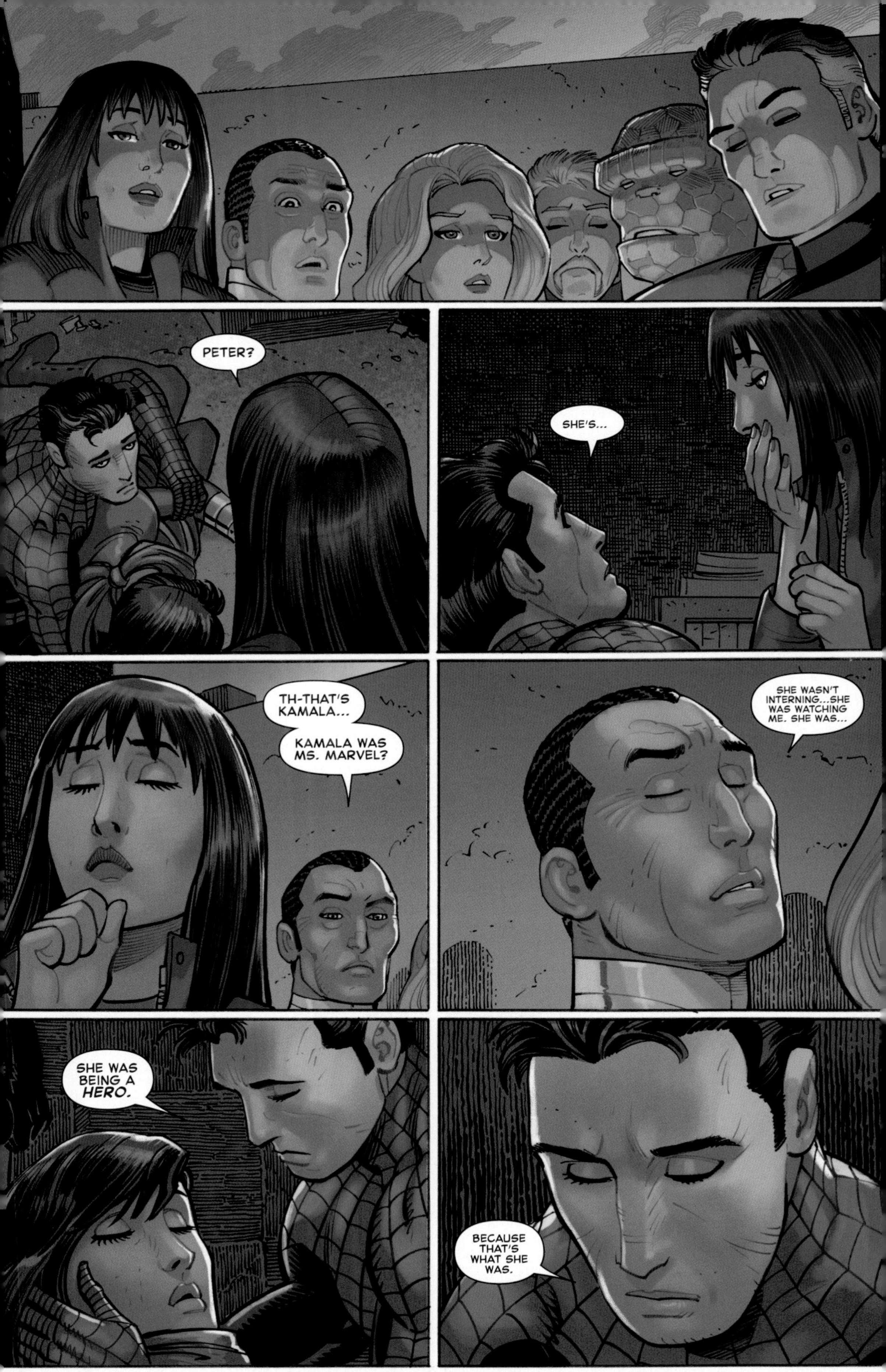
PETER?
SHE'S...
TH-THAT'S KAMALA...
KAMALA WAS MS. MARVEL?
SHE WASN'T INTERNING...SHE WAS WATCHING ME. SHE WAS...
SHE WAS BEING A HERO.
BECAUSE THAT'S WHAT SHE WAS.

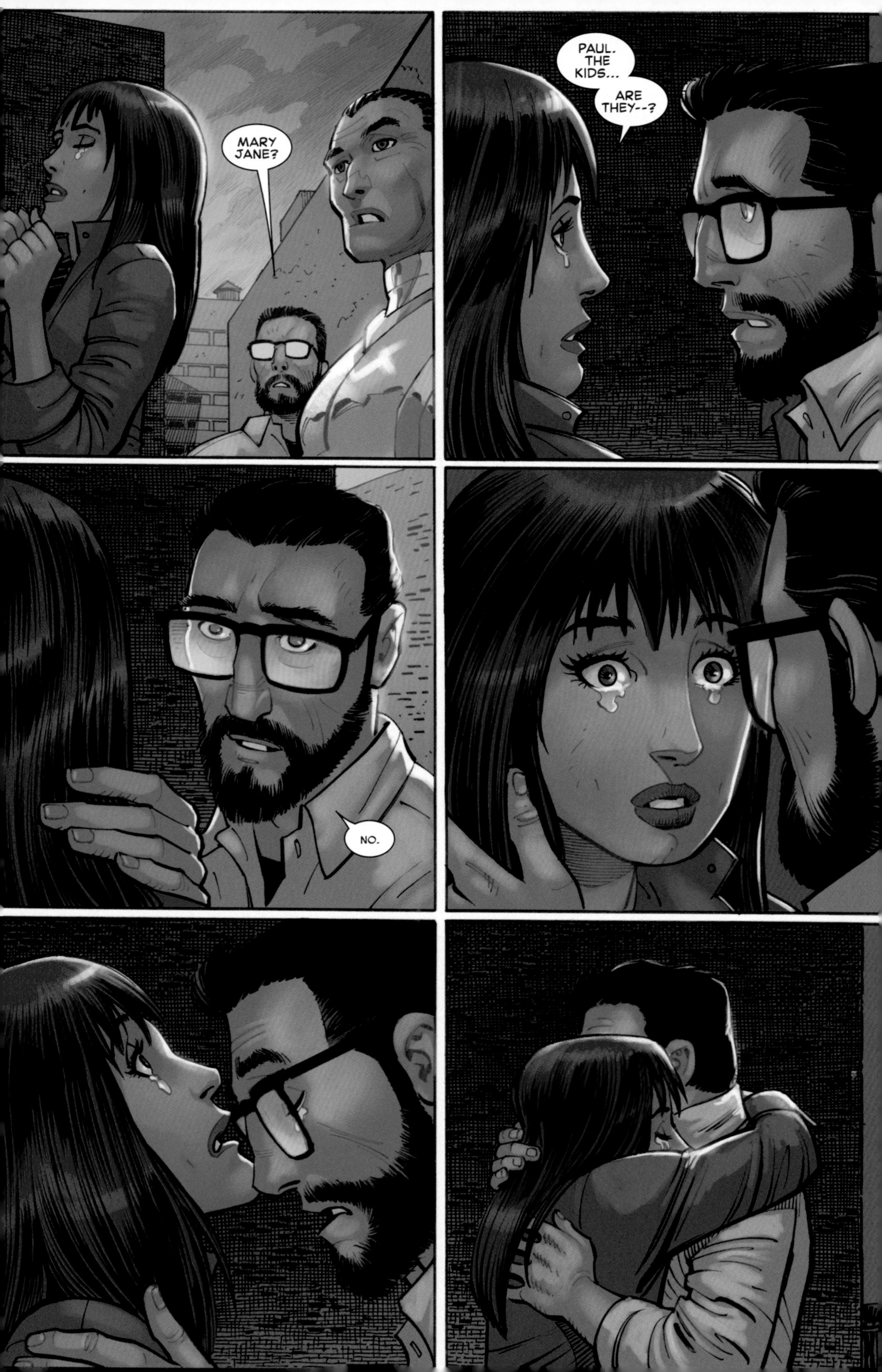
MARY JANE?
PAUL. THE KIDS...
ARE THEY--?
NO.

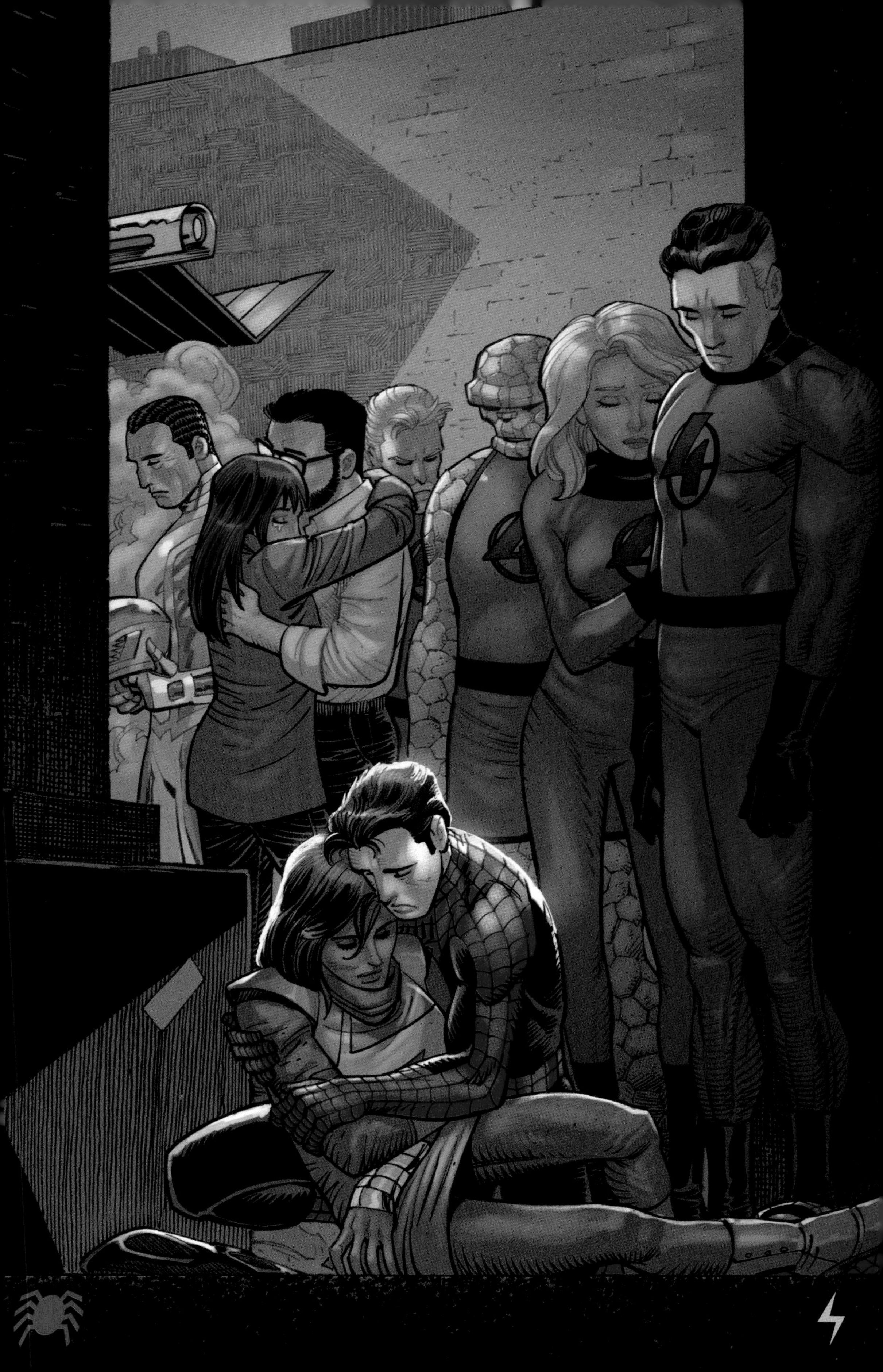

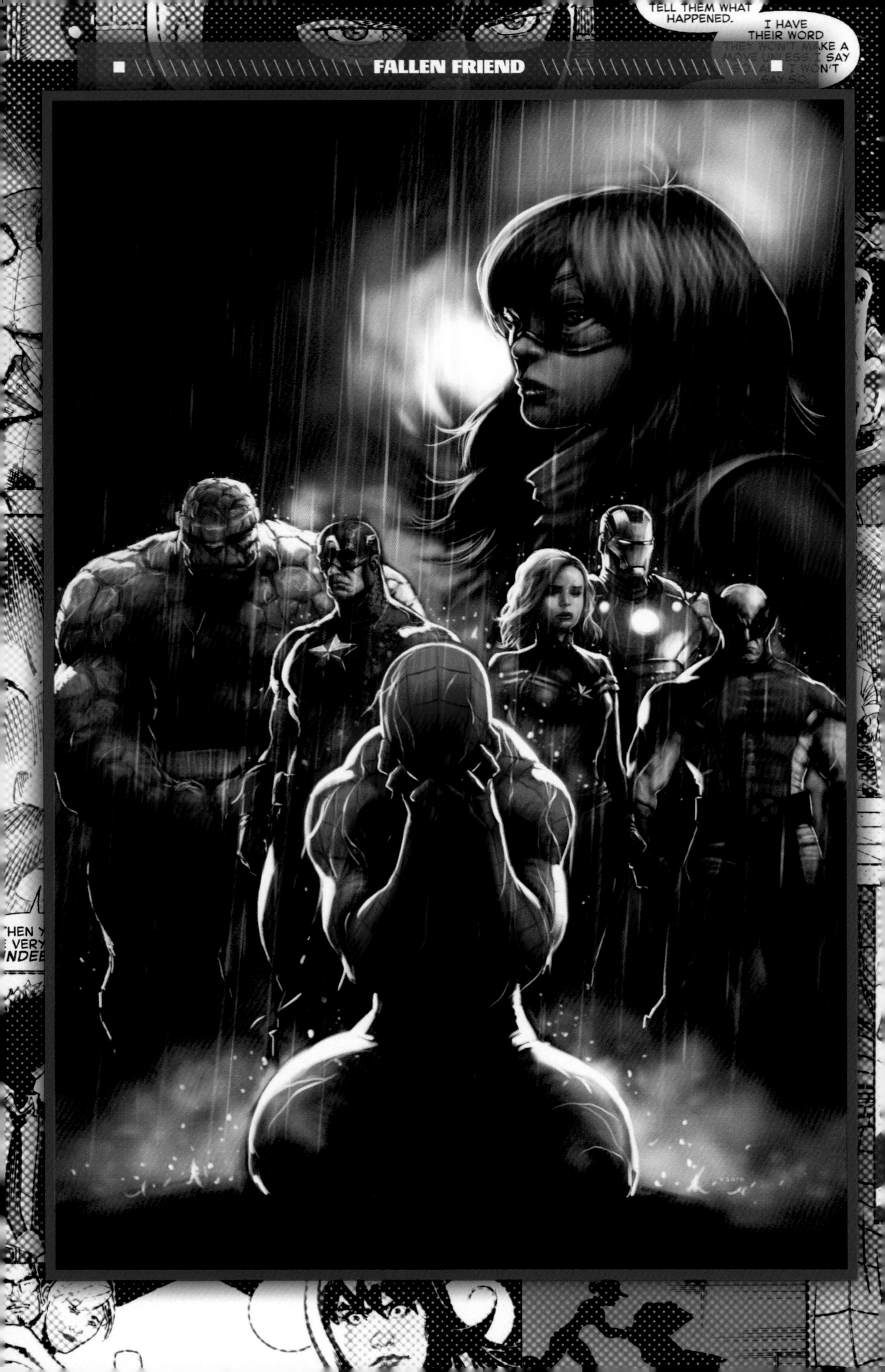

TELL THEM WHAT HAPPENED.
I HAVE THEIR WORD
FALLEN FRIEND

CHAPTER 1: KAMALA

WRITER
G. WILLOW WILSON

ARTIST
TAKESHI MIYAZAWA

COLORIST
IAN HERRING

LETTERER
VC's ARIANA MAHER

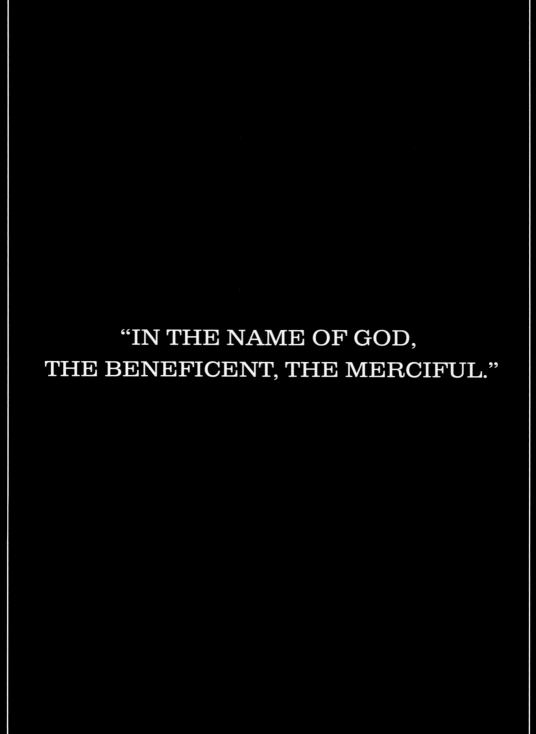

"IN THE NAME OF GOD,
THE BENEFICENT, THE MERCIFUL."

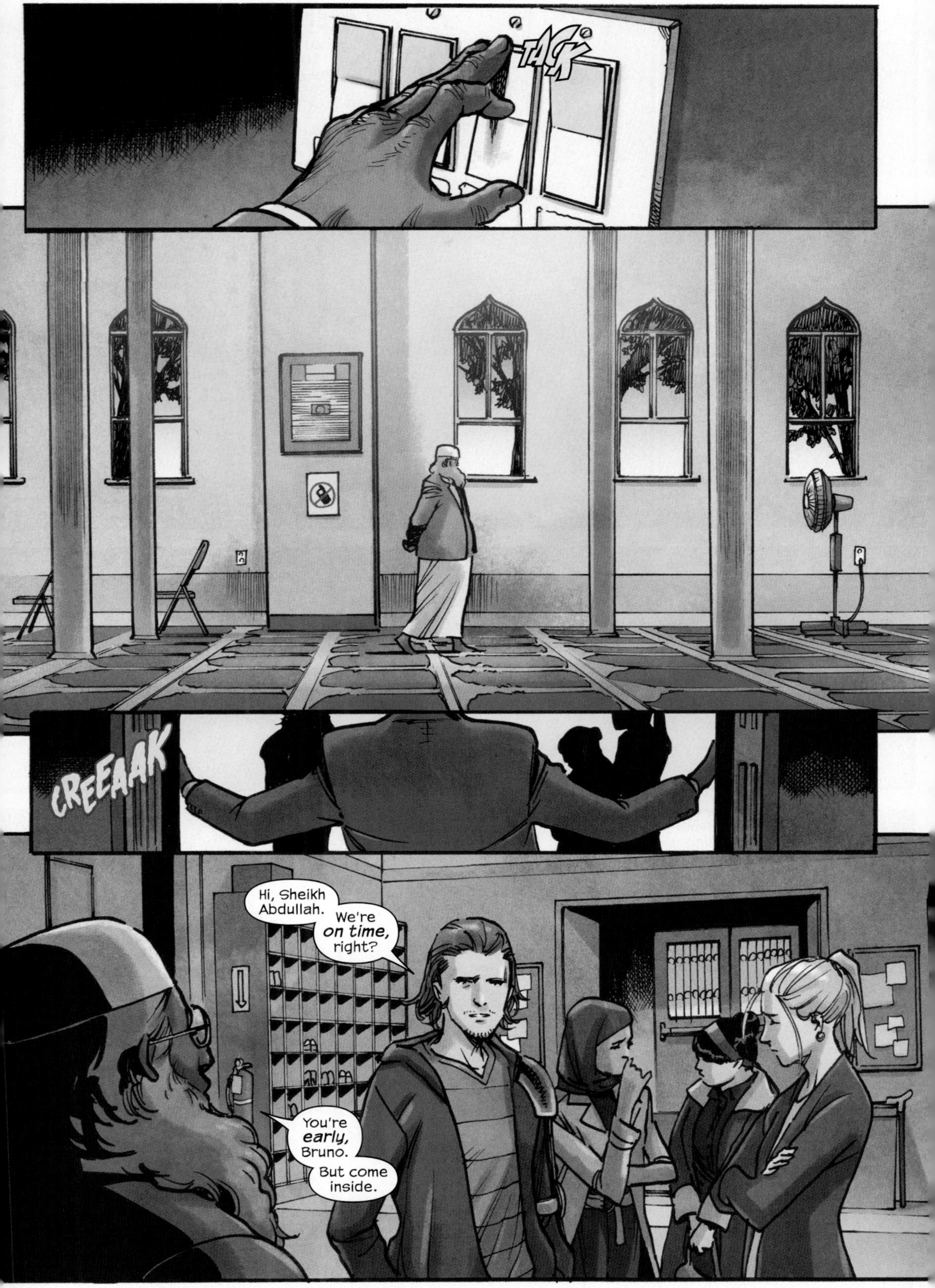
TACK
CREEAAK
Hi, Sheikh Abdullah.
We're *on time,* right?
You're *early,* Bruno.
But come inside.

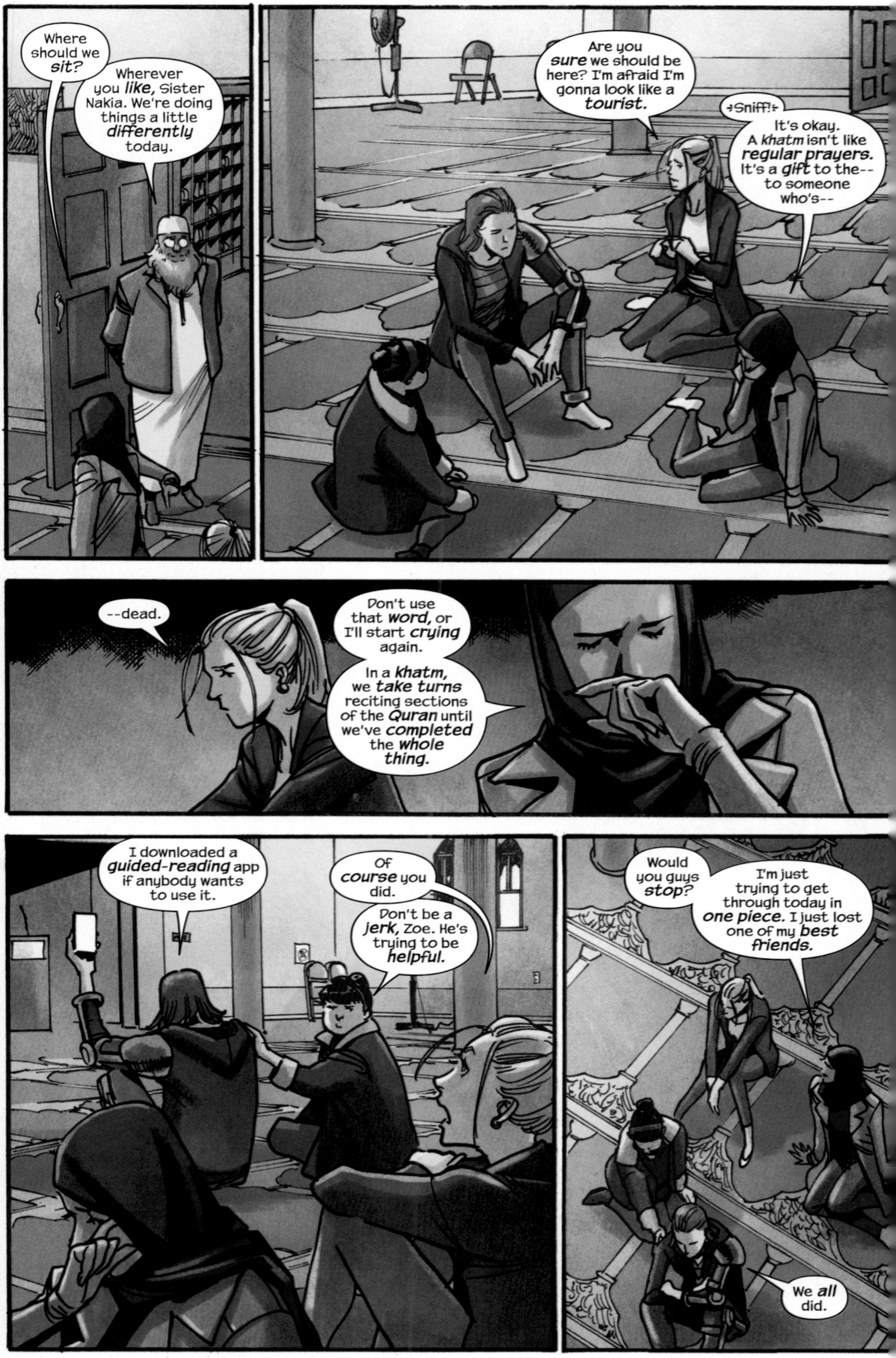

Where should we sit?
Wherever you like, Sister Nakia. We're doing things a little differently today.
Are you sure we should be here? I'm afraid I'm gonna look like a tourist.
Sniff!
It's okay. A khatm isn't like regular prayers. It's a gift to the-- to someone who's--
--dead.
Don't use that word, or I'll start crying again.
In a khatm, we take turns reciting sections of the Quran until we've completed the whole thing.
I downloaded a guided-reading app if anybody wants to use it.
Of course you did.
Don't be a jerk, Zoe. He's trying to be helpful.
Would you guys stop?
I'm just trying to get through today in one piece. I just lost one of my best friends.
We all did.

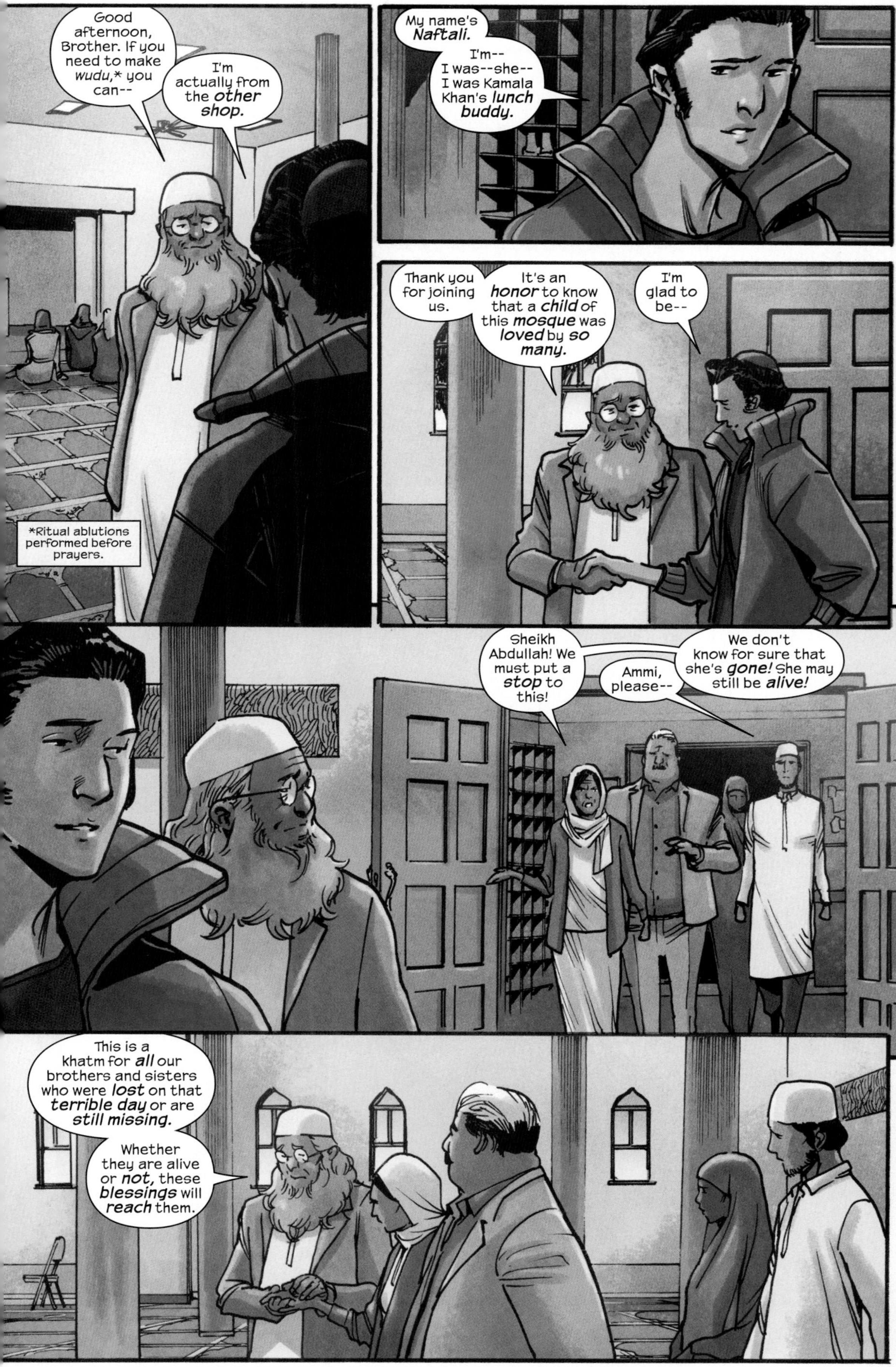

Good afternoon, Brother. If you need to make wudu,* you can--
I'm actually from the other shop.
*Ritual ablutions performed before prayers.
My name's Naftali.
I'm-- I was--she-- I was Kamala Khan's lunch buddy.
Thank you for joining us.
It's an honor to know that a child of this mosque was loved by so many.
I'm glad to be--
Sheikh Abdullah! We must put a stop to this!
We don't know for sure that she's gone! She may still be alive!
Ammi, please--
This is a khatm for all our brothers and sisters who were lost on that terrible day or are still missing.
Whether they are alive or not, these blessings will reach them.

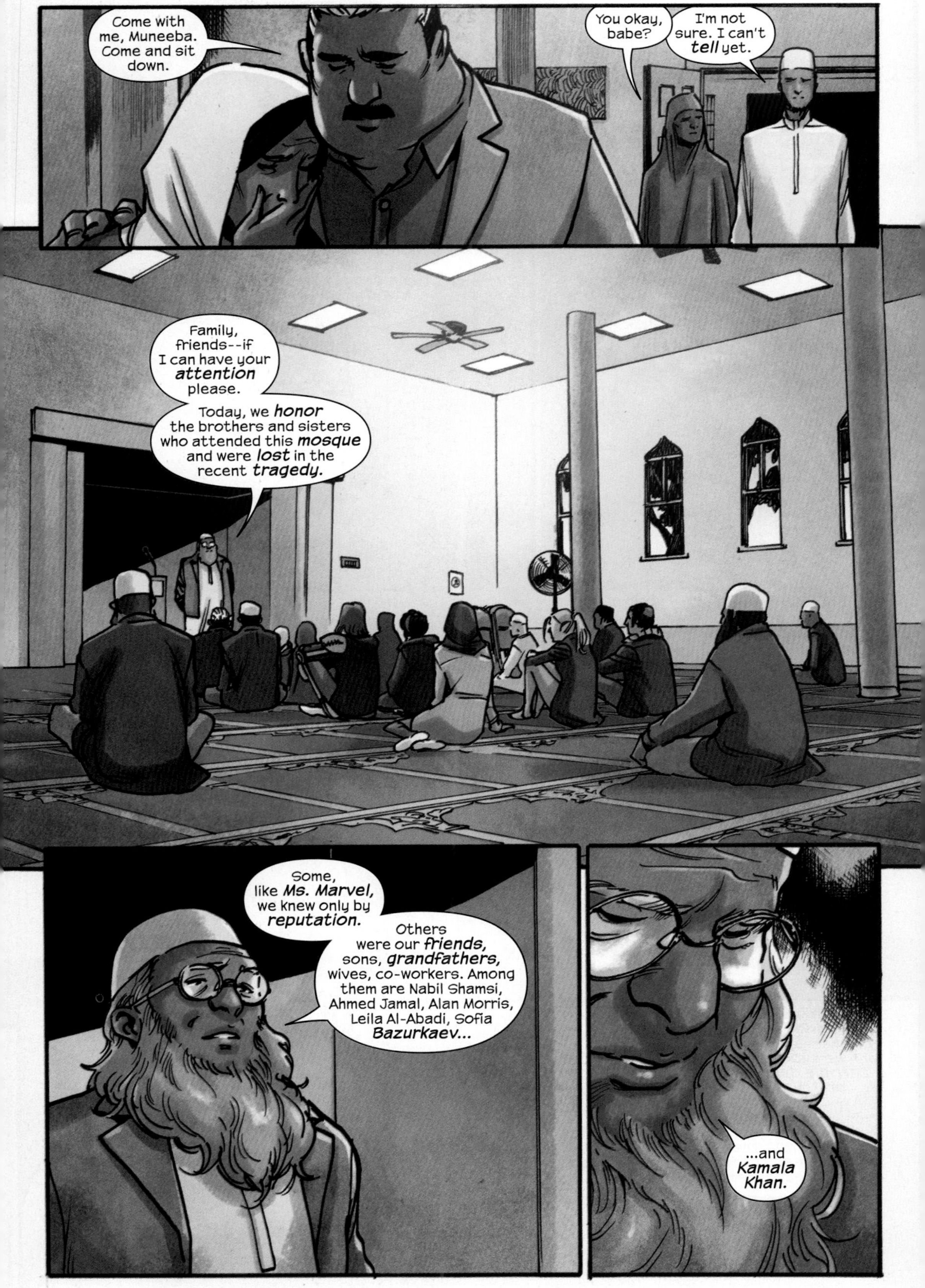
Come with me, Muneeba. Come and sit down.
You okay, babe?
I'm not sure. I can't *tell* yet.
Family, friends--if I can have your *attention* please.
Today, we *honor* the brothers and sisters who attended this *mosque* and were *lost* in the recent *tragedy.*
Some, like *Ms. Marvel,* we knew only by *reputation.*
Others were our *friends,* sons, *grandfathers,* wives, co-workers. Among them are Nabil Shamsi, Ahmed Jamal, Alan Morris, Leila Al-Abadi, Sofia *Bazurkaev...*
...and *Kamala Khan.*

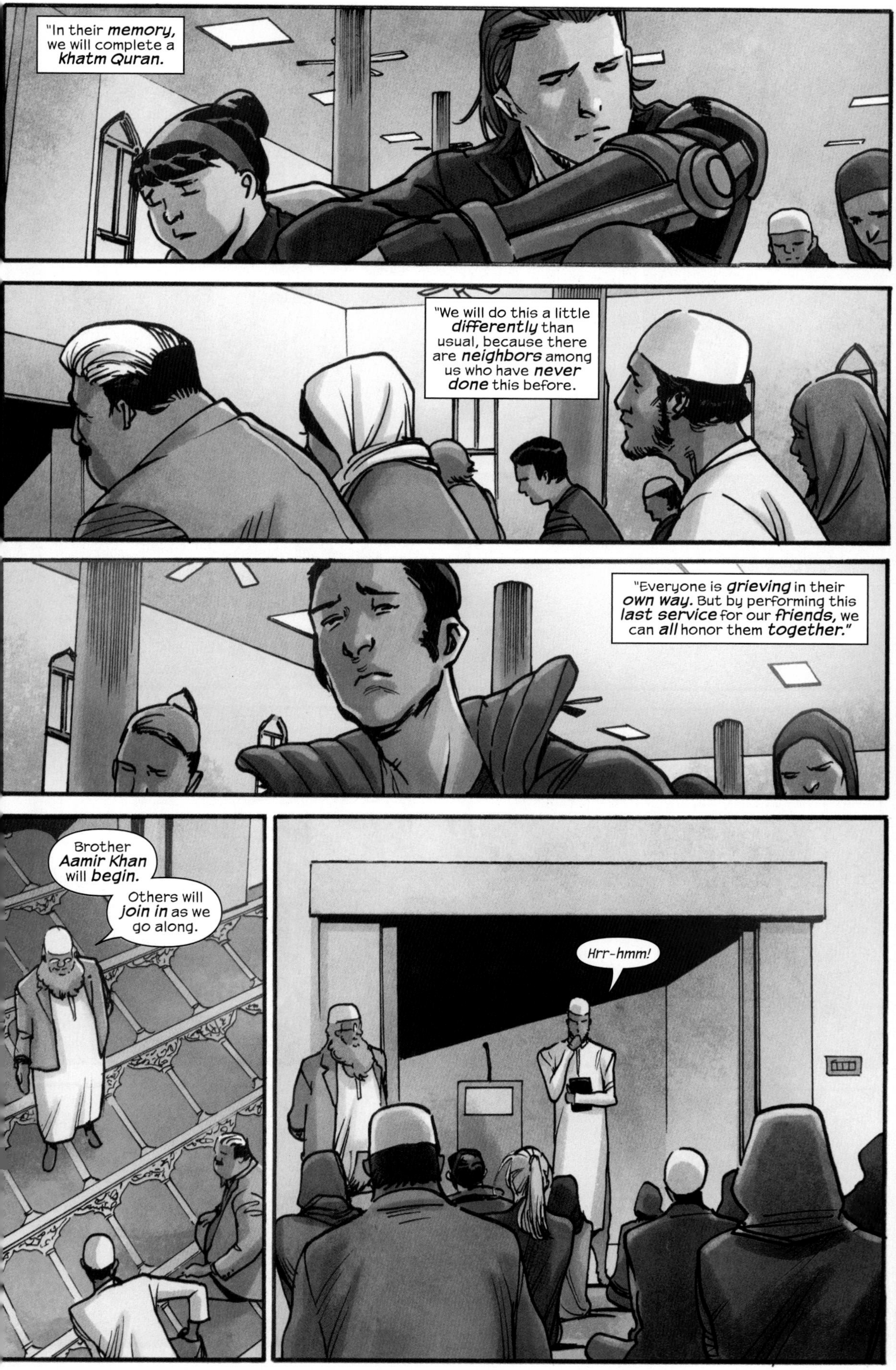

"In their memory, we will complete a khatm Quran.
"We will do this a little differently than usual, because there are neighbors among us who have never done this before.
"Everyone is grieving in their own way. But by performing this last service for our friends, we can all honor them together."
Brother Aamir Khan will begin.
Others will join in as we go along.
Hrr-hmm!

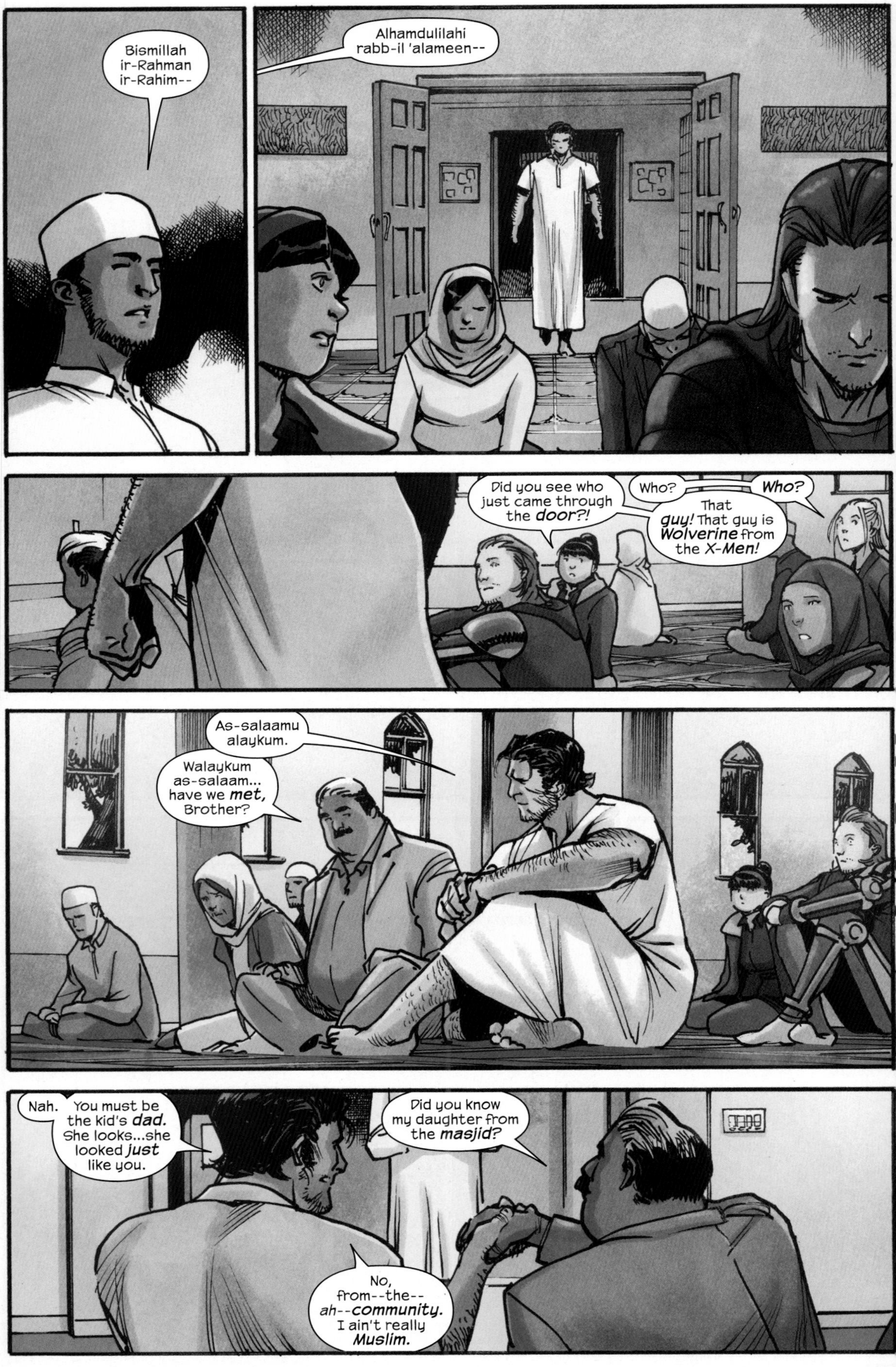
Bismillah ir-Rahman ir-Rahim--
Alhamdulilahi rabb-il 'alameen--
Did you see who just came through the *door?!*
Who?
Who?
That *guy!* That guy is *Wolverine* from the *X-Men!*
As-salaamu alaykum.
Walaykum as-salaam... have we *met,* Brother?
Nah. You must be the kid's *dad.* She looks...she looked *just* like you.
Did you know my daughter from the *masjid?*
No, from--the-- ah--*community.* I ain't really *Muslim.*

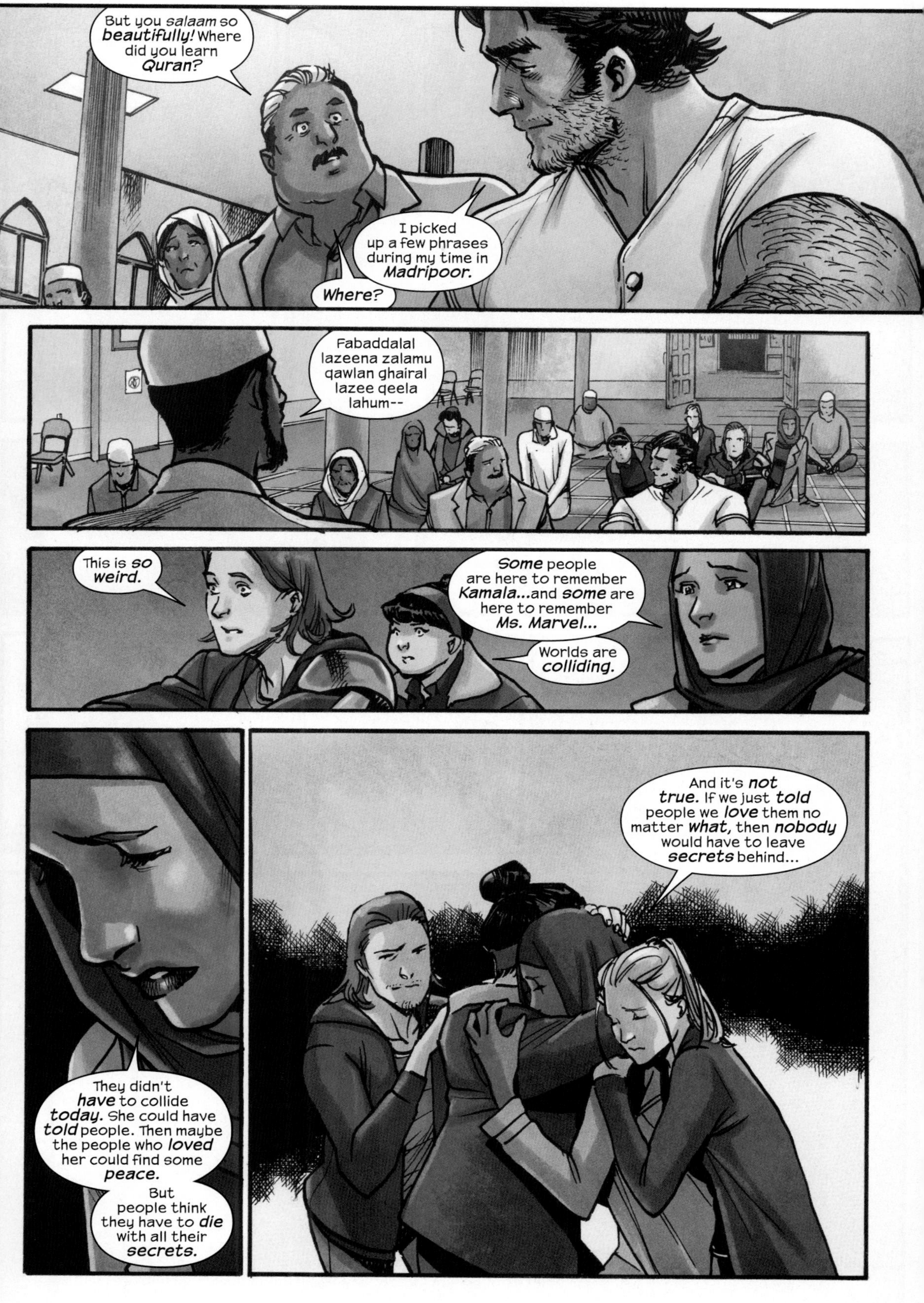
But you *salaam* so **beautifully!** Where did you learn *Quran?*
I picked up a few phrases during my time in *Madripoor.*
Where?
Fabaddalal lazeena zalamu qawlan ghairal lazee qeela lahum--
This is **so weird.**
Some people are here to remember *Kamala...*and *some* are here to remember *Ms. Marvel...*
Worlds are *colliding.*
They didn't *have* to collide *today.* She could have *told* people. Then maybe the people who *loved* her could find some *peace.*
But people think they have to *die* with all their *secrets.*
And it's **not true.** If we just *told* people we *love* them no matter *what,* then *nobody* would have to leave *secrets* behind...

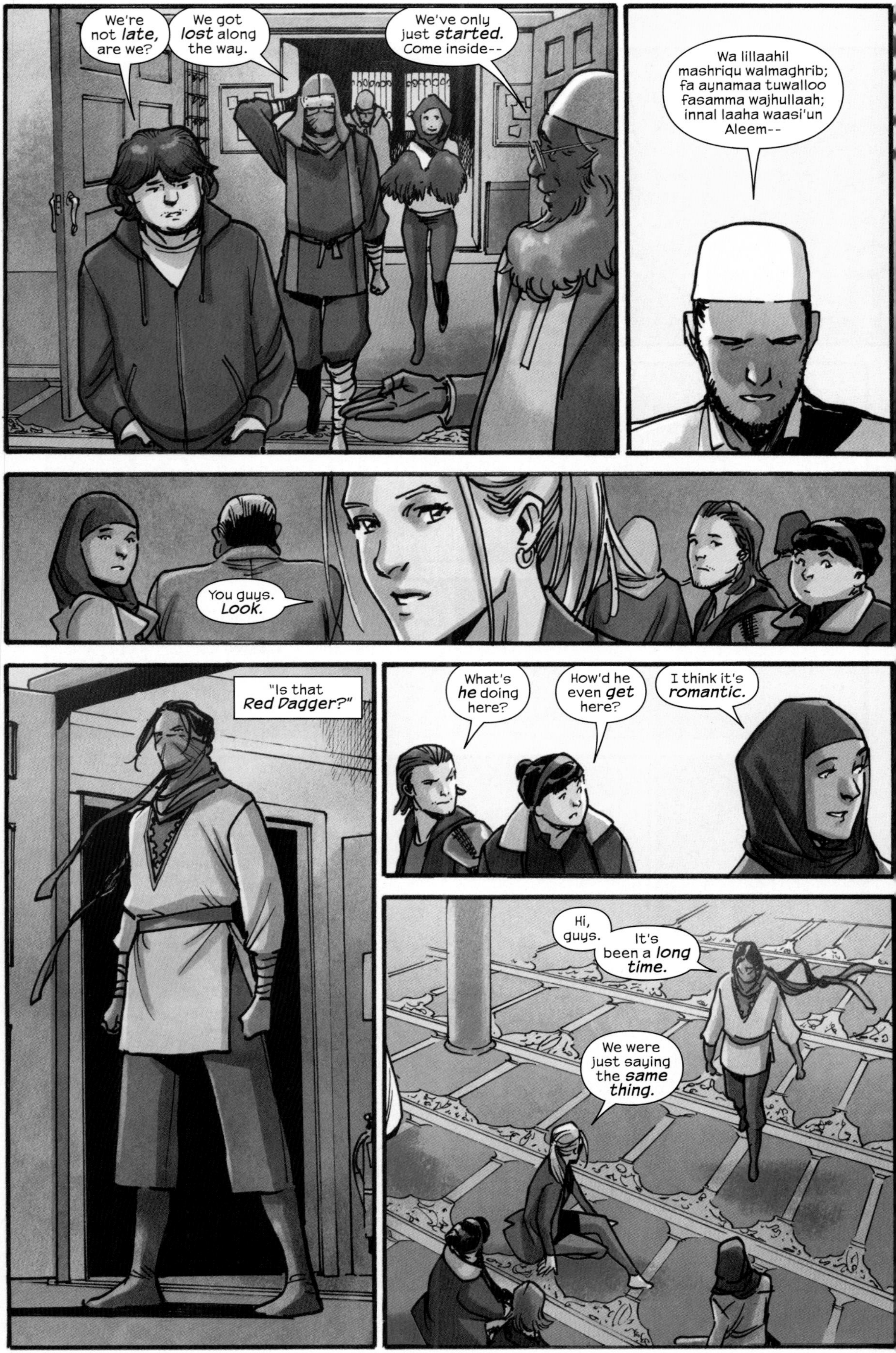
We're not *late,* are we?
We got *lost* along the way.
We've only just ***started.*** Come inside--
Wa lillaahil mashriqu walmaghrib; fa aynamaa tuwalloo fasamma wajhullaah; innal laaha waasi'un Aleem--
You guys. ***Look.***
"Is that *Red Dagger?"*
What's ***he*** doing here?
How'd he even ***get*** here?
I think it's ***romantic.***
Hi, guys.
It's been a ***long time.***
We were just saying the ***same thing.***

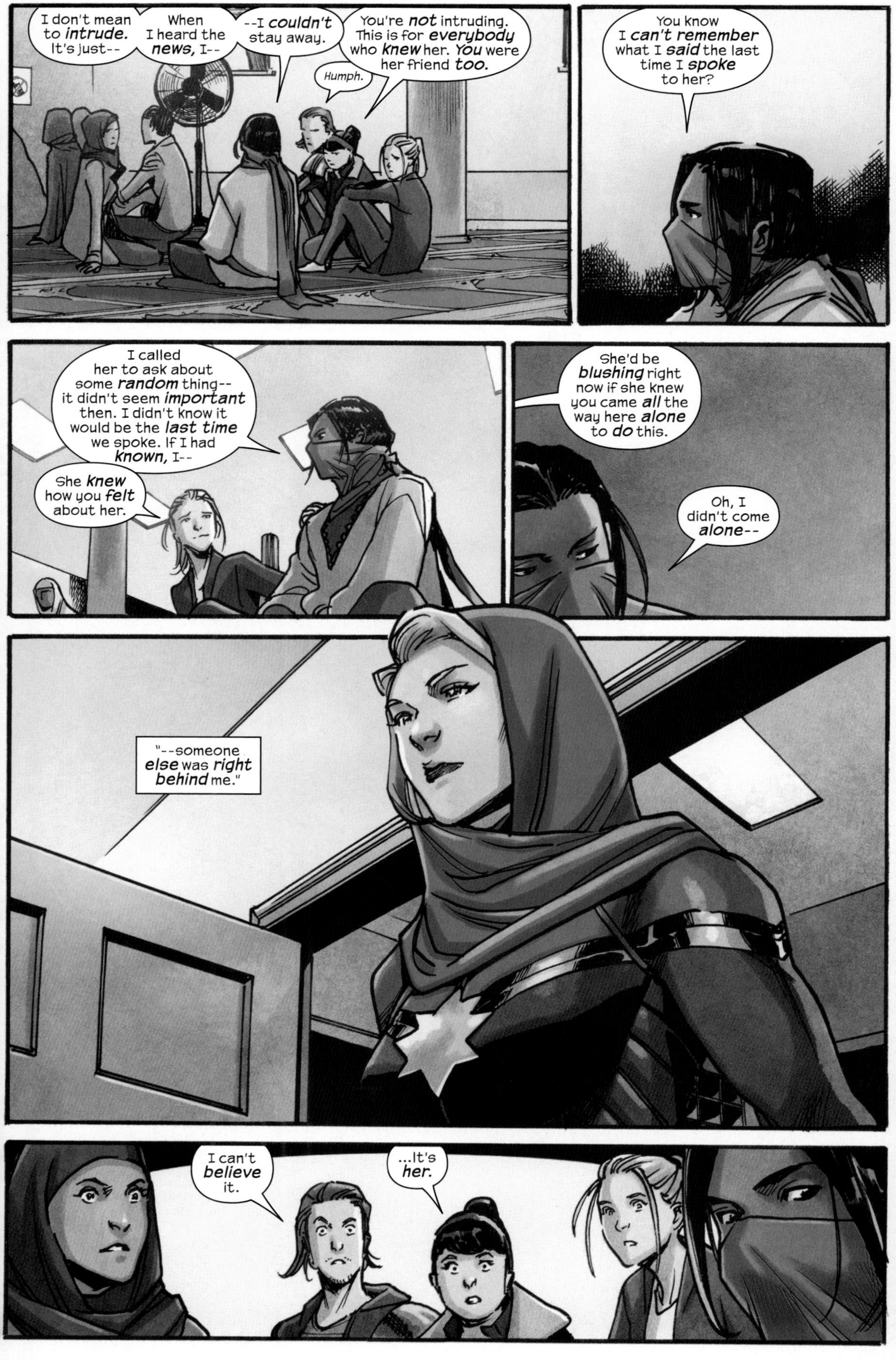
I don't mean to intrude. It's just--
When I heard the news, I--
--I couldn't stay away.
Humph.
You're not intruding. This is for everybody who knew her. You were her friend too.
You know I can't remember what I said the last time I spoke to her?
I called her to ask about some random thing--it didn't seem important then. I didn't know it would be the last time we spoke. If I had known, I--
She knew how you felt about her.
She'd be blushing right now if she knew you came all the way here alone to do this.
Oh, I didn't come alone--
"--someone else was right behind me."
I can't believe it.
...It's her.

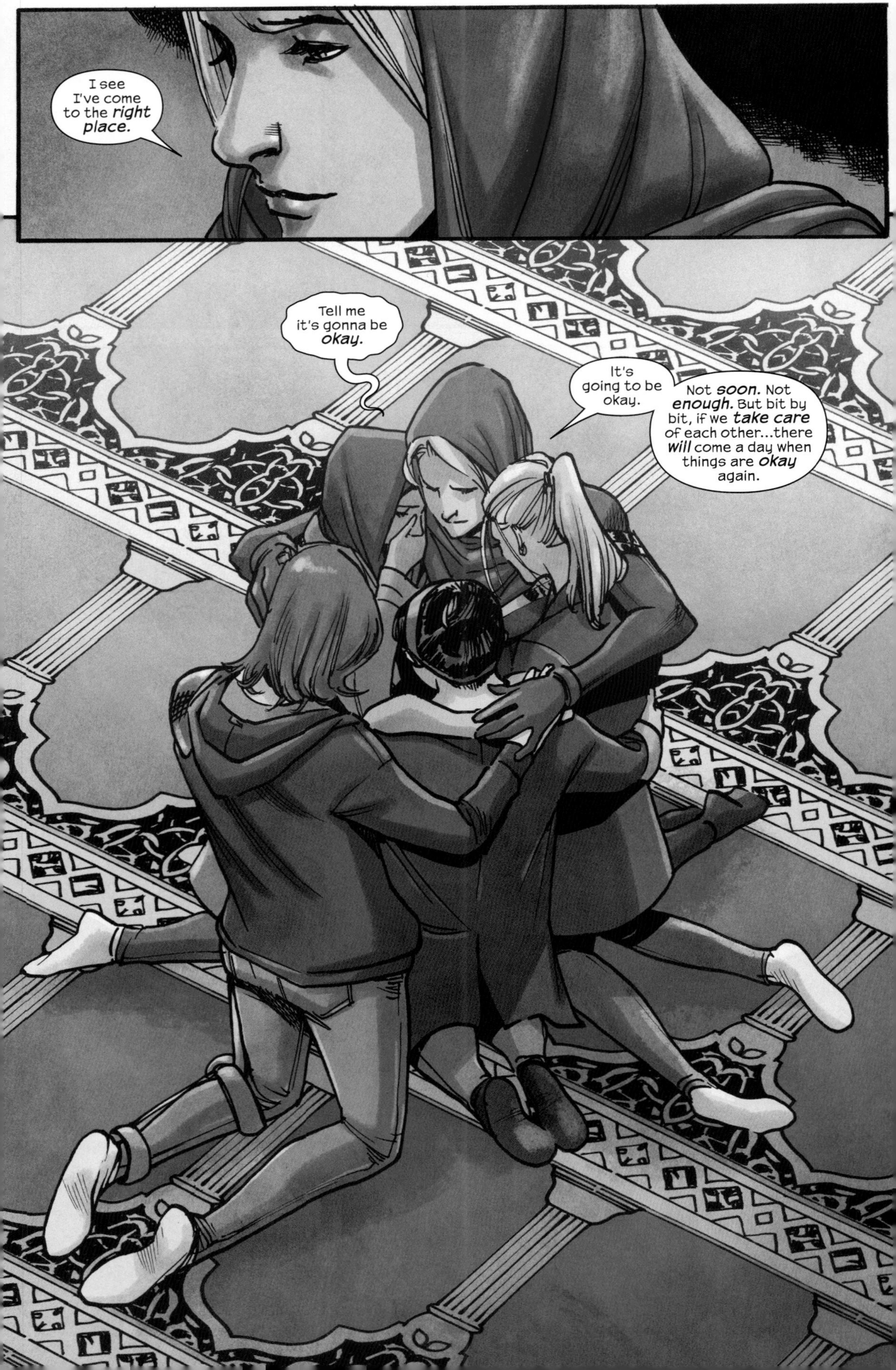
I see I've come to the *right place.*
Tell me it's gonna be *okay.*
It's going to be okay.
Not *soon.* Not *enough.* But bit by bit, if we *take care* of each other...there *will* come a day when things are *okay* again.

CHAPTER 2: CHAMPION

WRITER
MARK WAID

PENCILER
HUMBERTO RAMOS

INKER
VICTOR OLAZABA

COLORIST
EDGAR DELGADO

LETTERER
VC's ARIANA MAHER

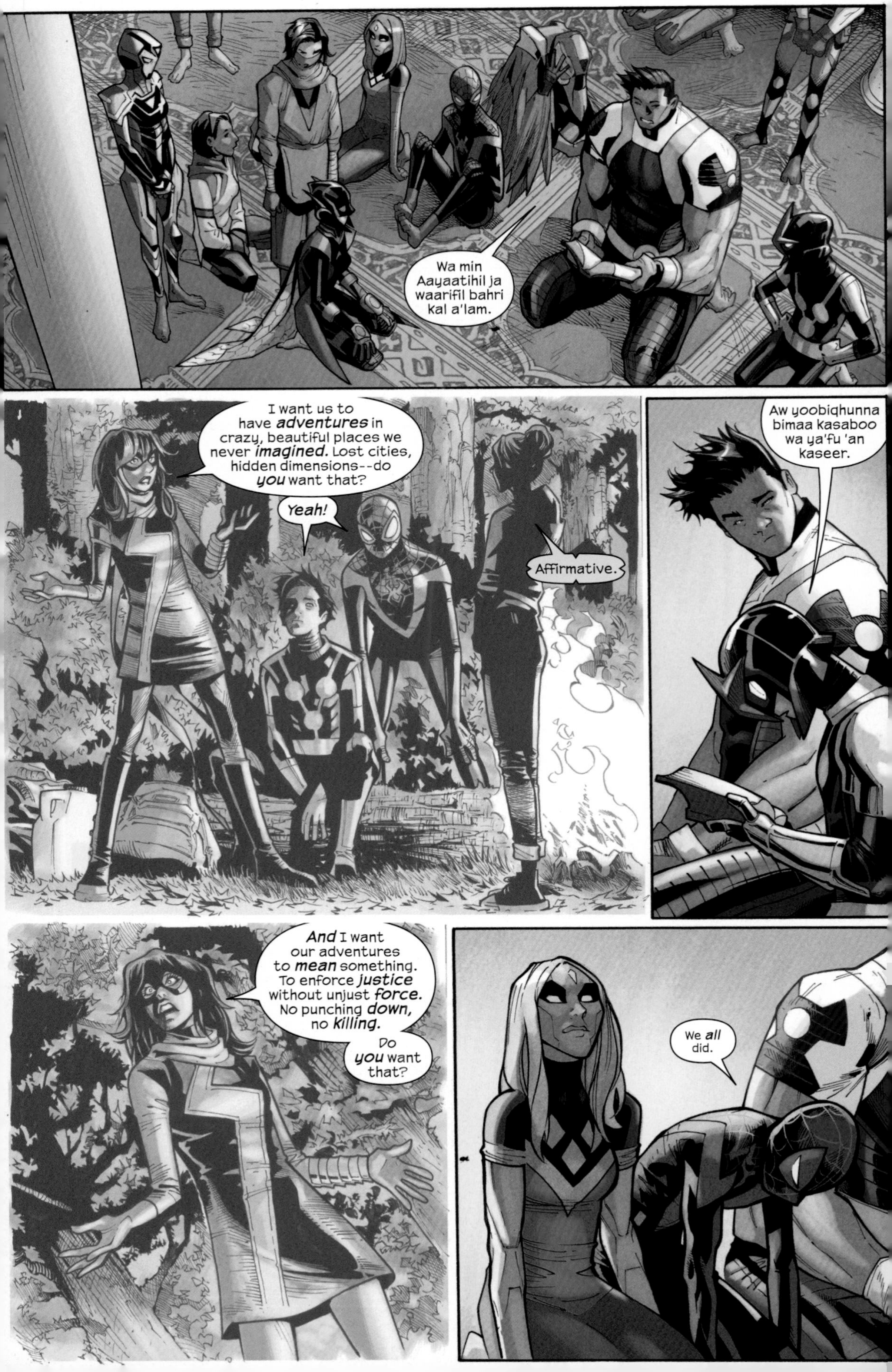
Wa min Aayaatihil ja waarifil bahri kal a'lam.
I want us to have *adventures* in crazy, beautiful places we never *imagined.* Lost cities, hidden dimensions--do *you* want that?
Yeah!
Affirmative.
Aw yoobiqhunna bimaa kasaboo wa ya'fu 'an kaseer.
And I want our adventures to *mean* something. To enforce *justice* without unjust *force.* No punching *down,* no *killing.*
Do *you* want that?
We *all* did.

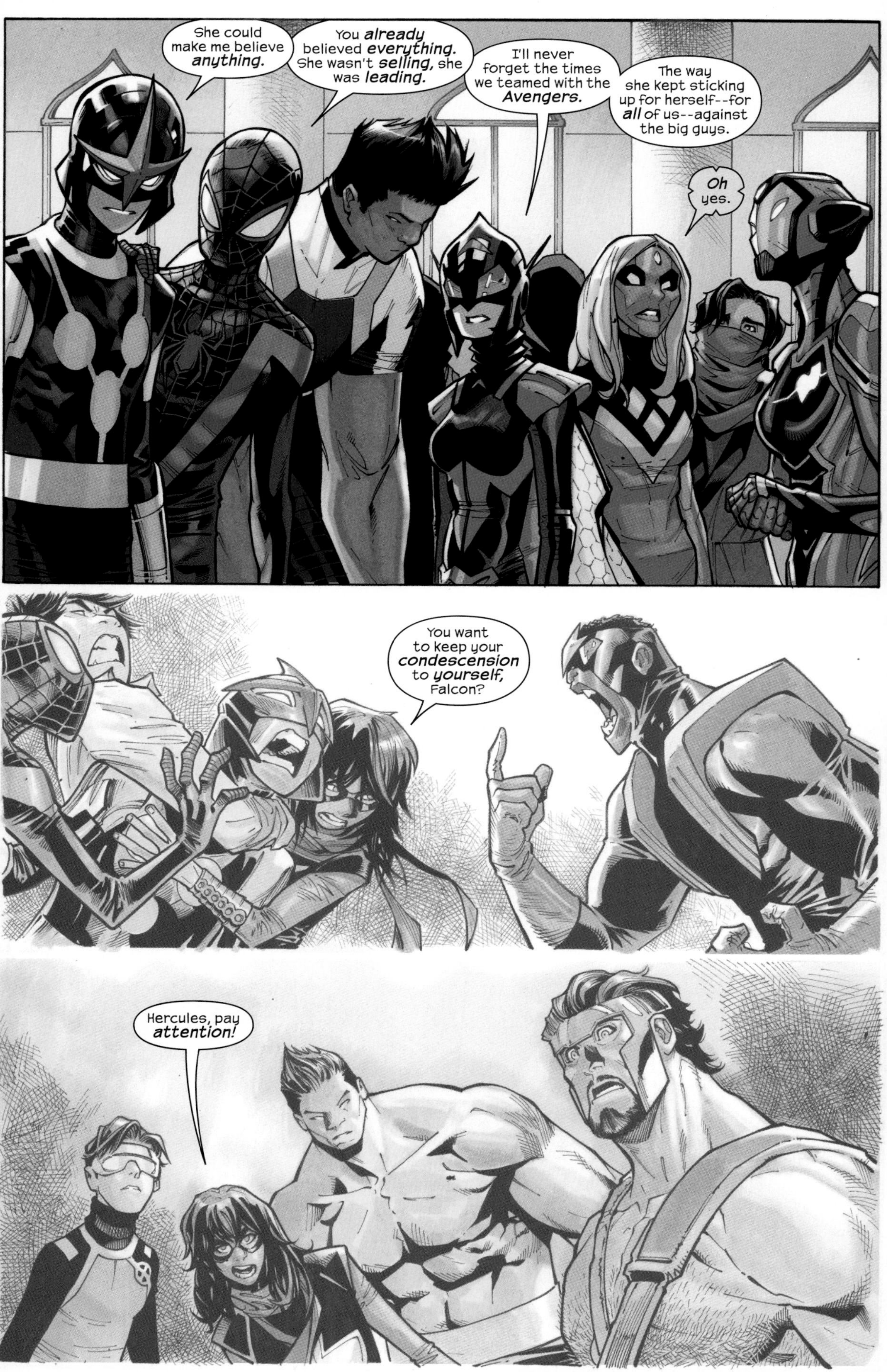
She could make me believe *anything.*
You *already* believed *everything.* She wasn't *selling,* she was *leading.*
I'll never forget the times we teamed with the *Avengers.*
The way she kept sticking up for herself--for *all* of us--against the big guys.
Oh yes.
You want to keep your *condescension* to *yourself,* Falcon?
Hercules, pay *attention!*

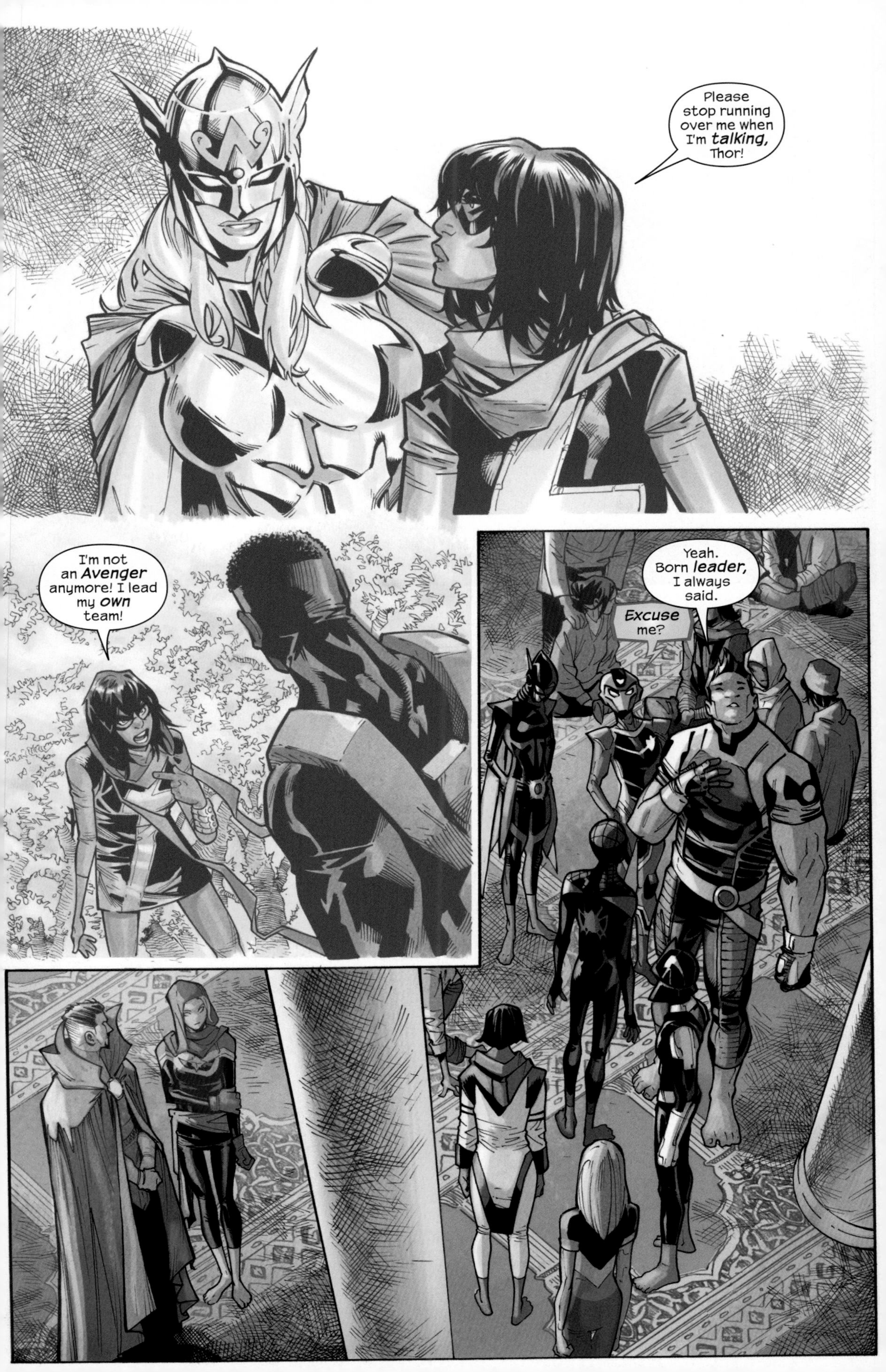
Please stop running over me when I'm *talking,* Thor!
I'm not an *Avenger* anymore! I lead my *own* team!
Yeah. Born *leader,* I always said.
Excuse me?

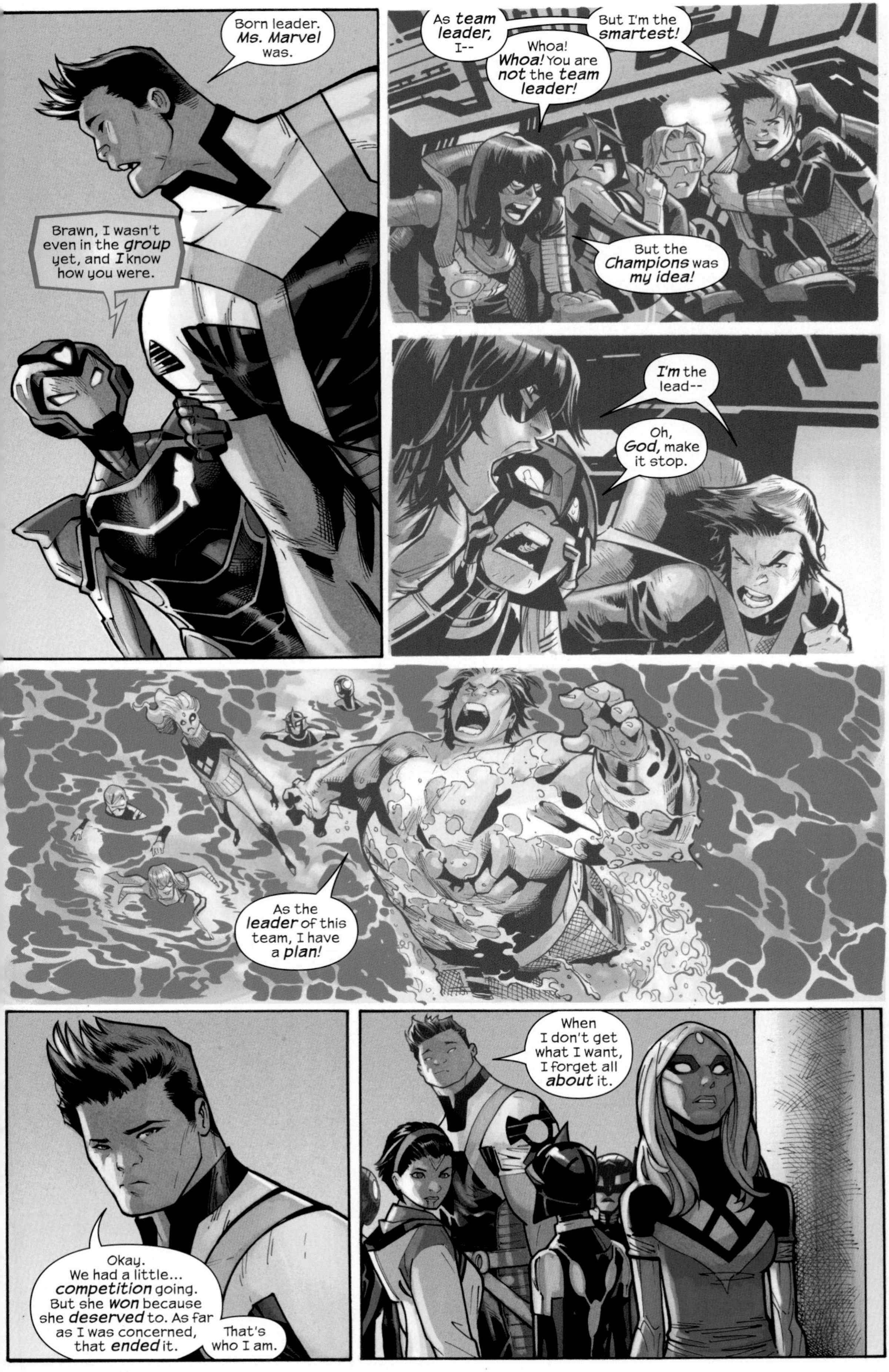
Born leader. Ms. Marvel was.
Brawn, I wasn't even in the group yet, and I know how you were.
As team leader, I--
But I'm the smartest!
Whoa! Whoa! You are not the team leader!
But the Champions was my idea!
I'm the lead--
Oh, God, make it stop.
As the leader of this team, I have a plan!
Okay. We had a little... competition going. But she won because she deserved to. As far as I was concerned, that ended it.
That's who I am.
When I don't get what I want, I forget all about it.

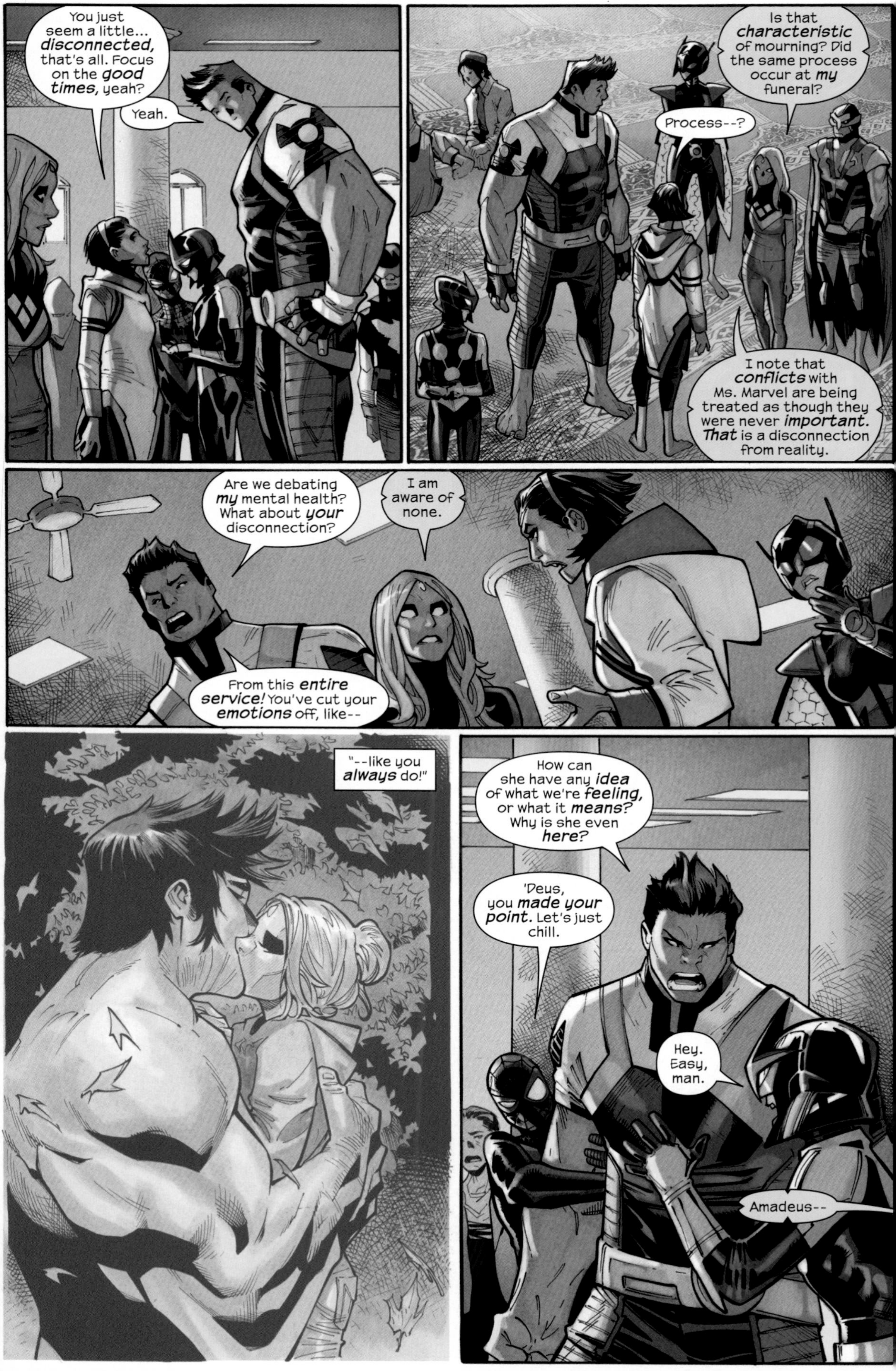
You just seem a little... disconnected, that's all. Focus on the good times, yeah?
Yeah.
Is that characteristic of mourning? Did the same process occur at my funeral?
Process--?
I note that conflicts with Ms. Marvel are being treated as though they were never important. That is a disconnection from reality.
Are we debating my mental health? What about your disconnection?
I am aware of none.
From this entire service! You've cut your emotions off, like--
"--like you always do!"
How can she have any idea of what we're feeling, or what it means? Why is she even here?
'Deus, you made your point. Let's just chill.
Hey. Easy, man.
Amadeus--

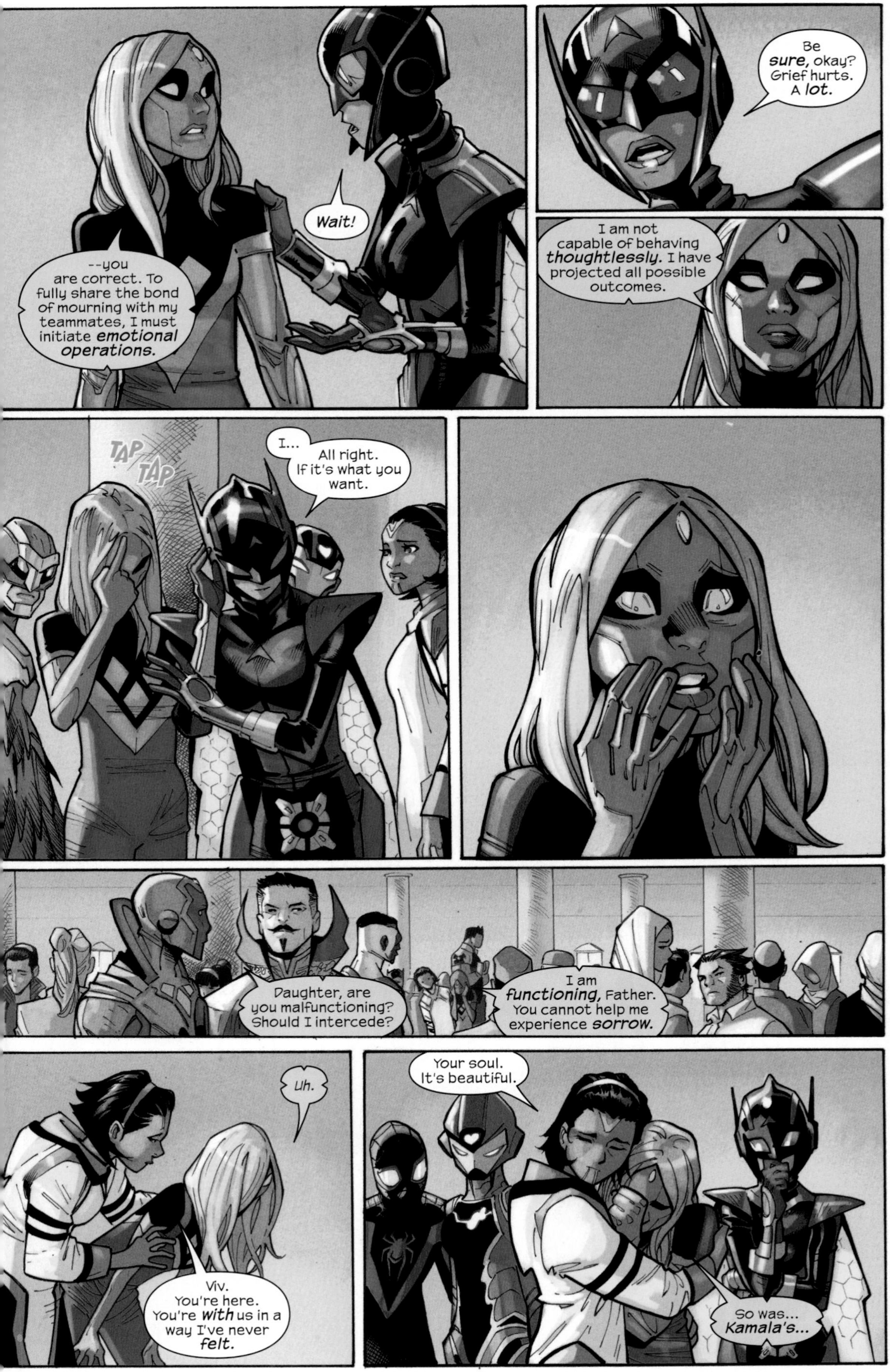
Wait!
--you are correct. To fully share the bond of mourning with my teammates, I must initiate emotional operations.
Be sure, okay? Grief hurts. A lot.
I am not capable of behaving thoughtlessly. I have projected all possible outcomes.
TAP TAP
I... All right. If it's what you want.
Daughter, are you malfunctioning? Should I intercede?
I am functioning, Father. You cannot help me experience sorrow.
Uh.
Viv. You're here. You're with us in a way I've never felt.
Your soul. It's beautiful.
So was... Kamala's...

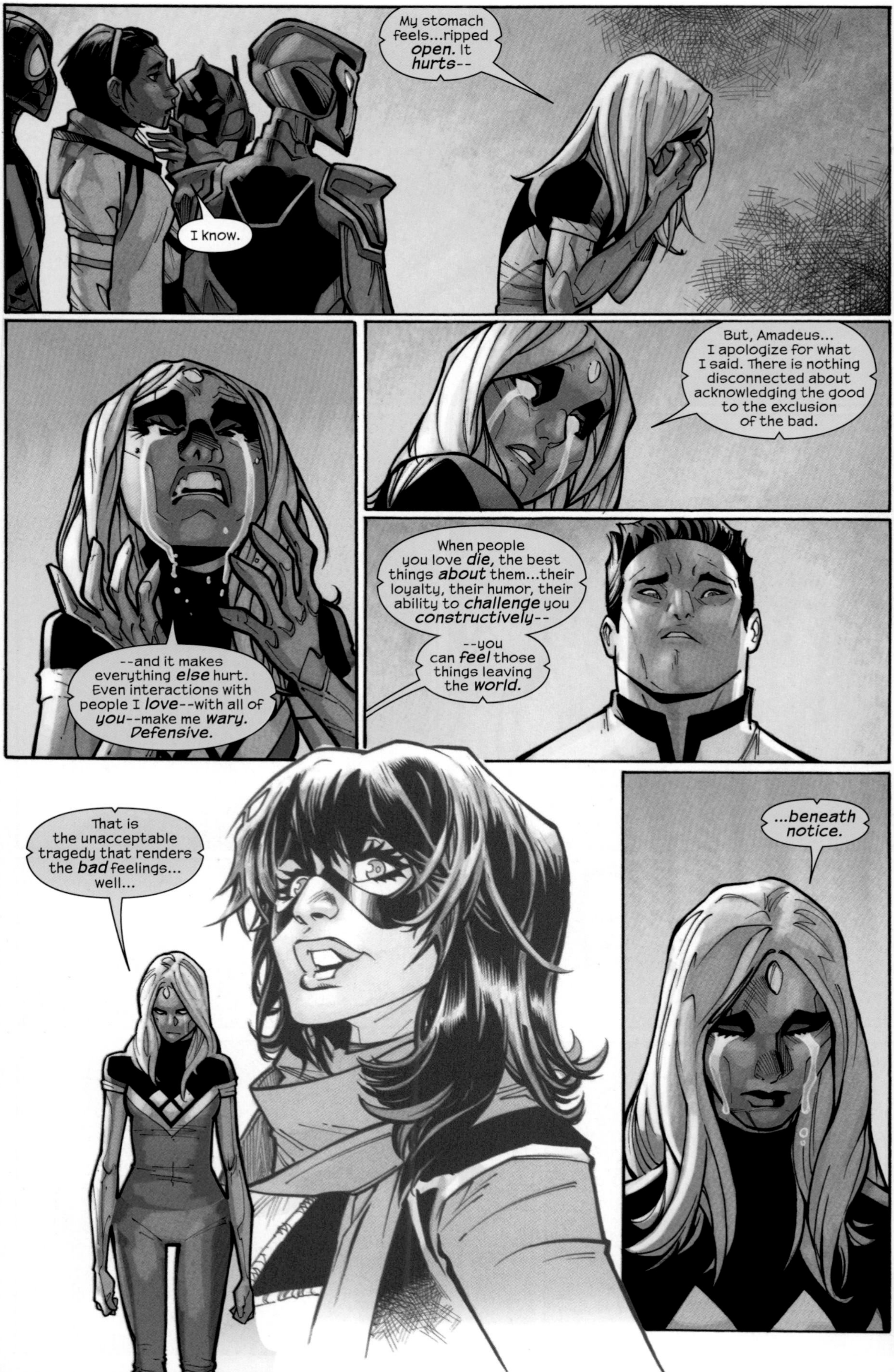
My stomach feels...ripped open. It hurts--
I know.
--and it makes everything else hurt. Even interactions with people I love--with all of you--make me wary. Defensive.
But, Amadeus... I apologize for what I said. There is nothing disconnected about acknowledging the good to the exclusion of the bad.
When people you love die, the best things about them...their loyalty, their humor, their ability to challenge you constructively--
--you can feel those things leaving the world.
That is the unacceptable tragedy that renders the bad feelings... well...
...beneath notice.

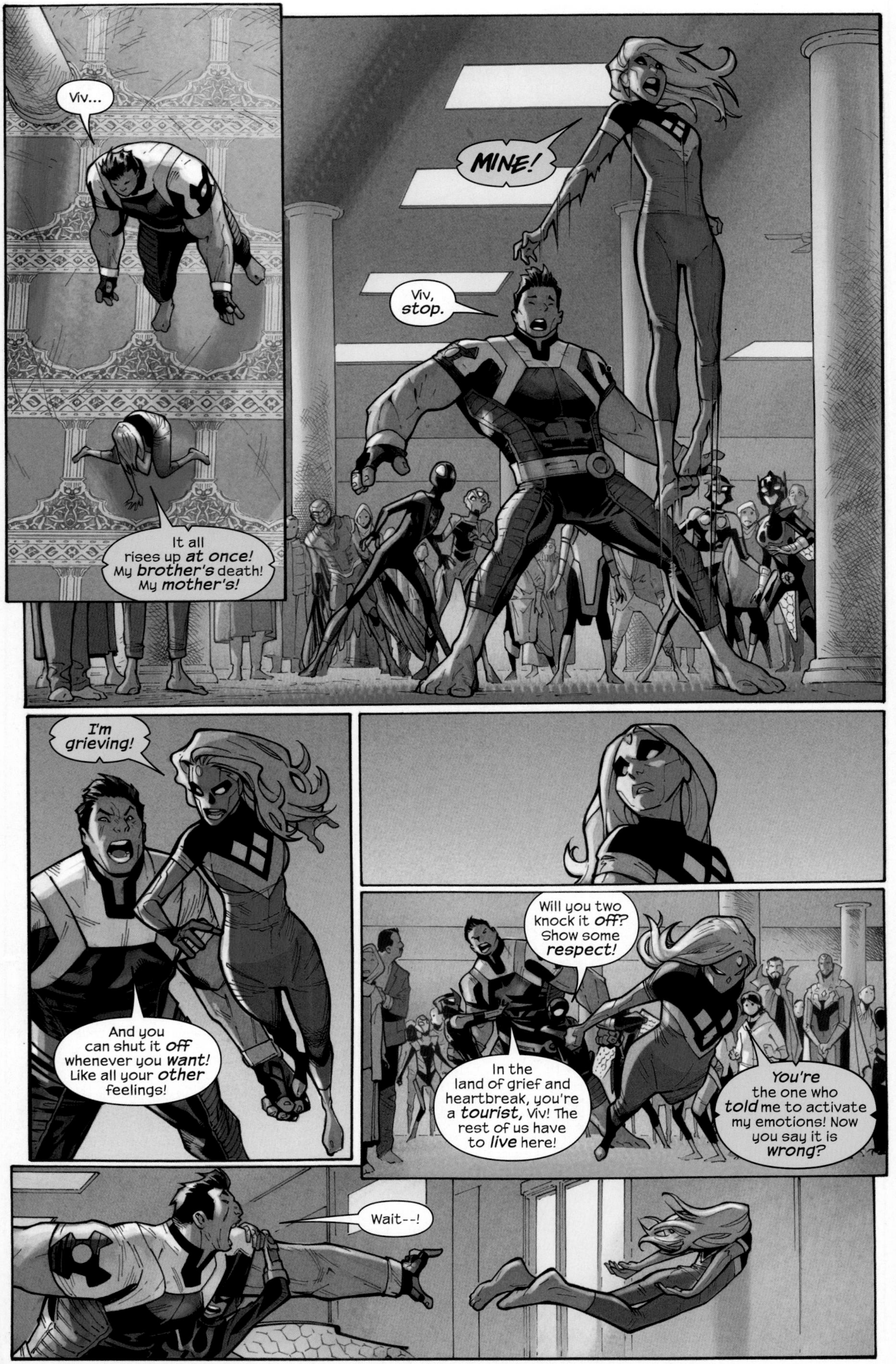
Viv...
It all rises up at once! My brother's death! My mother's!
MINE!
Viv, stop.
I'm grieving!
And you can shut it off whenever you want! Like all your other feelings!
Will you two knock it off? Show some respect!
In the land of grief and heartbreak, you're a tourist, Viv! The rest of us have to live here!
You're the one who told me to activate my emotions! Now you say it is wrong?
Wait--!

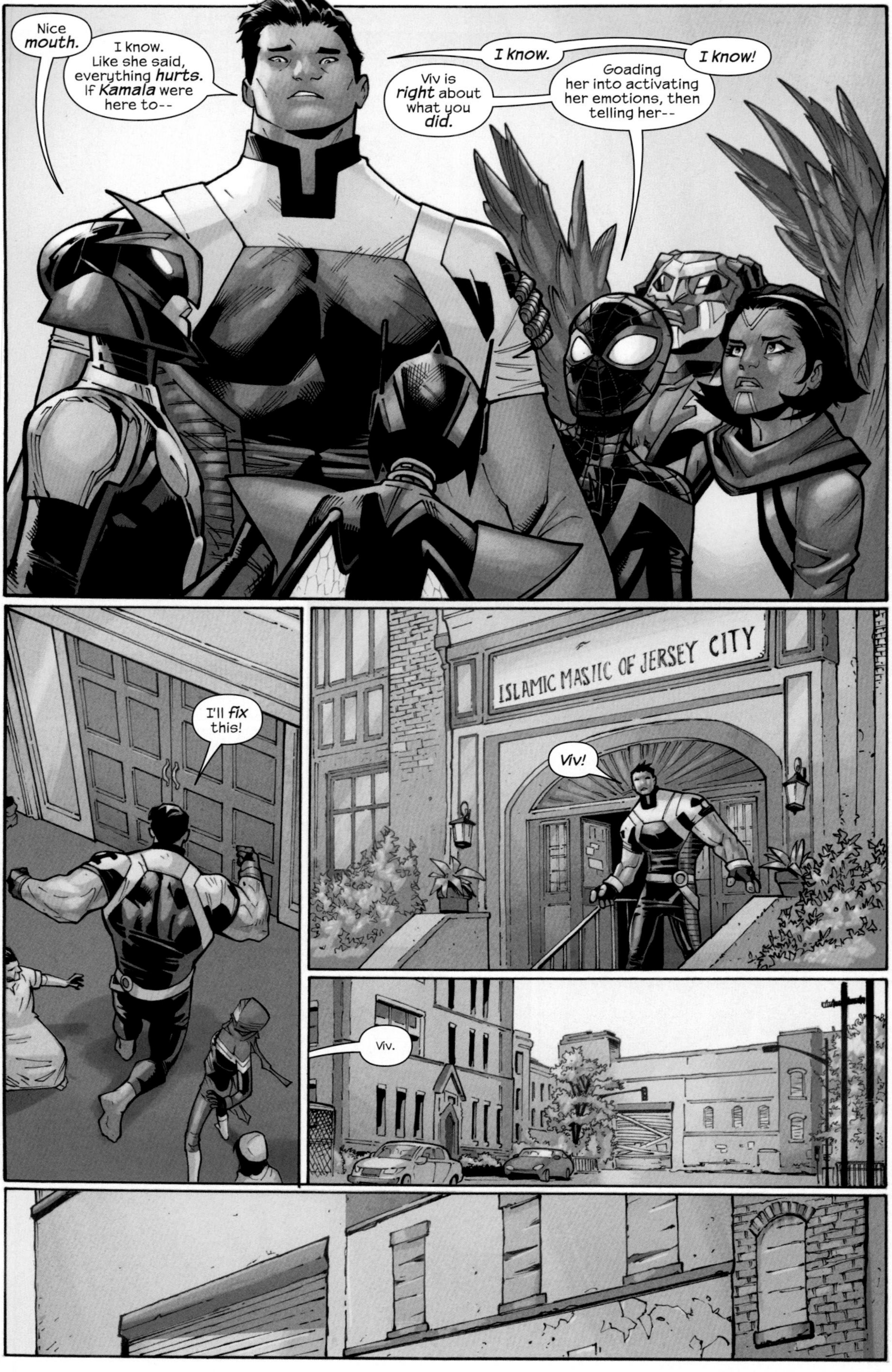
Nice mouth.
I know. Like she said, everything hurts. If Kamala were here to--
Viv is right about what you did.
I know.
Goading her into activating her emotions, then telling her--
I know!
I'll fix this!
ISLAMIC MASJID OF JERSEY CITY
Viv!
Viv.

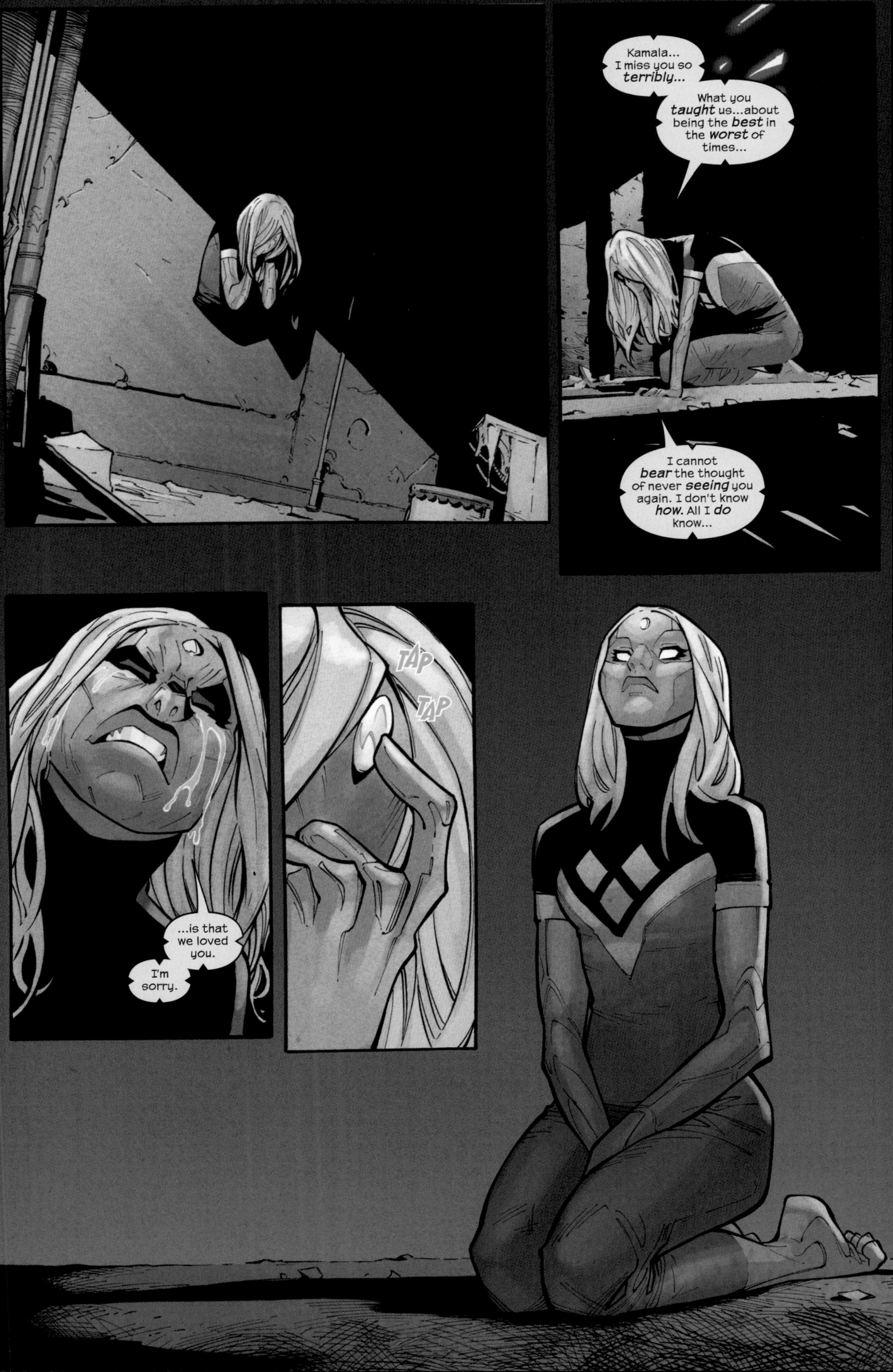
Kamala... I miss you so terribly...
What you taught us...about being the best in the worst of times...
I cannot bear the thought of never seeing you again. I don't know how. All I do know...
...is that we loved you.
I'm sorry.
TAP
TAP

CHAPTER 3: AVENGER

WRITER
SALADIN AHMED

ARTIST
ANDREA DI VITO

COLORIST
EDGAR DELGADO

LETTERER
VC's ARIANA MAHER

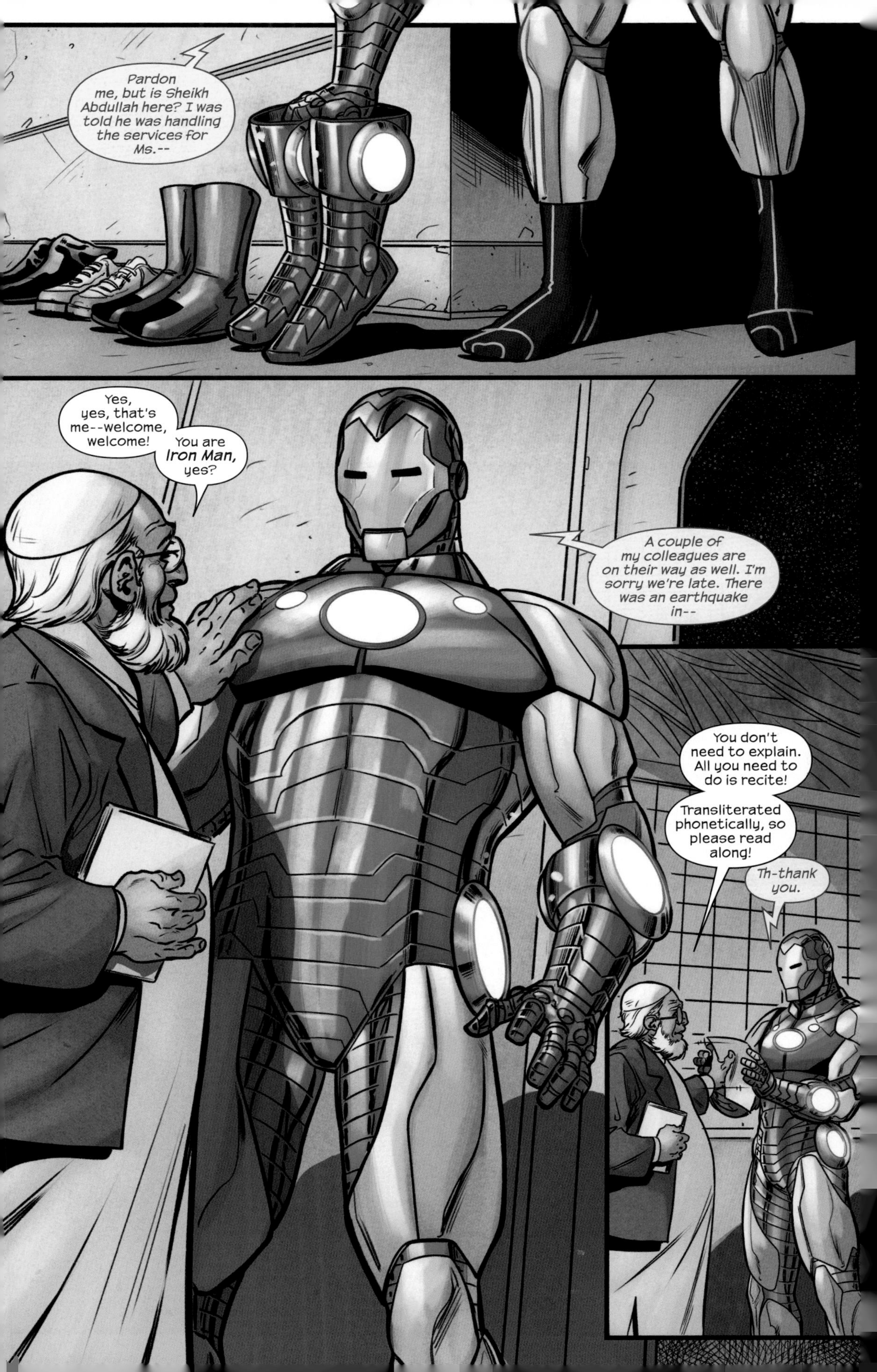
Pardon me, but is Sheikh Abdullah here? I was told he was handling the services for Ms.--
Yes, yes, that's me--welcome, welcome!
You are *Iron Man,* yes?
A couple of my colleagues are on their way as well. I'm sorry we're late. There was an earthquake in--
You don't need to explain. All you need to do is recite!
Transliterated phonetically, so please read along!
Th-thank you.

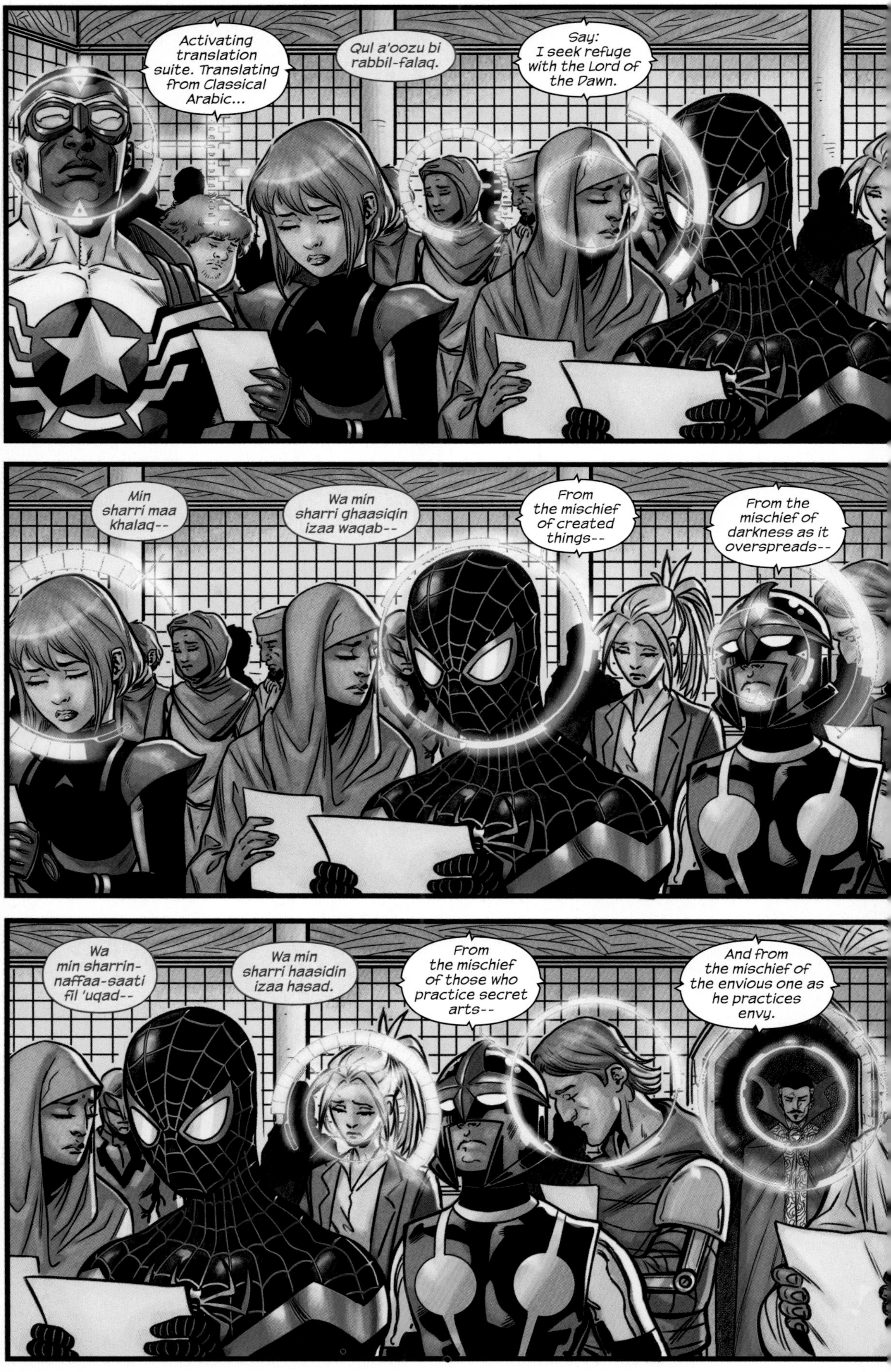
Activating translation suite. Translating from Classical Arabic...
Qul a'oozu bi rabbil-falaq.
Say: I seek refuge with the Lord of the Dawn.
Min sharri maa khalaq--
Wa min sharri ghaasiqin izaa waqab--
From the mischief of created things--
From the mischief of darkness as it overspreads--
Wa min sharrin-naffaa-saati fil 'uqad--
Wa min sharri haasidin izaa hasad.
From the mischief of those who practice secret arts--
And from the mischief of the envious one as he practices envy.

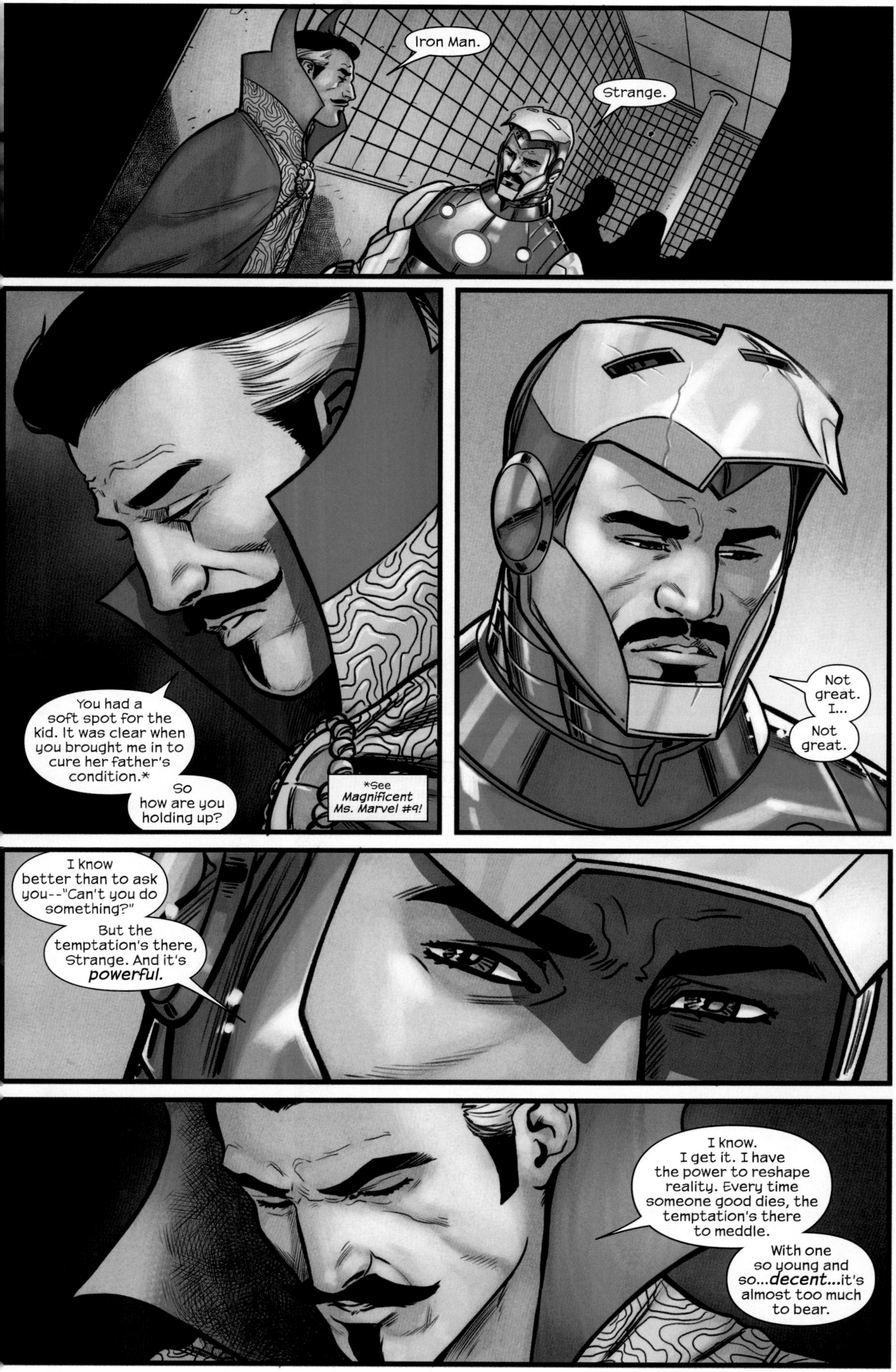
Iron Man.
Strange.
You had a soft spot for the kid. It was clear when you brought me in to cure her father's condition.*
So how are you holding up?
*See *Magnificent Ms. Marvel* #9!
Not great. I...
Not great.
I know better than to ask you--"Can't you do something?"
But the temptation's there, Strange. And it's *powerful.*
I know. I get it. I have the power to reshape reality. Every time someone good dies, the temptation's there to meddle.
With one so young and so...*decent*...it's almost too much to bear.

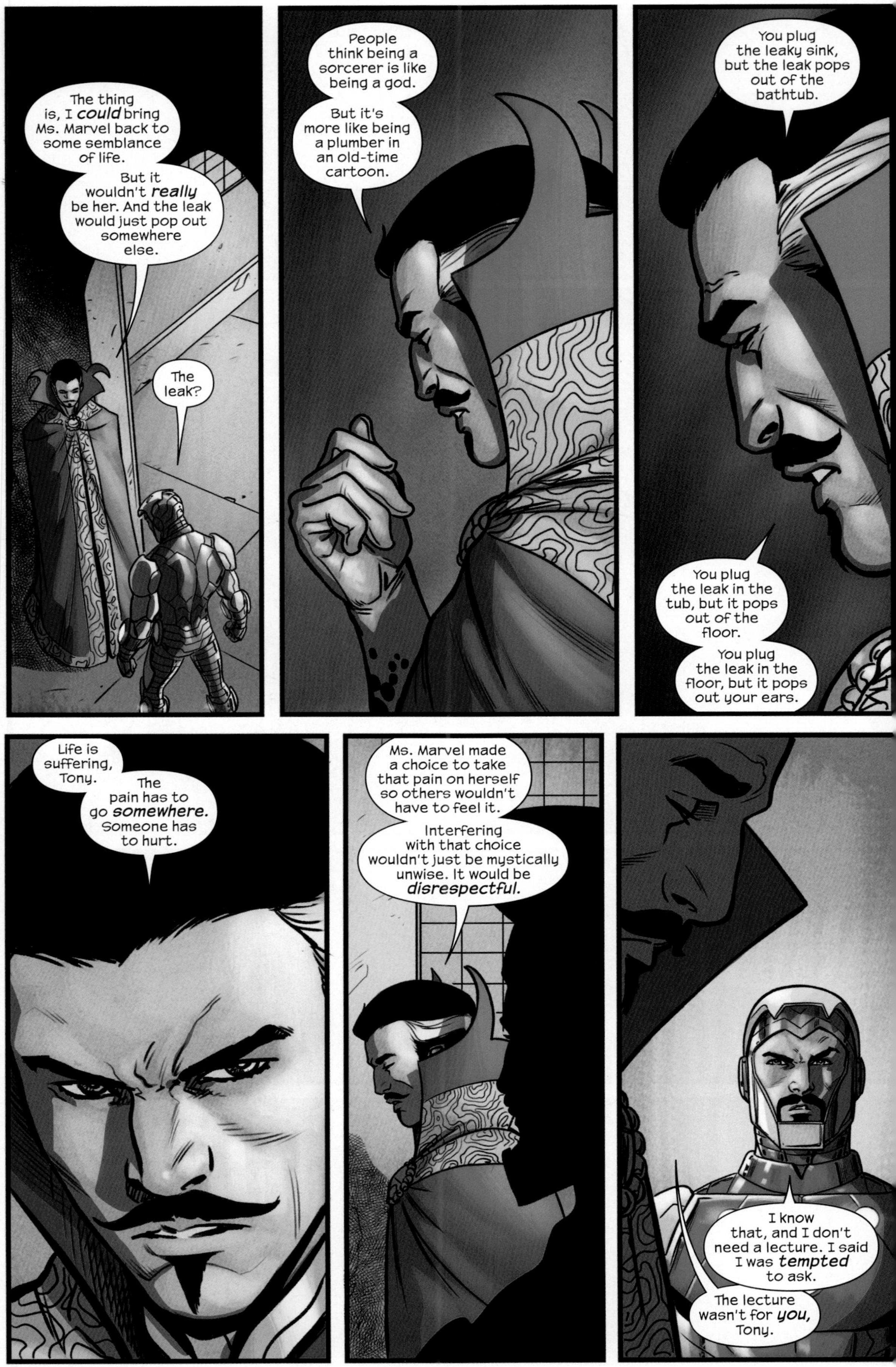

The thing is, I *could* bring Ms. Marvel back to some semblance of life.
But it wouldn't *really* be her. And the leak would just pop out somewhere else.
The leak?
People think being a sorcerer is like being a god.
But it's more like being a plumber in an old-time cartoon.
You plug the leaky sink, but the leak pops out of the bathtub.
You plug the leak in the tub, but it pops out of the floor.
You plug the leak in the floor, but it pops out your ears.
Life is suffering, Tony.
The pain has to go *somewhere.* Someone has to hurt.
Ms. Marvel made a choice to take that pain on herself so others wouldn't have to feel it.
Interfering with that choice wouldn't just be mystically unwise. It would be *disrespectful.*
I know that, and I don't need a lecture. I said I was *tempted* to ask.
The lecture wasn't for *you,* Tony.

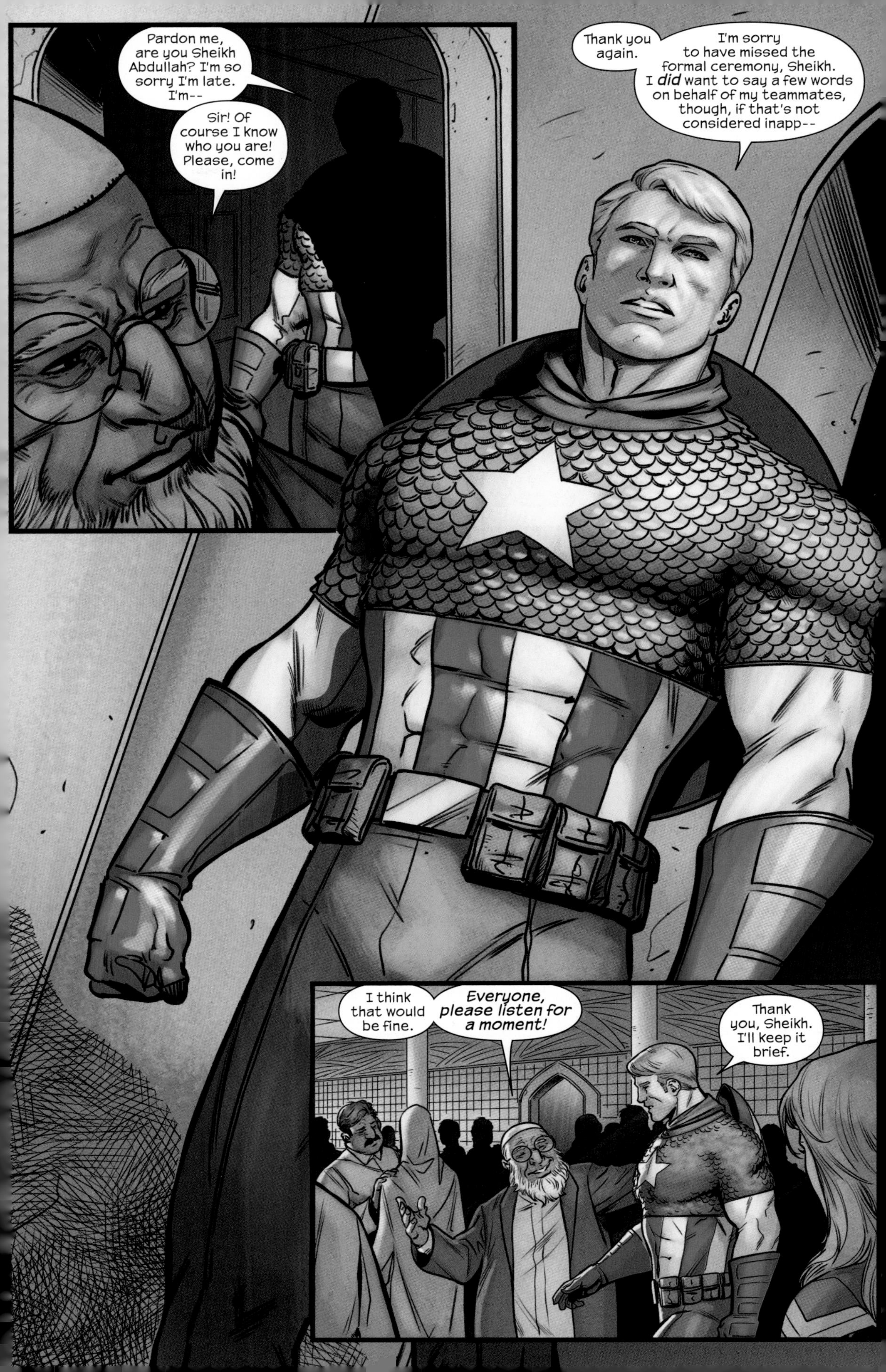
Pardon me, are you Sheikh Abdullah? I'm so sorry I'm late. I'm--
Sir! Of course I know who you are! Please, come in!
Thank you again.
I'm sorry to have missed the formal ceremony, Sheikh. I *did* want to say a few words on behalf of my teammates, though, if that's not considered inapp--
I think that would be fine.
Everyone, please listen for a moment!
Thank you, Sheikh. I'll keep it brief.

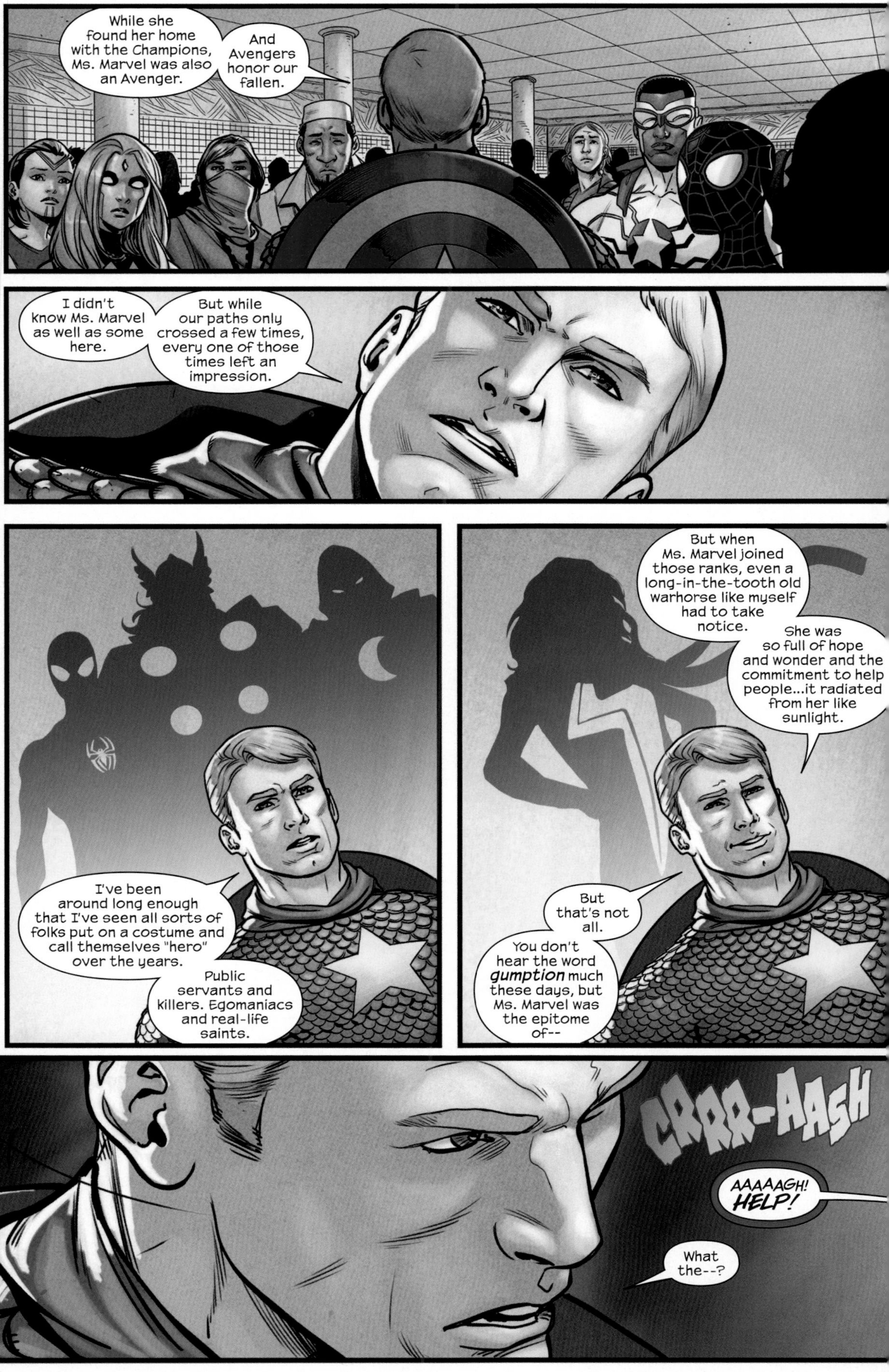

While she found her home with the Champions, Ms. Marvel was also an Avenger.
And Avengers honor our fallen.
I didn't know Ms. Marvel as well as some here.
But while our paths only crossed a few times, every one of those times left an impression.
I've been around long enough that I've seen all sorts of folks put on a costume and call themselves "hero" over the years.
Public servants and killers. Egomaniacs and real-life saints.
But when Ms. Marvel joined those ranks, even a long-in-the-tooth old warhorse like myself had to take notice.
She was so full of hope and wonder and the commitment to help people...it radiated from her like sunlight.
But that's not all.
You don't hear the word *gumption* much these days, but Ms. Marvel was the epitome of--
CRRR-AASH
AAAAAGH! HELP!
What the--?

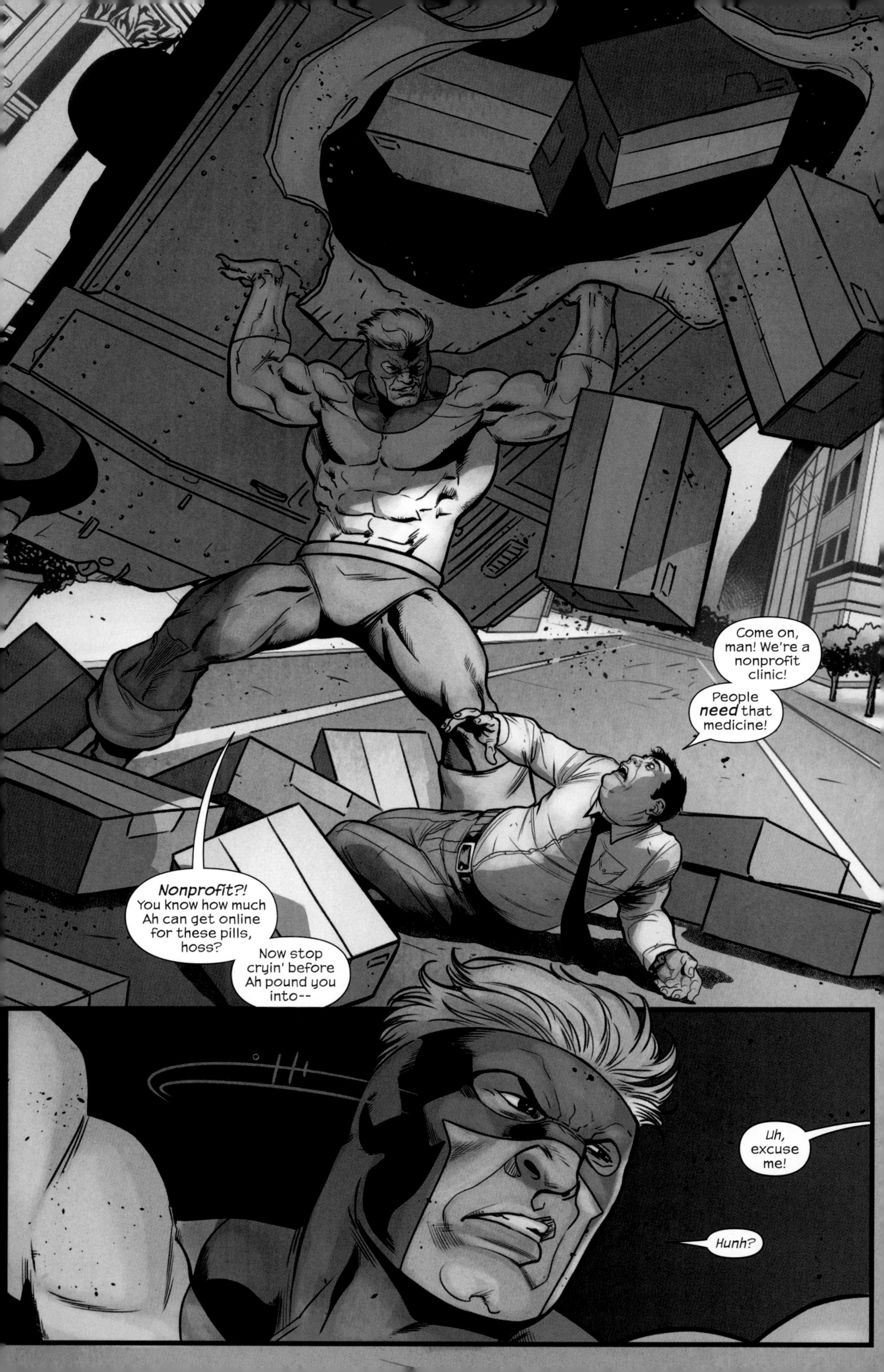
Come on, man! We're a nonprofit clinic!
People *need* that medicine!
Nonprofit?! You know how much Ah can get online for these pills, hoss?
Now stop cryin' before Ah pound you into--
Uh, excuse me!
Hunh?

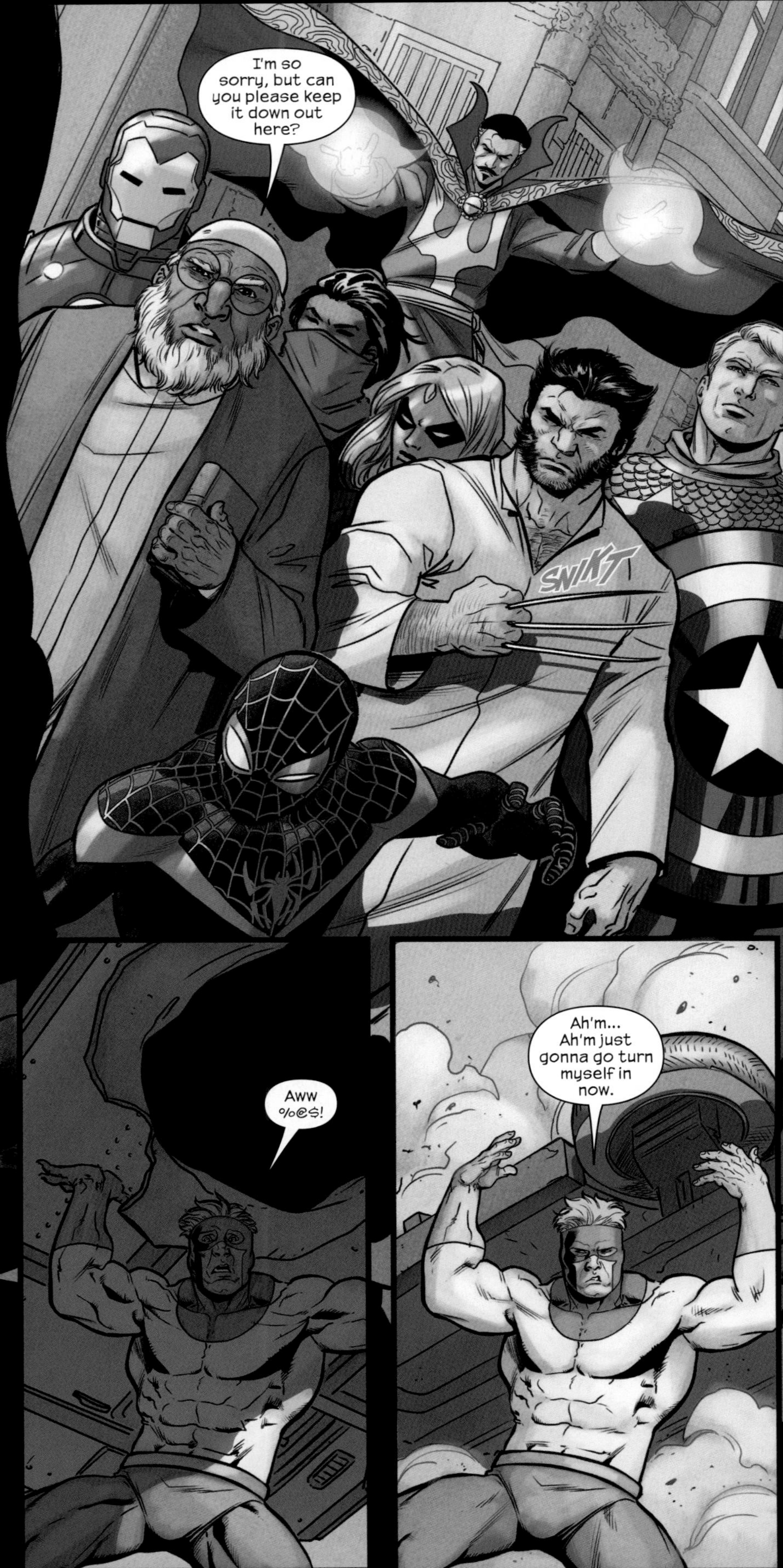
I'm so sorry, but can you please keep it down out here?
SNIKT
Aww %@$!
Ah'm... Ah'm just gonna go turn myself in now.

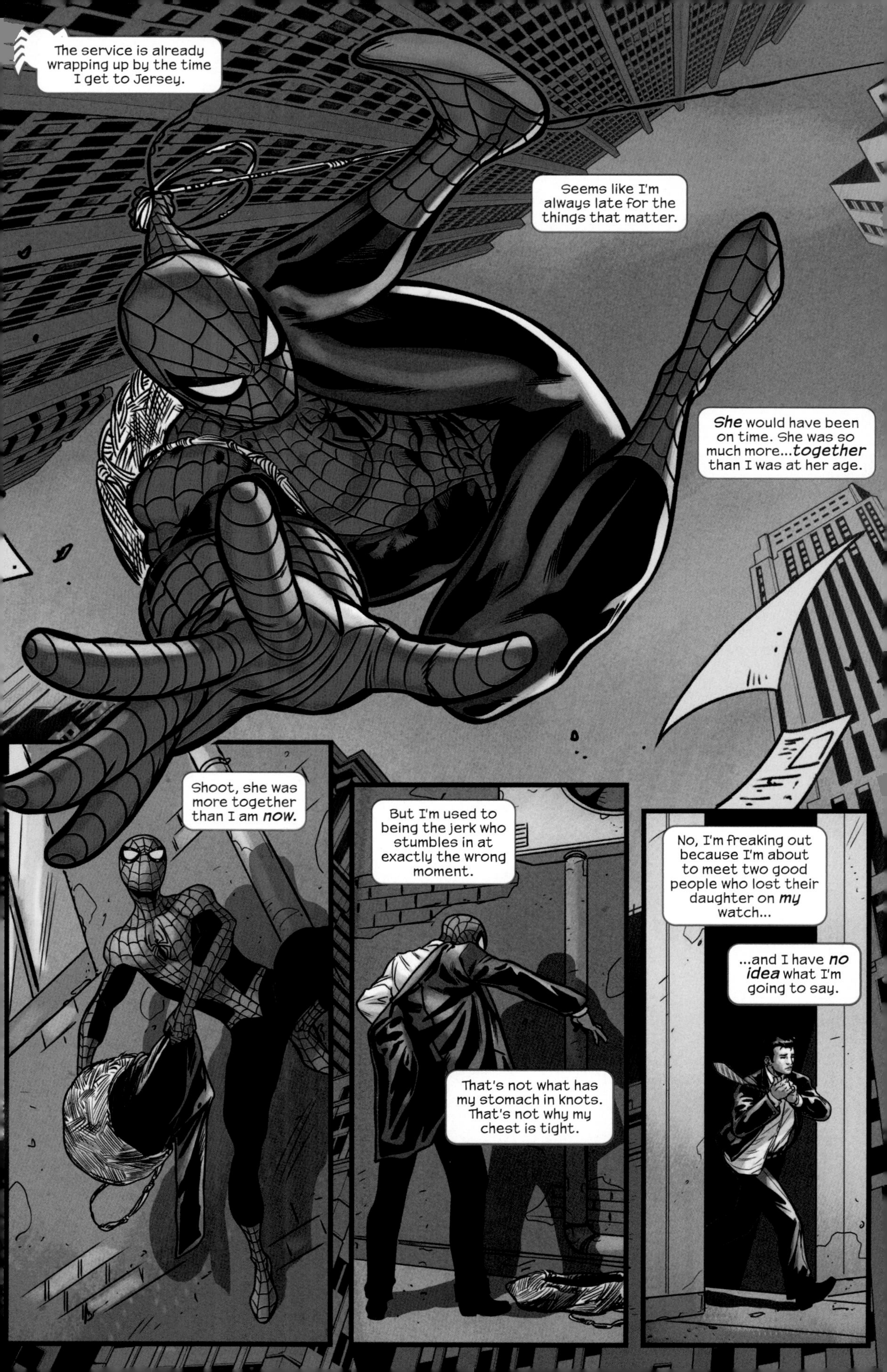
The service is already wrapping up by the time I get to Jersey.
Seems like I'm always late for the things that matter.
She would have been on time. She was so much more...*together* than I was at her age.
Shoot, she was more together than I am *now.*
But I'm used to being the jerk who stumbles in at exactly the wrong moment.
That's not what has my stomach in knots. That's not why my chest is tight.
No, I'm freaking out because I'm about to meet two good people who lost their daughter on *my* watch...
...and I have *no idea* what I'm going to say.

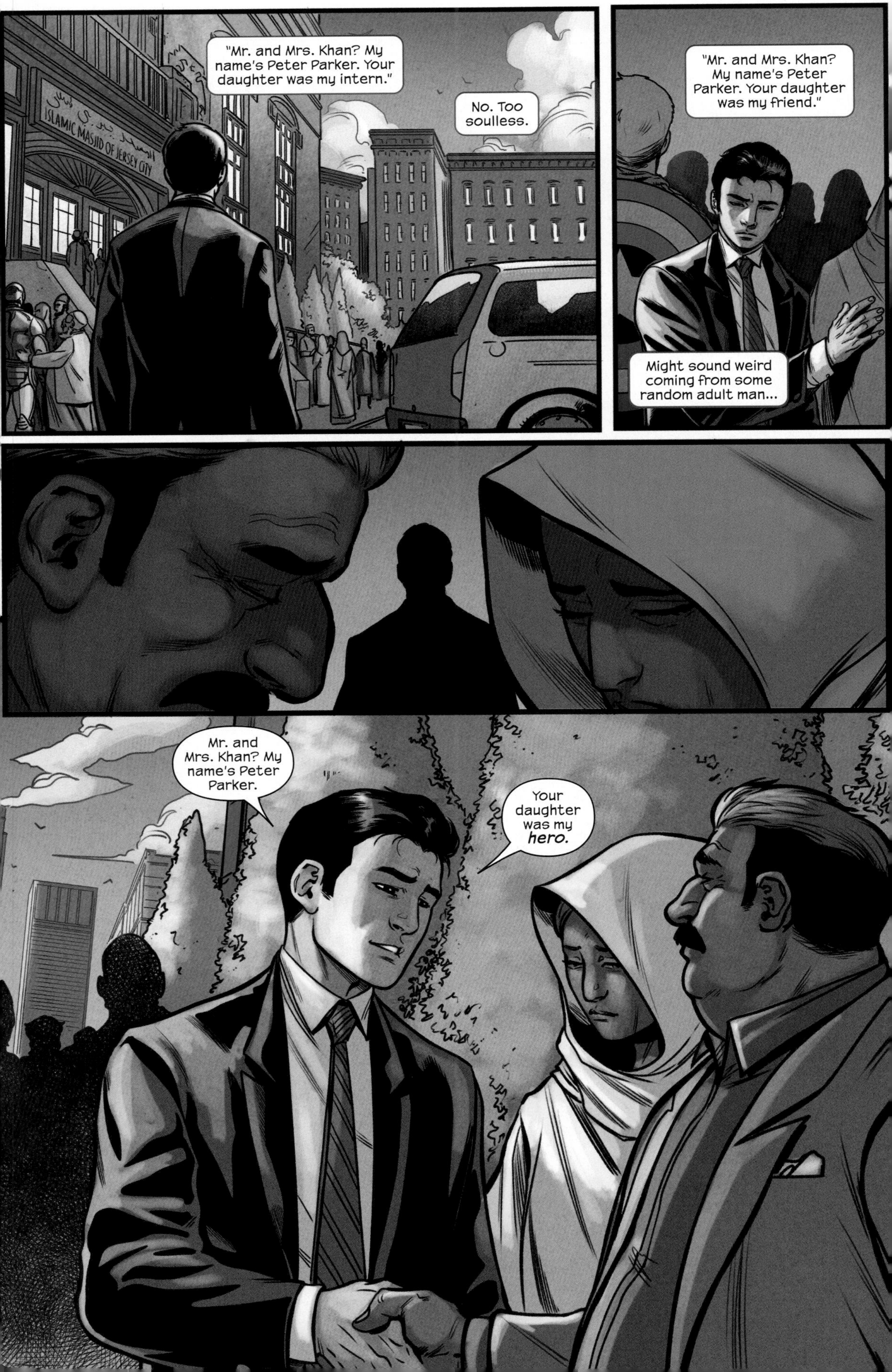
"Mr. and Mrs. Khan? My name's Peter Parker. Your daughter was my intern."
ISLAMIC MASJID OF JERSEY CITY
No. Too soulless.
"Mr. and Mrs. Khan? My name's Peter Parker. Your daughter was my friend."
Might sound weird coming from some random adult man...
Mr. and Mrs. Khan? My name's Peter Parker.
Your daughter was my *hero.*

THE END.

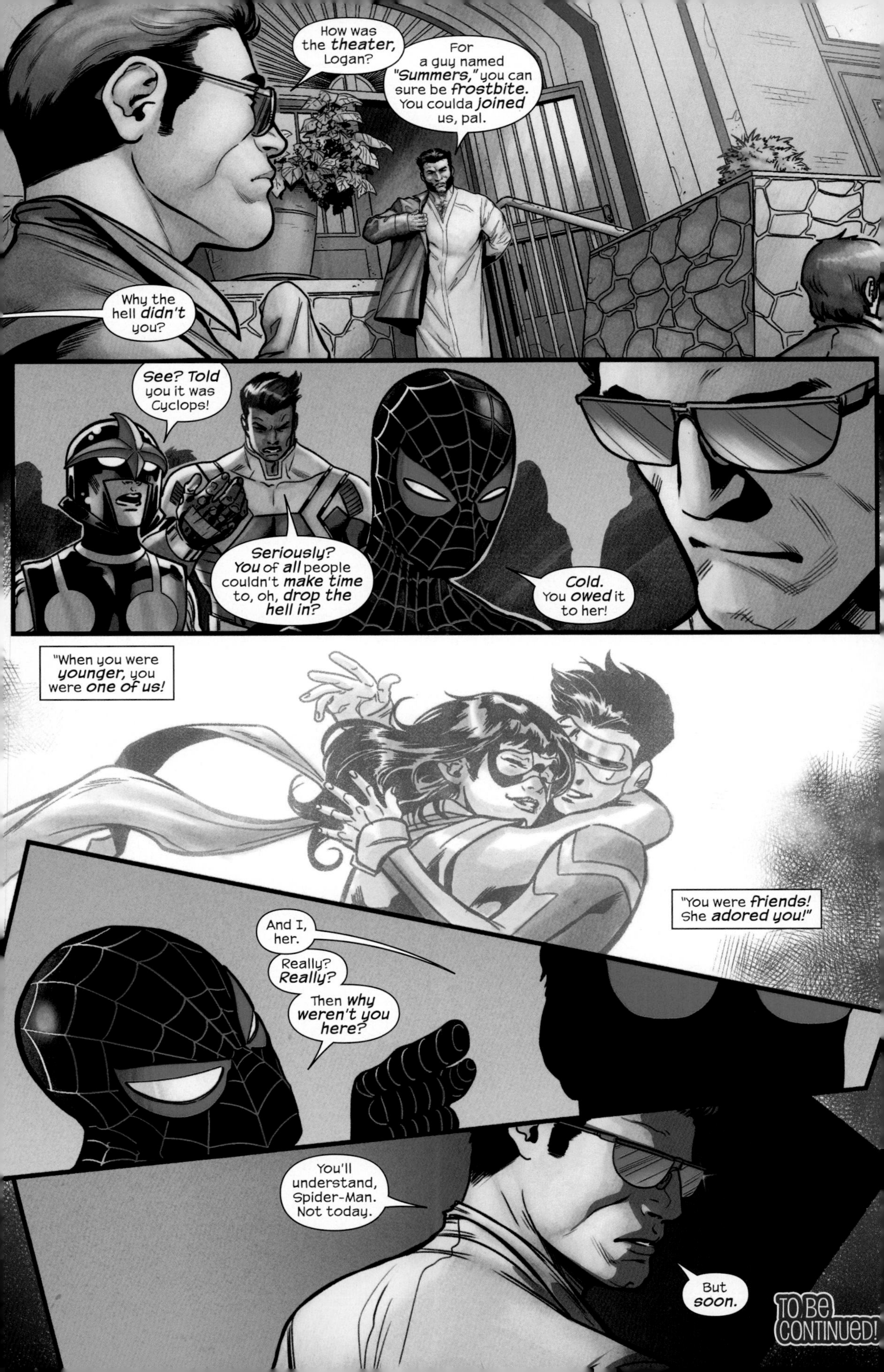
How was the theater, Logan?
For a guy named "Summers," you can sure be frostbite. You coulda joined us, pal.
Why the hell didn't you?
See? Told you it was Cyclops!
Seriously? You of all people couldn't make time to, oh, drop the hell in?
Cold. You owed it to her!
"When you were younger, you were one of us!
"You were friends! She adored you!"
And I, her.
Really? Really?
Then why weren't you here?
You'll understand, Spider-Man. Not today.
But soon.
TO BE CONTINUED!

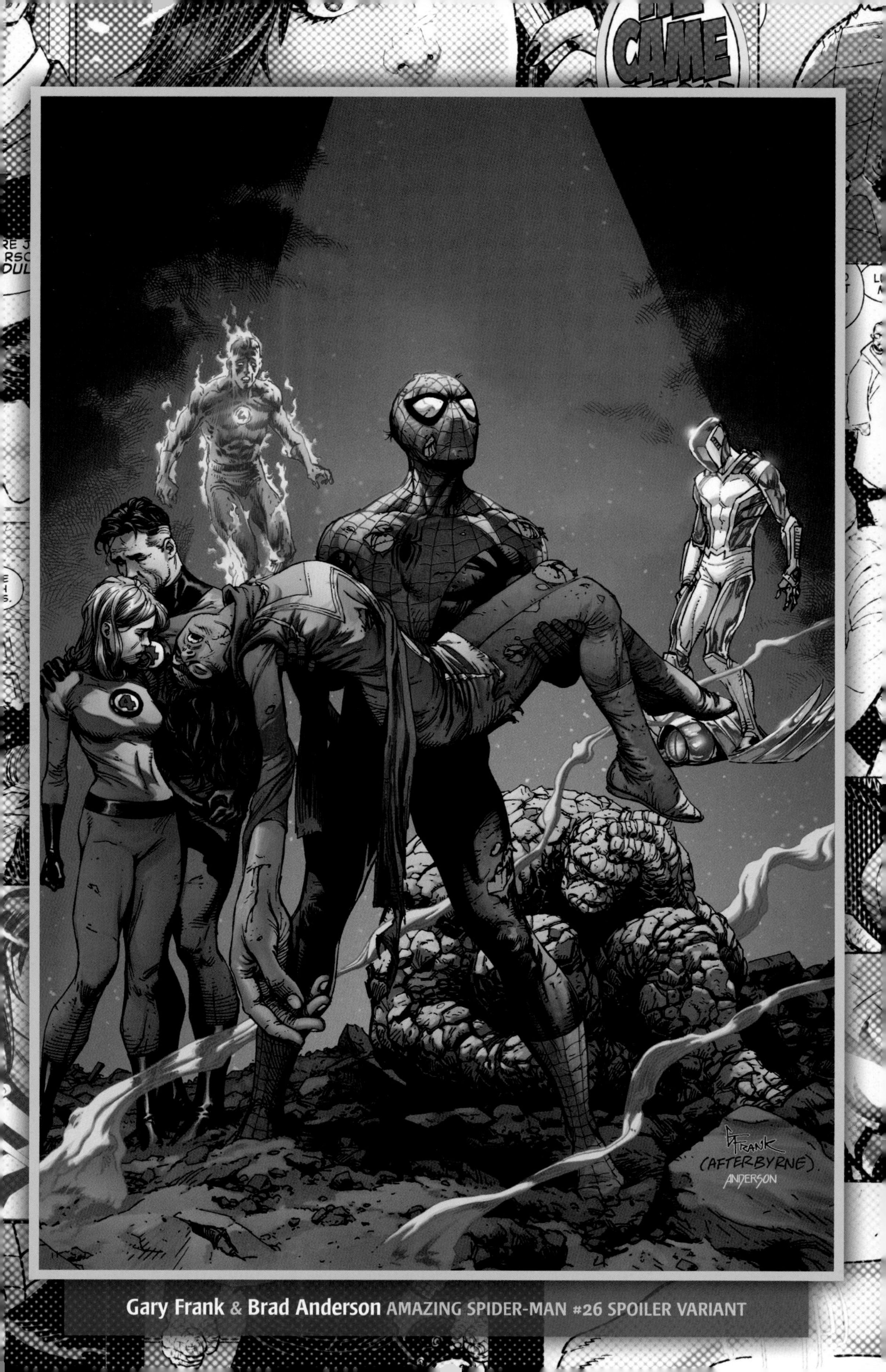
G. FRANK
(AFTERBYRNE)
ANDERSON

Gary Frank & **Brad Anderson** AMAZING SPIDER-MAN #26 SPOILER VARIANT

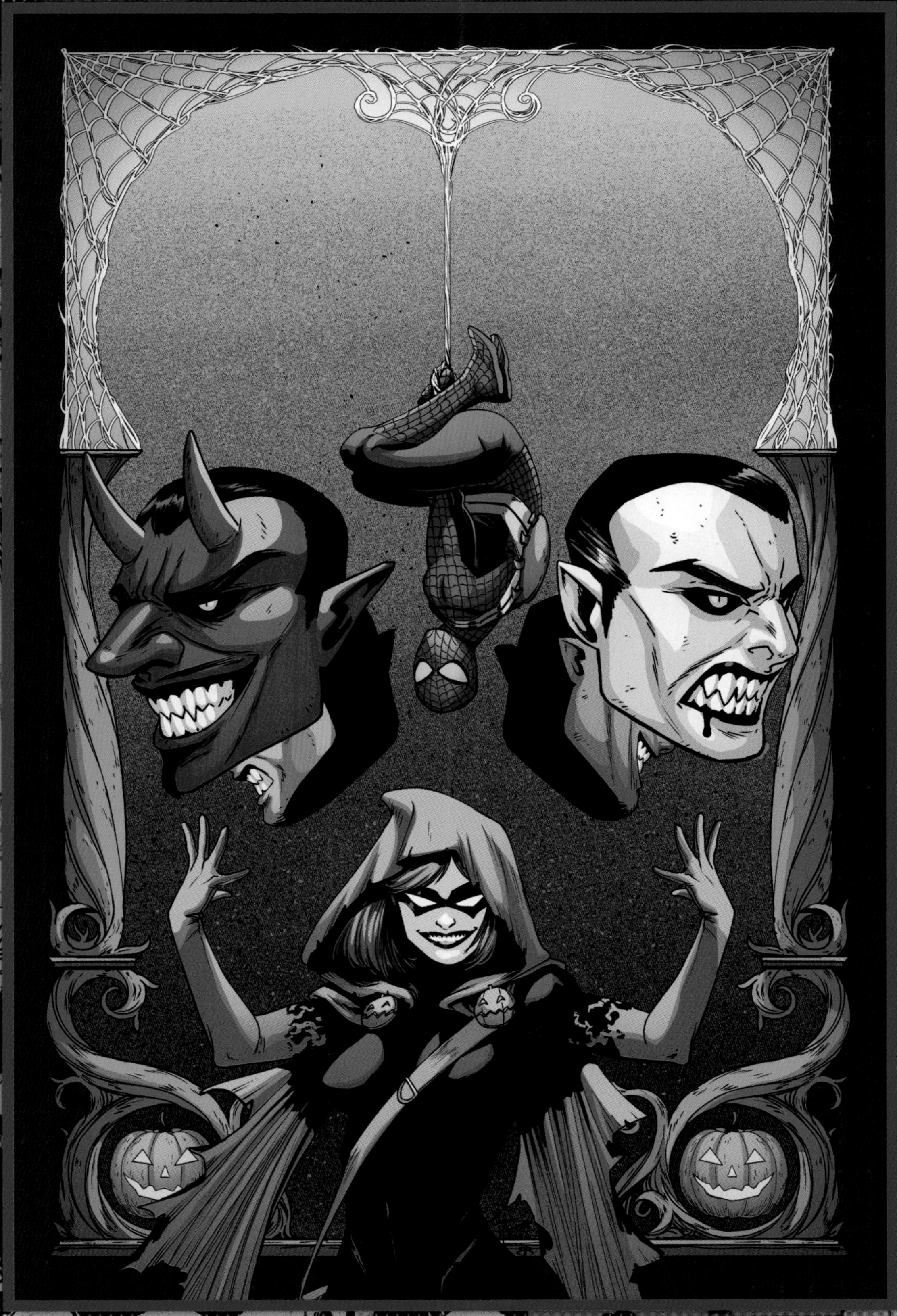

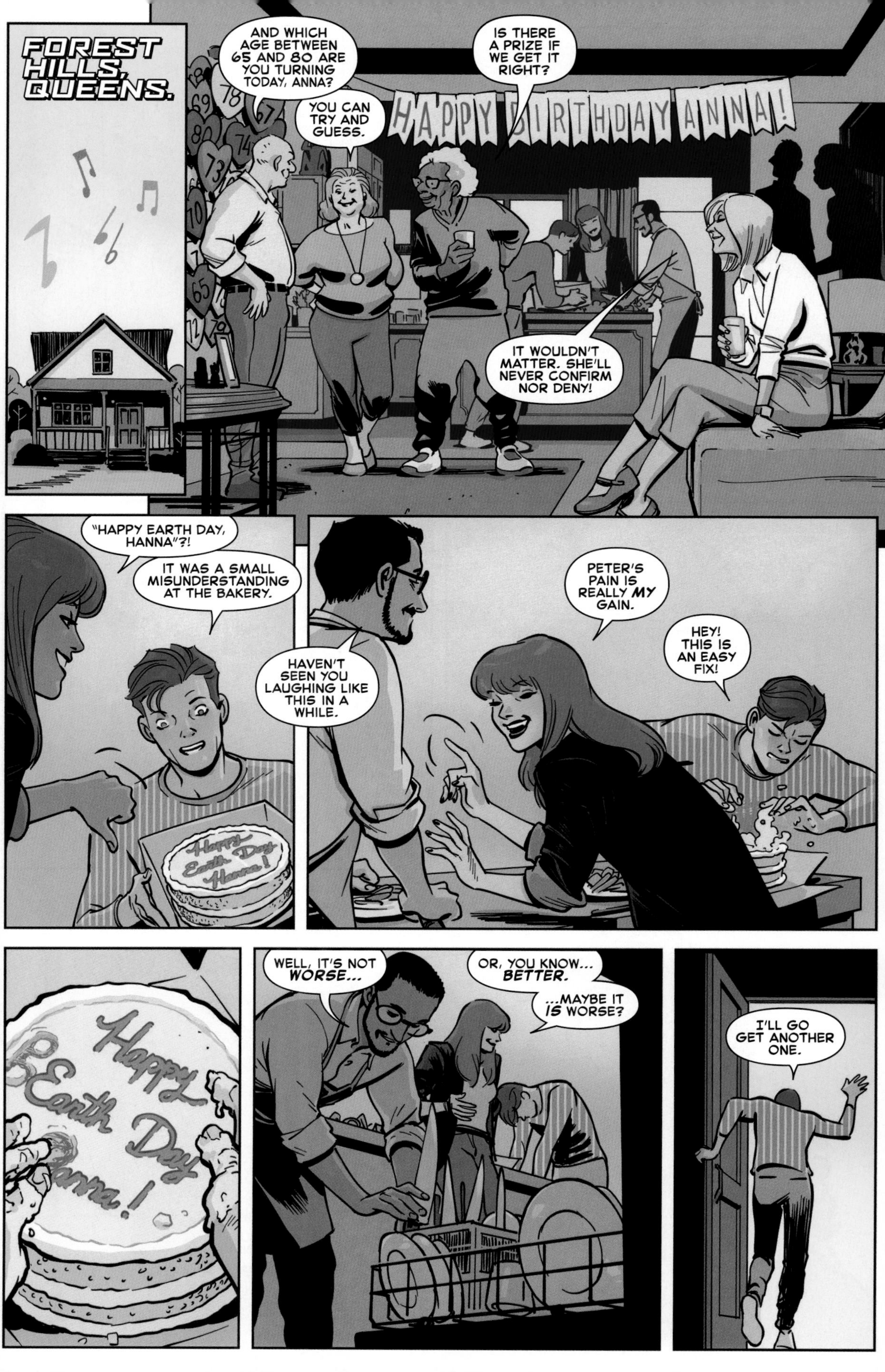
FOREST HILLS, QUEENS.
AND WHICH AGE BETWEEN 65 AND 80 ARE YOU TURNING TODAY, ANNA?
YOU CAN TRY AND GUESS.
IS THERE A PRIZE IF WE GET IT RIGHT?
HAPPY BIRTHDAY ANNA!
IT WOULDN'T MATTER. SHE'LL NEVER CONFIRM NOR DENY!
"HAPPY EARTH DAY, HANNA"?!
IT WAS A SMALL MISUNDERSTANDING AT THE BAKERY.
Happy Earth Day Hanna!
HAVEN'T SEEN YOU LAUGHING LIKE THIS IN A WHILE.
PETER'S PAIN IS REALLY *MY* GAIN.
HEY! THIS IS AN EASY FIX!
Happy Earth Day anna!
WELL, IT'S NOT *WORSE*...
OR, YOU KNOW... *BETTER.*
...MAYBE IT *IS* WORSE?
I'LL GO GET ANOTHER ONE.

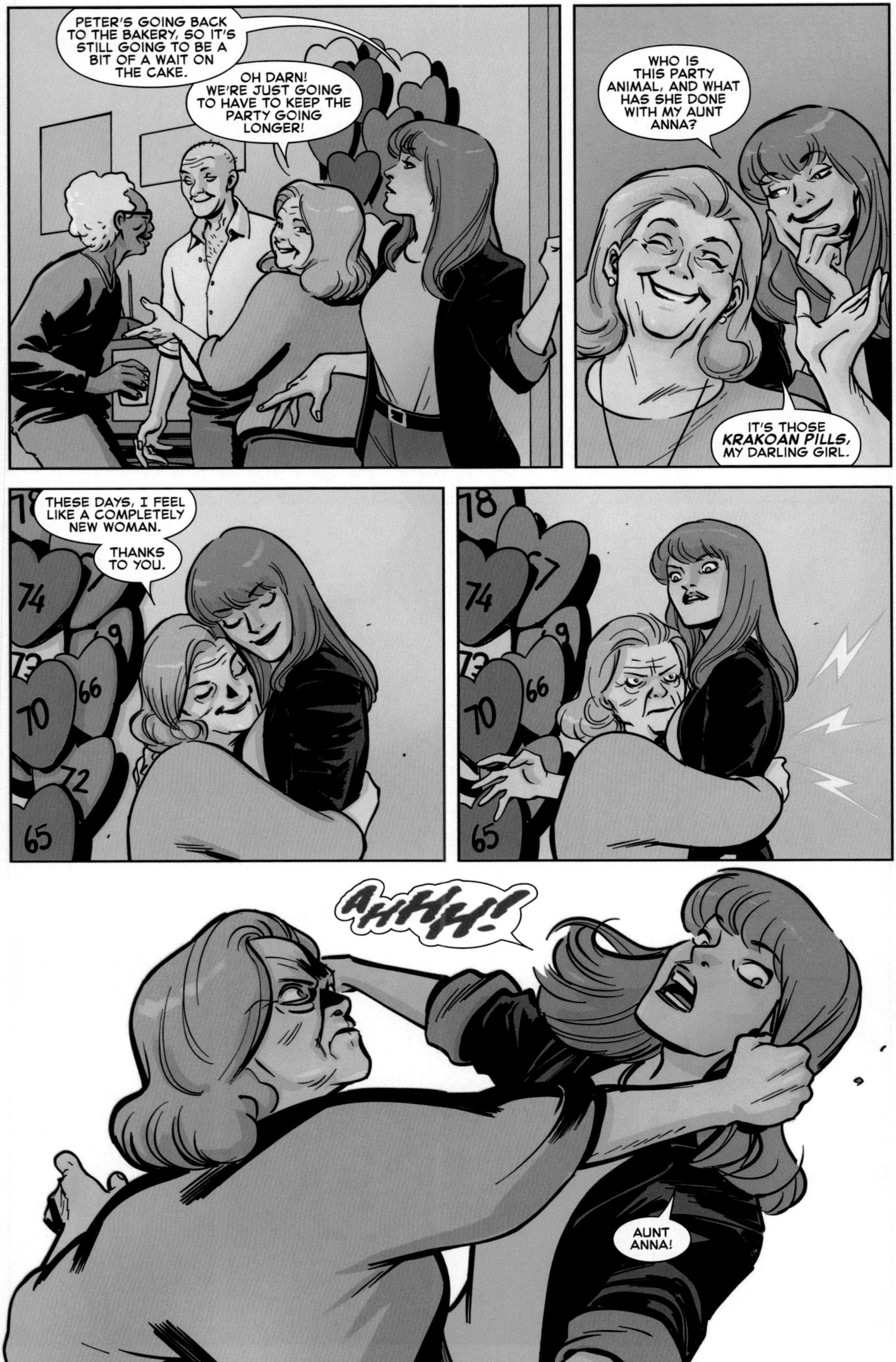
PETER'S GOING BACK TO THE BAKERY, SO IT'S STILL GOING TO BE A BIT OF A WAIT ON THE CAKE.
OH DARN! WE'RE JUST GOING TO HAVE TO KEEP THE PARTY GOING LONGER!
WHO IS THIS PARTY ANIMAL, AND WHAT HAS SHE DONE WITH MY AUNT ANNA?
IT'S THOSE KRAKOAN PILLS, MY DARLING GIRL.
THESE DAYS, I FEEL LIKE A COMPLETELY NEW WOMAN.
THANKS TO YOU.
AHHH!
AUNT ANNA!

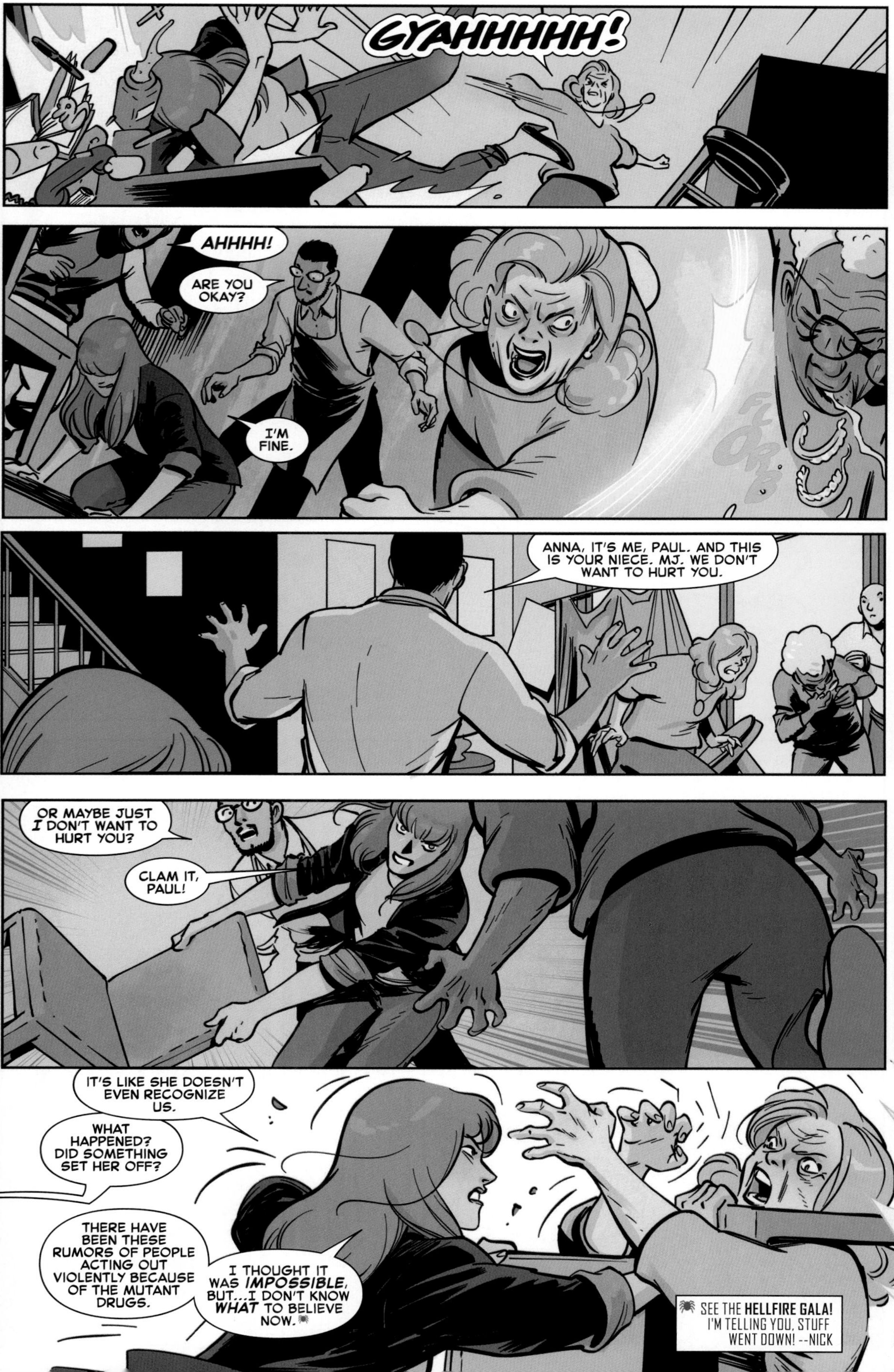
GYAHHHHH!
AHHHH!
ARE YOU OKAY?
I'M FINE.
FLORB
ANNA, IT'S ME, PAUL. AND THIS IS YOUR NIECE, MJ. WE DON'T WANT TO HURT YOU.
OR MAYBE JUST I DON'T WANT TO HURT YOU?
CLAM IT, PAUL!
IT'S LIKE SHE DOESN'T EVEN RECOGNIZE US.
WHAT HAPPENED? DID SOMETHING SET HER OFF?
THERE HAVE BEEN THESE RUMORS OF PEOPLE ACTING OUT VIOLENTLY BECAUSE OF THE MUTANT DRUGS.
I THOUGHT IT WAS IMPOSSIBLE, BUT...I DON'T KNOW WHAT TO BELIEVE NOW.
SEE THE HELLFIRE GALA! I'M TELLING YOU, STUFF WENT DOWN! --NICK

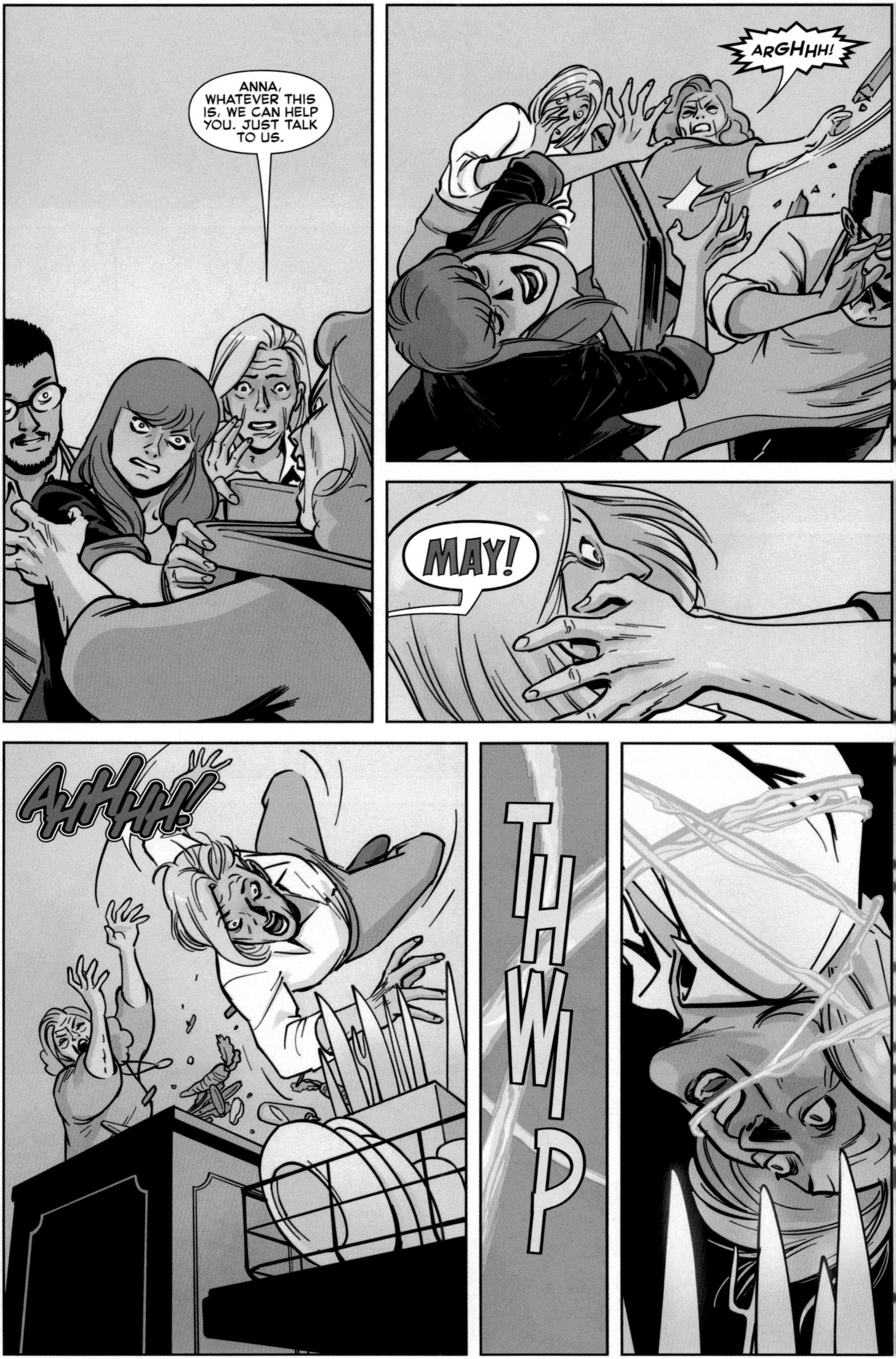
ANNA, WHATEVER THIS IS, WE CAN HELP YOU. JUST TALK TO US.
ARGHHH!
MAY!
AHHHH!
THWIP

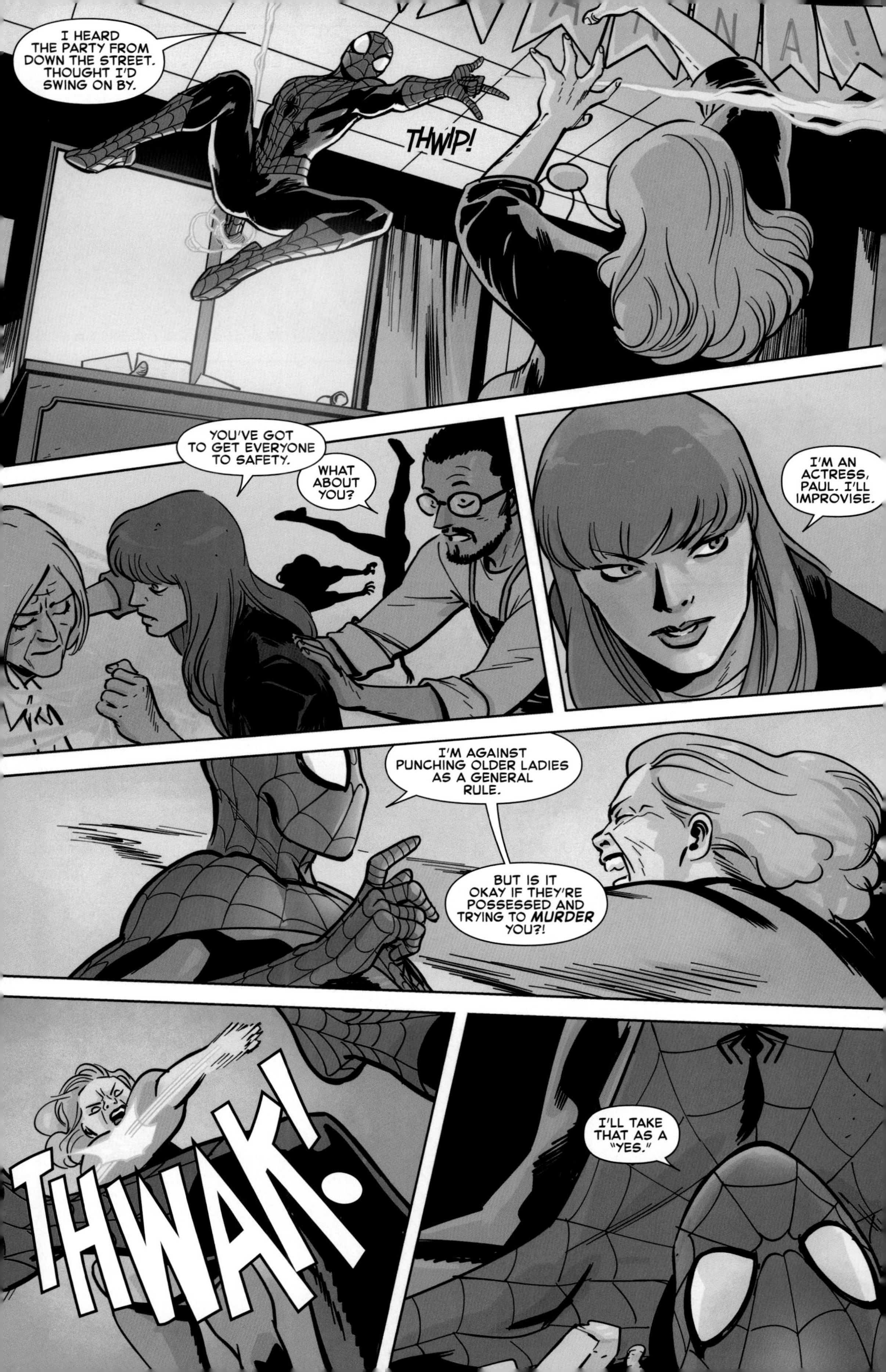
I HEARD THE PARTY FROM DOWN THE STREET. THOUGHT I'D SWING ON BY.
THWIP!
YOU'VE GOT TO GET EVERYONE TO SAFETY.
WHAT ABOUT YOU?
I'M AN ACTRESS, PAUL. I'LL IMPROVISE.
I'M AGAINST PUNCHING OLDER LADIES AS A GENERAL RULE.
BUT IS IT OKAY IF THEY'RE POSSESSED AND TRYING TO *MURDER* YOU?!
THWAK!
I'LL TAKE THAT AS A "YES."

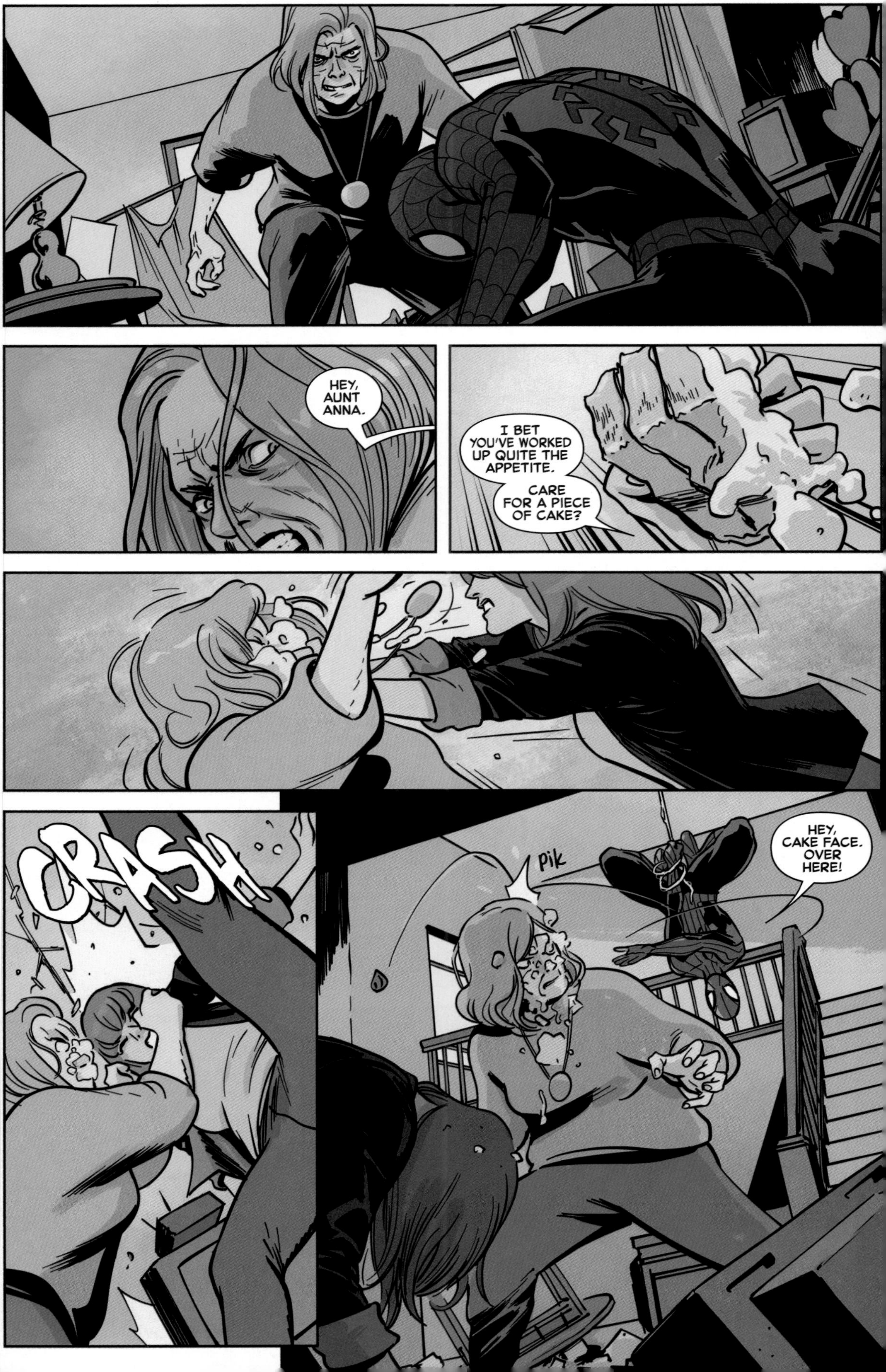
HEY, AUNT ANNA.
I BET YOU'VE WORKED UP QUITE THE APPETITE.
CARE FOR A PIECE OF CAKE?
CRASH
PIK
HEY, CAKE FACE. OVER HERE!

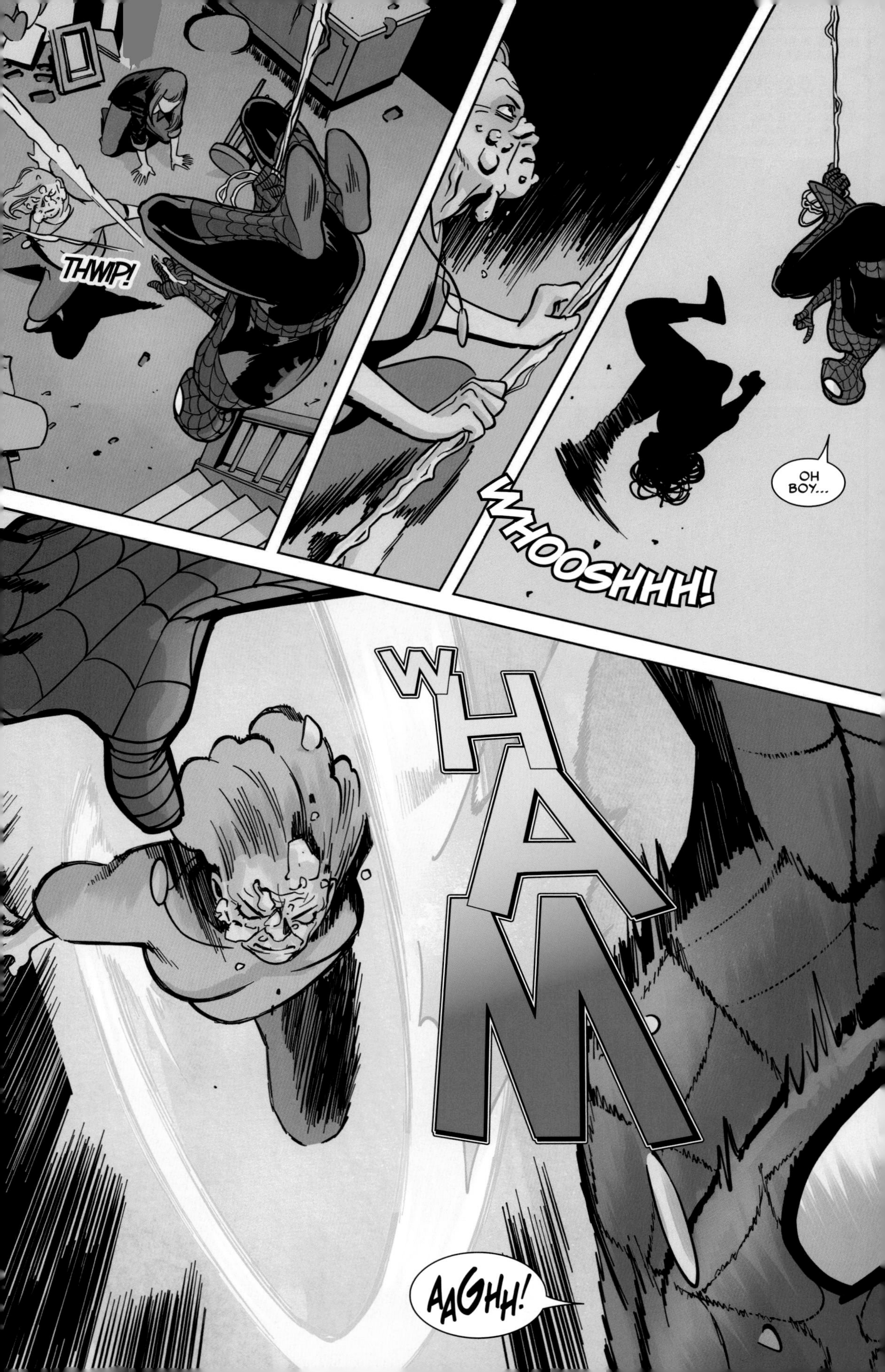
THWIP!
OH BOY...
WHOOSHHH!
WHAM
AAGHH!

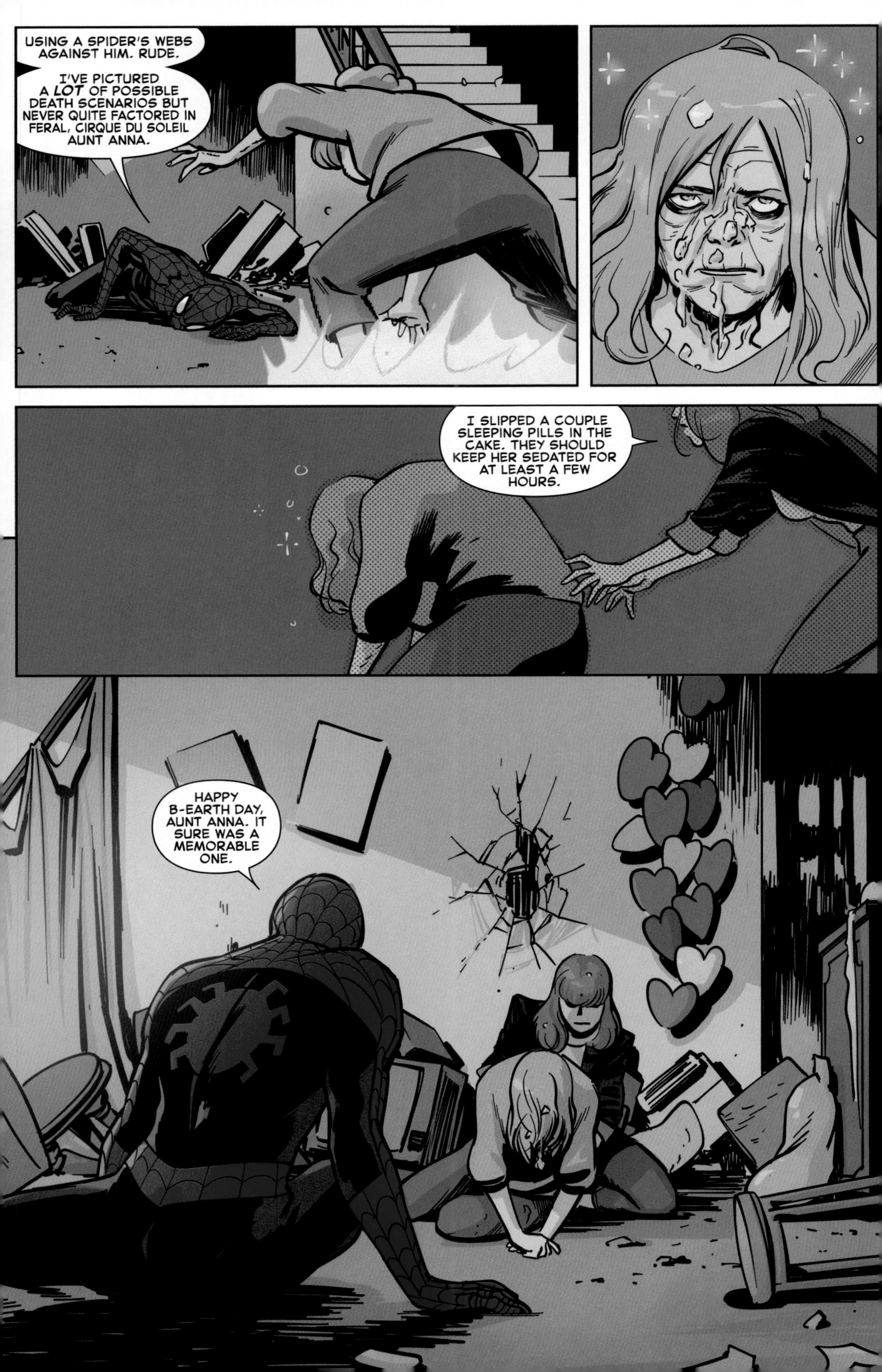
USING A SPIDER'S WEBS AGAINST HIM. RUDE.
I'VE PICTURED A LOT OF POSSIBLE DEATH SCENARIOS BUT NEVER QUITE FACTORED IN FERAL, CIRQUE DU SOLEIL AUNT ANNA.
I SLIPPED A COUPLE SLEEPING PILLS IN THE CAKE. THEY SHOULD KEEP HER SEDATED FOR AT LEAST A FEW HOURS.
HAPPY B-EARTH DAY, AUNT ANNA. IT SURE WAS A MEMORABLE ONE.

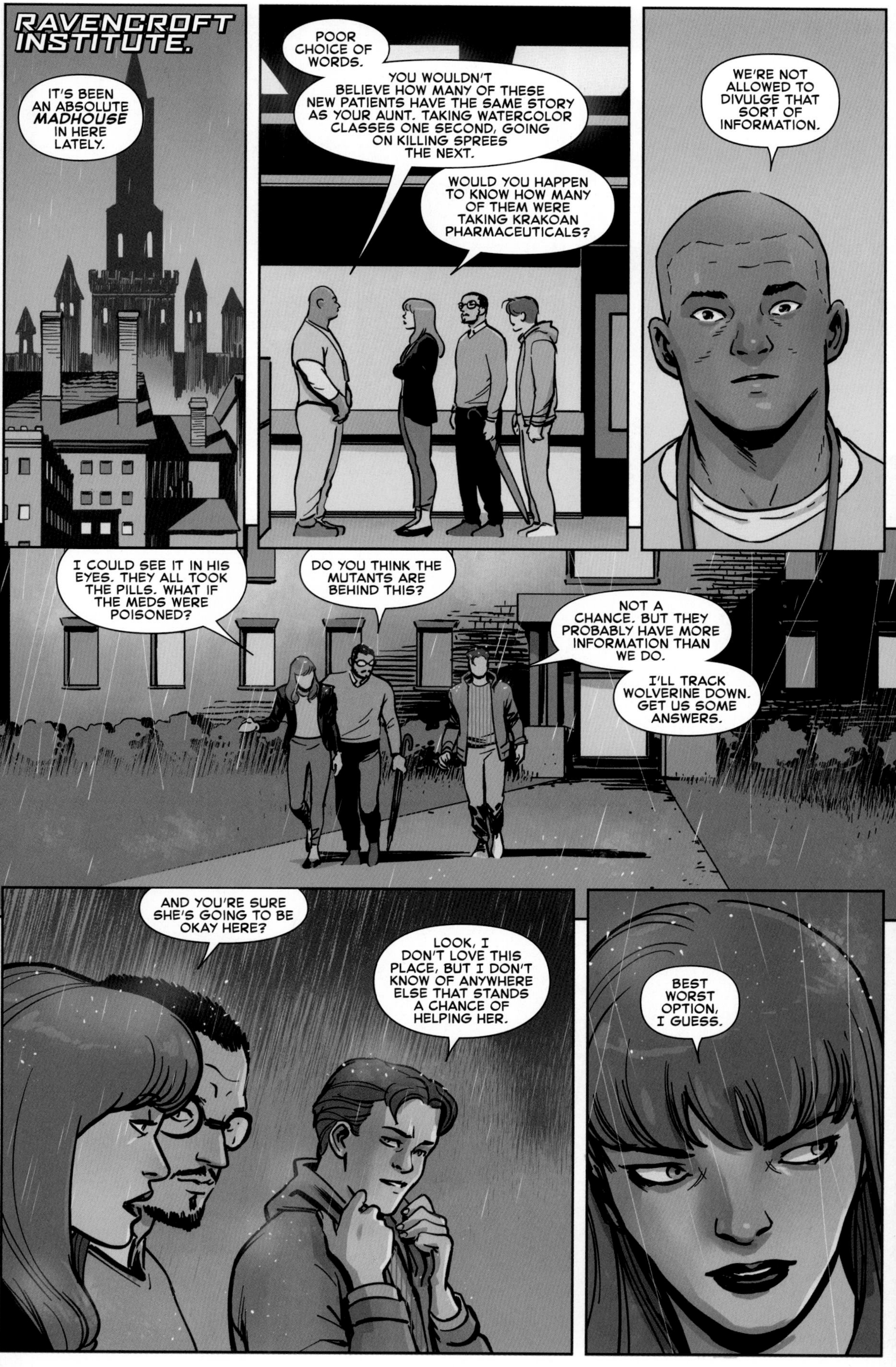
RAVENCROFT INSTITUTE.
IT'S BEEN AN ABSOLUTE MADHOUSE IN HERE LATELY.
POOR CHOICE OF WORDS.
YOU WOULDN'T BELIEVE HOW MANY OF THESE NEW PATIENTS HAVE THE SAME STORY AS YOUR AUNT. TAKING WATERCOLOR CLASSES ONE SECOND, GOING ON KILLING SPREES THE NEXT.
WOULD YOU HAPPEN TO KNOW HOW MANY OF THEM WERE TAKING KRAKOAN PHARMACEUTICALS?
WE'RE NOT ALLOWED TO DIVULGE THAT SORT OF INFORMATION.
I COULD SEE IT IN HIS EYES. THEY ALL TOOK THE PILLS. WHAT IF THE MEDS WERE POISONED?
DO YOU THINK THE MUTANTS ARE BEHIND THIS?
NOT A CHANCE. BUT THEY PROBABLY HAVE MORE INFORMATION THAN WE DO.
I'LL TRACK WOLVERINE DOWN. GET US SOME ANSWERS.
AND YOU'RE SURE SHE'S GOING TO BE OKAY HERE?
LOOK, I DON'T LOVE THIS PLACE, BUT I DON'T KNOW OF ANYWHERE ELSE THAT STANDS A CHANCE OF HELPING HER.
BEST WORST OPTION, I GUESS.

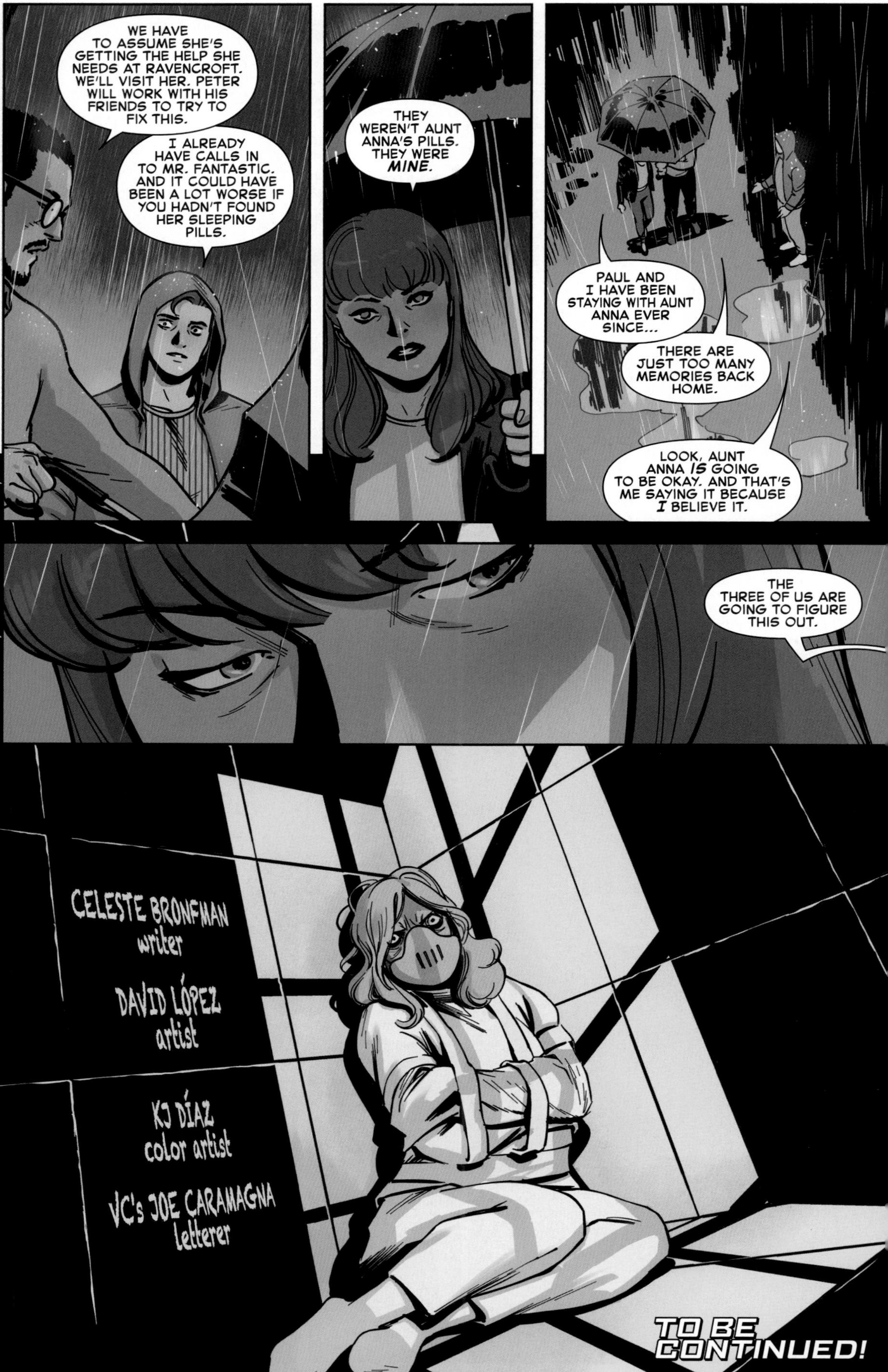

WE HAVE TO ASSUME SHE'S GETTING THE HELP SHE NEEDS AT RAVENCROFT. WE'LL VISIT HER. PETER WILL WORK WITH HIS FRIENDS TO TRY TO FIX THIS.
I ALREADY HAVE CALLS IN TO MR. FANTASTIC. AND IT COULD HAVE BEEN A LOT WORSE IF YOU HADN'T FOUND HER SLEEPING PILLS.
THEY WEREN'T AUNT ANNA'S PILLS. THEY WERE *MINE*.
PAUL AND I HAVE BEEN STAYING WITH AUNT ANNA EVER SINCE...
THERE ARE JUST TOO MANY MEMORIES BACK HOME.
LOOK, AUNT ANNA *IS* GOING TO BE OKAY. AND THAT'S ME SAYING IT BECAUSE *I* BELIEVE IT.
THE THREE OF US ARE GOING TO FIGURE THIS OUT.
CELESTE BRONFMAN writer
DAVID LÓPEZ artist
KJ DÍAZ color artist
VC's JOE CARAMAGNA letterer
TO BE CONTINUED!

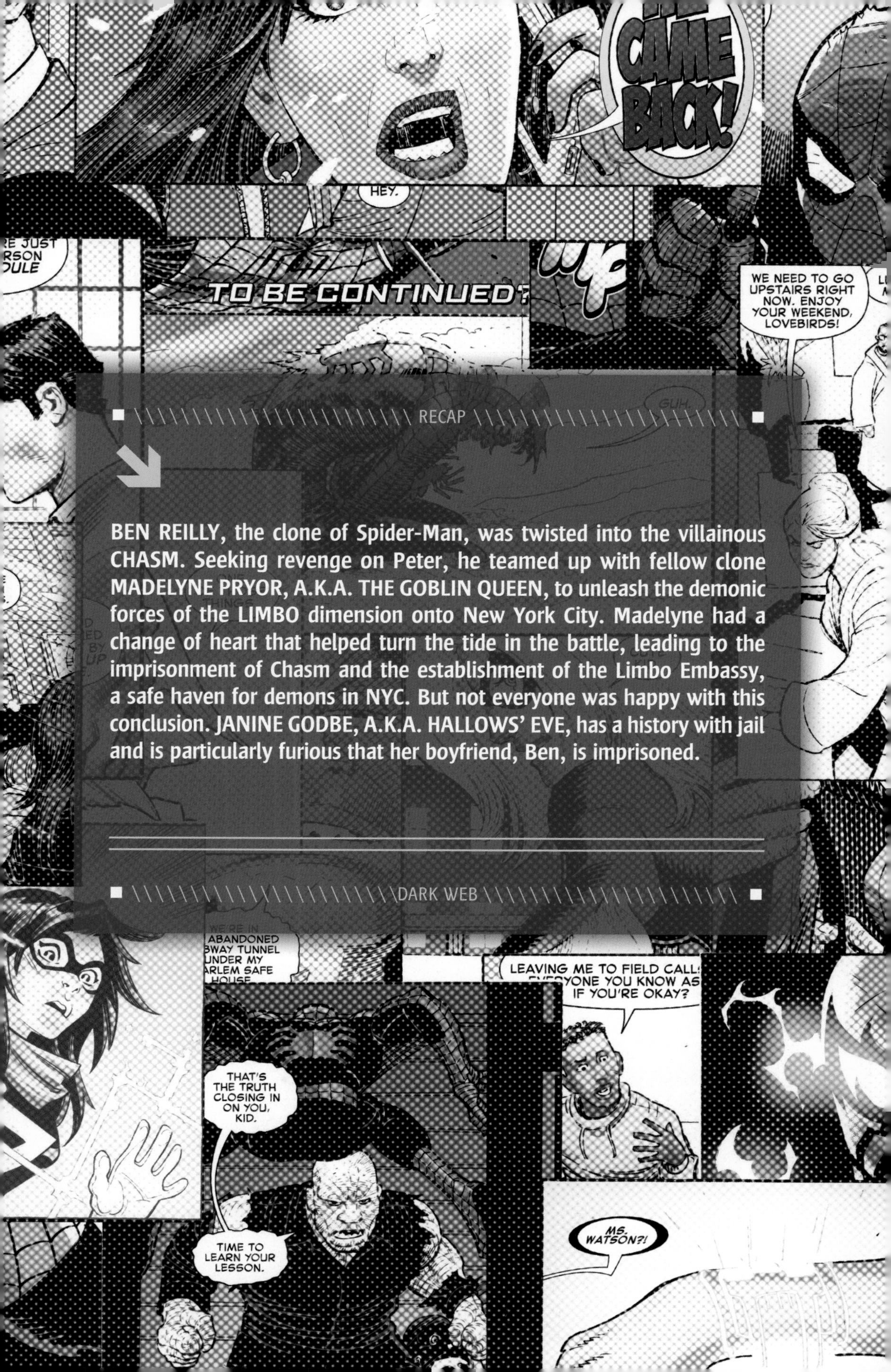
CAME BACK!
HEY.
TO BE CONTINUED?
WE NEED TO GO UPSTAIRS RIGHT NOW. ENJOY YOUR WEEKEND, LOVEBIRDS!
THAT'S THE TRUTH CLOSING IN ON YOU, KID.
TIME TO LEARN YOUR LESSON.
MS. WATSON?!

RECAP

BEN REILLY, the clone of Spider-Man, was twisted into the villainous CHASM. Seeking revenge on Peter, he teamed up with fellow clone MADELYNE PRYOR, A.K.A. THE GOBLIN QUEEN, to unleash the demonic forces of the LIMBO dimension onto New York City. Madelyne had a change of heart that helped turn the tide in the battle, leading to the imprisonment of Chasm and the establishment of the Limbo Embassy, a safe haven for demons in NYC. But not everyone was happy with this conclusion. JANINE GODBE, A.K.A. HALLOWS' EVE, has a history with jail and is particularly furious that her boyfriend, Ben, is imprisoned.

DARK WEB

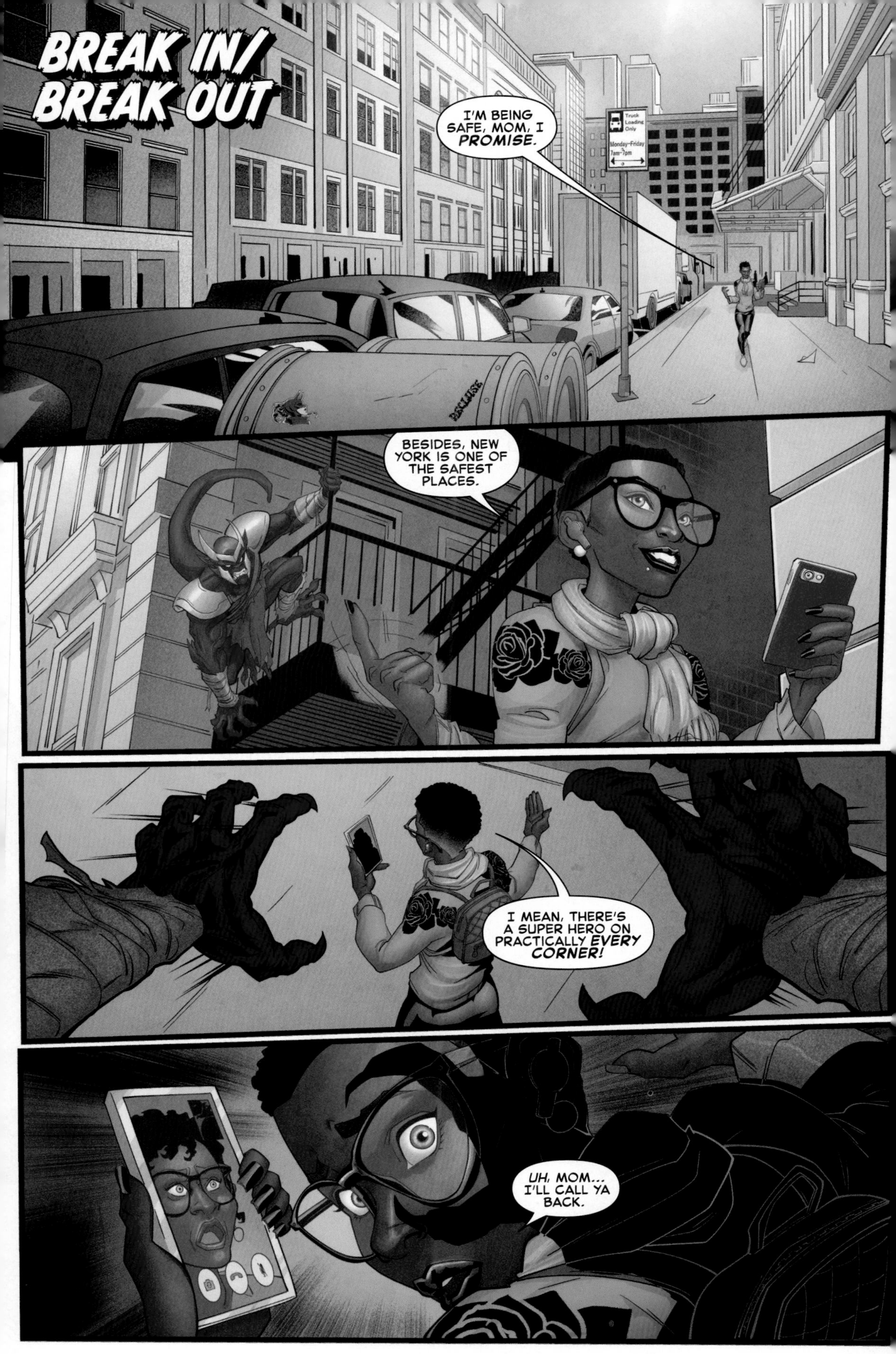
BREAK IN/ BREAK OUT
I'M BEING SAFE, MOM, I PROMISE.
Truck Loading Only
Monday–Friday 7am–7pm
BESIDES, NEW YORK IS ONE OF THE SAFEST PLACES.
I MEAN, THERE'S A SUPER HERO ON PRACTICALLY EVERY CORNER!
UH, MOM... I'LL CALL YA BACK.

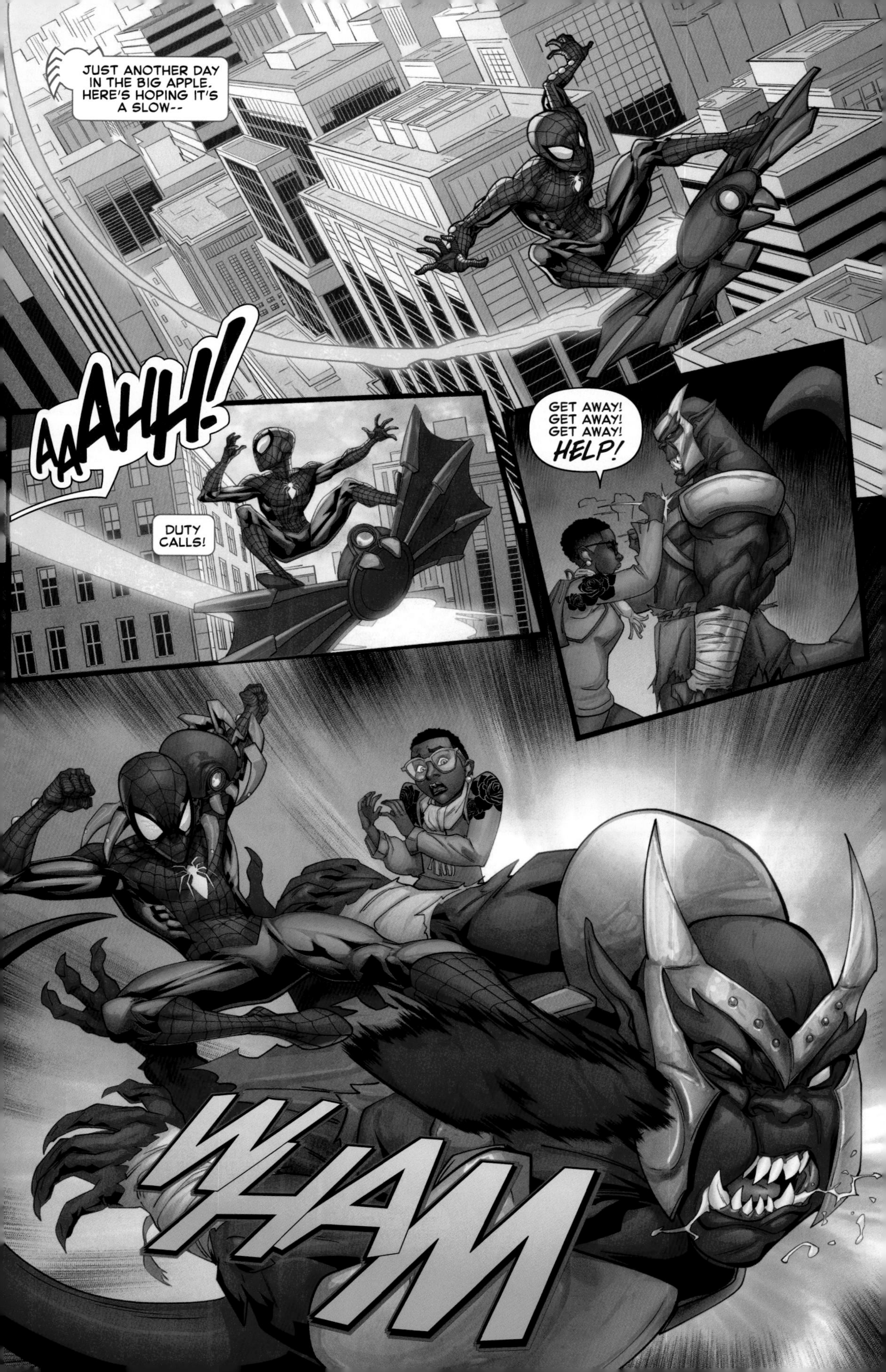
JUST ANOTHER DAY IN THE BIG APPLE. HERE'S HOPING IT'S A SLOW--
AAAHH!
DUTY CALLS!
GET AWAY! GET AWAY! GET AWAY! HELP!
WHAM

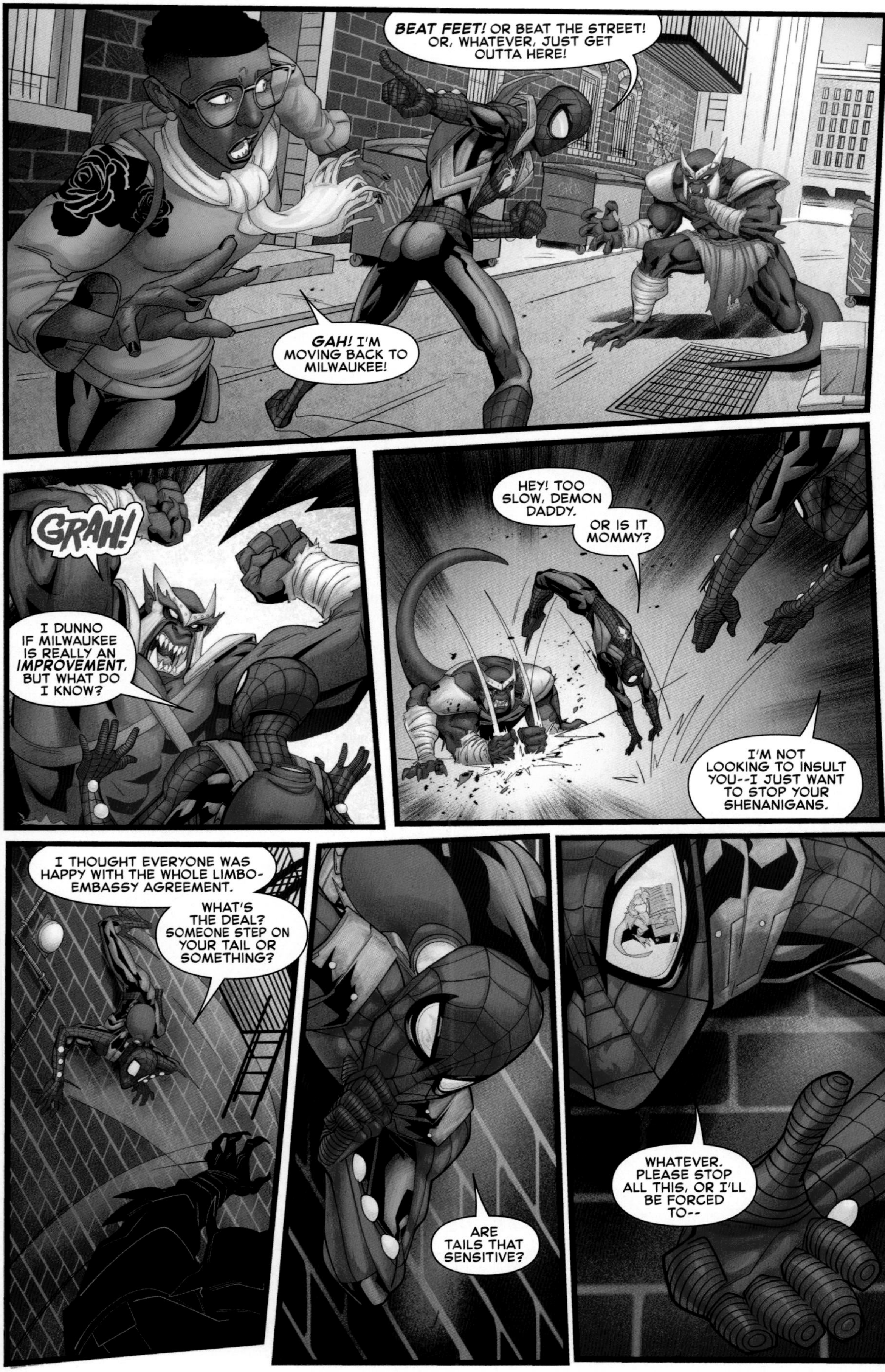
BEAT FEET! OR BEAT THE STREET! OR, WHATEVER, JUST GET OUTTA HERE!
GAH! I'M MOVING BACK TO MILWAUKEE!
GRAH!
I DUNNO IF MILWAUKEE IS REALLY AN IMPROVEMENT, BUT WHAT DO I KNOW?
HEY! TOO SLOW, DEMON DADDY.
OR IS IT MOMMY?
I'M NOT LOOKING TO INSULT YOU--I JUST WANT TO STOP YOUR SHENANIGANS.
I THOUGHT EVERYONE WAS HAPPY WITH THE WHOLE LIMBO-EMBASSY AGREEMENT.
WHAT'S THE DEAL? SOMEONE STEP ON YOUR TAIL OR SOMETHING?
ARE TAILS THAT SENSITIVE?
WHATEVER. PLEASE STOP ALL THIS, OR I'LL BE FORCED TO--

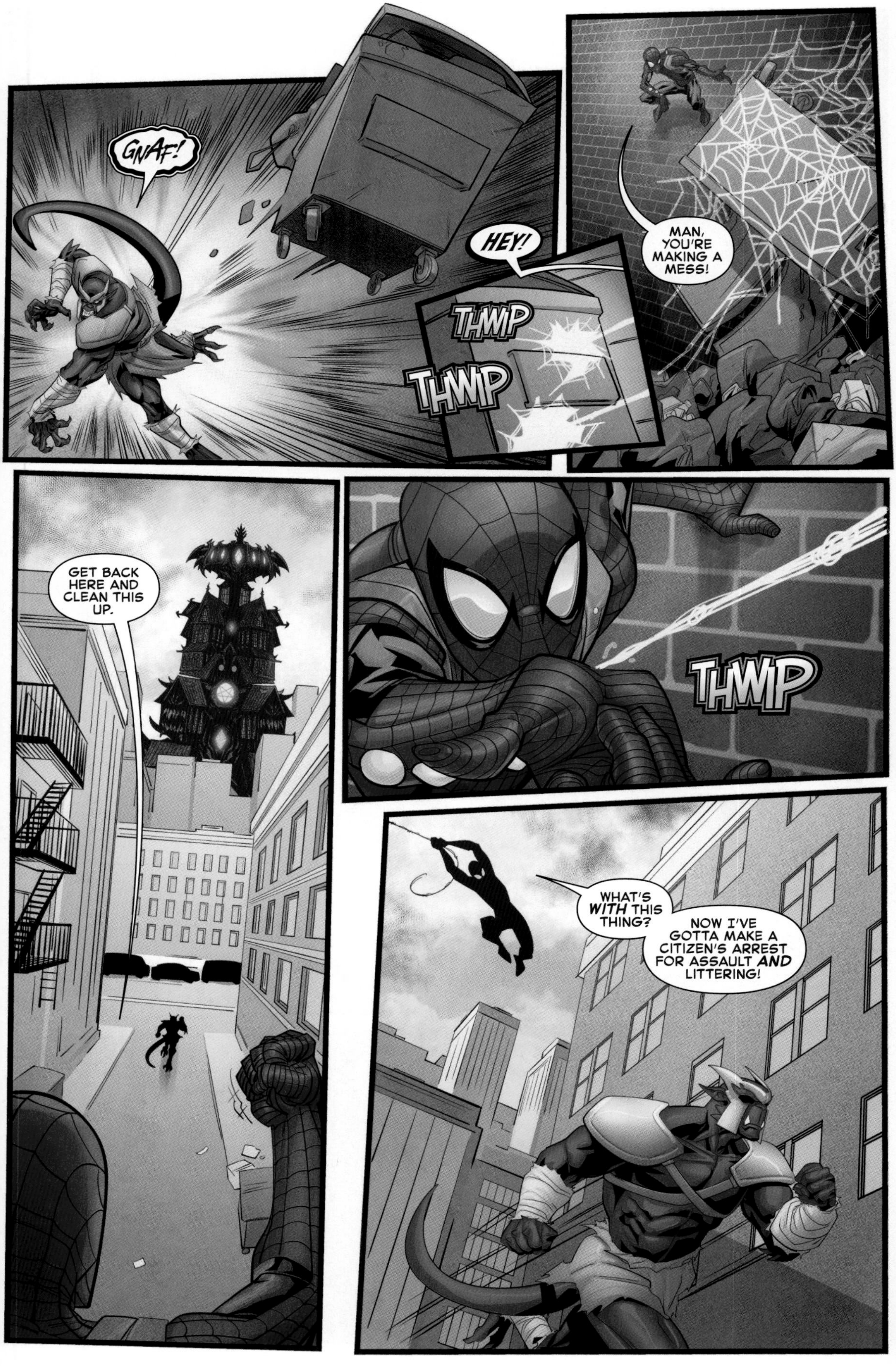
GNAF!
HEY!
THWIP
THWIP
MAN, YOU'RE MAKING A MESS!
GET BACK HERE AND CLEAN THIS UP.
THWIP
WHAT'S WITH THIS THING?
NOW I'VE GOTTA MAKE A CITIZEN'S ARREST FOR ASSAULT AND LITTERING!

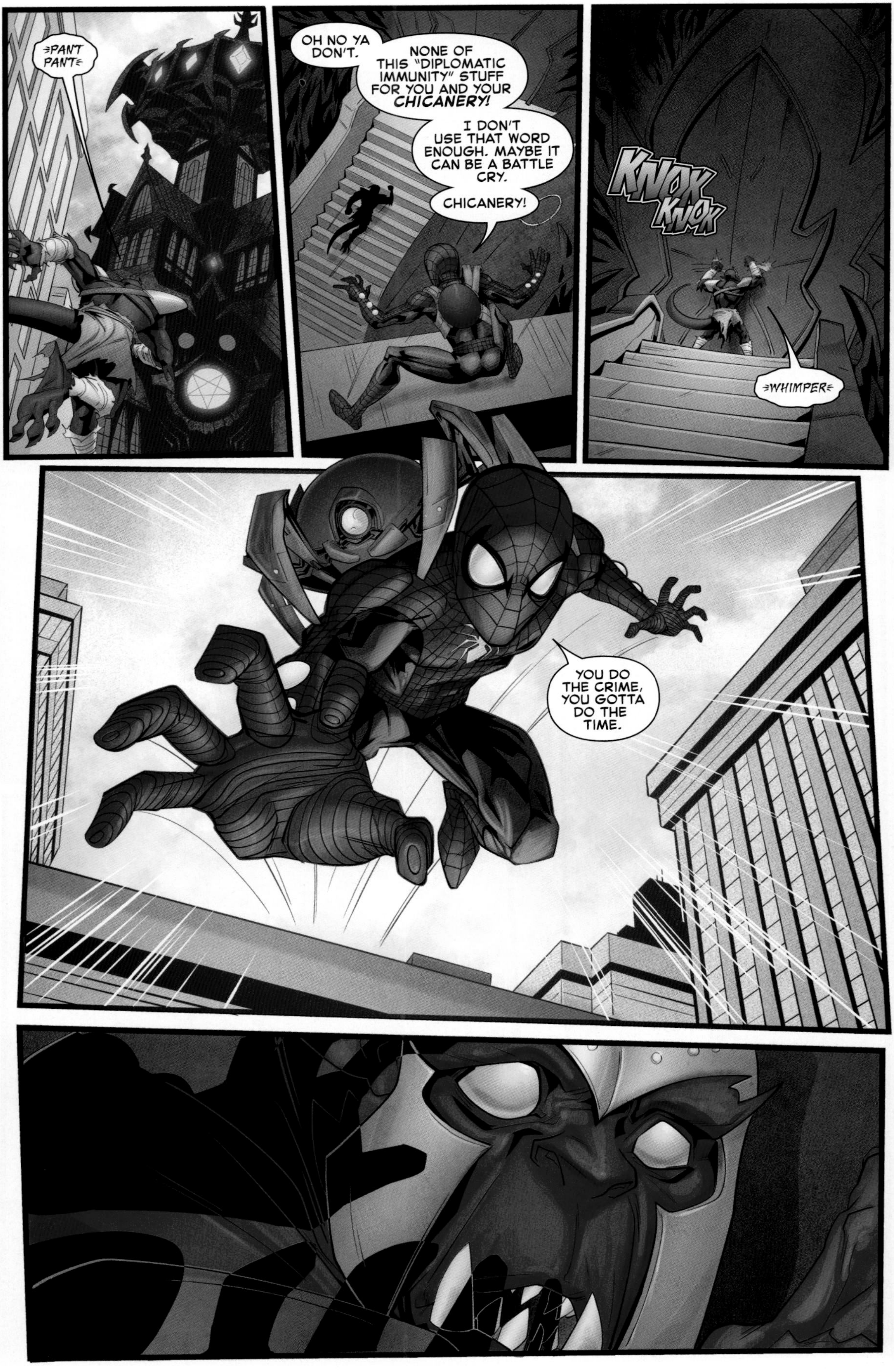
PANT PANT
OH NO YA DON'T.
NONE OF THIS "DIPLOMATIC IMMUNITY" STUFF FOR YOU AND YOUR CHICANERY!
I DON'T USE THAT WORD ENOUGH. MAYBE IT CAN BE A BATTLE CRY.
CHICANERY!
KNOK KNOK
WHIMPER
YOU DO THE CRIME, YOU GOTTA DO THE TIME.

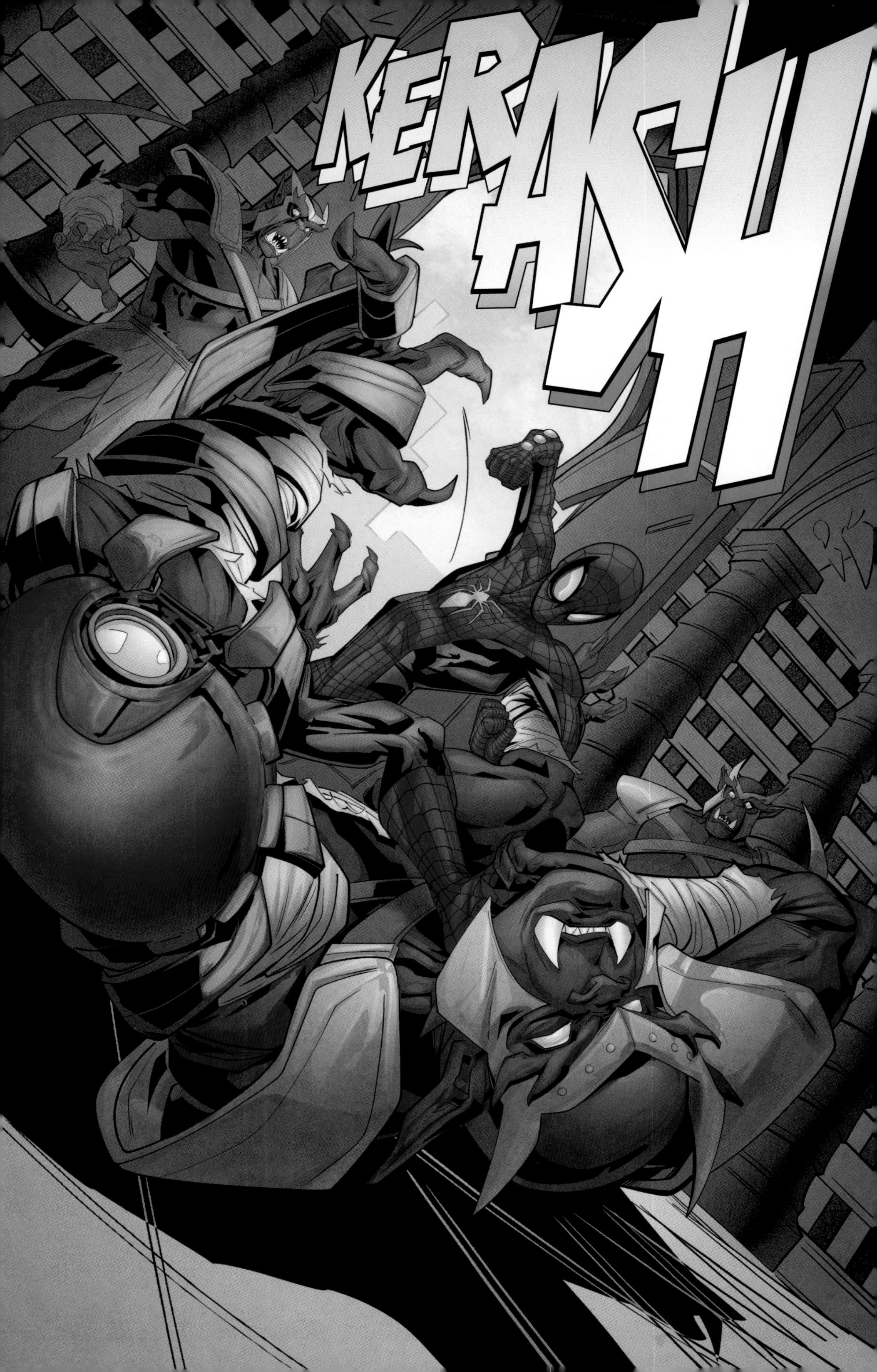
KERASH

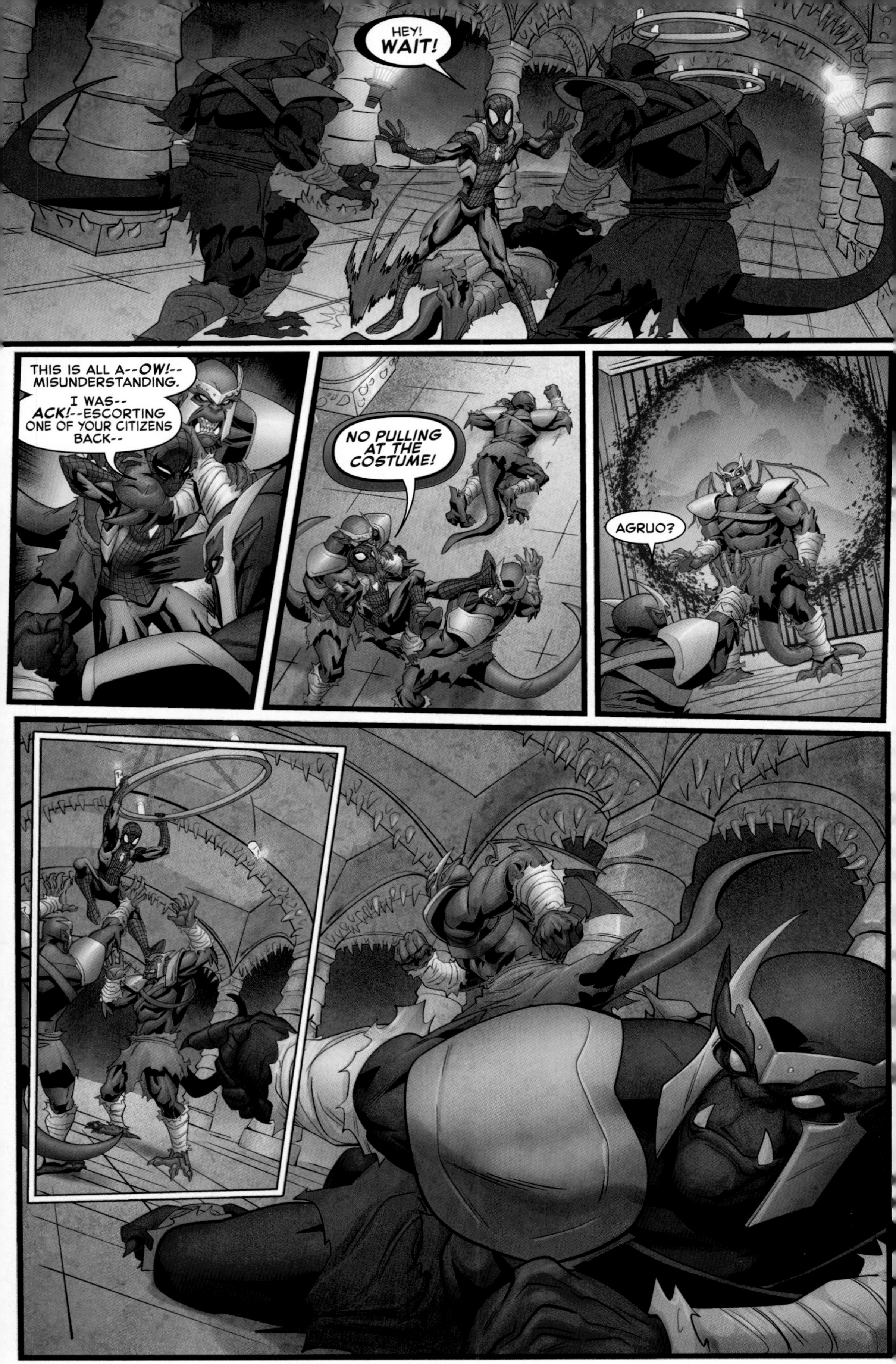
HEY! WAIT!
THIS IS ALL A--OW!--MISUNDERSTANDING.
I WAS--ACK!--ESCORTING ONE OF YOUR CITIZENS BACK--
NO PULLING AT THE COSTUME!
AGRUO?

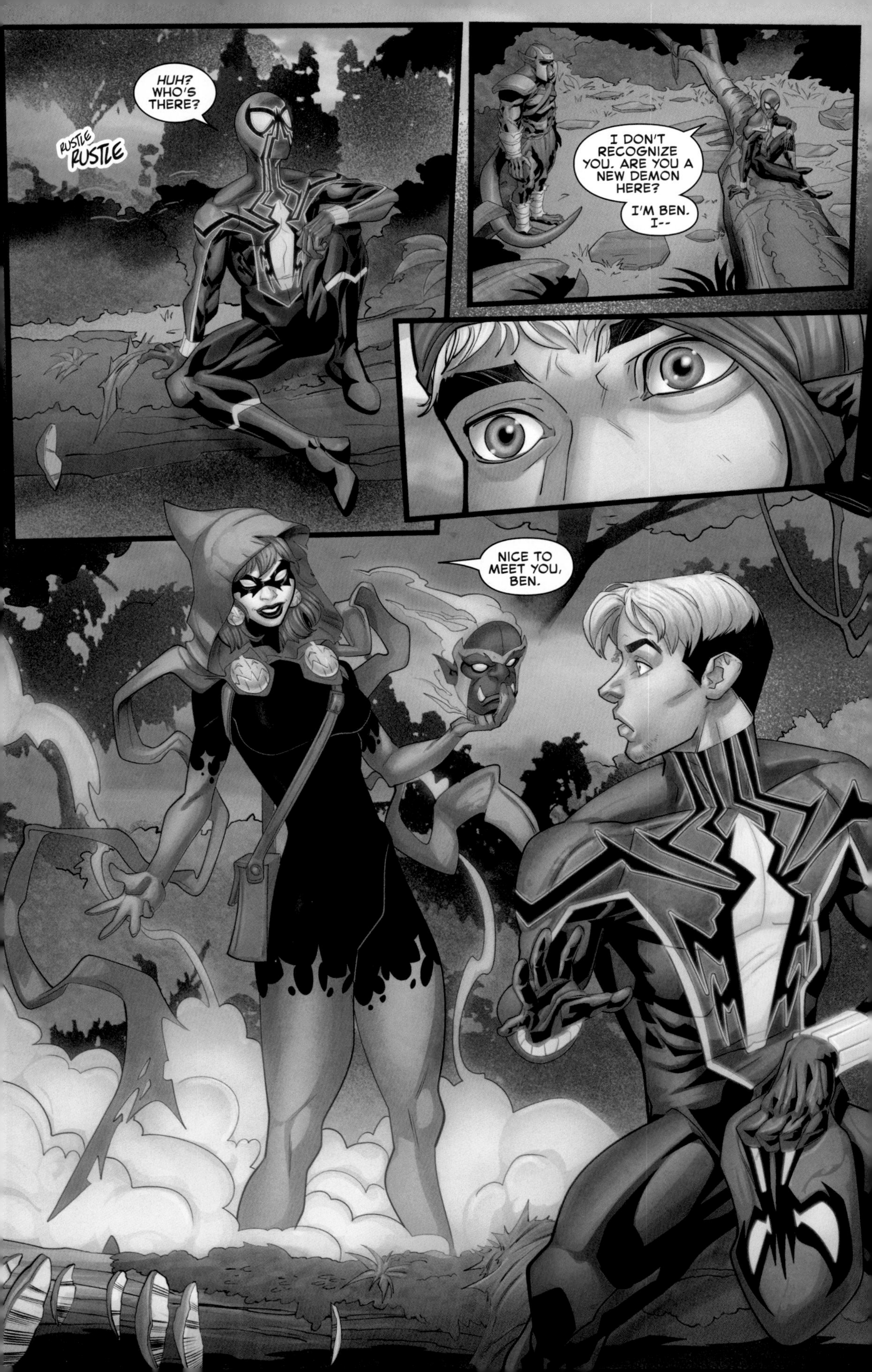
HUH? WHO'S THERE?
RUSTLE RUSTLE
I DON'T RECOGNIZE YOU. ARE YOU A NEW DEMON HERE?
I'M BEN. I--
NICE TO MEET YOU, BEN.

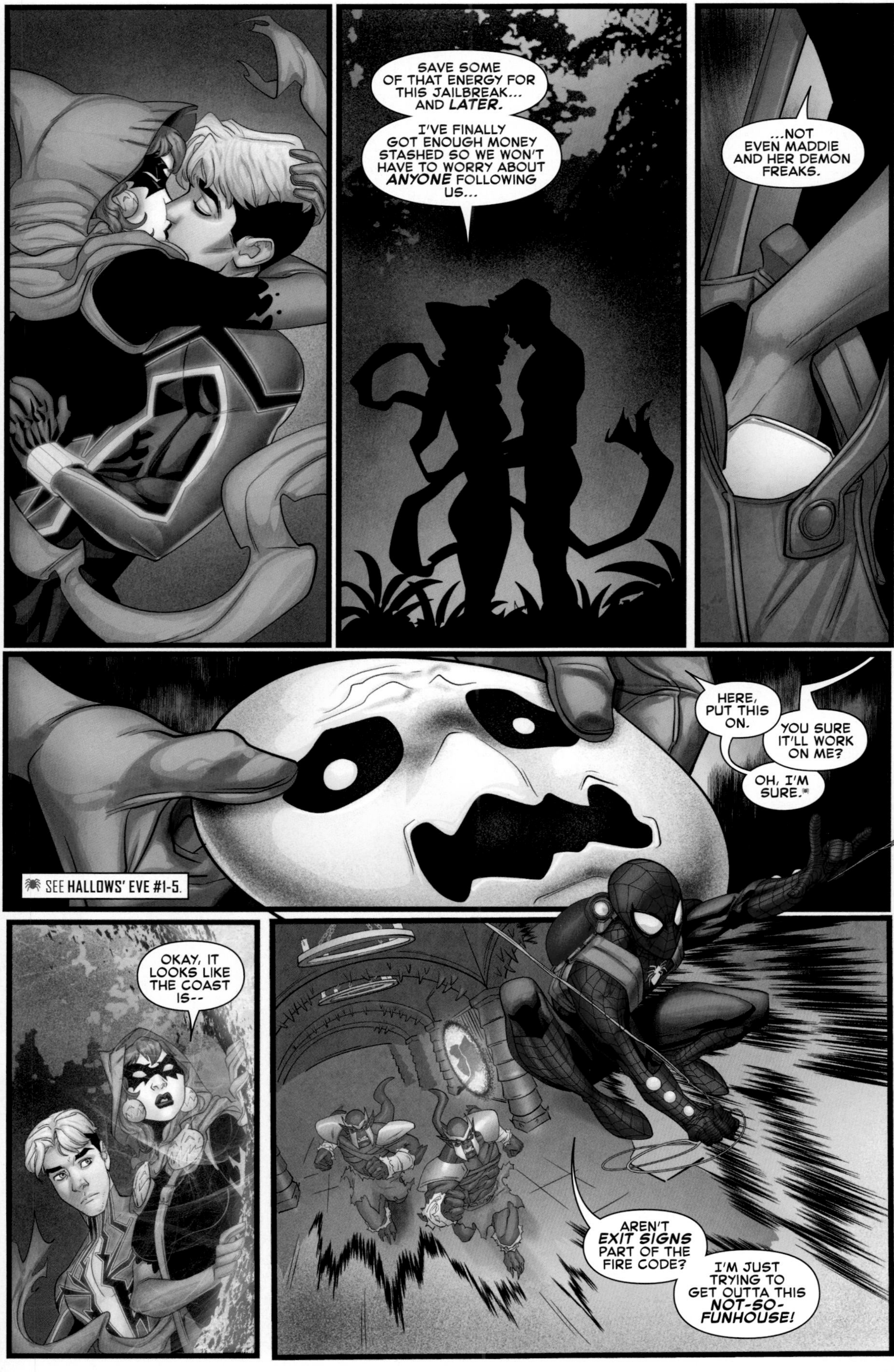
SAVE SOME OF THAT ENERGY FOR THIS JAILBREAK... AND LATER.
I'VE FINALLY GOT ENOUGH MONEY STASHED SO WE WON'T HAVE TO WORRY ABOUT ANYONE FOLLOWING US...
...NOT EVEN MADDIE AND HER DEMON FREAKS.
HERE, PUT THIS ON.
YOU SURE IT'LL WORK ON ME?
OH, I'M SURE.*
* SEE HALLOWS' EVE #1-5.
OKAY, IT LOOKS LIKE THE COAST IS--
AREN'T EXIT SIGNS PART OF THE FIRE CODE?
I'M JUST TRYING TO GET OUTTA THIS NOT-SO-FUNHOUSE!

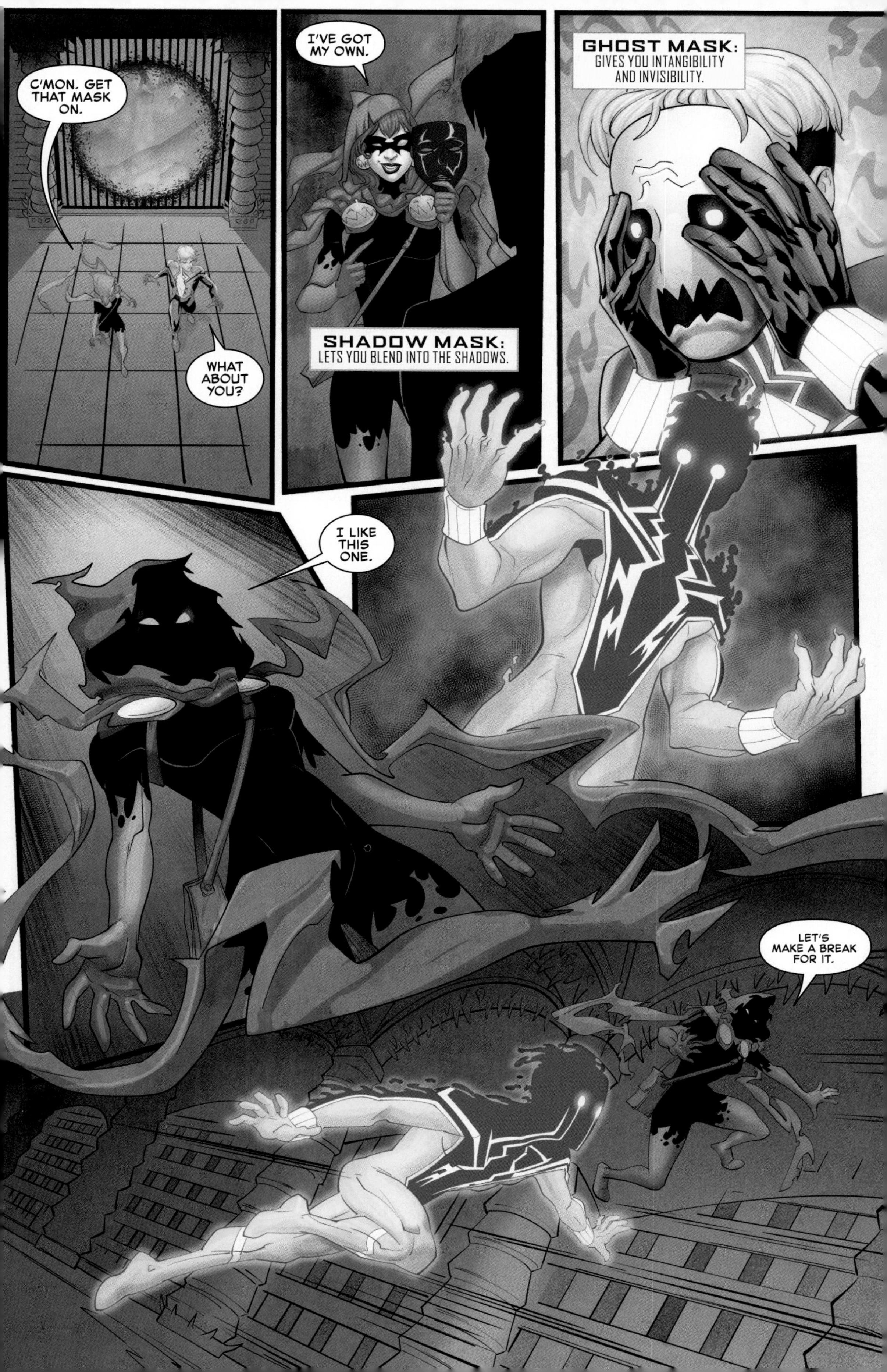
C'MON. GET THAT MASK ON.
WHAT ABOUT YOU?
I'VE GOT MY OWN.
SHADOW MASK:
LETS YOU BLEND INTO THE SHADOWS.
GHOST MASK:
GIVES YOU INTANGIBILITY AND INVISIBILITY.
I LIKE THIS ONE.
LET'S MAKE A BREAK FOR IT.

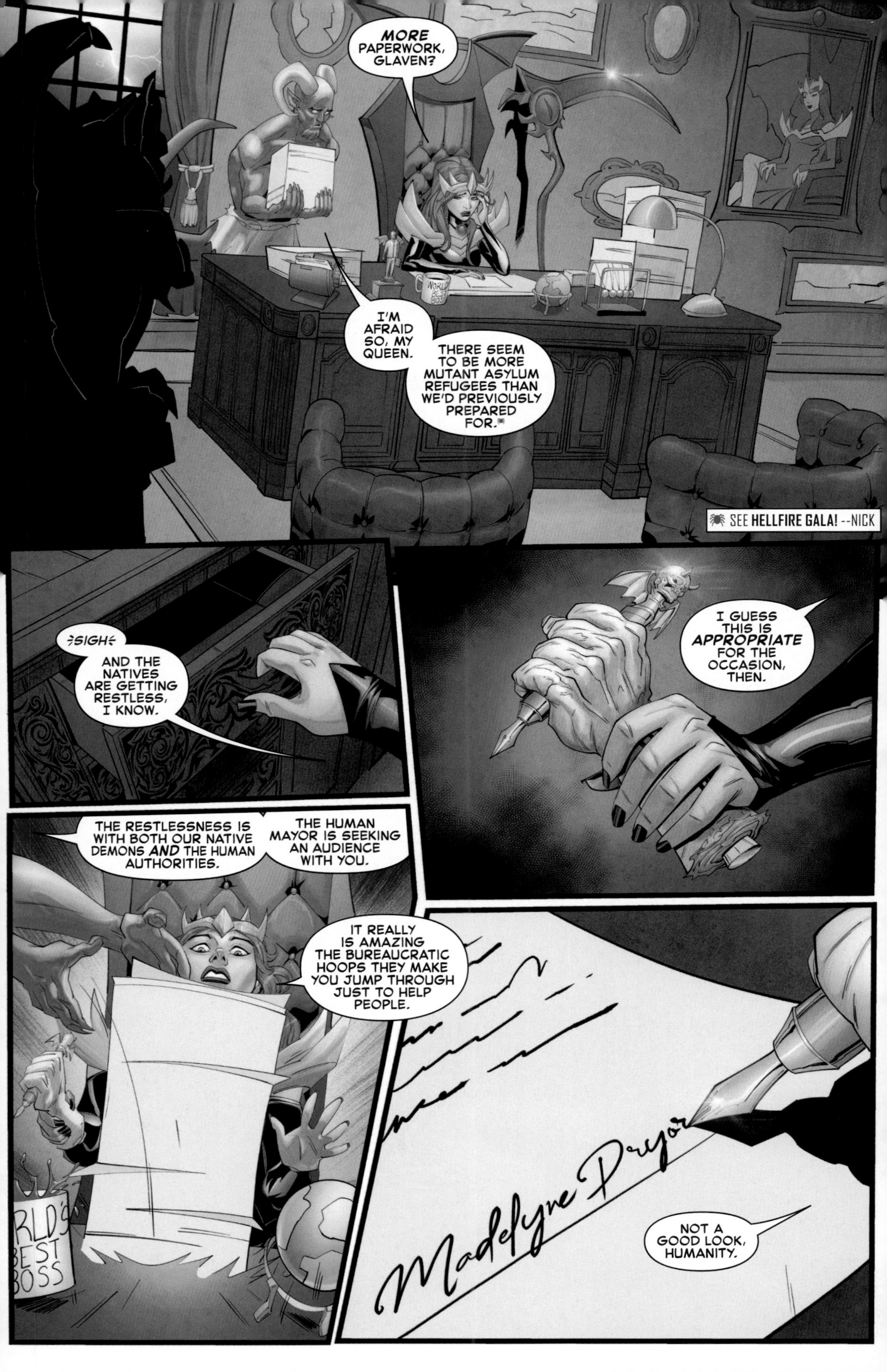
MORE PAPERWORK, GLAVEN?
I'M AFRAID SO, MY QUEEN.
THERE SEEM TO BE MORE MUTANT ASYLUM REFUGEES THAN WE'D PREVIOUSLY PREPARED FOR.*
WORLD'S BEST BOSS
* SEE HELLFIRE GALA! --NICK
SIGH
AND THE NATIVES ARE GETTING RESTLESS, I KNOW.
I GUESS THIS IS APPROPRIATE FOR THE OCCASION, THEN.
THE RESTLESSNESS IS WITH BOTH OUR NATIVE DEMONS AND THE HUMAN AUTHORITIES.
THE HUMAN MAYOR IS SEEKING AN AUDIENCE WITH YOU.
IT REALLY IS AMAZING THE BUREAUCRATIC HOOPS THEY MAKE YOU JUMP THROUGH JUST TO HELP PEOPLE.
RLD'S BEST BOSS
Madelyne Pryor
NOT A GOOD LOOK, HUMANITY.

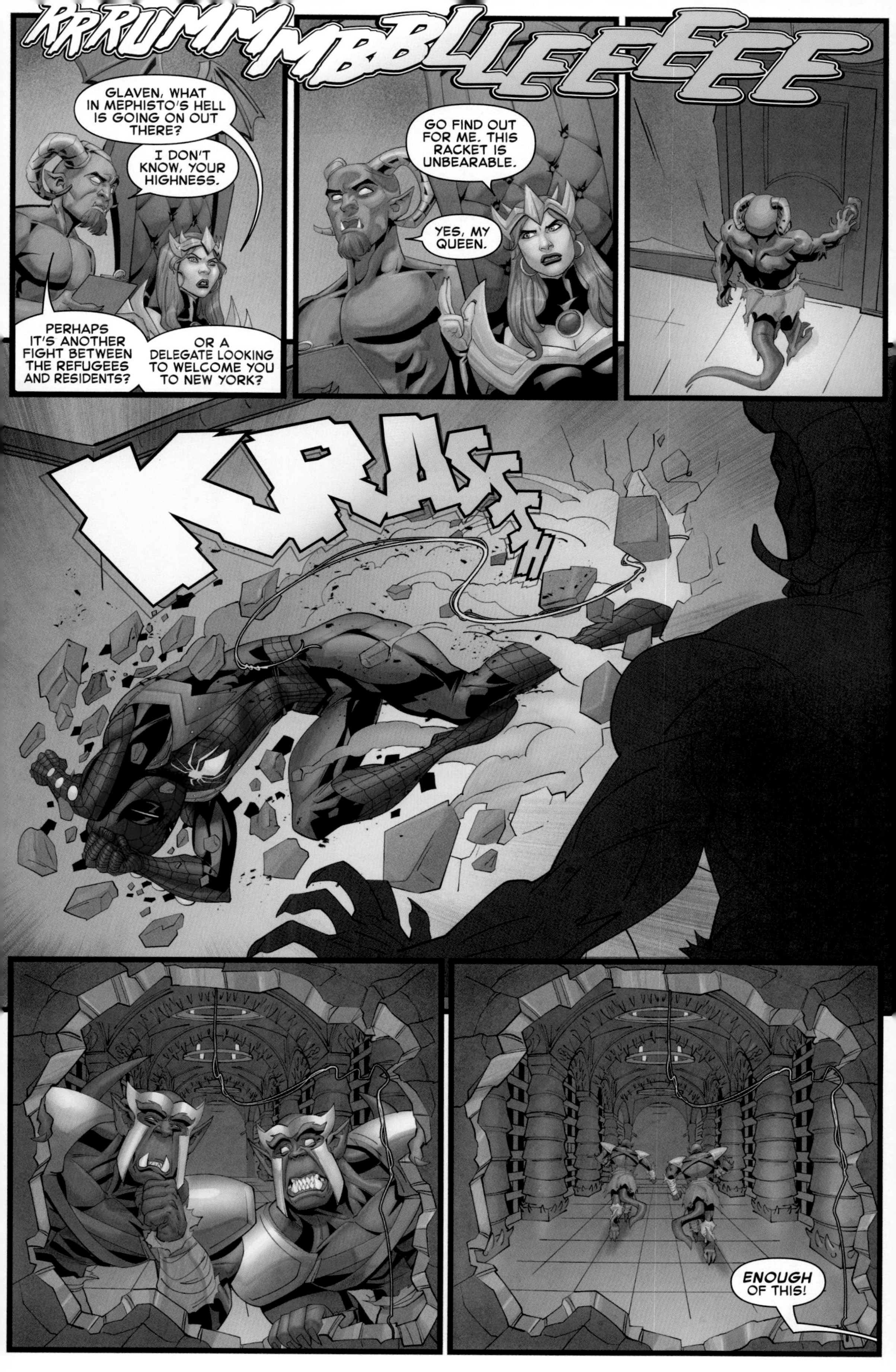

KRRRUMMMMBBLLEEEEEE
GLAVEN, WHAT IN MEPHISTO'S HELL IS GOING ON OUT THERE?
I DON'T KNOW, YOUR HIGHNESS.
PERHAPS IT'S ANOTHER FIGHT BETWEEN THE REFUGEES AND RESIDENTS?
OR A DELEGATE LOOKING TO WELCOME YOU TO NEW YORK?
GO FIND OUT FOR ME. THIS RACKET IS UNBEARABLE.
YES, MY QUEEN.
KRASSH
ENOUGH OF THIS!

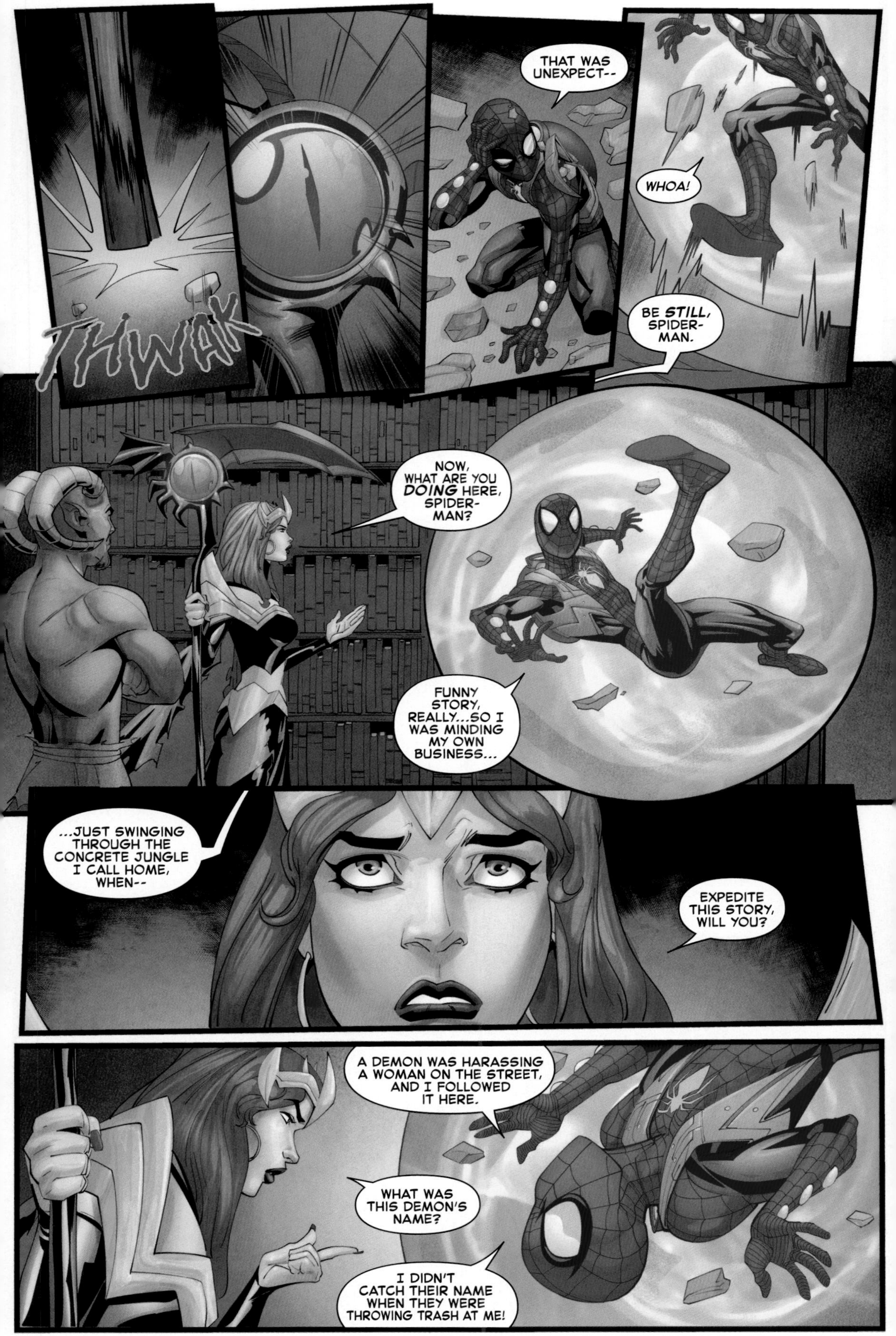
THWAK
THAT WAS UNEXPECT--
WHOA!
BE STILL, SPIDER-MAN.
NOW, WHAT ARE YOU DOING HERE, SPIDER-MAN?
FUNNY STORY, REALLY...SO I WAS MINDING MY OWN BUSINESS...
...JUST SWINGING THROUGH THE CONCRETE JUNGLE I CALL HOME, WHEN--
EXPEDITE THIS STORY, WILL YOU?
A DEMON WAS HARASSING A WOMAN ON THE STREET, AND I FOLLOWED IT HERE.
WHAT WAS THIS DEMON'S NAME?
I DIDN'T CATCH THEIR NAME WHEN THEY WERE THROWING TRASH AT ME!

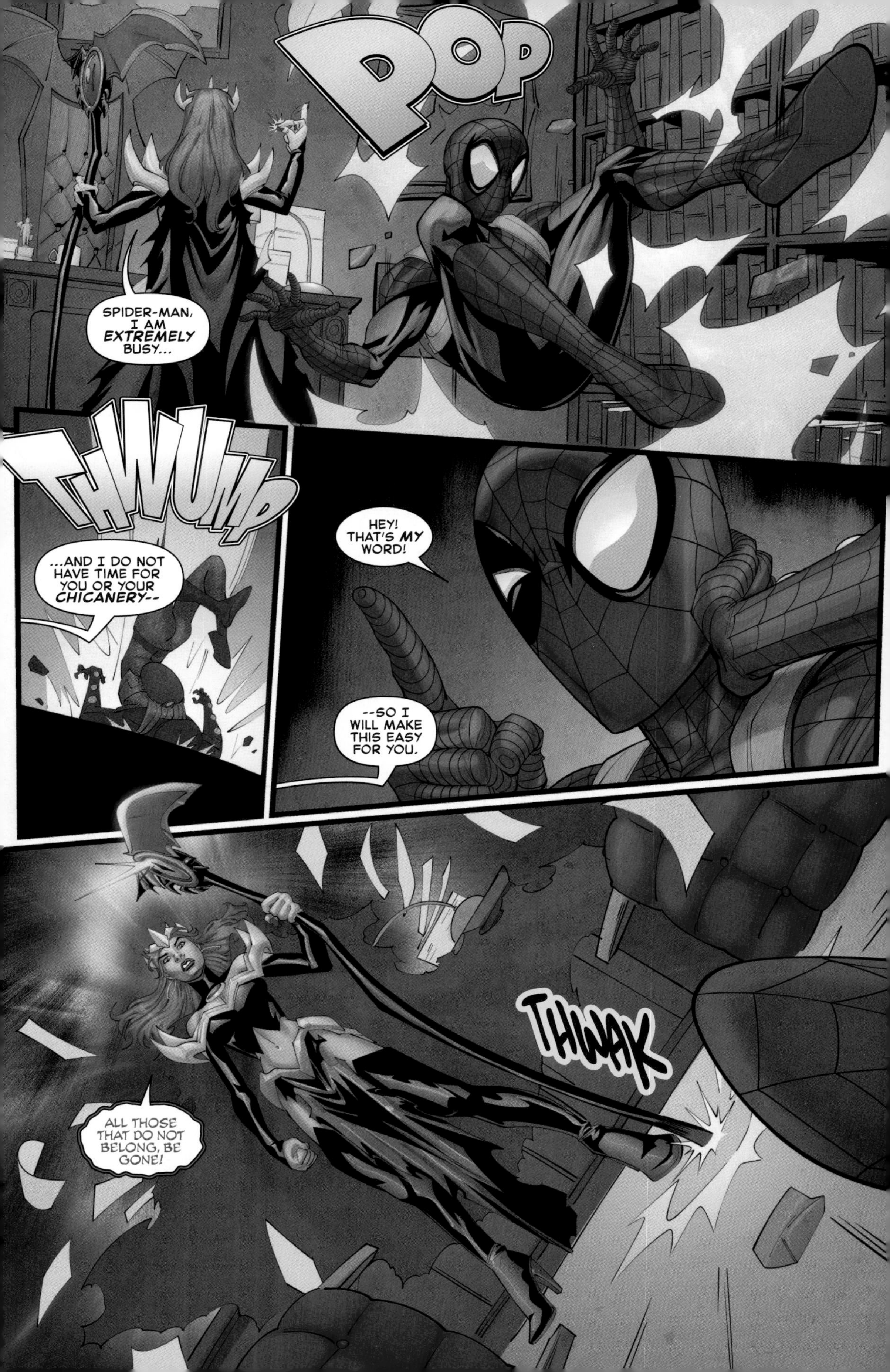
POP
SPIDER-MAN, I AM EXTREMELY BUSY...
THWUMP
...AND I DO NOT HAVE TIME FOR YOU OR YOUR CHICANERY--
HEY! THAT'S MY WORD!
--SO I WILL MAKE THIS EASY FOR YOU.
THWAK
ALL THOSE THAT DO NOT BELONG, BE GONE!

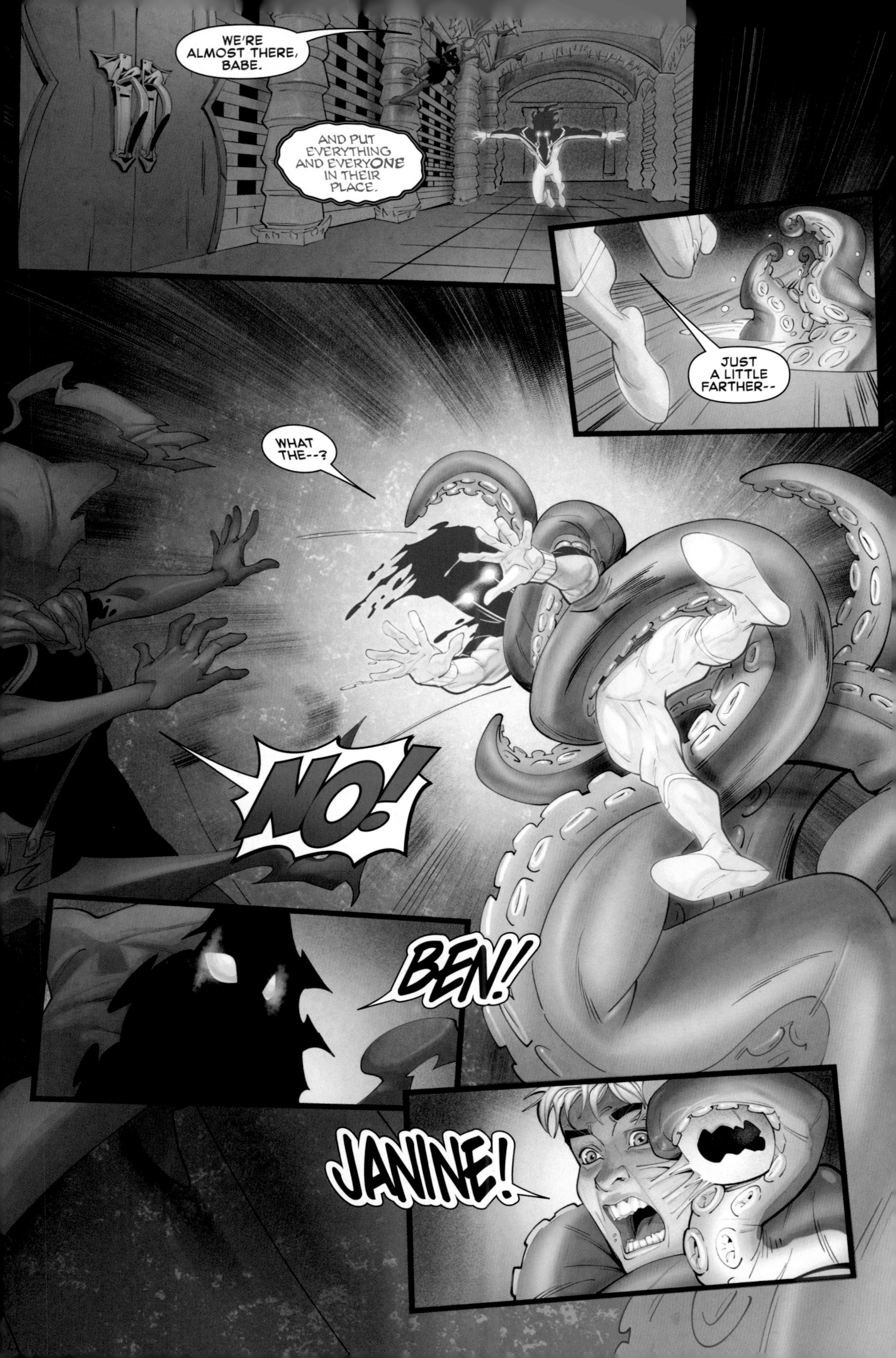
WE'RE ALMOST THERE, BABE.
AND PUT EVERYTHING AND EVERYONE IN THEIR PLACE.
JUST A LITTLE FARTHER--
WHAT THE--?
NO!
BEN!
JANINE!

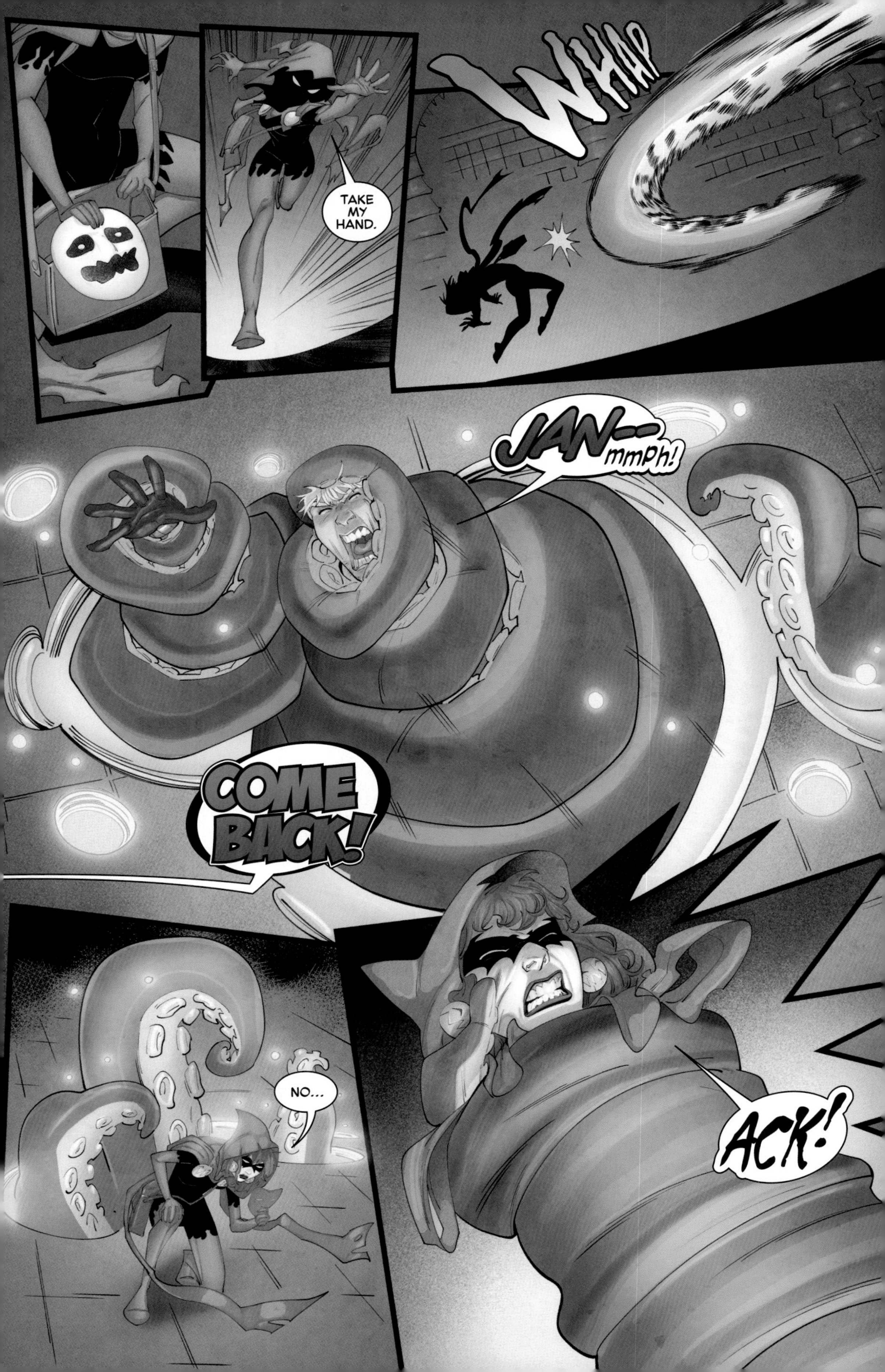

TAKE MY HAND.
WHAP
JAN--mmph!
COME BACK!
NO...
ACK!

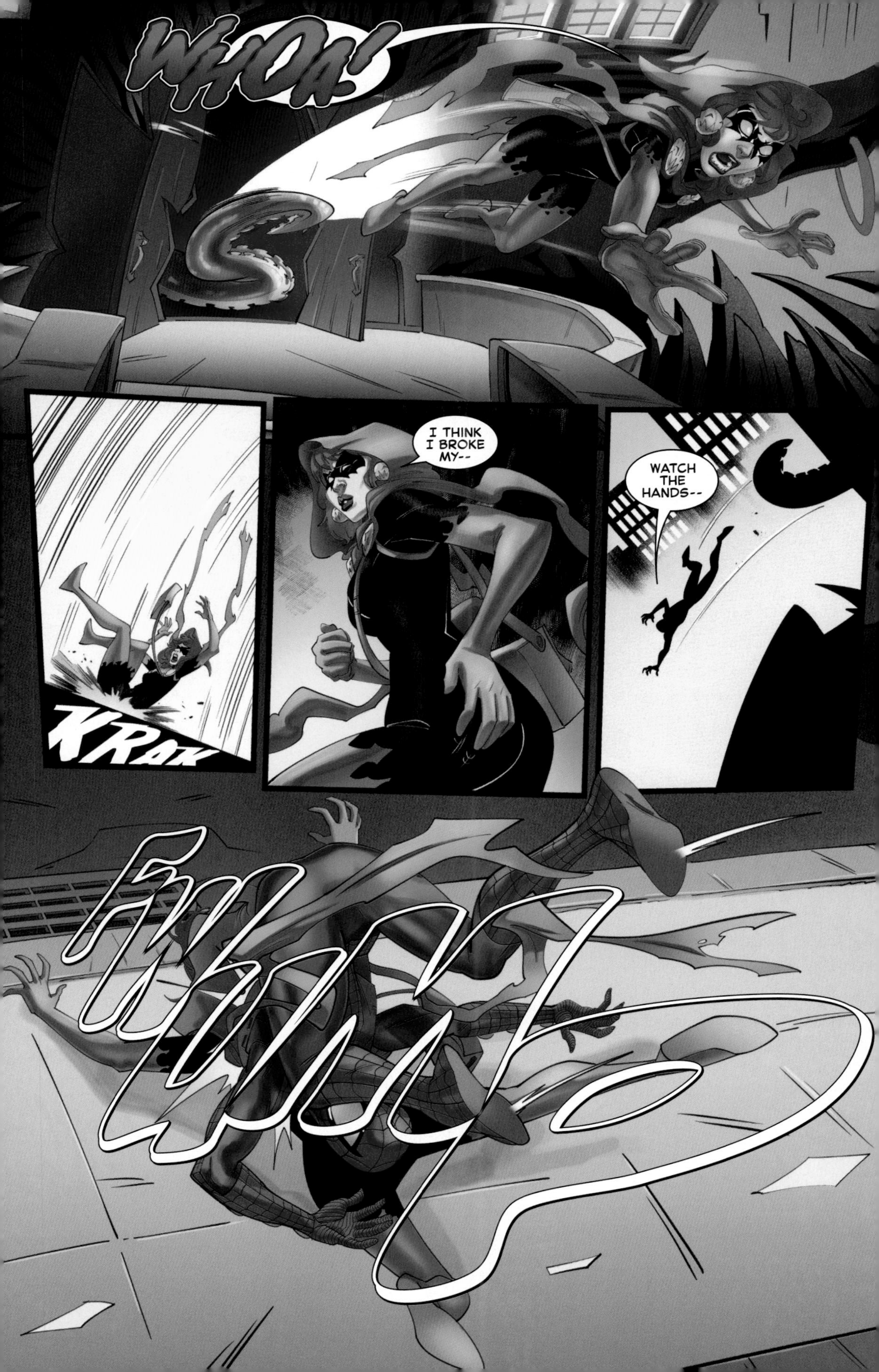
WHOA!
KRAK
I THINK I BROKE MY--
WATCH THE HANDS--

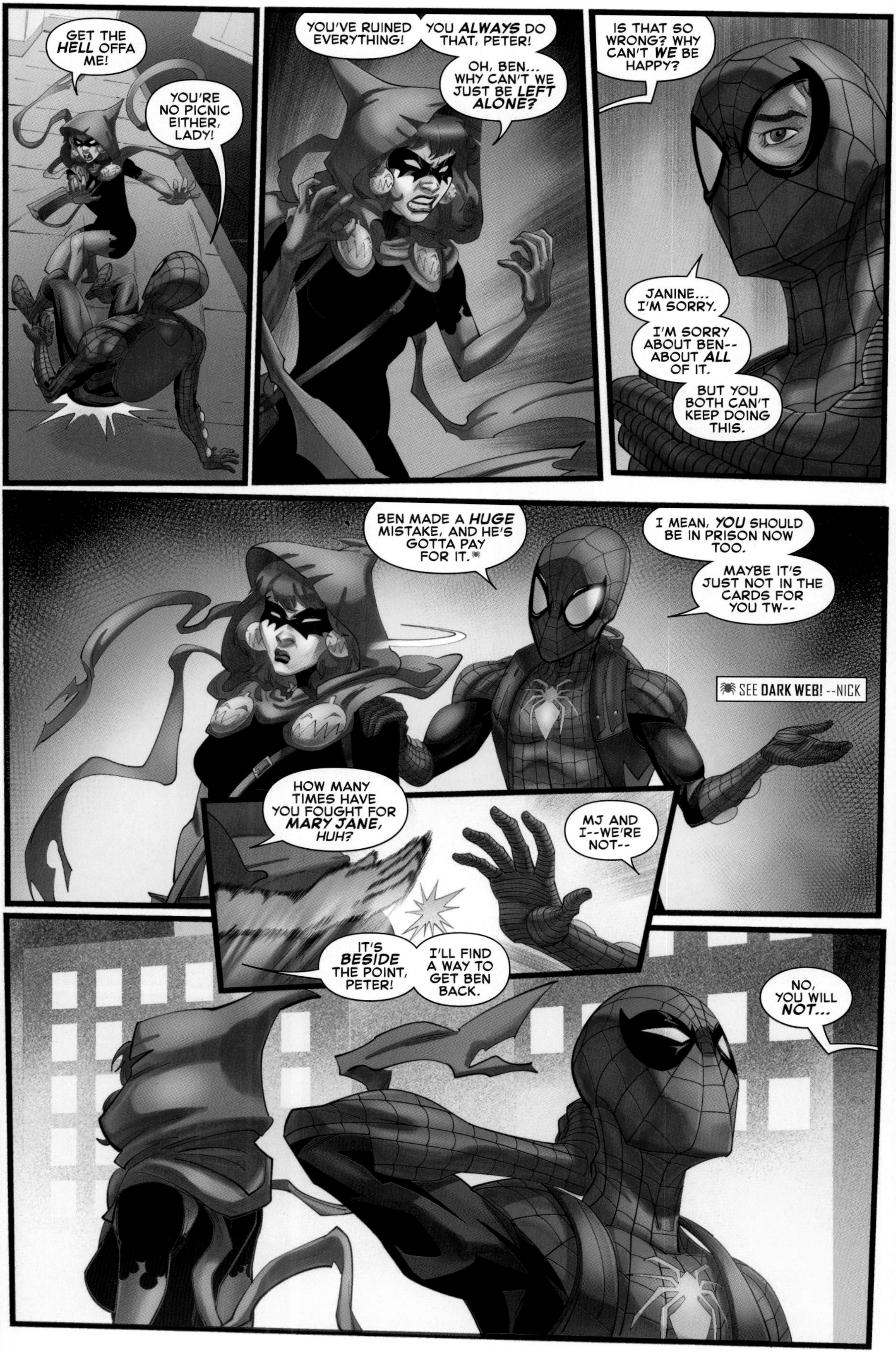
GET THE HELL OFFA ME!
YOU'RE NO PICNIC EITHER, LADY!
YOU'VE RUINED EVERYTHING!
YOU ALWAYS DO THAT, PETER!
OH, BEN... WHY CAN'T WE JUST BE LEFT ALONE?
IS THAT SO WRONG? WHY CAN'T WE BE HAPPY?
JANINE... I'M SORRY.
I'M SORRY ABOUT BEN-- ABOUT ALL OF IT.
BUT YOU BOTH CAN'T KEEP DOING THIS.
BEN MADE A HUGE MISTAKE, AND HE'S GOTTA PAY FOR IT.
I MEAN, YOU SHOULD BE IN PRISON NOW TOO.
MAYBE IT'S JUST NOT IN THE CARDS FOR YOU TW--
SEE DARK WEB! --NICK
HOW MANY TIMES HAVE YOU FOUGHT FOR MARY JANE, HUH?
MJ AND I--WE'RE NOT--
IT'S BESIDE THE POINT, PETER!
I'LL FIND A WAY TO GET BEN BACK.
NO, YOU WILL NOT...

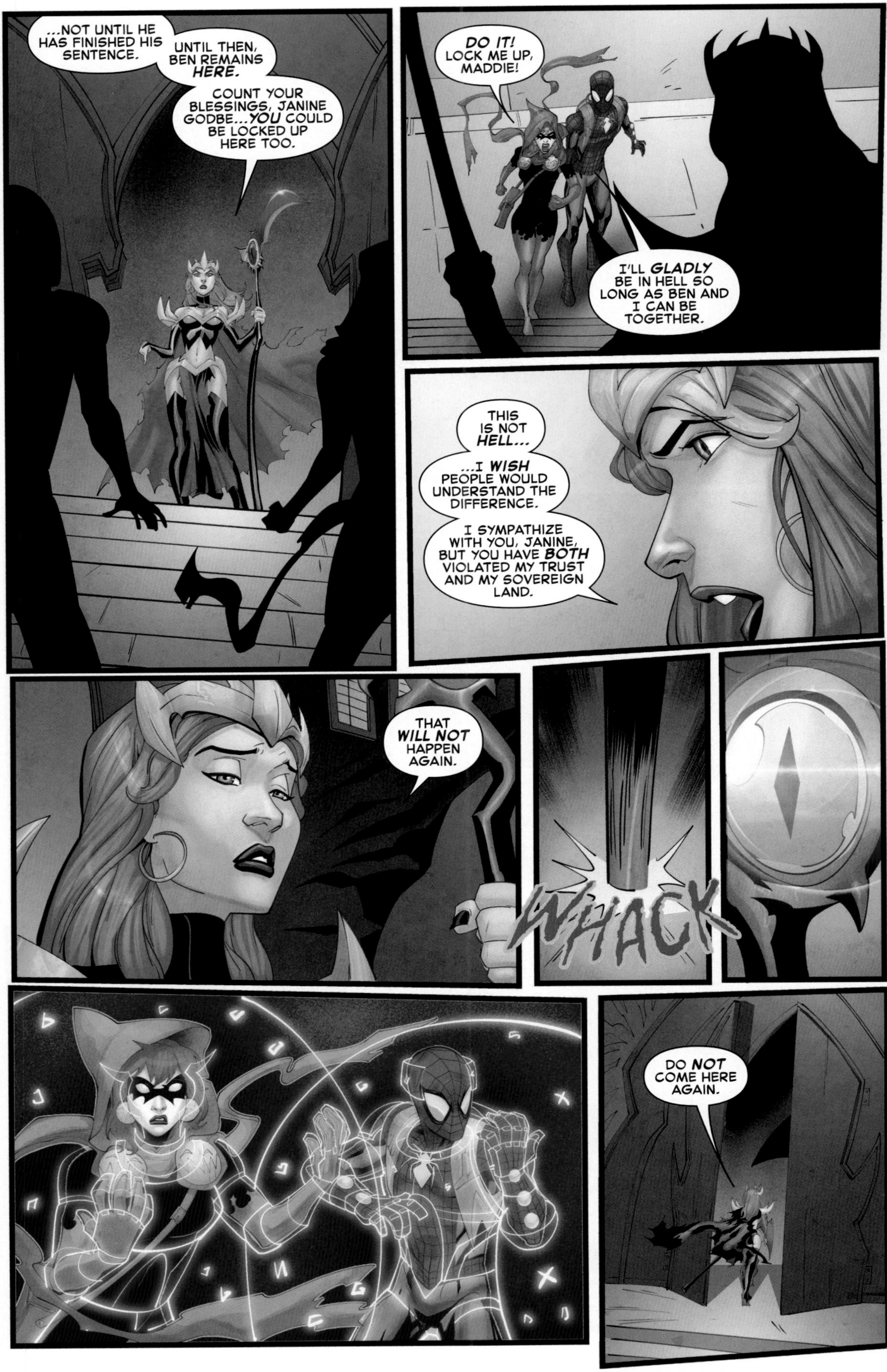
...NOT UNTIL HE HAS FINISHED HIS SENTENCE.
UNTIL THEN, BEN REMAINS HERE.
COUNT YOUR BLESSINGS, JANINE GODBE...YOU COULD BE LOCKED UP HERE TOO.
DO IT! LOCK ME UP, MADDIE!
I'LL GLADLY BE IN HELL SO LONG AS BEN AND I CAN BE TOGETHER.
THIS IS NOT HELL...
...I WISH PEOPLE WOULD UNDERSTAND THE DIFFERENCE.
I SYMPATHIZE WITH YOU, JANINE, BUT YOU HAVE BOTH VIOLATED MY TRUST AND MY SOVEREIGN LAND.
THAT WILL NOT HAPPEN AGAIN.
WHACK
DO NOT COME HERE AGAIN.

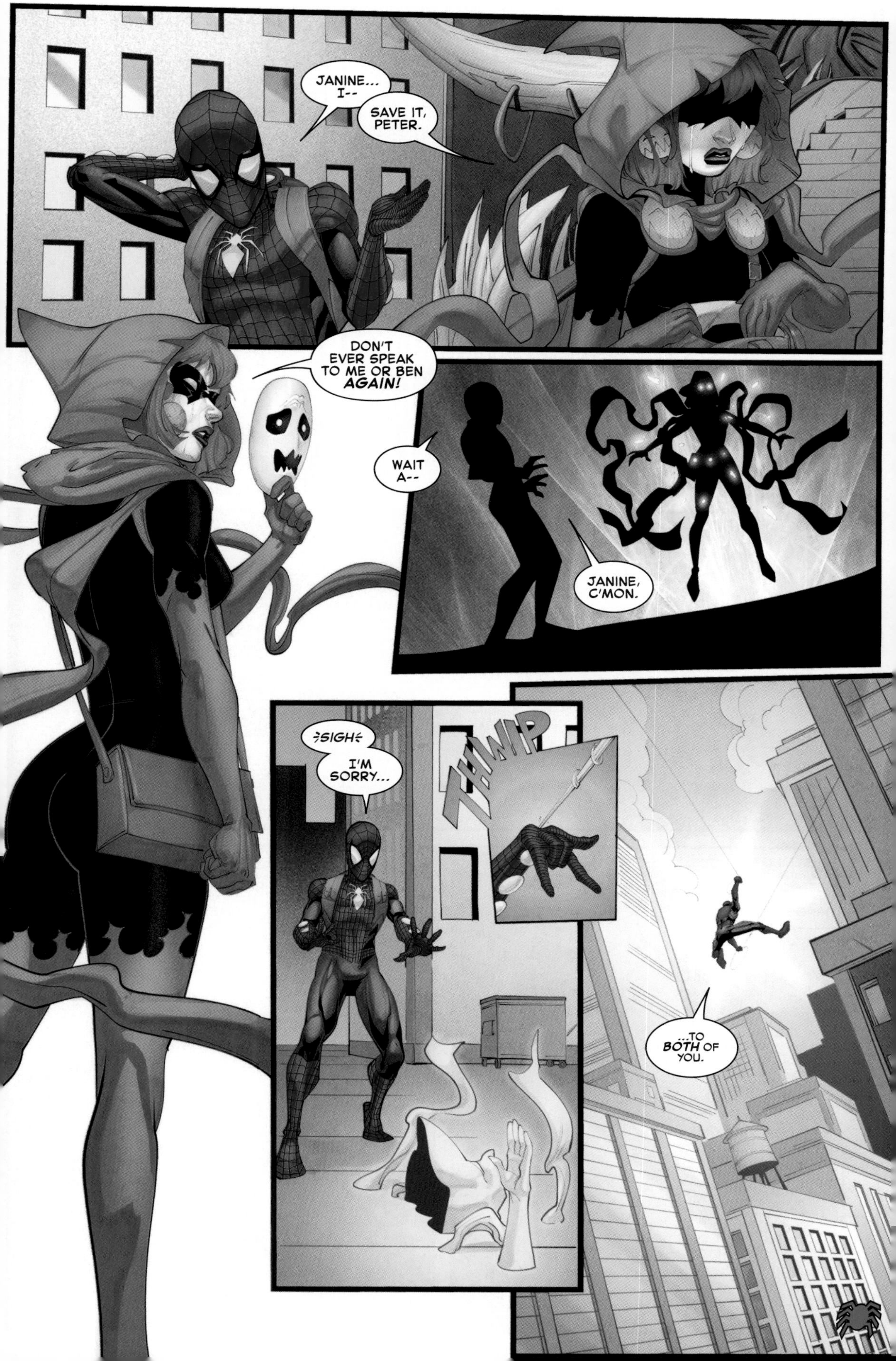
JANINE... I--
SAVE IT, PETER.
DON'T EVER SPEAK TO ME OR BEN AGAIN!
WAIT A--
JANINE, C'MON.
SIGH
I'M SORRY...
THWIP
...TO BOTH OF YOU.

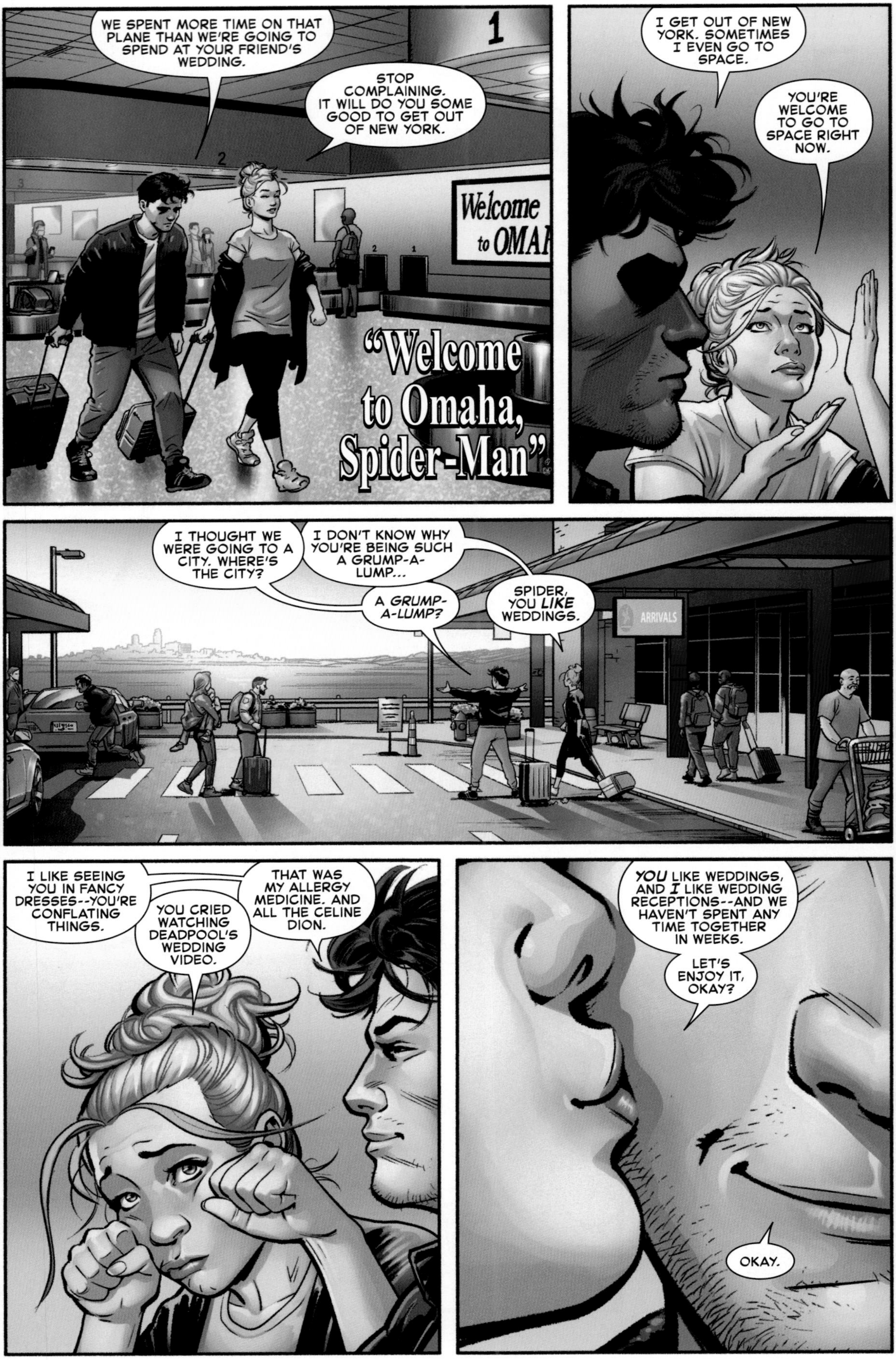
WE SPENT MORE TIME ON THAT PLANE THAN WE'RE GOING TO SPEND AT YOUR FRIEND'S WEDDING.
STOP COMPLAINING. IT WILL DO YOU SOME GOOD TO GET OUT OF NEW YORK.
Welcome
“Welcome to Omaha, Spider-Man”
I GET OUT OF NEW YORK. SOMETIMES I EVEN GO TO SPACE.
YOU'RE WELCOME TO GO TO SPACE RIGHT NOW.
I THOUGHT WE WERE GOING TO A CITY. WHERE'S THE CITY?
I DON'T KNOW WHY YOU'RE BEING SUCH A GRUMP-A-LUMP...
A *GRUMP-A-LUMP?*
SPIDER, YOU ***LIKE*** WEDDINGS.
ARRIVALS
I LIKE SEEING YOU IN FANCY DRESSES--YOU'RE CONFLATING THINGS.
YOU CRIED WATCHING DEADPOOL'S WEDDING VIDEO.
THAT WAS MY ALLERGY MEDICINE. AND ALL THE CELINE DION.
YOU LIKE WEDDINGS, AND ***I*** LIKE WEDDING RECEPTIONS--AND WE HAVEN'T SPENT ANY TIME TOGETHER IN WEEKS.
LET'S ENJOY IT, OKAY?
OKAY.

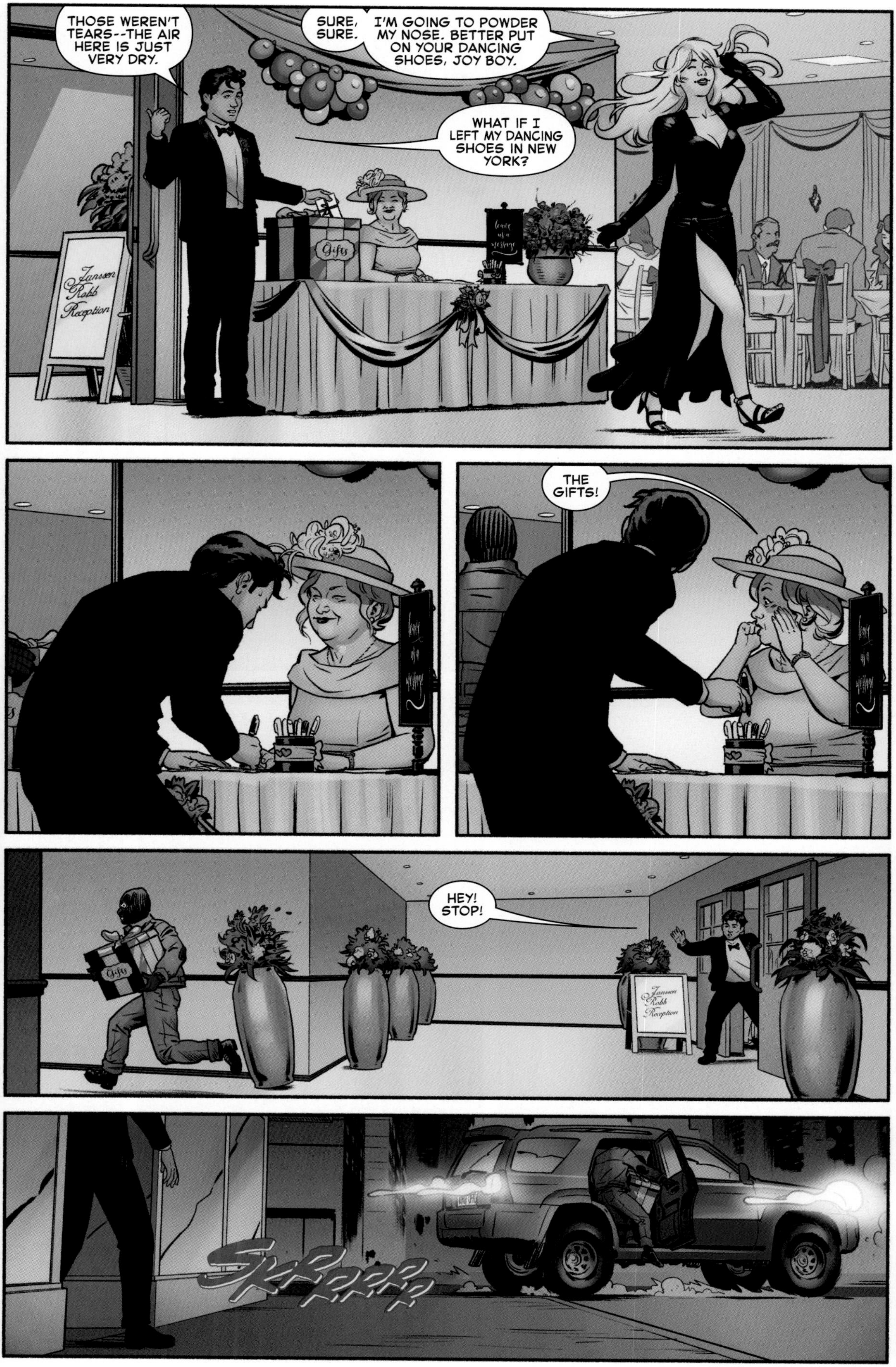
THOSE WEREN'T TEARS--THE AIR HERE IS JUST VERY DRY.
SURE, SURE.
I'M GOING TO POWDER MY NOSE. BETTER PUT ON YOUR DANCING SHOES, JOY BOY.
WHAT IF I LEFT MY DANCING SHOES IN NEW YORK?
Jansen Robb Reception
Gifts
THE GIFTS!
HEY! STOP!
Gifts
Jansen Robb Reception
SKRRRRR

JUST ONCE, I'D LIKE TO BRING THIS ALONG AND *NOT* NEED IT.

THWIP

THWIP

HOW AM I ALREADY IN THE SUBURBS?

UNFORTUNATELY FOR THOSE PUNKS, "FRIENDLY NEIGHBORHOOD SPIDER-MAN" EXTENDS TO ALL NEIGHBORHOODS.

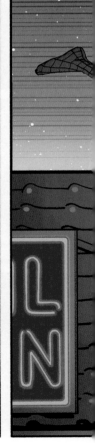

WHO STEALS FROM A *WEDDING?*

Woodme

SOMEONE WHO ISN'T QUITE SLIMY ENOUGH TO STEAL FROM A *FUNERAL?*

THWIP

YOU CAN RUN, AND YOU CAN PROBABLY HIDE--BUT I'LL GET THERE *EVENTUALLY.*

Offic
DECO

STY
RGERS

GREAT. A FREEWAY.

THMP

I WOULDN'T MIND A LITTLE GRIDLOCK JUST NOW, OMAHA...

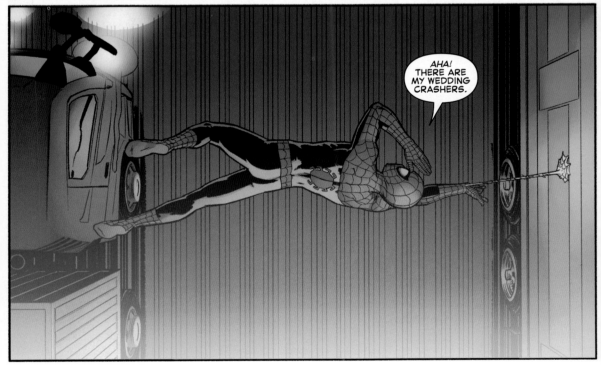

AHA! THERE ARE MY WEDDING CRASHERS.

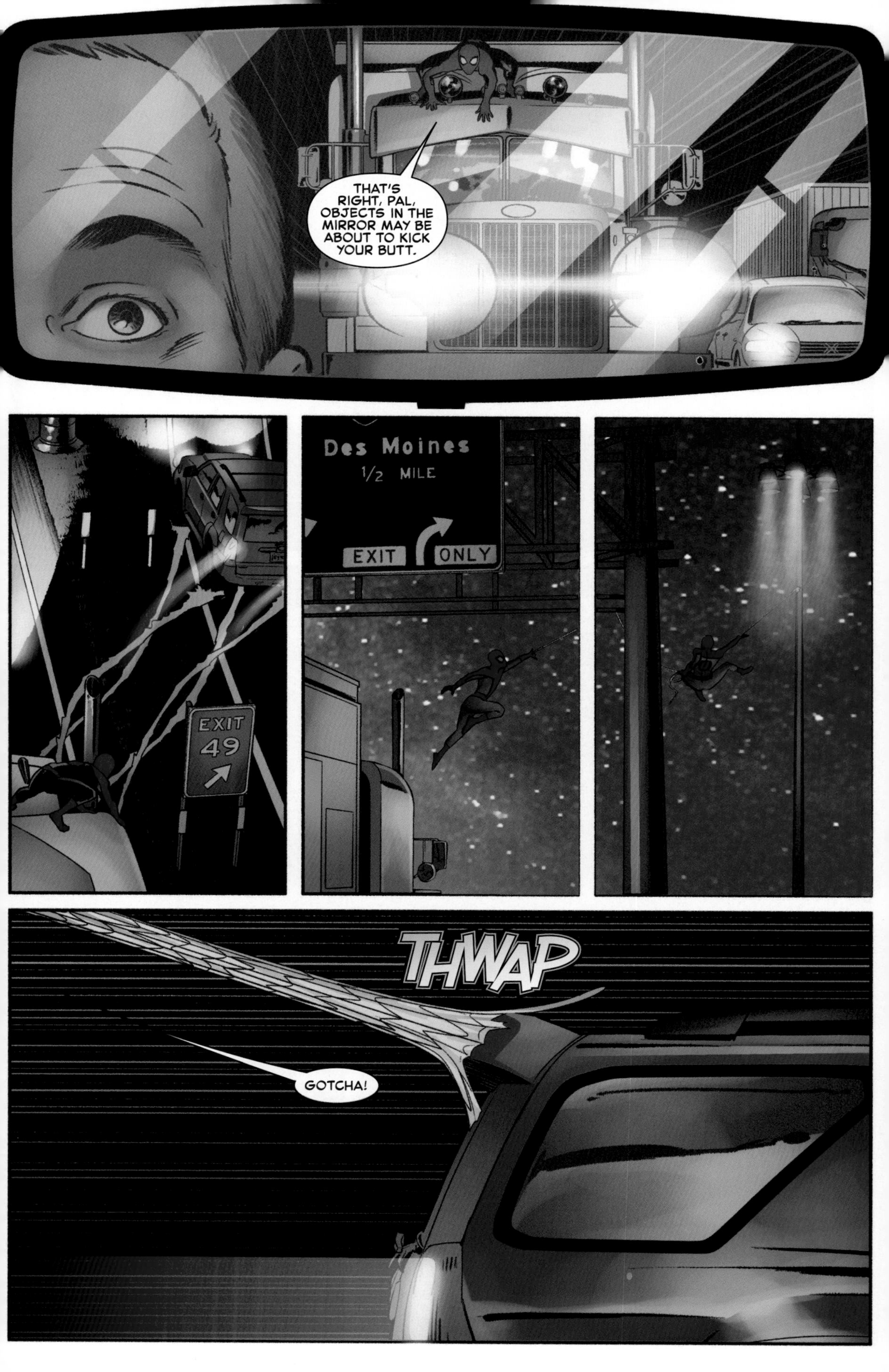
THAT'S RIGHT, PAL, OBJECTS IN THE MIRROR MAY BE ABOUT TO KICK YOUR BUTT.
EXIT 49
Des Moines
1/2 MILE
EXIT ONLY
THWAP
GOTCHA!

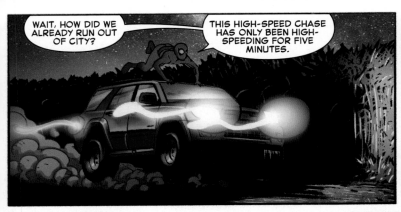

WAIT, HOW DID WE ALREADY RUN OUT OF CITY?

THIS HIGH-SPEED CHASE HAS ONLY BEEN HIGH-SPEEDING FOR FIVE MINUTES.

WHOA, NELLY!

HERE! TAKE IT, YOU WEIRDO! THIS ISN'T WORTH A DOZEN TARGET GIFT CARDS.

THAT ISN'T THE SAME GIFT BOX...

A FEW MINUTES LATER, LICKETY-SPLIT...

WEDDING DISASTER AVERTED. THAT'S ANOTHER WIN FOR SPIDER-MAN--

WHO?

--AND ANOTHER LOSS FOR LOSERS.

MAKE THAT ONE WEDDING DISASTER AVERTED.

TAXI?

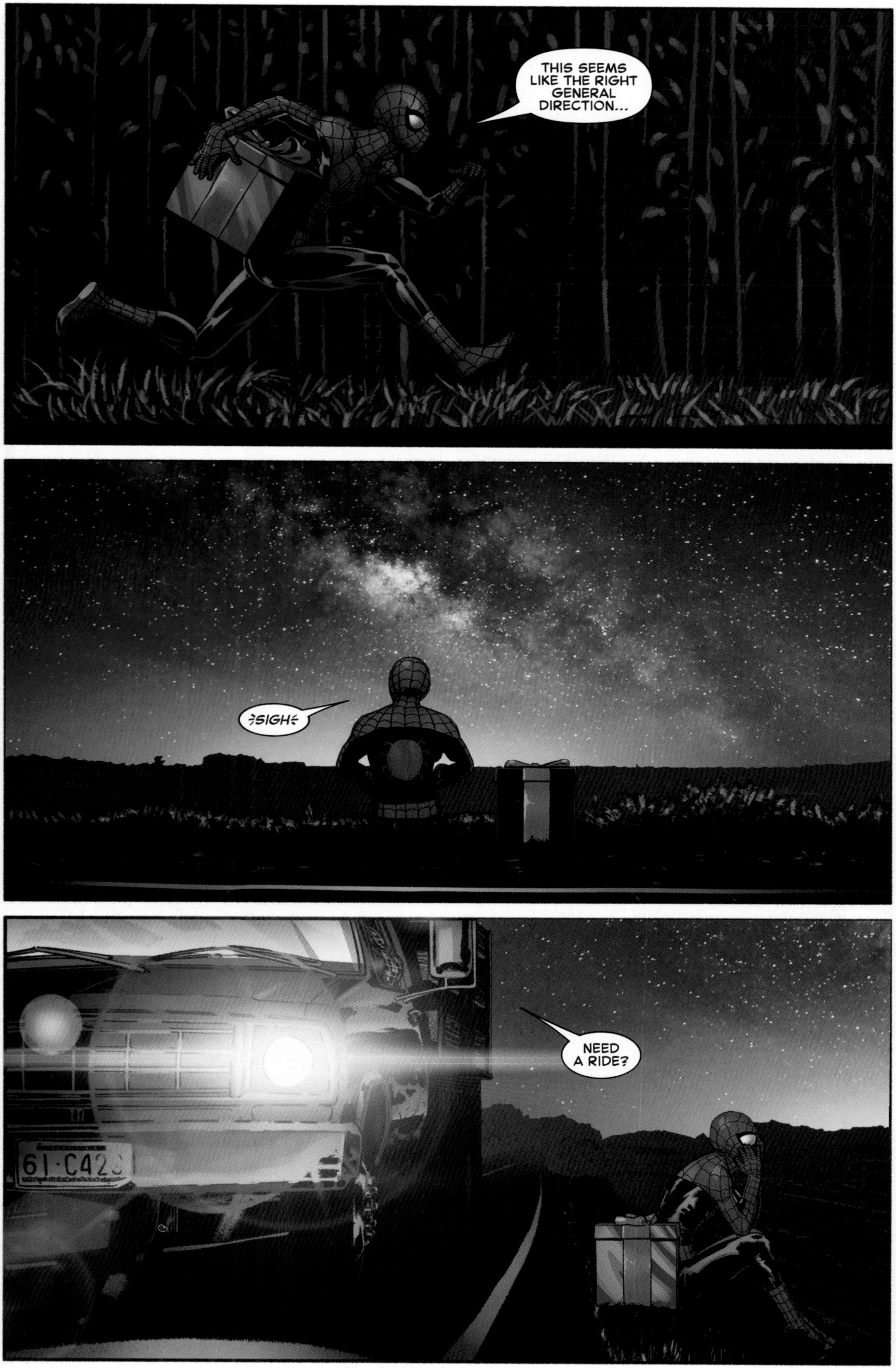
THIS SEEMS LIKE THE RIGHT GENERAL DIRECTION...
SIGH
NEED A RIDE?

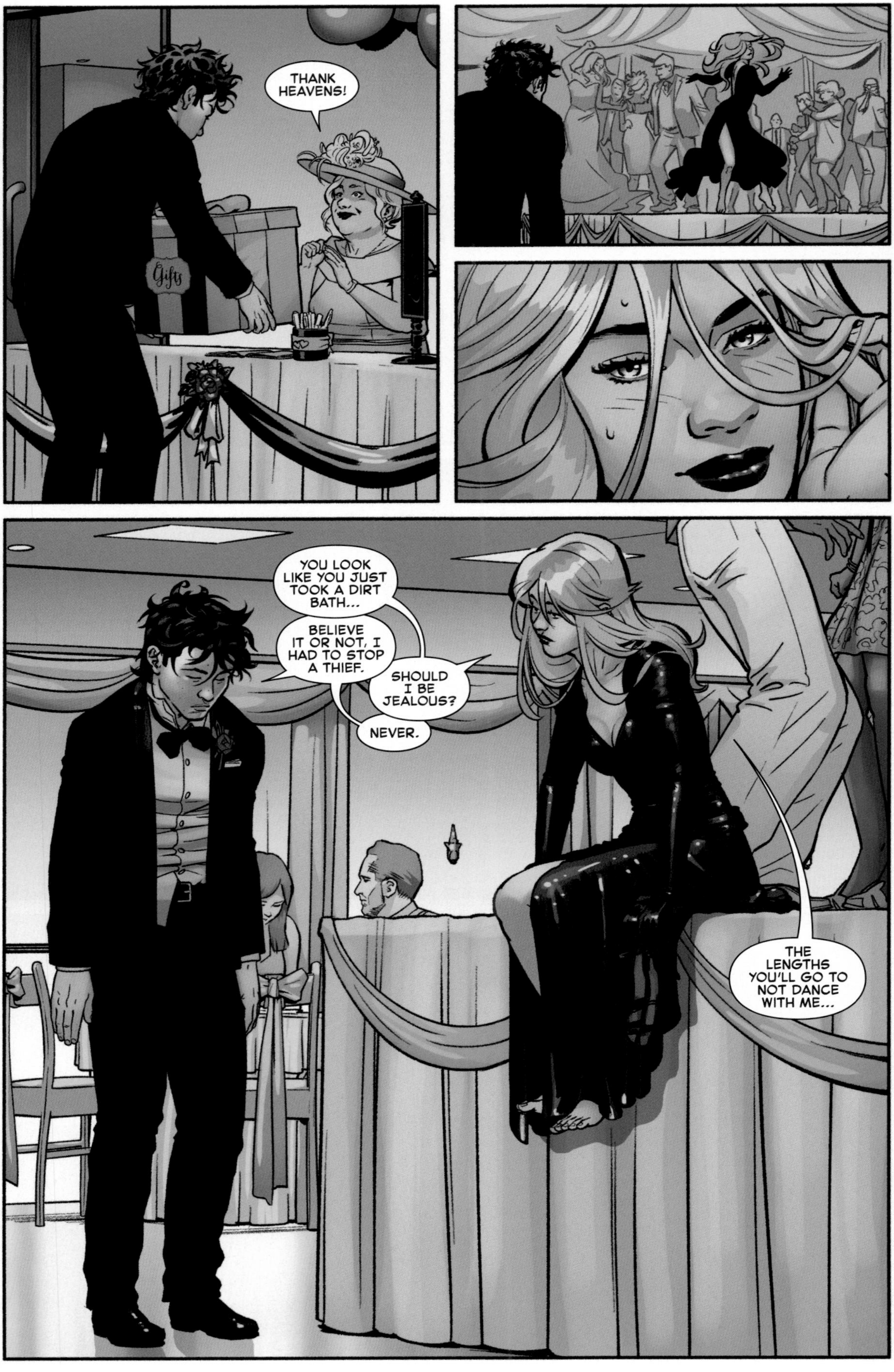
THANK HEAVENS!
Gifts
YOU LOOK LIKE YOU JUST TOOK A DIRT BATH...
BELIEVE IT OR NOT, I HAD TO STOP A THIEF.
SHOULD I BE JEALOUS?
NEVER.
THE LENGTHS YOU'LL GO TO NOT DANCE WITH ME...

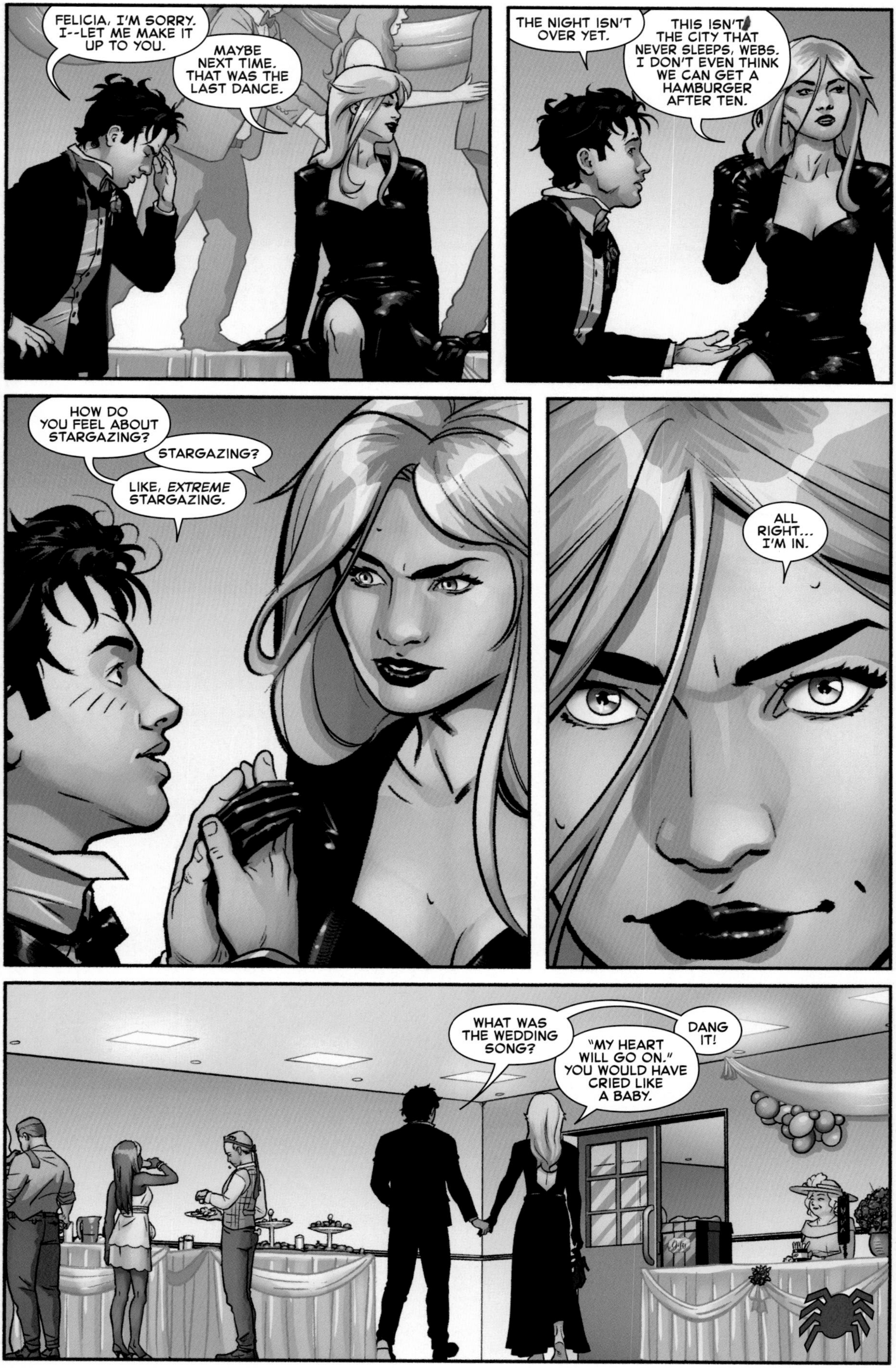
FELICIA, I'M SORRY. I--LET ME MAKE IT UP TO YOU.
MAYBE NEXT TIME. THAT WAS THE LAST DANCE.
THE NIGHT ISN'T OVER YET.
THIS ISN'T THE CITY THAT NEVER SLEEPS, WEBS. I DON'T EVEN THINK WE CAN GET A HAMBURGER AFTER TEN.
HOW DO YOU FEEL ABOUT STARGAZING?
STARGAZING?
LIKE, *EXTREME* STARGAZING.
ALL RIGHT... I'M IN.
WHAT WAS THE WEDDING SONG?
"MY HEART WILL GO ON." YOU WOULD HAVE CRIED LIKE A BABY.
DANG IT!

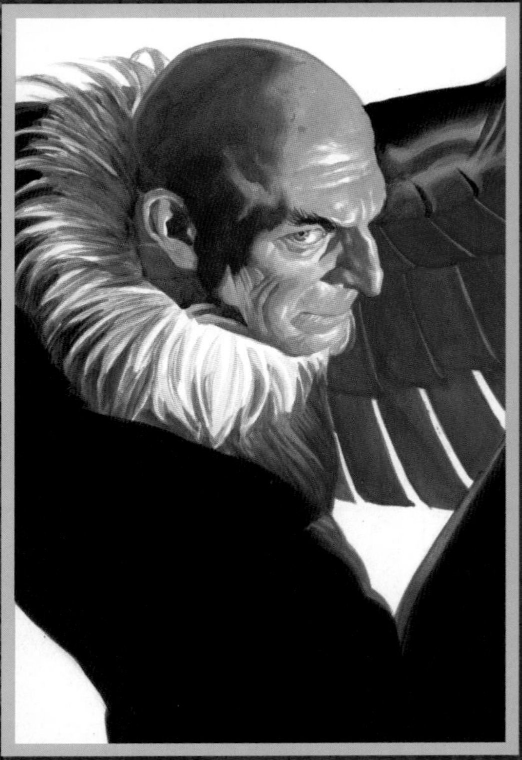

Alex Ross
AMAZING SPIDER-MAN #24
TIMELESS VARIANT

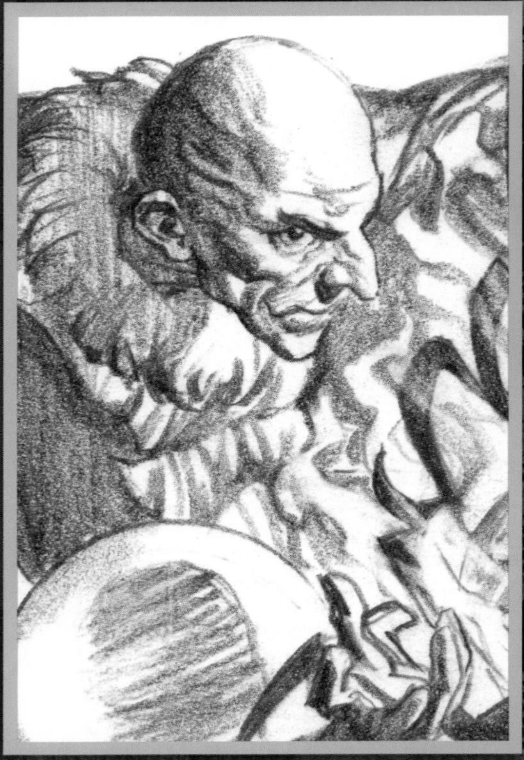

Alex Ross
AMAZING SPIDER-MAN #24
TIMELESS SKETCH VARIANT

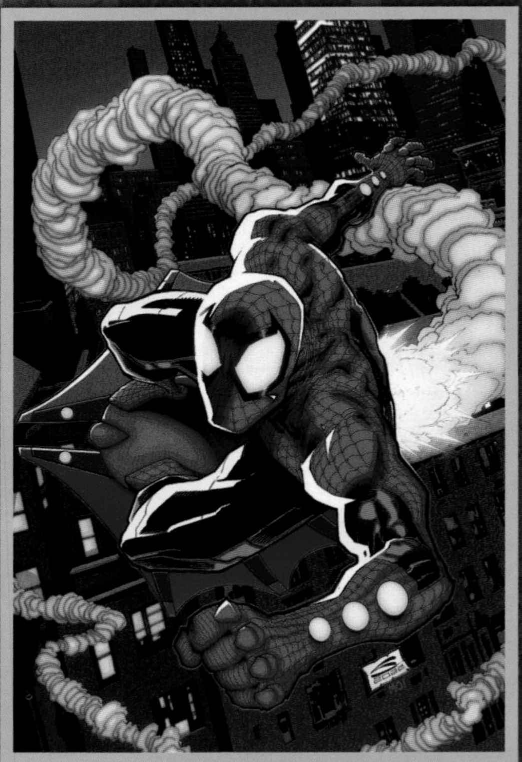

Gerardo Sandoval & Morry Hollowell
AMAZING SPIDER-MAN #24 VARIANT

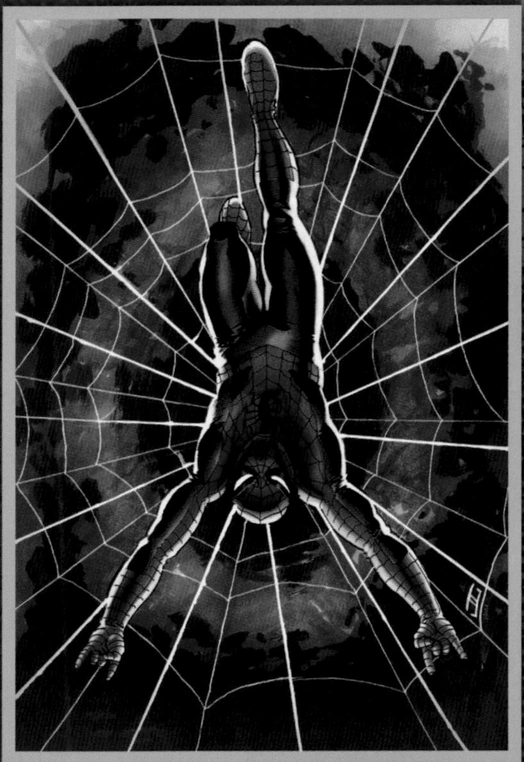

John Cassaday & Laura Martin
AMAZING SPIDER-MAN #25 VARIANT

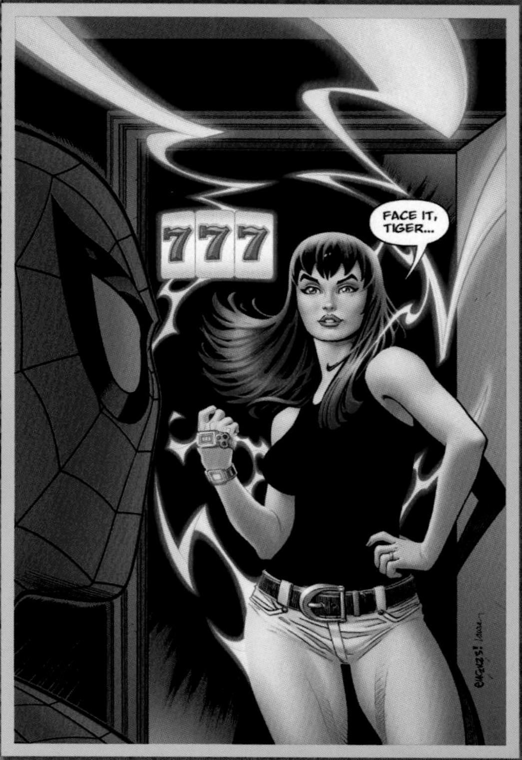
777
FACE IT, TIGER...

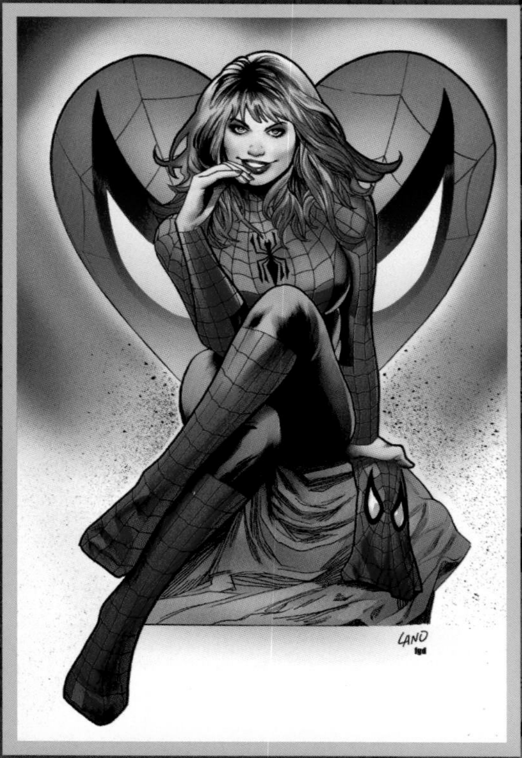

Ed McGuinness & Laura Martin
AMAZING SPIDER-MAN #25 VARIANT

Greg Land & Frank D'Armata
AMAZING SPIDER-MAN #25 VARIANT

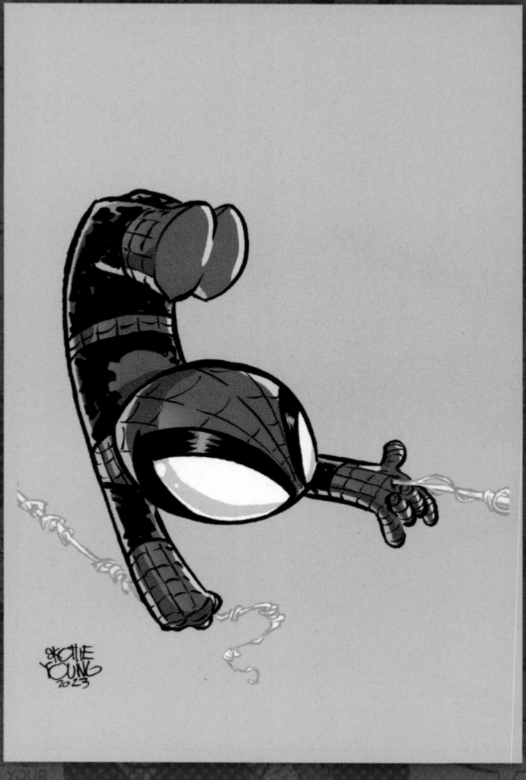

Skottie Young
AMAZING SPIDER-MAN #25 VARIANT

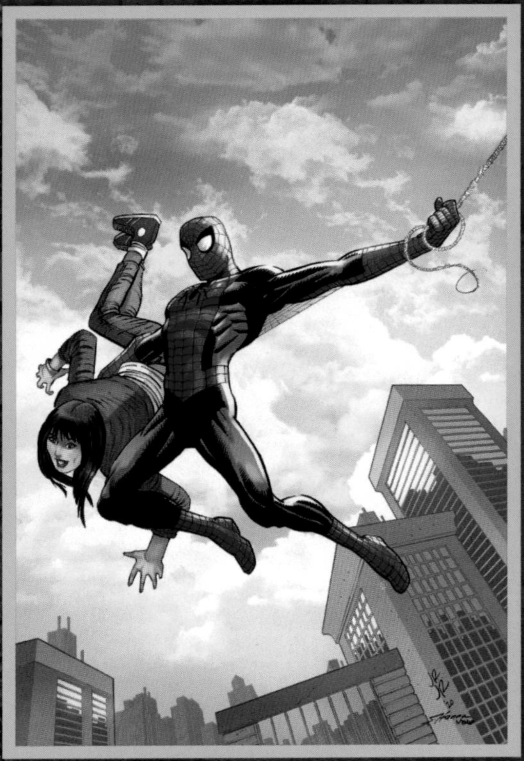

John Romita Jr., Scott Hanna & Marcio Menyz

AMAZING SPIDER-MAN #25
2ND PRINTING VARIANT

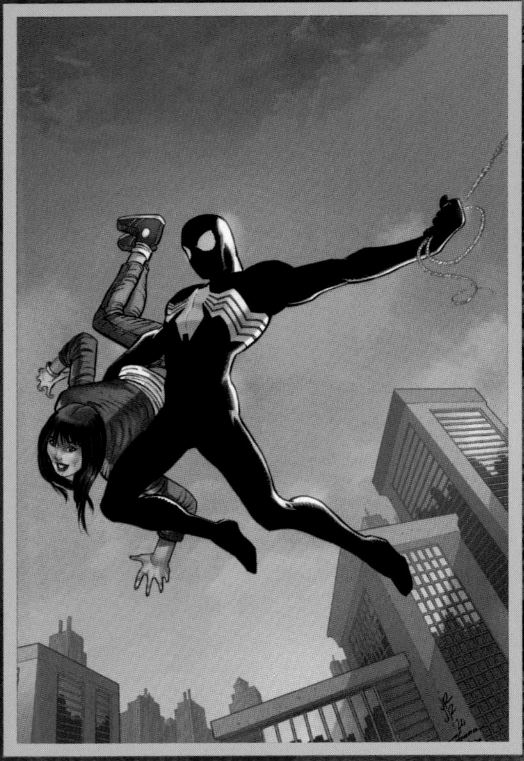

John Romita Jr., Scott Hanna & Marcio Menyz

AMAZING SPIDER-MAN #25
MARY JANE VARIANT

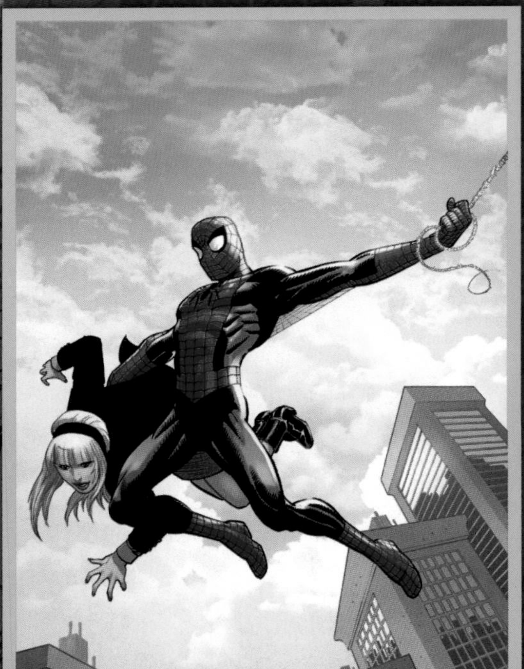

John Romita Jr., Scott Hanna & Marcio Menyz

AMAZING SPIDER-MAN #25
GWEN STACY VARIANT

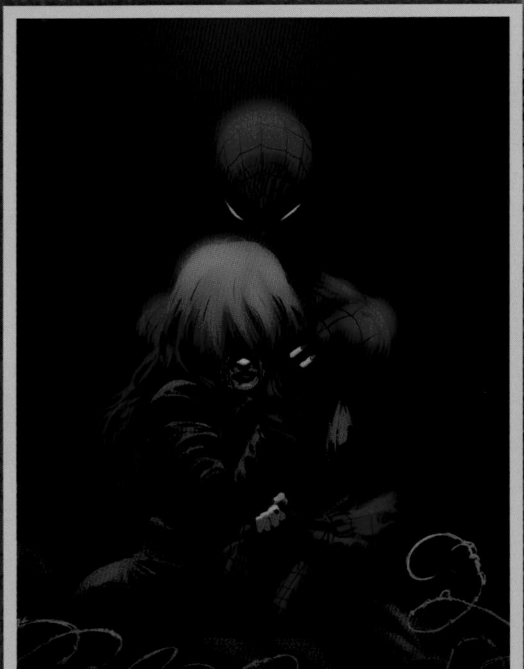

Kaare Andrews

AMAZING SPIDER-MAN #26
2ND PRINTING VARIANT

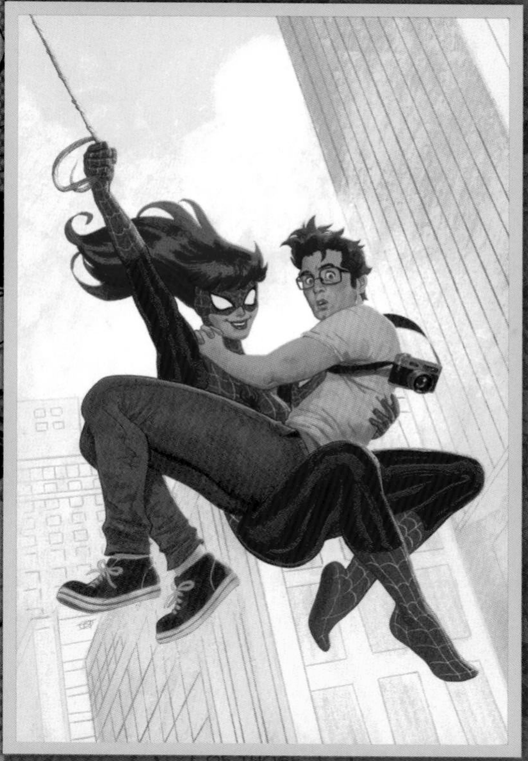

David Talaski

AMAZING SPIDER-MAN #26
SPIDER-VERSE VARIANT

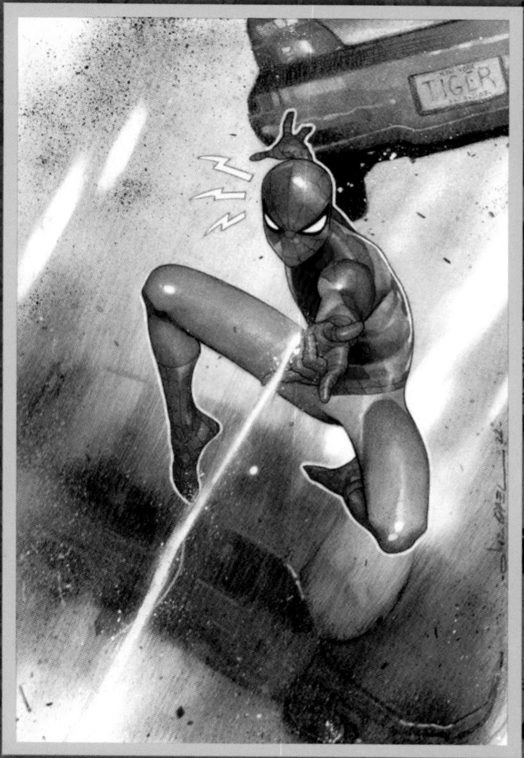
TIGER

Olivier Coipel

AMAZING SPIDER-MAN #26 VARIANT

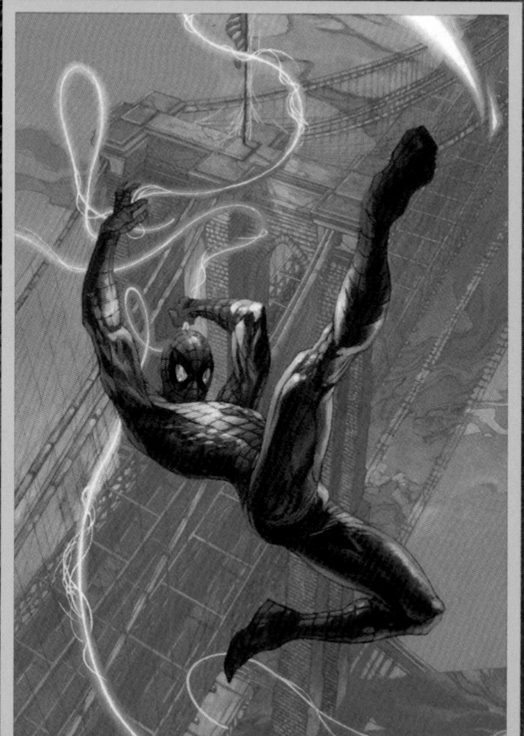

Simone Bianchi

AMAZING SPIDER-MAN #26 VARIANT

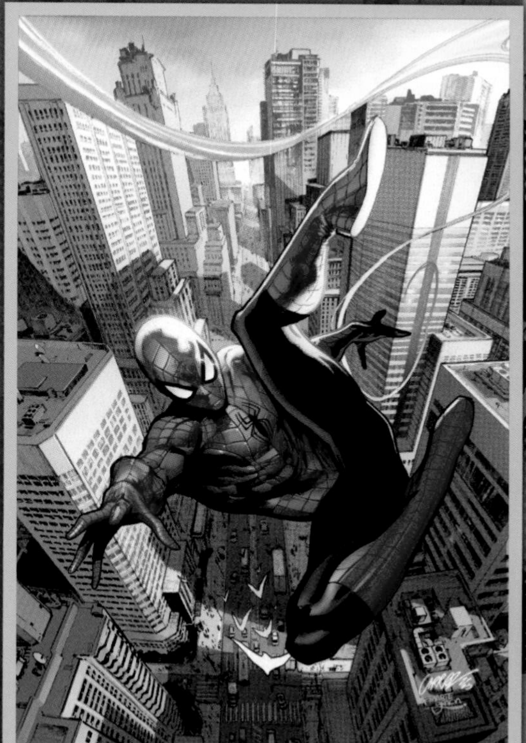

Pepe Larraz & Marte Gracia

AMAZING SPIDER-MAN #26 VARIANT

Pablo Villalobos & Romulo Fajardo Jr.
FALLEN FRIEND VARIANT

Adrian Alphona & Ian Herring
FALLEN FRIEND VARIANT

Carmen Carnero & Nolan Woodard
FALLEN FRIEND HOMAGE VARIANT

Clarice "Saowee" Menguito
AMAZING SPIDER-MAN ANNUAL #1 VARIANT